SUICIDE
AND THE
INNER
VOICE

SUICIDE
AND THE
INNER
VOICE

Risk Assessment, Treatment,
and Case Management

ROBERT W. FIRESTONE

SAGE Publications
International Educational and Professional Publisher
Thousand Oaks London New Delhi

For information:

SAGE Publications, Inc.
2455 Teller Road
Thousand Oaks, California 91320
E-mail: order@sagepub.com

SAGE Publications Ltd.
6 Bonhill Street
London EC2A 4PU
United Kingdom

SAGE Publications India Pvt. Ltd.
M-32 Market
Greater Kailash I
New Delhi 110 048 India

Printed in the United States of America

Library of Congress Cataloging-in-Publication Data

Main entry under title:

Firestone, Robert W.
    Suicide and the inner voice: Risk assessment, treatment, and case
management / author, Robert W. Firestone.
        p. cm.
    Includes bibliographical references and index.
    ISBN 0-7619-0554-5 (cloth). — ISBN 0-7619-0555-3 (pbk.)
    1. Suicide.   2. Suicidal behavior.   3. Suicide—Prevention.
I. Title.
RC569.F57 1997
197dc21   96-51212

    98 99 00 01 02 03 10 9 8 7 6 5 4 3 2

Acquiring Editor:	Jim Nageotte
Editorial Assistant:	Kathleen Derby
Production Editor:	Sanford Robinson
Production Assistant:	Denise Santoyo
Typesetter/Designer:	Marion Warren
Indexer:	Janet Perlman
Cover Designer:	Ravi Balasuriya
Print Buyer:	Anna Chin

Contents

Foreword   xi
  Pamela Cantor

Acknowledgments   xvi

1. Introduction   1

I. General Approach

2. The Self and Antiself   15

  Martin R.   17
  Sharon S.   19
  The Self and Antiself Systems   24
  Origins of the Core Conflict   29
  Conclusion   33

3. Suicidal Signs and Suicide Prevention:
  Inwardness—Personality Traits That
  Predispose Suicide   35

  Observable Signs of Inwardness   36
  Conditions Conducive to the Development of Inwardness   38
  Open/Outward Lifestyle Versus an Inward State   39
  Manifestations of the Inward State   40
  Summary and Implications for Suicide Prevention   56

4. Brief Review of Psychoanalytic and Cognitive
  Approaches to Suicide   59

  What Is Suicide?   59

Psychoanalytic/Object-Relations Approaches   61
Cognitive Approaches   62
The Interrelatedness of Self-Destructive Behavior   65
Summary   66

5. **The Epidemiology of Suicide and Brief**
   History of Methods for Assessing Risk   **68**

Demographic Factors for Suicide in the United States   68
Suicide Among Women   70
Suicide Among Children   70
Multicultural Issues in Suicide   73
A Brief History of Methods Used to Assess Suicide Risk   78
Conclusion   80

6. **Suicide Among Adolescents**   **82**

Adolescents' Discussion About Suicide   84
Continuation of Adolescents' Discussion   87
Interview About Adolescent Suicide   94
Sexuality and Suicide in Adolescence   98

7. **Suicide Among Older People**   **104**

Psychological Factors Associated With Elderly Suicide   105
Developmental Crises in Adulthood That Contribute to
     Hopelessness and Despair   109
The Psychodynamics of Elderly Suicide and Indirect
     Self-Destructive Behavior   110
Societal Influences on Suicidal Tendencies in
     Middle-Aged and Older Individuals   113
Treatment of the Suicidal Elderly   114
The Right to Die Controversy   116
Conclusion   118

II. Indirect Suicide

8. **Microsuicide**   **123**

Separation Anxiety and Death Anxiety   124
The Interrelatedness of Self-Destructive Behavior   126

The Dynamics of Microsuicide 126
Microsuicides of Everyday Life 127
The Manipulative Aspects of Microsuicidal Behavior 138
Summary 138

9. The Relationship Between Guilt and the Suicidal Process **140**

The Relationship Between Guilt and Religious Training 141
The Relationship Between Death Anxiety and Guilt 142
The Voice and the Two Modes of Guilt Reactions 143
Conclusion 157

10. Regression Precipitated by Positive Circumstances **160**

The Bipolar Causality of Regression 160
Regression as a Defense Mechanism 162
Stages in the Regressive Process Following Positive
Events 168
Episodic Regression Due to Positive Events 171
Conclusion 176

III. Theory of Defense Formation

11. The Voice Process and the Fantasy Bond **181**

Origins of Psychological Pain 182
The Basic Defense System 183
The Paradox of Defenses 185
The Core Conflict 187
Effects of Defenses on Interpersonal Relationships 188
The Universality of Child Abuse 189
The Voice and the Intergenerational Transmission of
Negative Parental Traits and Defenses 193
Resistance 194
Summary and Goals of the Therapeutic Approach 195

12. Couple and Family Relationships **198**

Psychodynamics of the Fantasy Bond: Brief Review of
the Literature 198
The Fantasy Bond in Marital Relationships 201

Family Bonds   210
Friendship and Love Relationships   212
Therapeutic Approaches   213
Conclusion   214

IV. Assessment and Treatment

**13. Identification of the Suicidal Individual: The Development
of the Firestone Assessment of Self-Destructive Thoughts   217**

Background of the Study   217
Theoretical Basis of the Study   221
The Initial Study   221
Findings From Inpatient Study   224
Clinical Findings Supported by Exploratory Factor
    Analysis   224
Empirical Findings Related to Increasing Levels of
    Self-Destructiveness   226
The Suicide Intent Composite of the FAST   227
The Total Score Composite of the FAST   227
Discussion   227
Application of the Concept of the Voice to the Assessment
    of Violence Potential   228
Conclusion   229
Research Notes   230

14. Treatment Strategies and Malpractice Issues   233

General Discussion   233
Acceptable Standards of Care   235
Treatment Strategies Based on Theoretical Models   245
Personality of the Therapist Treating Suicidal Patients   247
Dynamic Issues in Postvention   248
Conclusion   251

**15. Voice Therapy Methodology in the Treatment
of the Suicidal Patient   253**

Use of Voice Therapy Methodology in Crisis Intervention
    and the Intake Interview   255

Use of Voice Therapy Methodology in Treatment   262
Overview of Voice Therapy Methodology   272
Termination   274
Conclusion   274

V. Conclusion

**16. Guidelines for Primary Prevention
of Suicide and Summary**   **279**

Guidelines for Primary Prevention in Childhood   280
Dimensions of a Lifestyle That Counters Suicidal Trends   286
Summary   293

Appendix: Supplementary Resource Material   **297**

References   **299**

Name Index   **315**

Subject Index   **321**

About the Author   **333**

Foreword

What is it that drives people to suicide? Edwin Shneidman, the father of suicide prevention, believes it can be summed up in one word, "psychache." Ed believes a person can suffer from psychological pain so unbearable as to make him choose to end his life. Those who hold a different point of view believe that only those with some kind of illness will commit suicide. Still others believe society is at fault: poverty and intolerable living conditions; frequent mobility; the availability of handguns and other lethal weapons; the demise of religion; the dissolution of the two-parent family and of multigenerational support; the rise in drug and alcohol abuse; the escalation of violence; the industrialization, impersonalization, and rapidity of change in modern society cause suicide. Still others believe it is a lack of self-esteem and resiliency in our children that leads them to take their lives.

I have been a researcher, a clinician, and a teacher in the field of suicidology for over 25 years, and I hate to admit I do not know the answer. Biology and genetics shape us to a large degree, and inherited vulnerabilities play a larger role in emotional illnesses such as depression and anxiety than anyone realized a few decades ago. This understanding, however, does not eradicate the significance of both psychological and social factors. Although guns and other lethal weapons do not cause suicide, they do make it easier for an impulsive, despondent, or drunk youngster to commit suicide. There is no gene for suicide, only a genetic predisposition for certain mental illnesses. Human support and comfort can alleviate emotional pain; a lack of it, especially at critical times in development, can cause horrendous and sometimes irreparable damage.

However one gets there, whether it is a biologically determined mental illness, a physical illness, or a situationally caused state of depression or anxiety, there is little dispute that unbearable psychological pain is at the crux of the decision to commit suicide. We must remember, however, that what is unbearable for one person is not necessarily unbearable for another. The front page story in this morning's *Boston Globe* illustrates this point. The headline is "A family struggle ends in tragedy in Florida, a young boy dies along with his shattered parents." The picture accompanying it is of a distinguished older gentleman in his blue blazer and striped tie, a handsome little boy in his blue blazer with his school emblem and striped tie, and a beautiful younger woman posed with her head gently touching her son's. Their Florida mansion is in the background. The article reads, "Eight-year-old Jeffrey McIntosh was a trophy child, the prized only son of a doting mother and a sun-kissed token of youth for his rich, elderly father.

But on January 8, in the garage of his family's sprawling suburban home, Jeffrey begged for his life, snuggled between his parents in the back seat of their leased Cadillac as it slowly filled with carbon monoxide. His parents tearfully agreed, tucked him in for a fitful night of sleep, and the normally outgoing boy never mentioned it to anyone.

Then, with the same meticulousness with which they videotaped Jeffrey's first haircut, planned his annual birthday bash, and selected his private school, the parents finished what they set out to do. Last Monday, Bob McIntosh, 72, shot the sleeping Jeffrey, his willing wife and himself." The article explains Mr. and Mrs. McIntosh could not continue to live with their reduced financial circumstances. They had gone from great wealth to moderate wealth. Mr. McIntosh could not tolerate seeing his oldest son flush with money while he and his new family suffered financial strains. Mr. McIntosh blamed his 44-year-old son, stating in one of his suicide notes that his intentions were to die on his estranged elder son's birthday. His wife arranged for photos to be sent to the paper for her obituary; she did not want any unflattering pictures.

How do we explain, or understand, this murder-suicide? Mr. McIntosh killed his family and himself, and Mrs. McIntosh planned it along with him, willingly wrapping china and her son's toys and writing notes to make sure each survivor received exactly what she wanted them to. Was Mr. McIntosh suffering from a biological depression? Would he have profited from medication or therapy? Or did he kill himself because he felt rejected by his son and ashamed of his business failure without which he would not have been depressed? What prompted his wife to be willing to end her life and kill her young child as well? Was she mentally unbalanced? Or was she suffering so much unendurable psychological pain that, at that moment, she could not cope? What kind of emotional pain and constricted vision could bring two loving parents to kill their eight-year-old son? Were these people "pathologically disturbed" or "normal" people who hit a snag they could not cope with?

How would Robert Firestone explain these suicides? The newest book of this insightful and prolific author approaches the question of suicide from the psychoanalytic and existential point of view. His many years of clinical experience are woven with his experiences and those of his associates to formulate a theory—a theory that is truly the logical outgrowth of his earlier books. In *Compassionate Child-Rearing,* Firestone posed the seemingly obvious theory that parents who are kind to each other, to family members, and to those outside the family usually raise children who are caring towards themselves and others. Inhumane parents have a seriously destructive effect on their children, and these negative traits are generally passed on to the next generation. Harsh, critical parents produce harsh, critical children who often speak to themselves with harsh internalized words, and treat other children the same way their parents treated them. Alice Miller's *For Your Own Good: Hidden Cruelty in Child-Rearing and The Roots of Violence* proposes a similar theory. Somehow this message needs to reach the public, but sadly those who need to see it most are least likely to read these books.

In his newest book, *Suicide and the Inner Voice: Risk Assessment, Treatment and Case Management,* Firestone proposes the theory that in each suicidal person there is a voice that is the essential part of the destructive suicidal process. The voice is a continuous, although not always conscious, process that is carried inside one's head but usually not open to external interpretation because it remains unspoken. Voice Therapy is the process by which people can expose and come face to face with the demons they carry. Perhaps Mr. McIntosh carried a voice that propelled him to succeed in business, but then reduced his options to murder and suicide when his financial success crumbled. Voice Therapy shows how maladaptive behaviors and attitudes are rooted in childhood and how therapist and patient can work together to face and then change these destructive patterns. One can only wish that Mr. McIntosh and his wife had had the opportunity to work with Dr. Firestone. Perhaps he could have changed the voices that berated them enough to avoid the tragic outcome.

Firestone explains how the recognition of this internal destructive voice should change the therapist's approach to psychotherapy for suicidal individuals. One of his most interesting descriptions is of how a patient moves into a "trance-like suicidal state" when confronting these self-destructive, negative, hostile voices. It is these voices, Firestone believes, that cause the regressions that are precipitated by positive events and help explain the suicides of people who have accomplished a great deal in their lives, either through their work or in their relationships. I have heard patients tell me that they did not deserve their success, or that they must have earned it through specious or fraudulent means, because they could not possibly be worthy of it. I have also heard patients say that they would die only when they had reached the state they feel is closest to perfection, because then all they could have left is failure.

Firestone's greatest contribution, in my opinion, is what appears to be the original and sustaining focus of his life's work, that is, illuminating the inward patterns that begin with a lack of compassion in child-rearing and result in a predisposition to self-destructive thoughts and behaviors.

Firestone's application of this theory to suicide continues the work of Karl Menninger, Edwin Shneidman, and Norman Farberow. His description of the fantasy bond and voice process shows how the damage done in early childhood, combined with concerns about death and aloneness, set the stage for an individual's retreat into an inward, self-protective lifestyle of alienation and indifference. Here he builds on the works of theoretical giants such as Bettelheim, Miller, Kohut, Laing, Winnicott, and of course, Freud. Thus, he weds the theoretical perspectives of psychoanalysis, object relations, and existential psychology.

The author points out that the most significant signs of suicide are part of an identifiable inward lifestyle, an inwardness which children are forced to build out of the necessity to protect themselves against pain early in life when they are most vulnerable and malleable.

The inward child, and later the adolescent and adult, is involved in a lifestyle that includes a strong preference for living in fantasy, treating oneself and others as if they were objects, having little regard for others' feelings or acknowledgment of one's own feelings, suffering from low self-esteem, and harboring a profound cynicism toward others.

Everyone has negative voices—we would not be human without them—but people who are suicidal, according to Dr. Firestone, have negative voices that dominate their thinking and block the ability to think positively or even rationally. These voices create a person who is essentially turned against himself or herself. When faced with failure, rejection, illness, loss, or shame, this person has the potential to take action against himself. Could this theory explain the death of Mr. McIntosh?

If only Bob Firestone could have exposed the voices and challenged the self-attacks, perhaps he could have helped Mr. McIntosh to oppose the surrendering of his life. One of my patients, who is a therapist, told me she would not be willing to live with a mental illness. I would not wish to live with certain physical limitations or illnesses. Mr. and Mrs. McIntosh did not wish to live with reduced financial circumstances. Voices? Values? Mental illness? Biological depression? What is the answer? All we have in this case are the suicide notes the parents left. I wish we could have actually heard the spoken words. If the voice could be recognized before the suicidal act, if insights could be obtained by uncovering the "voices" that are driving a person toward suicide, the clinician would have a vantage point unavailable by other means and would have a new window into the "suicidal mind" (as Shneidman calls it), or the "suicidal state of mind," as I would prefer to call it.

Treating a suicidal patient is a most difficult task. It is frightening, demanding, and draining. I am not sure why we clinicians do it. Yet the experience of connecting with a person who is struggling to decide whether to continue with the rest of his life, and then helping this person to make a positive decision, is the only gratification I need to continue to do this trying work.

Robert Firestone is a compassionate, dedicated clinician who will leave as his legacy sound ideas about child rearing and innovative therapeutic techniques to help individuals avoid an inward, self-destructive lifestyle. I hope many parents and clinicians will read this book and put into practice his ideas about compassionate child rearing, the elimination of negative voices, and the substitution of the caring, supportive voices of parents and professionals whose sole desire is to help their children and patients let go of the words and thoughts that choke them.

Pamela Cantor, Ph.D.
Lecturer in Psychology, Dept. of Psychiatry
The Cambridge Hospital, Harvard Medical School
Past President, American Association of Suicidology

Acknowledgments

I would like to express my appreciation to Richard Seiden, Ph.D., M.P.H., for sparking my concern about the painful reality of the increased suicide rates in our society. As friend and esteemed colleague, it was invaluable to critically evaluate my theoretical concepts with him. In the same genre, I would like to thank Jean-Pierre Soubrier, M.D., president of the International Association for Suicide Prevention, for his intelligent discussion and profound interest regarding the subject of suicide.

I am grateful to former Surgeon General C. Everett Koop for inspiring the empirical research that led to the development of a scale to determine suicide risk in patients (the Firestone Assessment of Self-Destructive Thoughts), and to Lisa Firestone, Ph.D., my daughter, for her collaborative work in developing and testing the reliability and validity of our scale with over 1,000 subjects. My thanks to Susan Short, M.A., for her personal revelations contributing to the documentary film, *The Inner Voice in Suicide,* that so carefully explained the voice process in suicide.

I want to thank Jim Nageotte, acquisitions editor at Sage Publications, for his request for a concise and powerful book on suicide and his ongoing commentary. My appreciation goes to Joyce Catlett, M.A., for her painstaking efforts in collaborative writing on this project, and to Tamsen Firestone, Jo Barrington, and Marty Zamir for reviewing the material and helping with the final editing. Special thanks to the Glendon Association for their continued support and dedication, in particular to Anne Baker and Irma Catlett, Jerome Nathan, Ph.D., Catherine Cagan, Ana Blix, and Jina Carvalho, for helping with the manuscript and the dissemination of my ideas.

I would like to express my gratitude to Pamela Cantor, Ph.D., who has supported my work over the years, for her generosity in contributing her clinical expertise in writing the Foreword to this book.

1   Introduction

> Our life is what our thoughts make it.
> Marcus Aurelius, *Meditations*

In the United States, every 17 minutes a person acts on the resolve to terminate his or her existence. The problem of suicide and the attempts to understand this seemingly perverse antilife phenomenon are of immense concern to practitioners in the mental health field. You can imagine my excitement in discovering a unique window into this complex riddle. In penetrating the negative thought processes or internal voices manifested in the suicidal patient, my colleagues and I have developed a theoretical framework and psychotherapeutic methodology that illuminates the psychodynamics of self-destruction.

People acquire a sense of self in an interpersonal context. Unfortunately, it is this same social milieu in which this delicate sense of self is fractured. Painful experiences suffered in the developmental years lead to varying degrees of depersonalization and alienation. In the course of defending themselves from the onslaught of negative stimuli, children establish a fundamental ambivalence toward themselves that eventuates in an essential split in the psyche. Both sides of this division of the mind—the self and the antiself—are dynamic systems that have their own integrity and boundaries. People are both friend and intimate enemy to themselves. In the case of suicide, this enmity reaches epic proportions.

Suicide is the ultimate abrogation of self; as such, it represents the extreme end of the continuum of self-destructive mental processes. Because it represents the extreme, we would do well to study this phenomenon as it also sheds light on the entire gamut of mental illness. Furthermore, the alarming increase of suicide, together with the importance of sparing even a single life or spirit, compels us to search for the underlying dynamics.

The explanatory principle that I term the *voice* represents the language of the defensive process. It may be defined as an organized system of internalized thoughts and associated affects alien or hostile to a person's self-interest. Negative thought processes, or voices, are made up of conscious and unconscious components that obstruct the ongoing motivational field and cause varying degrees of maladjustment.

I refer to the system of thoughts that defines the defensive function of the personality as the "voice process" because all people are involved in an internal dialogue; that is, they are always talking to themselves about the ongoing events and experiences in their lives. Indeed, negative events, rejection, or hurt feelings are not nearly as harmful as what we tell ourselves about them. Because human beings have the unique ability to conceptualize, we are capable of responding to ourselves as an object. This dynamism is at once a remarkable asset and a curse. Internalized thoughts are experienced in the form of emotionally loaded statements about the self as though another person were talking to us. The thoughts have the character or feeling of being "heard," yet they are fundamentally different from the hallucinated voices of the psychotic individual. To clarify the complex issues outlined above, I will trace the development of the voice concept in my own history.

In December 1976, my wife Tamsen and I, along with a group of close friends, were transiting the Panama Canal on the first stage of a round-the-world sail. We were impressed by the scenic beauty we encountered as our oceangoing schooner sailed through the freshwater lake on the journey from the Pacific to the Atlantic Ocean.

This notable event was marred by the emotional background of the occasion. Tamsen was feeling bad and was in a confused state psychologically. Her reactions had been fitful and erratic for the past month or so, ever since we had begun talking about starting a family. Something about procreation terrified her and, although she strongly wanted to have children with me, she was virtually in a state of panic. When she wasn't acting nervous, she was distracted and remote. We were all disconcerted. In a conversation with friends, Tamsen overreacted when a woman friend suggested that the fear of having a child might be related to Tamsen's dread of turning out to be like her own mother. Tamsen was furious and lashed out at her innocent assailant—a style of defensive behavior that was entirely out of character for her. I was very worried and pondered the circumstances, searching desperately to reach an understanding.

I thought back to a pet theory I had developed from my own experience. I remembered that once, in a group meeting of colleagues, a woman had censured me for being a dominant figure: "Beware of the Bob Firestones of this world and their power needs." I was taken aback by the severe attack and felt misunderstood.

During the days that followed, I reviewed the scene over and over in my mind but continued to feel awful. I took myself to task and decided to attempt complete objectivity in an effort to understand my reaction. In all fairness, I did not see myself as having behaved in an aggressive or dominant role in the situation. On the contrary, I had been particularly sensitive and kind and had responded to the woman in question with empathy and compassion. But if she was wrong about me or had a distorted impression, why was I so hurt and insulted by her attack?

Finally it dawned on me that her accusation must have echoed something negative I thought about myself. I recognized that people are not necessarily hurt by the truth of the charges that are leveled against them but by whether the external attacks coincide with their internal self-attacks. They can be badly hurt even when the allegations are false, if unconsciously they themselves agree with the criticism.

On the basis of this insight, I went on to explore my self-attacks in a unique manner. I decided to meticulously record my own negative views of myself. In the process, I realized that I had strong internal voices that accused me of being "bossy and dominating." These voice attacks confused any positive leadership qualities I had with underhanded aggressive practices, and tore me apart. I wondered where in hell these internalized negative attitudes came from.

My mind flashed on a scene from my childhood in Brooklyn. I was playing in the alley with two of my chums when a voice rang out from an upstairs window. It was Barbara, the older sister of one of the boys, and she hated me. I remember her yelling out to her brother, "You don't have to listen to Bob's ideas all of the time! Who does he think he is, anyway?" This incident had been very hurtful and stuck in my mind.

I remembered too that my father often accused me of being selfish and demanding. He defined any desire or willfulness on my part as intrusive or bossy. He accused me of being a big shot.

These childhood experiences tied in with the woman's assault on my character and explained my overreaction in the group situation. On some level, I agreed with her. In essence, I was telling myself that I was a dominating, authoritarian person who was a bad influence. In working through the problem, I had not only helped myself emotionally, I had also stumbled on the insights that brought me to the brink of an important psychological discovery.

In recalling these events, I recognized continuity between my own experience and Tamsen's defensive anger in the travelers' discussion group. I wondered what destructive things she was telling herself about becoming a mother. At that point, I had the idea that she might want to reveal her self-attacks in the form of a dialogue or voice. She could say her thoughts as though she were talking to herself as an outsider.

Now let me place the events at the canal in context. Tamsen and I were part of a social group that actively dealt with psychological ideas, and we all talked about our thoughts and feelings (Endnote 1). She was a highly respected, intelligent, and outspoken member admired for her intuitive psychological insights and ideas. But for the time being, she was stuck in a quandary, feeling bad. Nevertheless, she was intrigued by my account of my experience with my own self-attacks and decided to pursue this avenue of exploration for herself. She sensed that I was on the right track, and was eager to uncover the cause of feeling lost or removed from herself and others. Once she grasped the idea, she was anxious to try out the technique.

Tamsen began the exercise in a calm voice, reciting her self-attacks about becoming pregnant. "I'm not fit to be a mother. I don't know the first thing about it and will probably mess up. I'm afraid of having a baby, like I'm losing something."

A colleague interrupted, "That's not exactly the technique. Say your self-attacks as though they were coming from an outside person. Try to say them as though you were talking to yourself. Like, 'You don't deserve to have a baby. You would be a lousy mother,' and so on."

Tamsen composed herself and attempted to comply. She started off tentatively repeating, "You're not fit to be a mother," then went on and gained momentum. "You don't deserve to have a child. You don't know a damn thing about children. Who do you think you are, anyway? You think you're better than me?"

As Tamsen expressed these self-attacks, her face grimaced, her speech pattern changed, and she sounded exactly like her mother. This transition seemed eerie to her friends. "You always were selfish and superior," she went on. "You little bitch, you were born with a silver spoon in your mouth. You were so pretty and your father always made over you, you're so smug." By this time, Tamsen's expressive movements revealed a combination of rage and agonizing sorrow as she exploded with the torrent of emotional abuse. "Just wait until you have children, you little shit. You'll see what it's like going through the delivery! Just wait until you feel the pain! Then maybe you'll understand what I went through. I just wish the same burden on you. Kids just take, take, take! There's nothing left for you! You never did appreciate me, you little bitch. Just wait until you have kids; they'll make you sorry you were ever born! You can never do enough for them, nothing's good enough!" This powerful release of feeling left Tamsen exhausted but relieved. The experience was self-explanatory; there was no need for intellectual interpretation. Because of her courage and initiative, what my friends and I witnessed that day was an unintentional yet incredible "voice therapy" session that would later be duplicated many times over by others. The "voice" had evinced itself in a "laboratory procedure" for the first time. All who were present sensed that it was an important occasion, that this new methodology was a discovery of deep significance. Man's destructive propensities toward self could be accessed with this new procedure. The spontaneous flow triggered by the new format not only illuminated the content of self-attacks and permitted a feeling release of considerable magnitude, it also shed light on the source of negative introjects.

Incidentally, in the experimental sessions that followed, every time the second person format was used, there was a significant difference in affective expression. Participants demonstrated powerful emotions when addressing, rather than describing, themselves.

After the brief exercise in Panama City, Tamsen understood the destructive elements in her own personality. Before the experience with "Voice Therapy," she had had absolutely no awareness of why she was reacting negatively to having a child. She was a passive victim of an unconscious self-destructive process. When she finished the exercise, she was alert to vicious negative thoughts that punished her for competing with her mother in the area of motherhood and family. She concluded that her mother's jealousy toward her, based on immaturity and self-hatred, had obviously left an imprint. She understood that she had internalized the aggression her mother felt toward her as a child and had come to see herself as an unlovable and unworthy burden. She anticipated that having her own baby would be an imposition and unconsciously regarded the child as an unpleasant intruder who would repay her for the "trouble" she had caused her own mother.

From the experience of externalizing her voices, it was apparent to Tamsen that her mother harbored a good deal of resentment toward her and that she, Tamsen, had incorporated the malice into her own personality. In reflecting on what I had observed and on Tamsen's remarks, I thought, Where else could the negative thoughts or voices have come from? Why did her enunciation and general bearing resemble her mother's speech patterns and mannerisms when she entered the exercise? Why was there so much anger and rage at herself, and why was she so sad? Tamsen's conclusions seemed to make good sense.

As she came to understand the division in her personality, Tamsen began to feel better. She followed up with two similar sessions that were equally powerful and added support to the original theory that she was plagued by the internalization of her mother's attacks. Her problem relating to having a child had begun to be successfully resolved.

Tamsen and I left the sail on the Atlantic coast of the canal, planning to return at a later date. I had a feeling of panic that something would happen to me before I could record this recent discovery of the "voice" and "Voice Therapy." I could not rest easy until I had translated the new insights into a written form and had shared my ideas.

On my return to Los Angeles, I explored these concepts in a group context with friends and associates. Within days of my arrival, I was involved in the exploration of "voices" in the group meetings. Everyone was intrigued by the improvement in Tamsen due to the voice exercise as well as by my theoretical explanation of the dynamics. They were happy to observe her renewed state of comfort and easy friendliness. They wanted to explore the ideas for themselves.

In the first meeting, several people were able to get into the exercise using the technique of talking to themselves in the second person. As soon as one person caught on to the process, others quickly learned the new method of using the dialogue format. The results were shocking. One after the other, they launched intensive verbal attacks against themselves, which were accompanied by powerful emotions. First, there was a horrifying rage that was totally unexpected followed by an extremely painful sadness—a kind of primal crying.

One man in talking to himself said: "You're not that good of a person, you know; you don't amount to much. What have you got to show for your life?" He spoke slowly at first and without affect but gradually his verbalization accelerated and intensified. "You know no one would miss you if you weren't around. You don't have a wife or girlfriend like other guys. You're a nobody, that's all you are!" In relation to his work with heavy equipment, the voice taunted him, "Go ahead, just move a little closer to that blade! See how close you can get without cutting yourself. Come on, just stick your hand in there! Get closer, you bastard, just shove it in there!" His voice grew louder and more savage. "Ram it in there, you cowardly bastard, you don't deserve to live! You cowardly piece of shit!"

This man had borne no conscious malice toward himself when he began the exercise. He was not depressed or particularly upset. The same held true for others. They attacked their appearance, their work failures, their competence, and everything negative imaginable. Men and women attacked their sexuality and accused themselves of not measuring up to other members of their sex. All of this was accompanied by angry emotions and the ever-present sadness.

Everyone was impressed by the powerful episodes they witnessed. Within minutes, each participant in the exercise was able to mobilize and express his or her most severe self-doubts and most painful self-attacks. The specific content made sense to each of the parties involved and they intuitively recognized the source. In some cases, the verbal assaults were exact duplications of phrases their parents had uttered. In others, the attacks recaptured the emotional climate that they had grown up in and fit the images they had had of themselves in their families. Some attacks were so brutal that the participants associated them with covert malice that had been directed toward them as children.

My investigation of Voice Therapy subsequently confirmed the observations and hypotheses that came out of Tamsen's dialogues. We came to understand that parental ambivalence toward children is the rule rather than the exception. Consequently, when a person is doing a Voice Therapy exercise in a group, the rest of the group members identify closely and feel strong emotions in themselves. I discovered that no one was immune to destructive voices that act against the person's goal-directed activities. It appears that the degree to which alien elements are present in the personality correlates with the degree of physical, emotional, or sexual child abuse suffered by the individual during his or her formative years.

It was apparent to my associates and me that in growing up, every person incorporates negative attitudes and feelings into his or her personality that are alien and hateful to the self. Although these voices are harbored inside, they exert a profound limiting influence on each person's life. Some self-attacks are conscious and people recognize these self-critical thought patterns; others are more insidious, remaining unconscious and inaccessible yet doing an enormous amount of damage. With this new therapy procedure, I was able to study the impact of "voices" and estimate the deleterious effects on each person's personality and functioning level.

As clinical material of this nature accumulated, it became a logical extension of my work to study this voice process in depressed patients and in individuals who had a history of suicidal thoughts and attempted suicides. I explored the self-destructive thought patterns that seemed to influence and even control their life-threatening behaviors and lifestyles. When my colleagues and I interviewed depressed and/or suicidal individuals, we discovered that they were able to identify the contents of this inimical way of thinking about themselves. Although many interviewees had no previous knowledge of the concept of the voice, they usually related to the concept with familiarity and ease. I hypothesized that the thought process that I had observed in "normal" or neurotic individuals was essentially the same mechanism that leads to severe depressive states as well as to self-destructive behavior and suicide.

In the beginning of our studies, my associates and I had only scratched the surface of the phenomenon; the discovery of this important theoretical concept was in its infancy. Later, there would be considerable follow-up with a diverse population: patients, associates, children, teenagers, and adults. The conclusions that ultimately supported my theoretical position were based on observing several hundred participants in Voice Therapy sessions (Endnote 2).

My purpose in writing this book is to elucidate the manifestations of the voice and to advance our knowledge of suicide and other, less severe, forms of human self-destructiveness. In proposing a correlation between the voice and self-destructive behavior, I will describe and expand the laboratory procedures of Voice Therapy that have been used to elicit this hostile thought process, thereby bringing it more directly into consciousness. The empirical research that my associates and I have undertaken to examine and analyze this destructive point of view has led to the development of a scale for assessing suicide risk, the Firestone Assessment of Self-Destructive Thoughts (FAST) (Firestone & Firestone, 1996).

Items on the FAST are made up of actual "voice" statements reported by subjects in the earlier clinical studies. Results of reliability and validation studies show that the FAST effectively discriminates between suicidal and nonsuicidal subjects at a high level of significance.

Although it is impossible to describe my theoretical position and its applications in a few pages, I do want to create a perspective in the reader regarding the concepts and methods and to provide some background for the following chapters that deal with the dynamics of the suicidal process. My theoretical approach represents a broadly based coherent system of concepts and hypotheses that integrate psychoanalytic and existential frameworks yet should not be considered eclectic. The theory explains how early trauma leads to defense formation and how these original defenses are reinforced as the child gradually becomes aware of his or her own mortality (Firestone, 1990d). Existential issues continue to have an enormous impact, generally negative, on individuals throughout their lives, particularly in relation to generating defensive, self-destructive responses.

Historically, in their efforts to understand psychological pain and maladaptive behavior, psychoanalytic and object-relations theorists have investigated the effects of interpersonal trauma, while existentialists have directed their attention to issues of being and nonbeing (Endnote 3). Both systems of thought, psychoanalytic and existential, must be integrated to fully understand the dynamics of the suicidal process within the individual. Neither system deals sufficiently with the important concerns of the other, and to neglect or minimize either seriously impairs an understanding of psychological functioning.

From a psychoanalytic perspective, my thinking extends the formulations of Anna Freud (1966) and Sandor Ferenczi (1933/1955) regarding the defense of identifying with the aggressor to show the crucial part it plays in the process of ego fragmentation and the etiology of self-destructive thinking and behavior. The focus of my work has been on describing the interpersonal pain experienced by the child during the pre-Oedipal phases, an emphasis compatible with the developmental object-relations approach of Margaret Mahler (1961/1979) and D. W. Winnicott (1958), attachment theorist John Bowlby (1973), and self-psychologist Heinz Kohut (1971). My conceptualization of the antiself system (Chapter 2) is congenial with the construct of the antilibidinal ego developed by Fairbairn (1952) and Guntrip (1969). The concepts of the fantasy bond and the voice process have also provided a cogent explanation of the psychodynamics involved in dysfunctional family systems described phenomenologically in the work of Alice Miller (1980/1984) and James Garbarino (Garbarino, Guttman, & Seeley, 1986), among others.

The distinctive features of my theoretical position are reflected in (a) my view of challenging psychological defenses, (b) the application of the concepts to an affective-cognitive methodology, and, as noted, (c) my strong emphasis on existential issues at every stage of individuation.

My view of psychological defenses differs substantially from the majority of psychoanalytic theorists in that it represents an ultimate challenge to the defense system. It is my belief that defenses are maladaptive because they cut deeply into an individual's life experience, and when they are maintained into adulthood, they eventually become the essential psychopathology. I feel that the reality of a person's experiences and emotions is primary; any defense mechanism that fragments or denies that reality or deprives the person of his or her experience is clearly destructive. At the same time, I understand that there is a natural tendency for people to resort to defenses to eliminate pain and anxiety. Ironically, defenses erected by children to protect themselves from a toxic environment and painful aspects of the human condition can become more damaging than the original trauma (Endnote 4). Therefore, the aim of my therapy is to help patients move toward a nondefensive lifestyle in general rather than to encourage their use of higher level defenses to replace more primitive mechanisms, which is the goal of many psychotherapeutic approaches.

The therapeutic methodology to which the concept of the voice has been applied is an affective-cognitive therapy. The purpose of Voice Therapy is to separate and bring out into the open elements of the personality that are antithetical to self as a result of the internalization of negative parental attitudes and damaging childhood experiences. The emphasis on exposing negative thought processes in my work overlaps cognitive theories and therapies to a certain extent, yet my approach is very different in that the methods deal more with the expression of feeling than analysis of logic or illogic. The expression of affect that often accompanies the verbalization of the voice leads to unusual insights similar to those obtained in Primal Therapy (Janov, 1970). The unconscious material that emerges has had tremendous value in terms of its research potential. In my opinion, however, the basic theory underlying Voice Therapy is more important than the methodology, and my approach is not restricted or limited to specialized techniques.

In terms of existential systems of thought, my basic premise regarding the relationship between individuation and death anxiety can be distinguished from that of other existential psychotherapists. I disagree with the views held by Yalom (1980), Searles (1961), Hinton (1975), and others who propose that death anxiety is a manifestation of unfulfilled strivings in life (Endnote 5). My theory, derived from extensive clinical data, supports a converse proposition that death anxiety is closely related to the degree of individuation and self-actualization of the individual. The constructs are an outgrowth of ideas set forth by Otto Rank (1936/1972), Ernest Becker (1973), and Abraham Maslow (1968) concerning the close relationship between the fear of death and the fear of standing alone, as an individual. As people differentiate themselves from their original families and continue to evolve or individuate, they are confronted with separation anxiety at each stage. Indeed, painful feelings about death and dying appear to be in proportion to patients' freedom from neurotic propensities and restrictions. Improvement opens people up to feeling about their lives, both the bitter and the sweet; it brings about a sense of personal freedom that makes them more aware of potential losses.

Unfortunately, most individuals, beginning in early childhood, try to deny death on an immediate, personal level and gradually accommodate to the fear of death by seriously restricting the scope of their lives or giving up, which is part of a suicidal process. It's a suicide of the spirit. In their retreat from life, they are tortured by existential guilt about a life not fully lived and become progressively more demoralized.

To understand the voice process is to become aware of the source of the self-destructive apparatus within the personality. Negative voices have a powerful effect on human behavior and impose strong restrictions on each person's life. In the case of suicide, these voices determine a trancelike state of mind in which they become the only stimuli that the person is attending to in his or her downward spiral toward self-destruction.

Endnotes

1. This group is composed of psychiatrists, psychologists, associates, and friends who have studied together for 17 years, investigating psychological issues of personal and vocational concern. They have shared this information for 15 years through the Glendon Association, a nonprofit organization that has disseminated this body of knowledge through books, articles in professional journals, and documentary films to mental health professionals and the general public.

2. The conclusions we arrived at as a result of the longitudinal study are elaborated in *Voice Therapy: A Psychotherapeutic Approach to Self-Destructive Behavior* (Firestone, 1988) and *Combating Destructive Thought Processes: Voice Therapy and Separation Theory* (Firestone, 1997).

3. The original psychoanalysts theorized about the trauma and psychological conflict experienced in successive stages of psychosexual development, particularly during the Oedipal phases. Later, object-relations theorists concentrated on problems arising during pre-Oedipal phases. Others (Balint, 1952/1985; Fairbairn, 1952; Guntrip, 1961) described the split in ego function as children suffer blows to their dignity, personal freedom, and autonomy. Existential psychologists have written of people's attempt to transcend their dualistic nature and the fact of their mortality (Bugental, 1976; Frankl, 1946/1959; Laing, 1960/1969; Maslow, 1968; May, 1958; Yalom, 1980).

4. When viewed from an evolutionary perspective, defenses can be seen as having functional value during the child's early years because they protect the infant and young child against complete ego disintegration or even physical death under conditions of extreme stress. They help diminish the experience of excessive emotional pain and anxiety. In this sense, the formation of defenses early in life increases the probability that the child will survive psychologically, reach sexual maturity, reproduce, and contribute to the gene pool. Incidentally, the defense of identifying with the aggressor and other defenses such as dissociation are the only solutions available at the time because the child is helpless and dependent on his or her parents or caretakers.

5. There is considerable controversy in the field of existential psychotherapy regarding the relationship between death anxiety and life satisfaction, or degree of self-actualization (see "Toward a Comprehensive Model of Death Anxiety" by Tomer & Eliason, 1996). The theorists who propose that death anxiety is inversely proportional to life satisfaction may be confusing death

anxiety with the existential guilt inherent in withholding life's satisfactions from oneself. Examples of the clinical data supporting my hypothesis include (a) the reports of countless individuals who experienced increased death concerns, death dreams, or nightmares immediately following an especially happy or fulfilling experience; (b) serious, long-term regression following an unusual success or achievement in otherwise high-functioning adults (Chapter 10); and (c) negative therapeutic reactions in clients after significant improvement in psychotherapy.

PART I

GENERAL APPROACH

2 The Self
and Antiself

Suicide is caused by psychache. . . . Psychache refers to the hurt,
anguish, soreness, aching, psychological pain in the psyche, the
mind. It is intrinsically psychological—the pain of excessively felt
shame, or guilt, or humiliation, or loneliness, or fear, or angst, or
dread of growing old, or of dying badly, or whatever. When it
occurs, its reality is introspectively undeniable. Suicide occurs
when the psychache is deemed by that person to be unbearable.

Edwin Shneidman (1993, p. 51), *Suicide as Psychache*

At this point in the [suicidal] trance, the inner pull toward suicide
dramatically intensifies. Often it comes in the form of a voice. In
fact, mention of a voice is so common that I've learned to inquire
directly about this during interviews. This voice grows in volume
with the stress of the suicidal ordeal. It demands increasingly to be
heard above everything else, and it begins to occupy a greater part
of the person's psyche until it smothers more reasonable voices
altogether. Often people experience this voice as relentlessly
driving them toward self-destruction.

Richard A. Heckler (1994, p. 74), *Waking Up, Alive*

Suicide represents the final submission to self-destructive machinations. Negative reactions against the self are an integral part of each person's psyche,
ranging from critical attitudes and mild self-attacks to severe assaults on the
self. The latter includes feelings and attitudes that predispose physical injury
to the self and eventually the complete obliteration of self. No one reaches
maturity completely unscathed by their personal experiences during the
developmental years and no person is completely exempt from a suicidal
process that leaves its mark on every life.

15

Psychopathology, or "mental illness," can be more accurately conceptualized as a limitation in living imposed on the individual by inadequate,
immature, or hostile parenting, internalized in the form of negative thought
processes ("voices"), and later manifested in self-limiting and/or self-destructive lifestyles. In this sense, varieties of so-called mental illness could be
conceptualized as subclasses of suicide rather than the reverse.

All aspects of giving up of self, one's sense of reality, goal-directed
activity, and appropriate emotional responses represent a defensive, self-
destructive orientation toward life that leads to neurotic or psychotic symptom
formation. The extent of emotional deprivation and destructive parenting will
determine the degree of dependence on psychological defenses. Inimical
thought patterns and emotional attitudes are introjected or incorporated into
the self system that strongly influence or control the relinquishing of one's
unique identity and the narrowing of life experiences; as such, suicide represents the ultimate renunciation of self.

It goes without saying that all mental and emotional phenomena are
psychosomatic; they involve both physical and psychological components. In
other words, all factors must be considered in understanding human behavior.
It is clear in this case that suicide, depression, and self-destructive actions are
multidetermined. Hereditary predispositions and biological components are
important factors in the etiology of suicidal behavior and represent a significant correlation in bipolar disorders. However, studies have also shown that
behavior patterns manifested by depressed and addicted patients are imitated
by their offspring. The process of identification and imitation may well be a
more powerful factor than genetic inheritability in the intergenerational
transmission of negative parental traits, behaviors, and defenses.

My expertise and approach to suicide is of a psychodynamic nature. In
the majority of cases that I have examined, the impact of psychological
elements on the child's development in all probability exceeds the influence
of innate predispositions. More specifically, self-destructive propensities and
suicidal actions appear to be overdetermined by interactions in the early
interpersonal environment.

This book represents a unique approach to suicide in that it focuses on
the internalized negative thought processes or "voices" that underlie suicidal
manifestations. As noted in the previous chapter, psychological pain and
anxiety derive from two major sources that affect the personality: interpersonal trauma and existential trauma. Destructive attitudes toward self are
incorporated under stressful conditions and become a separate and discrete,
alien part of the personality. The "voice" has been defined as an integrated
system of negative thoughts and attitudes, antithetical to the self and cynical
toward others, that is at the core of maladaptive behavior. Voices or negative

thought patterns are distinguishable from hallucinated voices in the psychoses, although they have the same character. In the case of the psychoses, hallucinated voices reflect a more drastic split within the personality. The voice reaches its most dangerous and life-threatening expression in suicidal acting-out behavior. Understanding the nature of suicidal thought processes or "voices" is fundamental in developing a therapy and a preventive mental hygiene program relevant to suicide. Our therapeutic methodology brings these introjected hostile voices to consciousness, which renders them accessible for treatment. Voice Therapy is not only valuable as a psychotherapeutic tool but is, in addition, an important laboratory for understanding self-destructive behavior.

All people are faced with a central existential conflict: They want to live their lives, act on their priorities, individuate, and find personal satisfaction, yet these goals are compromised by a fundamental ambivalence toward self. As a result, they vacillate between motives to actualize and to destroy themselves.

I will present two cases that clearly illustrate the core conflict and the essential polarities toward life and death manifested by the suicidal individual. In these two cases, both people made a serious suicide attempt yet, at the last minute, just as they were losing consciousness following a lethal dose of pills, they each tried desperately to arrest the process.

Martin R.

A mild-mannered, yet physically strong man of 38, Martin, an engineer by profession, was always uncomfortable with his anger. Despite his athletic ability and natural good looks, this discomfort gave him a humble, serious appearance. In December 1982, deeply troubled and humiliated by jealous feelings he was experiencing in relation to his wife's infidelity, he turned his anger against himself. He felt compelled to "get away" from friends who he feared might be able to detect his emotional turmoil. He convinced himself that he would find relief from his humiliation and shame if he could just get away for a while. He believed that a sunny place, a vacation spot where he had once enjoyed a relaxing week with his wife, might turn his mood around.

> *Martin:* At first I rationalized getting away by thinking, "You just need to get away where you can think things over. Find a warm, sunny place." Later, as I felt more and more ashamed of my jealous reactions, I thought: "You've just got to get away. You can't be around anyone when you're feeling like this. How

can you look anybody in the eye? They can tell how you're feeling. You have to get away."

At first I planned to go to San Diego, but I changed my mind and flew directly to Ixtapa, a place where I had a lot of good memories of romantic times. I was scared so I wanted to go to some place that was familiar. But even around perfect strangers, I felt paranoid. I couldn't look anybody in the face because I had started to develop the idea of killing myself, and I felt ashamed.

I was walking along the beach when I heard the voice really clear for the first time. I felt I had nowhere to go. "Why go anywhere? Why don't you just stop here?" As the week progressed, the voice, those thoughts, seemed to accelerate, to where I started to formulate a plan. I looked up at the hills and I could see all the shrubbery. I pictured myself just going up in the mountains and killing myself. The images got more vivid every day. I pictured myself in the bushes, sitting down and taking a knife and stabbing myself. And as it got more vivid, I got more scared.

I didn't feel angry at myself, I just felt worthless: "It would be better for everyone if you just disappeared." Then the voice started to taunt me: "You're too scared to kill yourself, you're yellow, you're not really going to kill yourself." It almost dared me, and I started to get worried that people would start wondering what I was doing there all by myself and I got more and more paranoid.

One interesting thing happened that week. I saw a girl on the beach and I started to think, well, maybe I could just talk to her. That thought caused me so much pain; I didn't want to "pollute" her with me. But at the same time, I was attracted to her. I felt rage toward myself because I didn't want to feel anything. I was cutting off more and more.

After the incident with the girl, the voices got even more intense: "You really have to kill yourself. Where are you going to get a knife?" But then I couldn't do it. I just couldn't do it. I don't know why. Finally I got to the point where I felt like doing it, and yet I couldn't. So I flew to San Diego and hung around there for a while. I just walked day and night.

I would have to figure out another way of doing it. I decided to take a train trip across the country. I started thinking about taking pills and at every station, I got off the train, went to a drugstore and bought sleeping pills. I bought more and more pills, but I guess I was kind of naive because I didn't know if they would kill me or not.

On the train, I stayed in my compartment, trying to read a book, but I couldn't concentrate on reading. I just watched the scenery go by. The voice said: "Just get more pills, get more pills!" Finally I stopped in Chicago and stayed there a while and felt really alone.

Then I went to New York and I started to think of all the different ways I could kill myself. "You can just walk the streets and get yourself run over."

But I was scared of that. The violence of it scared me. There was this dark underpass in a dangerous neighborhood. "You could just go under there and wait for it, maybe get killed." I terrified myself.

I tried to find my brother and his family. I actually walked over to his house, but he was away on a vacation, so I went back to the empty hotel. Again, it was a place where I had stayed during happier times.

I was sitting on the bed in the hotel room, all by myself and everything looked like it was closing in on me. "Now is a good time. Now is a good time. This is it! Just go ahead and do it. You just have to cut off feeling a little bit more to do it. You can make the walls shrink around you. Now's a good time. All you have to do is go to sleep and it'll be over. Now's a good time."

I went to the bathroom and got several glasses of water and started to take the pills. I don't know how many I swallowed. I don't remember anything for some time after that. Then the next thing I remember is throwing up violently. For a moment, I didn't know where I was. My first thought was a paranoid one—I wondered if anybody at the hotel had seen me and if I would get into trouble. I was very scared, but suddenly I realized with unusual clarity that I didn't want to kill myself anymore. I went right to the phone and called a close friend and headed back to Los Angeles.

I've never had voices like that since. I feel bad sometimes, but never like that. I guess I went through something that changed me. Funny, I still get angry at the kind of aliveness I feel when I am strongly attracted to a woman, like the time I saw that girl on the beach in Ixtapa. That's still with me.

This episode clearly illustrates the powerful conflict between forces in Martin that predisposed both annihilation of the self and survival of the self. Both systems were operant. Angry voices commanded Martin to destroy himself and yet his actions also revealed a desire for comfort and connectedness. He sought out familiar places with happy memories; he searched for his brother; and so on. Ultimately, his body rejected the lethal dose of pills and he clearly chose to live.

This pattern is repeated in our second case history, the case of Sharon S.

Sharon S.[1]

At 5:00 p.m. on October 10, 1976, Sharon drove her car to a hotel, registered, went to her room, and took a lethal dose of Seconal, Miltown, and Valium. At the last moment, before losing consciousness, she managed to pick up the

1. The material in this section is taken primarily from an article titled "The 'Inner Voice' in Suicide," *Psychotherapy, 23,* 439-447 (Firestone, 1986). Used by permission.

phone and reach an operator at a nearby university. Paramedics rushed to the scene, raced frantically through the hallways, and unlocked or banged loudly on every door until they finally found Sharon, lying unconscious across her bed. Fortunately, there was a hospital located directly across the street and they rushed her to emergency treatment. She remained on the critical list in the intensive care unit for the next 18 hours. Miraculously, she survived. From that time on, with the aid of psychotherapy, she steadily progressed and gradually resumed a normal life. Several years later, I interviewed her about the events leading up to the attempt to end her life.

Sharon was 30 years old when she made the decision to end her life. An exceptionally attractive, active young woman, she was highly successful in her career. However, she had become increasingly unhappy in a relationship that had been meaningful to her. A slow deterioration in feelings had occurred over a period of 2 years from the time the couple had first been very close. As the story unfolds, Sharon refers to a pattern of negative thoughts that almost completely dominated her thinking during this period in her life.

Sharon: The first thing I thought of was that that wasn't the only time I actually thought of killing myself. Even as a young child, I often thought about suicide when I felt really bad, which I did a lot of the time. I thought that if things really got bad enough I could just kill myself.

Dr. F.: What was tormenting you in your current situation that you wanted to get out of?

Sharon: I remember feeling depressed, down a lot. I felt like I was bad. Like there was something really bad about me that I couldn't fix. I couldn't stand myself, that's what I couldn't live with. It's hard to talk about this because I don't feel like this now.

Dr. F.: What kind of actual thoughts did you have about suicide? What form did these thoughts take?

Sharon: That I wanted to kill myself and I tried to get myself to the point that I didn't care enough about anything so that I could do it. Thoughts like, "You don't really like him. He doesn't matter that much to you. There are other people that he likes. You're so ugly. Who would choose you? There are other people important in his life. It doesn't matter. You don't matter that much to him. You don't matter to yourself. You don't matter to anybody. Who would care if you weren't around? People would miss you a little at the beginning but who would really care? You don't care." It's hard to believe I really thought these things, but I did.

I tried to get alone—because this process occurred when I was alone. The voice was weak when I was around other people, so the voice got me to be alone—saying: "Get alone. Look, don't you need some time for yourself? Get alone so you can think."

Then once I would get alone, either driving around somewhere or just walking around by myself, then these other voices, the more destructive ones, would start, like they took the form of, "If you don't matter, what does matter? Nothing matters. What are you waking up for? You know you hate waking up every morning. Why bother? It's so agonizing to wake up in the morning, why bother doing it? Just end it. Just end it. Stop it."

Dr. F.: Did you hear that voice like a hallucination, like somebody else saying it?

Sharon: No, it wasn't a hallucination at all. It was totally thoughts. It was thoughts in my head. Whenever I was alone, the voice was more vicious and angry: "You'd better do it! It's the only thing you can do. You'd better do it! I hate you! I hate you."

I just had a thought in relation to my mother. I'm remembering feelings directed toward me, when we were alone.

[Sharon relates an incident that occurred in the bathroom of her home, when she was 3 or 4 years old. Her mother screamed at her and beat her till she bled.]

I remember the hatred she directed toward me. "I hate you. I hate you." And that was like that voice—my own voice. It turned into my own voice when it was the most vicious, hating myself.

As Sharon made preparations to actually take her life, the voice became progressively dissociated from her own point of view and sounded monotonous, cold, and rational.

Sharon: I was so cut off that the voice seemed rational. "Here's the hotel. You gotta pull into the driveway. Be careful, you don't want to call any attention to yourself. Don't act stupid. Don't make this take longer than it has to. Now here is the key. Go to the elevator, go up to the room, and unlock the door." Which I did. Then I remember that I wanted to eat. I ordered a large room-service meal, which took some time.

At the last moment, when Sharon delayed taking the pills in order to eat the dinner she had ordered, the voice ridiculed her for procrastinating (an action that may have saved her life).

Sharon: Then afterwards, after eating the meal, "Okay, okay, you had the meal that you wanted. Now you can die in peace. Okay, go ahead now, you've got these pills. Go ahead, start taking them." This is something I haven't had a memory of before, of taking the pills. But I sort of remember it now. "Okay, you've had your meal. Now do it! Do it. Coward! Now do it already. You had your pleasure, now do it."

Dr. F.: Then, you almost died—you took a lethal dosage of pills and you almost died.

Sharon: I know that I took enough pills to kill myself. I also know that I called the information number of the university. I knew their number because I went to school there.

Dr. F.: After you took the pills.

Sharon: After I took the pills, I was lying on the bed.

Dr. F.: Were you getting drowsy?

Sharon: I can't remember, but I do know that it took every effort that I had to make the call.

Dr. F.: Something in you wanted to save yourself, obviously.

Sharon: At some point when I realized what was happening, that it was working, I thought, "My God, this is working! I don't want this to work." That wasn't a voice anymore. That was me.

Dr. F.: You could tell the difference.

Sharon: Yes.

The most important aspect of this interview is that Sharon chose to live and did save herself at the last moment. Her drive for survival overcame the self-destructive process, even though she came within inches of dying in spite of her call for help. Like Martin, her ambivalent attitudes toward herself were manifested in actions that played a role in saving her life. She chose to eat a big meal before ingesting the pills and this kept the pills from having a lethal effect. She chose a hotel adjacent to a hospital emergency room. And, finally, at the last minute, she called the university and reached out for help. Later, her desire for life was supported by her close circle of friends and a successful psychotherapy program.

It is vital to understand that in the majority of cases of suicidal acting-out behavior, harmful actions are based on the dictates of an insidious voice process. Heckler (1994), in interviewing 50 cases, observed the same pattern of voices. He described a suicidal trance state dominated by a compulsive self-attacking thought process that parallels my examples.

Prior to their suicide attempts, both Martin and Sharon seemed actually to be possessed by the voice, to be at the mercy of a point of view hostile to their own self-interest. Somewhere in the midst of the suicidal crisis, they found themselves and were no longer bound by the perverse desire to triumph over death by taking their fates into their own hands. Of interest, both parties felt enormously secretive and protective of the suicidal process, and their furtive plots were dominated by voice commands to hide their intentions from others. There was incredible guilt about their suicidal ideation and actions. In the early stages of the "suicidal trance," voices instructed them to isolate themselves and cut off emotional feelings for themselves and others. They turned inward and were resentful of experiences that intruded on their withdrawn state and their resolution to complete the act. Later, angry voices cajoled them to get on with the deed, and, finally, the voices drove them to the point of action.

Ambivalent attitudes and feelings are manifested at every stage of the suicidal process, and any event, either positive or negative, can tip the balance. For example, intoxication with alcohol or drugs will often predispose self-destructive actions. For this reason, it is important not to have weapons or other means available that could lead to an instant and irrevocable conclusion. Although depression seems interminable, even a deeply depressed individual is susceptible to extreme mood swings, and a compassionate, understanding person can often have a positive influence.

The road back to health after averting a suicidal crisis is not without adversity; it too is marked by ambivalent attitudes toward self. A year after her suicide attempt, Sharon confided in me that she felt incredible rage at the fact that she could no longer consider suicide as a viable alternative. She resented that her feelings of love and caring for her friends were a barrier to self-destructive action.

It was obvious that a hostile, defensive process was still operant. Her anger was manifested in irritable outbursts of meanness, which she learned to control until eventually the intensity of her negative affect toward those whom she cared for diminished. Indeed, Sharon felt angry at every concession that she made in the direction of investing loving feelings in others and in giving her own life value.

Martin too faced a core conflict on his way back to health. When he reported that he still felt rage when he was especially attracted to a woman, he exposed a negative attitude toward any inclination to become too excited about or involved in life's pursuits. Even now, he remains prone to depressive mood swings in which he is drawn toward isolation and self-attack but never to the level of their prior suicidal proportions.

We have shown examples of the extreme, conflicting attitudes toward life and death manifested by suicidal individuals. Now we must examine the psychodynamics that led to these extreme reactions, dynamics that play out their role not only in the personalities of disturbed people but in those of so-called normal persons as well.

The Self and
Antiself Systems

But when violence masquerades as love, once the fissure into self and ego, inner and outer, good and bad occurs, all else is an infernal dance of false dualities. (Laing, 1967, p. 75)

Under painful circumstances, children tend to depersonalize in an attempt to escape from painful emotions. Simultaneously, they internalize or incorporate the attitudes and feelings that are directed toward them. These negative parental introjects or voices lead to an essential dualism within the personality. This "division of the mind" reflects a primary split between forces that represent the self and those that oppose or attempt to destroy the self. These propensities can be conceptualized as the *self system* and the *antiself system*. The two systems develop independently; both are dynamic and continually evolve and change over time.

The *self system* consists of the unique characteristics of the individual including his or her biological, temperamental, and genetic traits, the synchronistic identification with parents' affirmative qualities and strivings, and the ongoing effects of experience and education. Parents' lively attitudes, positive values, and active pursuit of life are easily assimilated into the self system through the process of identification and imitation and become part of the child's developing personality, whereas internalized, negative parental traits remain alien.

There is also conflict within the self system. The self mediates between one's personal goals, one's conscience, and reality considerations. The superego, or value system conceptualized within the self system, is inner directed rather than imposed from the outside. In the developmental stages where circumstances are positive, issues of morality are harmoniously incorporated from the general demeanor and conduct of family members rather than from punitive treatment, lectures, or rigid object lessons. Value systems are derived more from lived example than from explicit training. Where there is discrepancy between words and actions, children inevitably suffer from internal conflict. Under negative environmental conditions, children generally fail to develop their own sense of values and tend to be outer directed, that is, constantly submitting to or defying parental prohibitions.

Living up to one's ego-ideal or expectations for oneself is seen as essential for maintaining a sense of integrity in relation to one's own system of beliefs and values. Behaviors are evaluated according to the criteria of the reality principle; that is, they must be appraised with respect to positive or negative consequences to oneself, others, and one's personal goals. Within the self system, aggression is appropriately directed at the sources of frustration. How it is dealt with and whether or not it is acted out are issues that generally comply with an adaptive ego function.

The *antiself system* refers to the accumulation of negative introjects or buildup of internalized cynical or hostile voices that represent the defensive aspect of the personality. The defensive process is influenced primarily by interpersonal pain that is reinforced and compounded by the suffering inherent in the human condition (illness, physical and mental deterioration, and death; poverty and economic recession; crime; natural disasters; and so on). Each person adapts to pain and stress to the best of his or her ability. Once a defensive solution is formed, people tend to protect the defensive apparatus at the expense of limiting their real lives and goal-directed activities. They exist in a state of defensive equilibrium. When this equilibrium is disrupted, it provokes a state of alarm or anxiety. Many times, people react to this state of anxiety before it reaches the threshold of conscious awareness. Often this unconscious motivation leads to defensive responses that are not adaptive or truly in their self-interest. For this reason, it is often difficult to identify the stimuli that precipitate regressive reactions.

Both positive and negative events that are unusual or especially significant will arouse anxiety and predispose a defended posture. The antiself system tends to predominate in these circumstances. Negative events that lead to regression are more easily recognized as a causative factor, whereas it is less generally recognized that unusually positive events can serve the same function. Both disturb the equilibrium and threaten the status quo. This fact explains why people are often refractory to affection, or even respond with hostility, when they are loved or valued. It helps to illuminate the mystery of why self-destructive behavior follows positive recognition and why suicidal acts are committed by individuals who manifest a high level of success or achievement.

One can differentiate two types of anxiety: positive and negative (Whitaker & Malone, 1981). There is always anxiety as an individual grows. A person must "sweat through" positive anxiety states to develop and achieve autonomy. On the other hand, negative anxiety aroused by traumatic or negative events is associated with the subsequent retreat to a more defended or self-destructive adaptation. For example, object loss or frustration in interpersonal relationships leads to anxiety that may necessitate the formation of a new psychological equilibrium that is more self-protective. In other words, anxiety can result from any situation that threatens the homeostatic balance.

When an individual depersonalizes or cuts off feeling in situations of stress and anxiety, there is an essential fragmentation of the personality into two elements: the helpless, needy child and the punishing, nurturing parent. This fragmentation or division of the self represents a polarization into both the powerful, punitive parent and the weak, repulsive child (at the same time the highest and the lowest) (Endnote 1).

In schizophrenia, we see a powerful split between grandiose fantasies on the one hand and extreme feelings of worthlessness on the other. The schizophrenic patient feels that he or she is both almighty God and the lowest scum. His or her break with reality and retreat into fantasy is characterized by both extremes. In this syndrome, the split affects the individual's capacity to regulate thought patterns along the lines of conventional logic and, as a result, the thought disturbances give rise to delusions, hallucinations, and other idiosyncratic phenomena.

In neurotic or normal individuals, the split is not as obvious or encompassing, yet there are unmistakable elements of the same division (nurturing-punishing parental aspects and infantile, helpless manifestations of the personality). Either aspect of the parent-child split may be extended or lived out in close associations. For example, in couple relationships characterized by a fantasy bond (Endnote 2), the individuals involved act out parental or childlike elements with each other as an ongoing pattern. Neither childlike nor parental manifestations reflect the true status of the individual. Both dominating and submissive aspects of the personality are essentially regressive. In each case, the individual is separated from his or her adult self.

The antiself system is an overlay on the personality representing the incorporation or introjection of negative, judgmental, and hostile views toward the self. There is strong affect associated with these negative attitudes. In Voice Therapy sessions where patients articulate their self-attacks and release the angry affect, these aggressive attitudes manifest themselves in a way that is dramatic, powerful, explicit, and easily identified in relation to their sources.

Depending on which element is ascendent in the personality at the time—self or antiself—an entirely different point of view will be manifested. People are very different when they "feel like themselves" than when they are dominated by the alien point of view. When they are themselves, they are generally relaxed and far more likable. When they are influenced by voices, they are typically more hostile, defensive, and toxic to be around. Basically, they act more like the people who damaged them. Everyone must be familiar with this phenomenon in relation to their loved ones. The entire countenance of the person reflects "the bad mood" or adversarial nature of the person. If we are reasonably sensitive, one look at the face of our loved one will tell the whole story.

It is interesting, although disconcerting, to observe negative traits of a parent intruding into the personality of an individual. I am reminded of a man of my acquaintance who exhibits two completely different personalities depending on whether he is "himself" or "not himself." At times, for no apparent reason, this typically congenial, sweet, lovable person is transformed into a paranoid, irritable, sadistic person. This man is so extreme in his differential reactions that his wife has given him two names: Sam, his real name, and "Fred Nurge" (his alter ego or antiself name). On one occasion, "Fred" became so enraged that his wife fled from the house in fear for her life and remained in her neighbor's home for the night. Finally, she tired of his meanness and temper and abandoned the relationship in spite of his good qualities. Incidentally, "Fred Nurge" is an exact replica of Sam's father at *his* worst. As Sam's father has grown older, his behavior has degenerated to the point where he lashes out in rage and actually hits other people.

People are most reluctant to recognize the essential division within their personalities because they are threatened to discover irrational, hostile attitudes toward themselves and others. They attempt to deny this fracture by identifying negative traits predisposed by the antiself system as their own. In refusing to tolerate the lack of integration, they tend to compromise their essential aliveness, spontaneity, and individuality and move in the direction of the prescriptions of the voice. Freud's recognition that unconscious motives determine human behavior was a threat to people's illusions of omnipotence and self-confidence. Discoveries made while using Voice Therapy procedures are even more threatening because they make us painfully aware of the aggression toward ourselves.

The malicious attitudes toward self manifested in the two case histories presented earlier are not separate, discrete, or qualitatively different than the voices of normal people in their everyday lives. All people have an enemy within that they fear. They worry that if they recognize hostile or suicidal inclinations in themselves, they will be more likely to act them out. Actually, the reverse is true; becoming aware of unconscious negative attitudes toward self and others allows us to achieve greater mastery of our lives.

Parental Ambivalence

**Parents both love and hate themselves and
extend both reactions to their productions, i.e., their children**

| **Parental Nurturance** | **Parental Rejection, Neglect, Hostility[2]** |
| | **Other Factors:**
Accidents, illnesses, death anxiety[3] |

| **Self System** | **Antiself System** |
| Unique makeup of the individual— physical, temperamental, genetic structure; harmonious identification and incorporation of parents' positive attitudes and traits; and the effect of experience and education on the maturing self system. | The Fantasy Bond (core defense) is a self-parenting process made up of two elements: the helpless, needy child, and the punishing, nurturing parent. Either aspect may be extended to relationships. The degree of defense is proportional to the amount of damage sustained while growing up. |

**Ego mediates between
(1), (2) and (3)**

(1) Personal goals: primary and secondary—primary goals include food, water, sex; secondary goals include affiliation with others, search for meaning, compassion for others.

(2) Superego or personal conscience: made up of individual's own ego-ideal and value system (inner-directed).

(3) Reality principle: actions are evaluated with respect to positive or negative consequences in relation to personal goals.

Copyright © 1996 by The Glendon Association

**The antiego is composed of
three primary factors or stages of self-attack[4]**

Voice Process	Behaviors	Source
(1) Critical thoughts toward self	Verbal self-attacks– a generally negative attitude toward self and others predisposing alienation.	Critical parental attitudes, projections, and unreasonable expectations.
(2) Microsuicidal injunctions	Addictive patterns. Self-defeating and self-limiting behaviors.	Identification with and imitation of parents' defenses.[5]
(3) Suicidal injunctions– suicidal ideation	Actions that jeopardize, such as carelessness with one's body. physical attacks on the self. and actual suicide.	Parents' covert and overt aggression (identification with the aggressor).

Figure 2.1. Division of the Mind[1]

1. Division as indicated on the chart is oversimplified, with abrupt boundaries for purposes of elucidation. Psychological functions are more complex, and mental events and internal conflict are always multidetermined.
2. I feel that psychological factors are more significant in emotional disorders than other factors—that is, inherited characteristics, biological states, and accidents, illness, and so on—are in affecting the human condition. Also, negative experiences in the family contribute most directly to human suffering. For example, in times of war, the suicide rate decreases, and in times of tragedy, there is not a corresponding increase in mental illness.
3. Despair is inherent in the human condition in relation to the fact of death. People feel scared of the unknown, and vulnerable. Death anxiety supports the defense system, particularly at the point in the developmental sequence when the child first becomes aware of death.
4. The three factors correspond to the patterns of negative thoughts accessed by the Firestone Assessment of Self-Destructive Thoughts (R. Firestone & L. Firestone, 1996).
5. The imitation of parents' attitudes and defenses is inevitable; it has a powerful survival function on a primitive level, as in the animal kingdom.

In Voice Therapy sessions, the enemy surfaces and can be studied. Recognition of the enemy within themselves enables patients to resist defensive behavior patterns and self-destructive tendencies, and helps them to attain greater personal power and make a better fight for their lives (see Figure 2.1, "Division of the Mind").

Origins of the Core Conflict

The division of the psyche into the self and antiself system occurs early in life, during the preverbal phase of development. In the face of intense emotional pain or intolerable anxiety, the child attempts to preserve some level of rationality and sense of unity. Efforts to maintain logic and systematic thought under unusual, stressful conditions lead to the specific defense of identifying with the aggressor. Rather than suffer complete ego disintegration, children make a strong identification with the same forces that produce the torment they are trying to escape.

In situations where there are deficiencies in the parental environment or where parents are punitive or abusive, the child ceases to identify with him- or herself as the helpless victim and assumes the characteristics of the powerful, hurtful, or punishing parent. This maneuver of splitting from the self partially alleviates the child's terror. However, in the process, the child takes on not only the parent's animosity and aggression directed toward him- or herself but the guilt, the fear, and, indeed, the total complex of the parent's defensive adaptation. Once incorporated, the process lends itself to a feeling of being invaded or possessed by an internal enemy. Feelings of demonic possession as demonstrated in films and other accounts are symbolic exaggerations of this phenomenon. Moreover, this internal complex of parental voices represents an integrated point of view, a systematic organization of feelings and attitudes toward the self that is relatively inflexible and becomes the core resistance to change and the opportunity for a better life.

The split within the personality develops when the child depersonalizes under circumstances that threaten his or her "going on being" (Winnicott, 1965). Ironically, the child's desperate struggle to preserve intactness and wholeness produces fragmentation and disintegration. As noted earlier, in forming this imagined connection or fusion with parents, the child fragments into becoming at once the weak, bad child and the strong nurturing/punishing parent, the transgressor and his or her severest critic. In this manner, children achieve an illusion of security and mastery, which relieves their anxiety to varying degrees. Thereafter, a strong sense of pseudoindependence and denial of external need develops within the child.

The process of "identification with the aggressor" was first described by Sandor Ferenczi (1933/1955). In portraying the child's reaction to incidents of incest or sexual abuse, Ferenczi wrote:

The weak and undeveloped personality reacts to sudden unpleasure not by defence, but by anxiety-ridden identification and by introjection of the menacing person or aggressor. (p. 163)

When the child recovers from such an attack, he feels enormously confused, in fact, split—innocent and culpable at the same time and his confidence in the testimony of his own senses is broken. (p. 162)

Anna Freud (1966) contended that the mechanism of identification or introjection combines with imitation "to form one of the ego's most potent weapons in its dealings with external objects which arouse its anxiety" (p. 110). "By impersonating the aggressor, assuming his attributes or imitating his aggression, the child transforms himself from the person threatened into the person who makes the threat" (p. 113).

I conjecture that covert or unspoken parental aggression or rage may be more threatening to the child than rage expressed in punitive or explosive actions. The child who is physically abused, although suffering pain, is aware of what is happening, and this awareness has a survival function (Endnote 3).

In general, children feel powerless and unconsciously identify with their parents, whether or not the situation is punitive. However, the more they feel victimized, the stronger the bond is with the parental power structure. Even when the prevailing family attitudes are positive, elements of parental insensitivity are introjected during infrequent stress situations. When conditions are miserable or terrifying, aspects of an observing, punishing, parental self combine with parts of the hurt, frightened child self to form the antiself system. In extreme cases, the incorporated parental aggression, murderous rage, and unconscious death wishes may be acted out later, in adolescence or adulthood, in the form of self-mutilation or suicide. In his analysis of patients who manifested serious self-destructive or suicidal behaviors, Bruno Bettelheim (1983) addressed this issue and posed the question:

Why should we incorporate into the essence of our being the desire of those who (at least once) wished to destroy us? . . .

[Because] the parent-child bond is powerful. . . . The younger we are, the more we respond to what we feel are the most powerful emotions of the person who is most important to us, and it does not matter what the nature of these emotions is. (p. 302)

R. D. Laing (1960/1969) has depicted this "take-over" of an individual's personality by the internalized parent as follows:

> A most curious phenomenon of the personality, one which has been observed for centuries, but which has not yet received its full explanation, is that in which the individual seems to be the vehicle of a personality that is not his own. Someone else's personality seems to "possess" him and to be finding expression through his words and actions, whereas the individual's own personality is temporarily "lost" or "gone." (p. 58)

Because human beings defend themselves under conditions of stress, children incorporate into themselves an image of their parents at their worst, that is, those occasions when they were the most defensive, the most aggressive, and the most feared. These parental introjects have a basic autonomy within the personality and may ultimately dominate the scene, as in a suicidal crisis.

Predisposing factors leading to the type of depersonalization and split described here were discernable in both Martin's and Sharon's family constellations. Martin reported that his mother lived on "a different level from other people—in the ether," and that her behavior was erratic and histrionic. As a youngster, whenever his behavior was construed as being so much as even a minor infraction of family rules, he had to face his mother's silent look of devastation, martyrdom, and tears. He remembered that her response frightened and enraged him. The fear of upsetting his mother's delicate balance made him susceptible to her manipulations, and he swallowed his anger. Her blackmailing tactics led him to turn his rage against himself, and he experienced feelings of confusion and disorientation. As an adult, when his anger was provoked by his wife's infidelity and the vacillations in her feeling toward him, Martin reverted to the state of mind he felt as a child. He could not get angry; he could only withdraw and turn his angry feelings against himself. (Martin also disclosed that his father was an extremely inward, miserable, angry man who spent most of his time in the garage in isolation from the rest of the family.)

In the second case, Sharon revealed that throughout her childhood, she had experienced both overt and covert anger directed toward her from her mother. The incident of physical abuse that she recalled during the interview represented an outward expression of the vindictive hatred her mother had characteristically felt toward her as a small child, which she had concealed under a veneer of oversolicitousness. Sharon remembered an especially threatening phrase, "You little brat, I'd like to wring your neck," routinely stated by her mother "at least ten times a day." Sharon took the threat literally and waited in tense anticipation for her mother to carry it out.

The dysfunctional family dynamics that contributed to Sharon's self-destructive propensity were in place before she was born. According to Sharon, her father had originally fallen in love with her aunt (her mother's younger sister) but had been rejected by her. He often praised the aunt's beauty and told Sharon that she bore a strong resemblance to this aunt. This accounts for some of the mother's jealous rage toward Sharon. When Sharon was 5 years old, her aunt committed suicide. It was around that time that Sharon first experienced suicidal thoughts. She reported that when her mother's temper was out of control, she felt unremitting fear from which there seemed to be no escape. Her only alternative was to identify with her attacker, at great expense to herself. Sharon's insight in the interview indicated that her mother's sadism and intrusiveness came to characterize Sharon's own attitudes toward herself. In a subsequent interview, Sharon disclosed contradictory, hostile attitudes she had had as a child. She recalled torturous, compulsive thoughts about being a murderer: "I was so angry I didn't know what to do with it. I was afraid that I'd really kill somebody. I lived as a kid, feeling like a murderer . . . or feeling that I should kill myself." The fundamental dynamic in this case was that Sharon internalized her mother's murderous rage in the form of a destructive thought process that ultimately commanded her to destroy herself. Rosenbaum and Richman (1970) noted that "death wishes [toward recovering suicidal patients] were implicit or explicit in many statements made by the relatives and were voiced with unexpected frequency. 'We'd all be better off if you were dead'; 'Next time pick a higher bridge' " (p. 1653) and other such malicious comments were sarcastically voiced to these patients by their parents. These researchers introduced their controversial paper by stating: "We believe that the clinician must ask . . . 'Who wished the patient to die, disappear, or go away?' " (p. 1652). In his other writings, Richman (1986, 1993) has noted that the suicidal person is blamed for all the ills in the family. In contrast to the psychotic person who is labeled as "sick," the suicidal person is singled out as "bad."

In suicidal patients, parental death wishes are incorporated as a voice, frequently in a disguised form. One patient was physically abused by her father on a number of occasions, and once he had tried to strangle her. This young woman secretly held a bizarre belief that she was filled with poison and thought of herself as "bad, evil, and contaminating." She made several attempts to commit suicide and said she had obeyed a voice that ordered her to "slash your wrists, get rid of the poison!" In this extreme case of pathological acting out, her father's death wishes had been translated into action. I have conjectured that parental death wishes are involved in the etiology of destructive voices that operate to reinforce the drive toward self-destruction.

Conclusion

The cases described in this chapter demonstrate that the suicidal individual is ambivalent up to the very last minute. Because ambivalence is always present within persons who are in a "suicidal trance," every opportunity must be offered to help them. As clinicians, it is incumbent on us to challenge every avenue that allows the suicidal patient to take action when he or she is faced with seemingly hopeless psychological circumstances. We must remove the means for committing suicide and at times provide practical assistance (when that is what is most needed) to make life feasible for the despairing, desperate person. In other words, we must make it as difficult as possible for the suicidal person to die and as desirable as possible for the suicidal person to live. We must refrain from responding in a manner that would increase his or her feelings of guilt or shame. It is vital to recognize that directive, judgmental attitudes toward patients concerning their negative thoughts and behaviors will only drive them further into the self-destructive process.

On the other hand, the clinician who understands the negative thought process and its impact on human behavior can often be instrumental in averting a suicidal crisis. Depressed or suicidal individuals are unusually aware of the destructive voices elicited in Voice Therapy sessions. These patients have reached a stage where the balance has shifted to such a degree that the alien point of view represented by the voice actually has become their own point of view. In other words, the severely depressed or suicidal person has adopted the voice, and its strictures, commands, and directives, as his or her own. Being allowed to express the negative parental introjects in the session helps the depressed person to perceive these cognitive distortions as coming from an external source so that he or she can begin to question and challenge their validity. The practitioner who is knowledgeable about the voice process is acutely sensitive to which aspect of self (the self or antiself) is being expressed or manifested by the patient. Patients feel exceptionally understood by therapists who recognize the voice process, and this helps them to establish good rapport for the treatment program.

Endnotes

---

1. I first described this split and the resultant parent/child elements that make up the "self-mothering process" in a theoretical doctoral dissertation, *A Concept of the Schizophrenic Process* (Firestone, 1957).

2. The *fantasy bond* refers to an illusion of connection formed with the mother or primary caretaker during infancy or early childhood and later extended to significant others in an adult's interpersonal environment (Firestone, 1984, 1985).

3. This statement does not deny the damage caused by overt physical and sexual abuse. For example, several studies have also demonstrated correlations between physical abuse in childhood and later suicide attempts (Frederick, 1985; Sabbath, 1969). On the other hand, the child sensing unconscious or covert malevolence in his or her parent or parents experiences intense anticipatory fear or terror without insight into its source.

3 Suicidal Signs and Suicide Prevention

Inwardness—Personality Traits That Predispose Suicide

> If the fear comes from the protector
> Who is there to protect you from this fear?
> Nagarjuna, *The Tree of Wisdom,* verse 79
> (cited by Laing, 1976, p. 89)

> The inner self seeks to live by certain (apparently) compensating
> advantages. Such a self cherishes certain ideals. . . . Anything may
> be concealed from others, but nothing must be hidden from
> himself. In this, the self attempts to become "a relationship which
> relates itself to itself" to the exclusion of everything and anything.
> R. D. Laing (1960/1969, pp. 82-83)

> Inwardness is an exile, an excommunication from life.
> Stephanie

The term *inwardness* refers to a state of mind and a corresponding way of living that has drawn my attention for many years. I have observed that a disturbing number of people exist in a dazed, emotionally deadened state, with little or no comprehension of the essential reality of their lives. They are unaware that they are involved in a process that significantly diminishes their humanness, that they have embarked on a path that is potentially suicidal. They fail to notice that their defenses predispose them to live out a destiny that is not truly their own. I have come to understand that this lack of awareness is a principal characteristic of an inward, impersonal style of living that affects the majority of individuals in our culture.

There are countless ways of eliminating those qualities that make one uniquely human. The workaholic rationalizes giving up his or her personal life by blaming the demands of his or her job; the drug addict escapes pain by wrapping him- or herself in a cocoon of oblivion; the loner avoids the congenial fellowship of potential friends; the cynic poisons him- or herself with suspicions; the businessman/woman develops colitis; and the despairing teenager contemplates suicide as the only way out. Oddly enough, most people are not particularly concerned about these adverse personality manifestations and often pride themselves on the very traits that seriously damage their chances in life.

The process of becoming inward and neutralizing experience cuts an individual off from feeling for him- or herself and other people. This self-protective state is characterized by self-consciousness rather than a sense of being conscious of self or centered in self. The person's gaze is focused inward, on him- or herself, rather than outward toward others. Events in the interpersonal environment are filtered through this distorted lens of self-absorption, transformed (given a negative loading) by the voice process, and responded to inappropriately in a self-defeating manner.

The ability to give and accept love is also seriously impaired when people are immersed in an inward existence. Satisfaction of wants and needs is sought internally; the inward person is ministered to and punished by an internal voice process. He or she relates to parental introjects instead of real objects, which results in the reduction of both giving and taking operations, thereby significantly diminishing transactions with others.

To comprehend this narrow focus, the loss of experience, and the propensity for self-destruction, it is necessary to take an incisive look at the characteristics of the inward person. In this chapter, I will attempt the following: first, to understand the symptomatology of the retreat from feeling and withdrawal from interpersonal relating; second, to provide ideas for counteracting each aspect of the inward lifestyle; and, third, to suggest guidelines for a more honest, open, and outward orientation to life.

Observable Signs of Inwardness

My concept of "inwardness" denotes a syndrome of specific personality traits and behavior patterns that play a central role in all forms of psychopathology

but that are particularly evident in suicidal individuals. The primary characteristics of the inward person are (a) a tendency toward isolation, (b) progressive denial of his or her priorities and withdrawal from favored activities and
relationships, (c) use of addictive substances or routines, (d) withholding
personal feelings, (e) a preference for seeking gratification in fantasy in place
of pursuing satisfactions in the real world, (f) marked feelings of self-hatred
and cynical attitudes toward others, and (g) a lack of direction in life leading
to a sense of despair and hopelessness.

It is necessary to distinguish the inward syndrome from self-reflection,
introspection, time spent alone for creative work or planning, contemplation
of nature, meditation, and other forms of spiritual or intellectual pursuits. By
contrast, the inward orientation to life represents a retreat into oneself based
on early attempts in childhood to avoid frustration and primal pain. What was
once an adaptive defense to stress, and functional as a survival mechanism,
remains in the personality as a dysfunctional, addictive habit pattern. For the
adult, the inward process causes far more problems than it resolves.

Most significantly, the traits and habit patterns of individuals who lead
an inward, self-protective lifestyle correspond directly to the precursors of
suicide as delineated by suicidologists including David Shaffer and Edwin
Shneidman (MacNeil-Lehrer Productions, 1987). They indicated that when
an individual moves toward increased isolation, resents social intrusion, and
becomes exceptionally quiet and withdrawn, one should be concerned. (This
is especially true when observing adolescents.) An alarm signal should sound
when one notices that a close friend or relative exhibits such telltale signs of
depression and hopelessness as losing interest and excitement in priorities,
dropping out of favored activities, or retreating from an important relationship
for no apparent reason. This alarm should intensify when behaviors such as
these are accompanied by an increased reliance on substances, that is, inordinate food intake or excessive drinking or drug usage. Preoccupation with
fantasy and a self-critical or victimized orientation round out the profile of
the presuicidal individual.

We must bear in mind that the suicidal person will do everything in his
or her power to conceal the suicidal motive by striving to appear as normal as
possible as he or she moves along the pathway toward complete self-
destruction. Yet a sensitive and caring friend or concerned outsider familiar
with the warning signs noted above might have the perceptiveness to see
through the deception and take appropriate action. In understanding the
dynamics involved in "inward personality disorders," we can challenge these
trends before they reach pathological proportions. Ideally, this task would be
avoided altogether if we adopted a sound approach to mental hygiene that

discourages children from using the defensive strategies that can ultimately lead to suicide. This approach would stress (a) avoiding the preconditions for developing inward personality traits and (b) helping children to alter such defensive patterns when they are manifested.

Conditions Conducive to the Development of Inwardness

It is apparent that no child grows up under perfect conditions; a certain amount of stress is inevitable as each person develops and becomes fully grown. Tension and anxiety result from delays and frustrations impinging on the basic drives of the individual. No parent, no matter how loving, mature, and involved, can meet all of the needs of the child in a timely manner that would eliminate this core anxiety. Beyond this unavoidable damage, however, children are caused a vast amount of unnecessary pain and distress as a result of their parents' ignorance, personal limitations, and aggressive tendencies toward them. Undeniably, there are vast differences in the emotional climate that children are exposed to in their formative years. The degree of stress suffered varies considerably from person to person; even children within the same home have diverse experiences.

Even in very young children, one can observe the early signs of withdrawal or retreat from self. By the time the individual reaches adulthood, these characteristics are deeply entrenched (see Figure 3.1). The inward person, whether child or adult, (a) is not centered in him- or herself; (b) tends to be excessively dependent or anxiously attached; (c) makes connecting responses that arouse guilt, emotional hunger, anger, and a sense of obligation in the other; (d) has a tendency to avoid genuine eye contact; and (e) is, to varying degrees, cut off from feeling or is inappropriate in his or her emotional responses. There are often melodramatic reactions to trivial or unimportant incidents yet little or no response to significant life events.

Retreat to an increasingly inward posture represents a form of controlled destruction of the self. Neurotic symptomatology, personality disorders, and repetitive, self-defeating behaviors are the inevitable result. A particular style or mode of defense will tend to generate specific symptoms, that is, compulsive-obsessional disorders, psychosomatic illnesses, delusions, or other forms of psychopathology. Patterns of defense tend to persist and become habitual, which leads to progressive deterioration in broad areas of functioning. For example, a person whose characteristic style of defense is one of emotional distancing will provoke negative responses and rejection from significant

Observable Signs of the Healthy Individual	Observable Signs of Fragmentation in Children and Adults
The healthy, spontaneous, centered individual seeks external gratification. Aggression is directed at the source of frustration.	The damaged or excessively defended individual seeks gratification internally in fantasy and tends to sabotage successes in reality. Aggression and rage are directed at self and others as an alienation process.
The healthy individual generally manifests	**The defended individual manifests**
(1) A self-possessed state, as contrasted with elevated anxiety states and emotional deadness (2) A lively, appealing quality (3) Eye contact—personal relating (4) Independence (5) Feeling responses	(1) A cutoff or agitated state (2) Unlikable characteristics—character defenses are etched into physical appearance, posture, and expressive movement (3) Lack of genuine eye contact—impersonal relating (4) Dependency relationships and connecting responses (5) A lack of or inappropriate affect

Figure 3.1. Manifestations of Mental Health (Self) and Fragmentation (Antiself) Systems)

others, which leads to a further retreat into fantasy or other self-protective mechanisms. The defended individual becomes imprisoned in a downward-spiraling cycle.

Open/Outward Lifestyle Versus an Inward State

Psychological functions and addictive propensities can be represented as opposite poles on a continuum, ranging from an outward lifestyle of pursuing goals in the real world to an inward lifestyle characterized by fantasy, passivity, and isolation (see Figure 3.2).

A number of the dimensions listed above are related to those delineated on the "Continuum of Negative Thought Patterns" (see Figure 13.1). In summary, every individual blocks out feelings and emotions to some degree and in a manner that causes him or her to deviate from the true course of his or her life. Each person tends to develop a specific, idiosyncratic method for dulling, deadening, and disconnecting from his or her experiences. The tragic fact is that most people live out their lives largely in the destructive antiself system or defended posture, resisting individuation and fulfilling experiences in life.

Manifestations of the Inward State

Indications of an inward state are not separate and discrete; they tend to overlap. For purposes of clarity and elucidation, however, they will be referred to as separate entities and illustrated by case material. At the end of the discussion of each category, I will offer corrective procedures. These suggestions will be expanded in Chapters 14 and 15.

Case Background

Stephanie, a youthful 50-year-old woman with a lively sense of humor, was seemingly outgoing and friendly. Despite her facade, her posture and mannerisms revealed the imprint of the abuse and neglect she had endured during her childhood. Extremely uncomfortable in social situations, her self-consciousness and low self-esteem were evident in the way she lowered her head and avoided direct eye contact and in her hesitant style of talking. At work, Stephanie experienced overwhelming feelings of claustrophobia and often left the office. At these times, she drove around aimlessly or wandered alone through a nearby shopping mall, seeking the comfort and relaxation she believed she could find only in isolation. Years ago, Stephanie sought further relief through increasingly frequent periods of drinking in isolation. Stephanie's childhood was chaotic, marked by physical mistreatment, indifference, and repeated separations.

Notes from Stephanie's journal tell her story:

My family was not accepted in the North Carolina town where I was born. The neighbor kids couldn't play with us because we weren't the "right kind

OPEN/OUTWARD VERSUS INWARD/SELF-PARENTING	
Goal-directed behavior Self-fulfillment Self-affirmation	Seeking gratification in fantasy Self-denial Self-destructiveness
Lack of self-consciousness Realistic self-appraisal Self-assertion	Exaggerated self-consciousness Hypercritical attitudes toward the self Passivity and victimized stance

Adaptability
Facing up to pain and anxiety
    with appropriate affect
    and response
	Nonadaptability
	Utilizing routinized habits,
	    addictive personal relationships,
	    and substances as painkillers

Relatedness to others Feeling state Social involvement	Impersonal relating Cutting off or withdrawal of affect Isolation

Genitality
 	
Maintaining a separate identity
Search for meaning and
    transcending goals
	Masturbatory and addictive
	    sexuality
	Merged identity and fusion
	Narrow focus

Figure 3.2. Open/Outward Lifestyle Versus Inward/Self-Parenting Lifestyle

of people." One of my first memories is of walking down the street and repeating to myself, "I don't care, I don't care."

My life was just me. I hardly remember ever talking to anyone, particularly in my family. My mother left before I can remember. One memory is more like a nightmare. I was in the back seat of a two-door car. Making noise, either crying or just laughing or something. She reached for me, angry. Then something was over my face. I was screaming and squirming.

I started to sink. I could feel my breath being taken away. I stopped, eyes open wide, as still as still can be. Not a breath or a sound. All was quiet. Then flashing lights and noises. I heard someone say, "She's not moving." Whatever was over my face was gone. I imagine my eyes wide open. My father was there and my mother was gone. Flashing lights scare me a lot. I don't remember talking much after that. And never looking anyone straight in the eyes. My eyes were too big; they knew too much. They knew about dying. She marked my soul.

I was left alone, living in fantasy. My father was unpredictable. He would either cook dinner for us or beat everyone in sight. I'd hide. Nights were filled with terror. Voices. In writing this I can feel the emotion of the memory of my father beating my sister. Of waking to see my sister's bed empty. There was nothing I could do to save her. I saved myself by being quiet.

A Tendency Toward Isolation

Recently, Stephanie met with me and described her isolated lifestyle. At the time of the interview, her defended solution was stabilized and she had managed to achieve psychological equilibrium. However, dissatisfied with this plateau of adjustment, she had expressed the desire to move forward in her life.

In the first part of the discussion, Stephanie reveals the state of mind that imprisoned her and the severe limitations it imposed on her. She goes on to explore the self-critical thoughts or voices that direct her to distance herself from close friendships and isolate herself in meaningless activities.

Dr. F.: What does "inwardness" mean to you when you think about it?

Stephanie: I know that it has caused me the most problems in my life, in relation to everything in my life, in relation to my children. Yet it feels like survival to me. Even in thinking of talking about it with you today, I felt hugely threatened.

Dr. F.: How does inwardness manifest itself in your life? How do you lead this inner life? What do you do?

Stephanie: I try to make myself okay. That's the thing that's utmost in my mind. I'm always thinking about how to improve myself. It can be the most simple thing. It can be cleaning off my desk, arranging my clothes.

Dr. F.: This time alone is spent working on yourself, fixing yourself. Why do you need to fix yourself?

Stephanie: I just feel like I'm such a poisonous person, like I'm just like the worst person. Everything is wrong with me, my looks, my thinking, my speech, and the best thing I can do is be quiet. The best thing I can do is just stay out of people's way. That's like the voice I listen to, "Don't cause any trouble."

Dr. F.: Try to say it as a voice. Try to say what you are telling yourself.

Stephanie: "Look, get everything straight. Stand up straight! Talk straight! Don't be so stupid."

(Stephanie sounds increasingly angry.)

> "You're so stupid all the time. Every word out of your mouth is stupid! You don't know how to speak. You don't know how to talk. You don't know the right words for things. You don't know the right things to do. You don't know how to touch people. You don't know how to love people. Just stay out of things, just stay out of it.
>
> "Just look at you. You're bothering everybody. You're bothering everybody. Don't look at people. You'd better not look at people, because then people will see. They'll see it in your eyes. They'll see deep down inside of you how really bad you are."
>
> The only thought I had about talking with you today was that I just wanted to hold my head up. I didn't want to keep my head down.
>
> *Dr. F.:* You didn't want to look like you believed those things.
>
> *Stephanie:* But I do. And I can never feel relaxed. It's like one or two times in my life I could remember feeling relaxed. But when I'm alone I feel more relaxed, when I'm reading or walking around alone.
>
> *Dr. F.:* You see it as a way of relaxing. But does it really work that way?
>
> *Stephanie:* It doesn't make me feel better, later when I'm not alone. It's just the absence of something.

Isolation is a key aspect of an inward, self-destructive lifestyle. It can be a significant sign of suicidal intent and a central element in actual suicide. As in Stephanie's case, self-critical attitudes and feelings of worthlessness lead to an avoidance of meaningful social relationships. However, the inward person rarely faces the extent of his or her self-hatred. Instead, rationalizations preclude awareness of the retreat from life: "I need some space, more quiet time or time alone to think things over," or simply, "I'm too busy," or "I don't have enough money to go places and do things."

Heckler (1994), in *Waking Up, Alive,* notes that the first step in the descent into the "suicidal trance" is characterized by withdrawal from social contact. This consists of

> a tangible, emotional, spiritual, and even physical pulling away from contact and connection [with others. It is not] a casual decision to remain aloof . . . it is an active response to intense unabated suffering. (p. 46)

Withdrawal may begin in small increments, and from the outside it may not be easy to detect: little things left unsaid, eyes that don't look up to meet your gaze, a faraway expression.

Withdrawal is a complex process, with two complementary mechanisms. It offers protection, a cloak in which one may take refuge from the impact and reverberations of overwhelming stress . . . [a normal response to trauma]. On the other hand, the withdrawal can become generalized—a habitual posture of retreat from the world, which insidiously becomes a lifestyle and then a trap. (pp. 49-50)

A demographic study by Gove and Hughes (1980) indicates that inwardness as exemplified in social isolation is related to self-destructive behavior. The authors demonstrate that alcoholism and suicide are two forms of social pathology that relate to social isolation, operationally defined as "living alone." They conclude that these two forms of self-destructive behavior are found to be much more prevalent in those living alone than in those who live with others. This conclusion agrees with findings from research relating high suicide rates to areas of low population density with their resultant physical and social isolation (Seiden, 1984a).

• *Corrective procedures:* Most patients report a decline in voice attacks when in the company of other people. Thus the corrective procedures would be to discourage time spent alone, encourage communication with a friend or ally, and help the patient schedule activities in a social context.

A Progressive Denial of Priorities and Withdrawal From Relationships and Favored Activities

Tendencies toward isolation can ultimately lead to the abandonment of friendships and significant relationships. Continually changing jobs or careers, as well as frequent moves to a new location, are other indications of a suicidal process or "trance." Losing interest in special activities, hobbies, or causes that previously brought pleasure to a person or that appeared to be an important part of his or her identity is evidence of a progressive descent into an inward state in which one no longer cares, where nothing matters.

At crucial points in her life, Stephanie's tendency to withdraw escalated into a pattern of running away. When her son was 2 years old, Stephanie left him with her husband and moved to a distant state to start life over on her own, thereby unconsciously repeating the rejection she had experienced from her own mother. In the interview, she refers to this method of escape and connects it to extremely self-depreciating voices.

Stephanie. If anyone is ever critical of me, then I just feel like, "You've got to go away. You've got to get out of here." It doesn't even have to be critical at all, even a slight request, "Would you move your chair over?" or something as innocuous as that. It's not at all like somebody being really critical.

Dr. F.: It takes nothing to set you off.

Stephanie: Right. If I come out of the inward state at all and then if there's anything that hurts my feelings, I mean even something like that, then I'm just set off and the voice starts again:

"You see, I told you. You're a weird person. You should just go off by yourself. Just get out of here."

That voice used to be much stronger in relation to running away. I've had a pattern where I ran away since I can remember. From the time I was able to walk I ran away. But as an adult, too, I ran away. It's like someone committing suicide except you just go away. It's not much different really, except you just don't kill yourself.

Dr. F.: It serves the same purpose.

Stephanie: And it feels as intense as suicide, but it's an exile. It's not a good thing. It's an exile. It's an excommunication from life. I guess that's what I feel I deserve for some reason.

As the interview progresses, Stephanie makes a connection between her impulse to run away as an adult and the fear that drove her to seek a "safe place" as a child.

Stephanie: In my house, it was very dangerous and it was much safer to go off by myself. There was a lot of violence.

Dr. F.: What do you mean by violence?

Stephanie: My father was a violent man. You never knew what he was going to do, if he was going to beat everybody up. There was no warning. He didn't drink or do anything where there was any warning. It just came out of nowhere.

If someone just coughed or made a little noise, anything would set him off. I don't really remember my mother. I was very afraid of her and she left before I can remember. But I know I have feelings of being very afraid of her. I have a lot of physical fear of her.

Dr. F.: So it paid to just hide and stay out of everybody's way.

Stephanie: It was very important to stay out of people's way. My sister didn't and she was beaten every day. My brother and I both went away. But in my present life, it doesn't make any sense.

It is difficult to predict at what point in an individual's life the pattern of social isolation will progress to more serious forms of self-destruction or take the form of a "substitute" suicide (running away and so on). Incidents of adolescents running away as well as of adults suddenly deserting their families are often symptomatic of serious pathology. Heckler (1994) provides a succinct analogy to explain this dangerous progression in an individual's journey toward suicide:

> One pulls further away from genuine interpersonal exchange and, over time, loses a sense of who or what could be helpful. It is as if a person has become lost in the forest and finds a cave in which to sleep for the night. The territory is foreign and the sounds alien. Every rustle of leaves or crack of a twig is interpreted as a sign that something alive and dangerous is drawing nearer, and one pulls back into the cave, withdrawing deeper and deeper. The further the person retreats from the cave's mouth, the less the possibility of his or her distinguishing fact from fear, help from danger. (p. 56)

• *Corrective procedures:* In therapy, one would encourage the client to maintain important priorities, as, for example, in Stephanie's case, to somehow "sweat out" the relationship with her family and her child and not retreat any further than necessary from responsibilities and areas of meaning in her life. It is important to search out patients' unique interests and find a means to help them to pursue any activity in which they have invested any modicum of energy and excitement. Movement away from one's predilections is demoralizing whereas positive movement generates increased vitality and a stronger desire for life.

The Use of Addictive Routines and Substances

Excessive alcohol use and drug use are associated with suicide attempts and completions. Maltsberger (1986) reports that

> one fourth of the patients who commit suicide are in fact alcoholics. . . . Suicide prone patients are likely to become addicted to all such substances [sedatives, barbiturates, the benzodiazepenes, cocaine, and so on], and it is easier to act suicidally when under the influence of any of the sedatives. (pp. 74-75)

In general, self-nourishing habits can be categorized as "egosyntonic" in that they are originally perceived as positive and arouse minimal conflict with normal ego functioning. Until their use clearly becomes self-destructive or potentially dangerous, they are in consonance with the person's ego (Freud, 1917/1963). However, well-established self-nurturing habits become progressively self-limiting and self-destructive because they interfere with a person's capacity to cope with everyday experience. As addictive habits become associated with a more generalized retreat from the real world, they no longer feel acceptable to the self and begin to cause the individual considerable guilt. The indulgence of one's addiction, followed by punishing voice attacks, increases psychological pain, which, in turn, necessitates the use of more drugs or alcohol and sets into motion an insidious cycle of guilt, perturbation, and inescapable psychological pain. In numerous cases of long-standing addictions to harmful physical substances, self-nourishing habits of this sort eventually lead to self-destruction.

Breaking a compulsive habit pattern or an addiction can be the most difficult task that a patient undertakes in therapy. Stephanie reveals that when she stopped drinking 2 years earlier, the world looked cold and foreboding to her. Here she compares inwardness to other addictions.

> *Stephanie:* Staying within myself is the most important thing in my life. When I stopped drinking, it was nothing in comparison to thinking about this. Even though that was a big thing and it was hard for me to do.
>
> *Dr. F.:* You mean being inward or into yourself seems more addictive than when you were drinking.
>
> *Stephanie:* There's no comparison. Stopping drinking was one of the hardest things that I ever did. I went through a period that I've almost never experienced. I was in the dark. I felt like I was in a dark, cold place and it didn't stop for a long time, and it hasn't stopped altogether yet.
>
> But stopping drinking was something I had to do for myself. Inwardness is like that. There's something that I have to decide for myself that I want. I've already taken an action of being closer to the people that I really like, but it's so different than anything that I've ever experienced.
>
> *Dr. F.:* So to feel people liking you causes you pain, instead of making you happy.
>
> *Stephanie:* It causes me incredible pain.
>
> *Dr. F.:* So in a way you have to go against that, you have to be willing to suffer that pain to come out of this defense.
>
> *Stephanie:* I feel that when a person breaks a habit or an addiction no matter how small or large, it's like you think you're never going to get to the other side of this huge ditch or canyon. I get confused because if I go away to get that comfort, it feels so compelling, and the other way, until you get to the other side of whatever you're trying to cross, is very different, it's full of dangers. But it's the difference between living in the real world and living in a nightmare.
>
> *Dr. F.:* That's right. You have to sweat it out.

Stephanie: That nightmare that people live in is so terrible. It may seem nice, because sometimes it's comfortable and it's familiar, but it's a nightmare. That's what people don't realize. You can see it more in an alcoholic. People like to say, "a disgusting alcoholic" or a "disgusting drug person" but they don't see people living inwardly as disgusting.

Dr. F.: Even though it's somewhat like that.

Stephanie: And it's so compelling, once you get into that state, you don't want to come out, and it's as compelling as a person on heroin. I imagine that that's the way they feel. It's no different.

Anxiety and other painful symptoms generally accompany withdrawal from addictive substances. Stephanie stresses that coming out of the inward state is similar to "going cold turkey." She emphasizes that she would have given up almost anything in life to hold on to her inward world and isolation because of the comfort and solace she found there as a child.

Dr. F.: So it's difficult to come out of this inward state. You hold on to it at practically all costs.

Stephanie: At all costs. Yeah, it's worth everything to me. I feel I would defend it to my death. It's worth more than my children, it's worth more than friends that I would say I love. But I would choose this over that, I would choose it over my children. I have. It doesn't make any sense, and so my whole life doesn't make any sense.

I think I have to do something about this, because it's not a thing that you can stay even with. It only gets worse. I've made strides, but I get to a point and I get scared or something happens and then I go back to them. I go back to the inward state, then I'm lost again.

Voices regulate and rationalize addictive habit patterns, then punish the person for indulging his or her habit. Voices that say, for example, "Have a drink," "You deserve to relax," "One drink can't hurt" seduce the inward person into abusing a substance and then assail him or her with severe self-recriminations: "You're so weak." "You have no willpower." "You've let your family down again!" Such examples provide evidence that the voice is a hostile process rather than a form of conscience or moral guideline. In other words, voices attack from both sides of the fence. For example, a schizophrenic girl listened to voices telling her to burn herself. After she complied with these injunctions, she turned on herself. "Look how insane you are! You burned yourself! Only crazy people do that."

• *Corrective procedures:* Discourage substance abuse or any other addictive patterns and encourage the patient to substitute activities and relationships that are real and constructive. In place of addictive patterns of inwardness, it is important for the patient to schedule time with others, struggling through the painful anxiety states involved in interpersonal contact. Helping the person to recognize angry voices instead of allowing them to have full reign in the personality is important. Simply being cognizant that one is attacking oneself is a valuable technique that intrudes on voice attacks. An understanding of negative voices helps patients to see the voice as external and separate rather than as a representation of their own point of view.

Withholding Personal Feelings

Withholding refers to a holding back of pleasure or fulfillment from the self as well as a withdrawal of emotional and behavioral responses from others. When hurt and frustrated, the child withdraws his or her emotional investment in objects; that is, a process of decathexis occurs. As noted, the inward person has converted his or her transactions from social exchanges in the interpersonal environment to exchanges with internalized parental introjects. The withholding person resists involvement in emotional interchange, refusing to take love in from the outside or offer love and affection to others. There are a variety of patterns that act to keep relationships at bay, which causes a generalized reduction of commerce with others. These patterns are characterized by the reluctance or outright refusal to interact or, in psychobiological terms, to engage in an exchange of products.

Inward people tend to hold back desirable qualities that receive recognition. For example, a clinician reported complimenting a disturbed patient on her appearance; within hours, she made a serious suicide attempt. In less extreme cases, people are also refractory to compliments and admiration. A husband told his wife he loved her beautiful long hair, only to be startled and disappointed when she cut it the very next day. An employer gave an employee a highly favorable review, after which the employee's performance dropped off dramatically.

In the following, Stephanie talks about her lack of tolerance for genuine interactions with the people closest to her.

> *Stephanie:* I feel like I almost can't stand to have a real interaction with another person.
>
> *Dr. F.:* So you're cheating yourself out of your real life.

Stephanie: Yes, but it's way beyond anything that people can imagine. I hardly speak to anybody really. I hardly have any interaction with anyone, even though I have a boyfriend. I have really close friends. I'm well liked. I have an important career. I have things that are important in my life, like life's dreams.

Dr. F.: But somehow they're lost.

Stephanie: But they're all lost to me because of the inwardness.

Dr. F.: It's like a shield.

Stephanie: Yeah. I always imagine in an intimate situation being close, I imagine that I could be close, that I could kiss someone and I could caress them and be tender, but in the actual situation, I feel like I could jump out of my skin. Maybe I accomplish it in that one little isolated situation, but then I never go back to that level of closeness. I don't want to go back. I'm scared to death to really relate on that level.

Wherever it manifests itself, withholding is governed by internal voices. Free-flowing feeling responses are inhibited by destructive thought patterns such as in the following: "Why should you go out of your way for her?" "She doesn't love you." "Your friends don't really care about how you feel." "Hell, who needs him, anyway?" The withholding individual may or may not be conscious of this underlying thought process, but it controls his or her destiny.

Patterns of withholding are also prevalent in the workplace, where passive-aggressive behaviors of procrastination, incompetence, and other nonproductive work styles are often manifested. Passive aggression may be directed outward toward others as a disguised form of hostility or inward against self as a pathological example of self-denial and self-limitation. The person who inhibits his or her responses, whether in the work arena or in personal relationships, needs to make sense out of his or her seemingly perverse tendency to avoid achieving essential goals. He or she uses ostensibly realistic reasons to justify behaviors that generate a restrictive, self-limiting lifestyle.

• *Corrective procedures:* It is important to point out withholding behavior patterns and the negative consequences they predispose. Many people hold back desirable qualities because of their basic intolerance of intimacy. In therapy, it is necessary to help patients recognize the anger involved in passive aggression. Patients should be encouraged to maintain generous attitudes and, at the same time, to develop the capacity for accepting kindness and generosity from others.

Preference for Fantasy Gratification in Place
of Pursuing Satisfactions in the Real World

Fantasy is a major defense against emotional pain, a self-soothing mechanism that is immediately rewarding. In choosing to defend against disappointment, sadness, anger, and other painful affects, the inward person gradually comes to prefer fantasy over active competition for life's rewards. Reliance on this type of gratification tends to be progressively incapacitating as it distorts everyday experiences, interferes with the active pursuit of goals, and leads to passivity. This preoccupation with fantasy is far more extensive than simple daydreams or idle ruminations and far more pervasive than is usually recognized. The key issue here is that fantasy and the habit patterns that support and supplement it deprive the individual of the necessary ingredients for a fulfilling life.

People who attempt to gratify their needs in fantasy are, on some level, aware of their retreat from others. They create and strive to maintain a facade composed of superficial interactions to disguise their lack of genuine involvement in close relationships.

> *Stephanie:* I feel like I still live in fantasy a lot. When I was a kid, I totally lived in fantasy. I get more gratification from that than I do from a real interaction with another person.

Stephanie goes on to describe how she retreated into an inward world of fantasy to escape the pain and guilt surrounding the recent suicide of her brother.

> *Stephanie:* I felt like I was getting somewhere in my life, and then when my brother died it felt like that was a good excuse to go back into that inner world, because I couldn't resolve his death. (sad)
>   I wasn't close to him in my adult life, but in my childhood I was. So I can't imagine if someone I care about now died. I can't imagine the pain.
> *Dr. F.:* So then you went even more inward after you heard about his death?
> *Stephanie:* I didn't want to feel anything. Nothing! When I came out of it a little bit, it seemed too painful. But it was a dramatic reaction, because I think it's not as painful if you put yourself back in the real situation. But if you withdraw into fantasy, you're in trouble. You have to put yourself back into the real situation or else you're dead. You have to put yourself back into the feelings.
> *Dr. F.:* You have to feel your pain in order to stay alive.
> *Stephanie:* Because if you withdraw you only keep withdrawing.

Dr. F.: So why are you going backward since his death?

Stephanie: Because I just haven't been brave enough to keep feeling.

People who live largely in fantasy are more concerned with image or appearance than with actual personal satisfactions. They refrain from initiating actions that might lead to real rewards because achieving their goals in reality threatens to disrupt the fantasy process. Passivity and indifference signify surrender to an unfeeling, deadened state in which the person experiences spontaneous activity or productive work as an unwelcome intrusion. A passive lifestyle also fosters a helpless, victimized, paranoid posture in which people perceive forces as acting on them rather than seeing themselves as being able to act upon the environment. In subverting their anger, they feel progressively more overwhelmed by negative events and an increasing sense of powerlessness and hopelessness.

• *Corrective procedures:* Expose the fantasy process and discourage its manifestation. Suggest real activities that are goal directed. Help patients to feel their pain, to face issues in their lives rather than retreating into fantasy. Guide the individuals toward relationships that are satisfying, and help them to avoid those that are toxic and justify their defenses. Friendship is therapeutic. In working with inward patients, the therapist ideally would be a positive "transitional object," a real person whom the patient can trust and depend on while breaking down the fantasy process.

• In relation to a paranoid, victimized orientation, the therapist would help the patient understand that feelings of right or wrong, just or unjust, are not the key issues. The key issue is survival and feeling the appropriate anger and rage rather than complaining about one's circumstances.

A Negative Self-Image and Cynicism Toward Others

One characteristic common to suicidal individuals is a deep sense of low self-esteem and shame. Such individuals tend to hold on to negative attitudes toward themselves and find it extremely difficult to adjust to a more positive or realistic point of view. The process of self-criticism is a direct consequence of the defense mechanism of idealizing parents and other family members. In Stephanie's case, this idealization was clearly associated with her low opinion of herself. Her sense of worthlessness and shame were compounded by guilt reactions in relation to her brother's suicide. Throughout her childhood, she worshiped him and wholeheartedly believed that he had been strong enough to escape the family unscathed. His suicide destroyed her idealized picture of him and precipitated guilt for surviving when he did not.

> *Dr. F.:* What voices do you think you had after you found that your brother had died? What did you tell yourself?
>
> *Stephanie:* It goes like, "How can you be alive, you're the fucked-up one, you're the one who never did anything right, never did anything responsible, never did anything. You never did anything, you never did anything and he did everything right. And he's dead. He's the one who's dead.
>
> "You should be dead! You're the one who should be dead, not him. He did everything right, he was smart, he did everything right. He had a family! He had a wife! He had everything!
>
> "*You're* the one who's supposed to be dead, you're the fucked-up one, you're the stupid one, you're the ugly one. You're the one who was never supposed to be born." (sobs deeply)
>
> I was never supposed to be born. I just kind of sneaked out, that's what I feel like. My whole life, I've felt like I just kind of sneaked in.
>
> I was never supposed to have a life, much less a life like I have now.
>
> *Dr. F.:* You feel like you're just not entitled to it.
>
> *Stephanie:* I wasn't even supposed to be born. Nobody was happy that I was born. So in a way I don't even believe people. I'm very skeptical that I could be a person that somebody would like or care about.

Stephanie's skepticism and distrust of others operate in conjunction with the disparaging thoughts she has toward herself. At times, when threatened by too much closeness, she exhibits an irritability and sarcasm uncharacteristic of her usual manner. Both views, self-critical attitudes and hostility toward others, are symptoms of a defended, alienated state of mind representative of negative parental introjects within the antiself system. Negative anticipations about the world are also based on early experiences within the family. When the general atmosphere at home is hostile and the parents inadequate or untrustworthy as they were in Stephanie's formative years, the child's feeling reactions to these conditions will later be transferred to new persons and relationships. As an adult, the person will distort people and events, responding to them with negative or fearful expectations.

• *Corrective procedures:* Help the patient realize that voice attacks both on the self and on others operate concurrently, and both predispose alienation.

Assist him or her in separating out realistic considerations from irrational self-attacks. It is important to help the patient realize that attacking oneself serves no purpose; rather, it is more productive to direct energy toward changing negative or dysfunctional behaviors.

• The therapist should point out paranoid distortions and demonstrate to patients that anger and cynicism are often projections onto others of parental attitudes, a process that leads to distortion in current personal relationships.

Lack of Direction in Life Leading to a Sense of Hopelessness and Despair

Most children grow up with a weakened, fragmented, and fragile sense of self. Early in life, the damaged child disconnects from him- or herself and, in the process, loses touch with his or her basic wants and priorities. Cut off from real experience, the inward person finds it more and more difficult to express or even define his or her emotions. Suicidologists have noted that an absence of desire or motivation characterizes the stage immediately preceding the suicidal act. If an individual loses touch with fundamental wants or strivings, he or she will find it impossible to identify the source of his or her angry feelings. Even if a person develops an "I don't care" attitude (as Stephanie did) and inhibits or represses his or her needs, they are still operant; when frustrated, they activate aggressive reactions. This reaction predisposes a state of agitation and bewilderment in the suicidal individual, with a corresponding depletion of energy and vitality. The process of progressive self-denial and loss of direction described here leads to a demoralized state of emptiness, hopelessness, and despair for the inward person.

Stephanie's family life was typified by both emotional and physical neglect. Her parents failed to teach her, either through role-modeling or explanation, any values or even any of the most fundamental ways of coping with life. Living in near poverty, and traumatized by the memory of her mother's overt act of aggression as well as the abandonment that followed, Stephanie grew up with a profound sense of deprivation. She failed to develop motivation to fulfill basic wants or needs. Heckler (1994) describes the child's reaction to this form of trauma as "the most dramatic form of loss which suicide attempters describe. The event, indelibly etched into the body and mind, represents the moment when the world ceases to be a nourishing place" (p. 19).

As the discussion drew to a close, Stephanie expressed her outrage at the effect the neglect and maltreatment she incurred early in life has had on her.

She has been handicapped in her capacity to direct her actions toward goals that would give her life meaning and purpose.

> *Stephanie:* Today I have a way better life than I ever imagined, but it's hard for me to accept it.
>
> *Dr. F.:* Still you're stuck in your inward style. And it still hurts you, you say.
>
> *Stephanie:* Yes, definitely, and there's a certain amount of anger that comes up in relation to this. I feel so split in it. On one hand, I keep telling myself these self-critical things all the time, and then on the other hand I'm very angry that anyone would ever think that about me.
>
> How could somebody treat a child like they treated me? How can somebody let a child grow up with such misperceptions and such, such a lost feeling of not even knowing the simplest thing about life? How could you not take a child's life seriously? How could you look at a child and let them grow up with nothing, not even a word? Not a reaction except anger.
>
> *Dr. F.:* So you're outraged.
>
> *Stephanie:* Yeah, on some level.
>
> *Dr. F.:* But it's weak, and it sounds like you can't quite take your part strongly. Why don't you try to take your part in it?
>
> *Stephanie:* I would be so outraged, it would be like murderous. For what they did to me, they deserve to die. They deserve torture. Just the simplest thing: I can't hold my head up, I can't hold my head up, I can't look at anybody!
>
> Don't you understand that? You stupid people! (loud, angry screaming) I can't hold my head up! I can't look at anybody! I can't have a life! I can't love my own daughter! I don't know how. I don't know how. She suffers because of you. You didn't even see me. I was alive!
>
> I was a person! I was trying to make sense of something, I had no sense. I have no sense of my life. I walk around all day trying to make sense of the slightest feeling of loving somebody or wanting to reach out to somebody. The slightest feeling causes me agony because these assholes didn't look up.
>
> They let my brother kill himself. They didn't look up, they were perfectly happy, they just let him die. That's a huge anger in me, and it wasn't just because he was sick. It's because he lived his life out the way he thought he should and then he just killed himself.
>
> So I'm doing the same thing. In a way maybe I'm just too guilty to do anything else, but it's not okay.
>
> *Dr. F.:* Or you can do something about it.
>
> *Stephanie:* I can do something about it. Because if I go away, it's such a nightmare. And the other way, you get to the other side of it. Yet it's full of dangers, it's full of hurts because somebody may die or . . .

Dr F.: Yeah, if you attach to people you really can be hurt again. (pause) How do you feel from talking?

Stephanie: I feel hugely relieved.

• *Corrective procedures:* Help the patient to discover the essential thing in life he or she cares about—a person, a cause, or raison d'étre. In *Man's Search for Meaning,* Viktor Frankl (1946/1959) emphasized the central importance of the search for meaning in life. This issue is of the greatest concern for people at risk for suicide. Loss of meaning and existential despair must be countered by encouraging emotional investment in oneself and others and helping the patient find transcending goals. A positive offering to others beyond his or her narrow self-interest builds up self-esteem in a person who is otherwise demoralized.

Summary and Implications for Suicide Prevention

The inward state is an addictive, painkilling mode of defense adopted by the child in the face of environmental deprivation and external threat. The child's renunciation of his or her true self and the retreat into an emotionally deadened existence is the best adaptation that he or she can make in the struggle to preserve a rudimentary sense of self in the midst of toxic influences. These self-protective measures help an individual to survive a grim or torturous childhood at the expense of a richer, fuller life as an adult. On an unconscious level, the inward person gradually gives up goal-directed activity and avoids real gratification so as to cling to the safety of an internal world over which he or she has complete control. The process of nurturing oneself in the inward state becomes addictive because it has immediately rewarding properties that dull psychological pain. Becoming aware of this process is essential for understanding and facilitating movement toward one's growth potential.

It is important to emphasize that people will encounter internal and external pressures as they emerge from the self-protective, inward state and will inevitably have to face painful truths about their lives. Understanding these dynamics is all the more important because the damage, whether clinical or subclinical, is far more extensive than one would like to believe.

Recognizing the signs of a potential suicide before they reach peak intensity is the most important factor in suicide prevention. One or more of the major inward personality traits delineated above may be exhibited in the premorbid condition. However, people who exhibit these traits often stabilize at varying levels along the continuum of self-destructiveness, and many will never become suicidal. At the time of Stephanie's interview, she had been stable for 10 to 15 years. Although considerably impaired in her ongoing life experience, she appeared to have found an alternative to complete self-destruction. Although it remains unlikely that she will become self-destructive to the point of inflicting injury on herself, she must continue to be on the alert for a buildup of inward patterns.

A significant increase in the intensity of inward characteristics sets into motion a negative spiral of self-absorption and increased voice attacks. A progression of this sort is the most blatantly obvious cause for alarm. It is important for suicidologists to widen their perspective and look beyond the destructive signs of inwardness manifested by disturbed individuals to recognize the core dynamics that predispose defensive, self-protective personality trends in "normals." These signs of inwardness are apparent early in life. Inimical voices are manifested in children as well as adults.

One day, I was showing a documentary on destructive voices to associates and visitors. Friends and their children, who were moving in and out of the large family room, overheard the film. Some of the children commented, "You know, I have these voices too." Finding it somewhat surprising, we inquired further about what the children meant. They went on to explain: "I have voices that tell me I'm bad. I also have voices that tell me that I'm ugly and stupid. I even have voices that tell me I don't deserve to live." Needless to say, their responses caused us concern, and we decided to investigate further. We discovered that in a group of children between the ages of 7 and 15, all were able to identify similar thoughts. There were strong parallels between parents' voices and their children's voices, suggesting a clear intergenerational link.

Recognizing inward, defensive patterns in our children that are based on internal voices can serve as the basis for a sound mental hygiene program. Inward patterns can be observed and dealt with using corrective procedures. Children who are withdrawn, spacey, preoccupied with fantasy, or seemingly lost can be helped before these patterns become rigid and impenetrable. Children who have too many accidents and who continually hurt themselves are a cause for concern. Children who are generally angry, self-critical, sullen, or always feeling rejected and sorry for themselves should be seen as in need of help, and appropriate measures should be taken.

Once we recognize how inward personality traits relate to various forms of psychopathology, we can identify both predisposing and precipitating causes of self-destructive behavior in our search for understanding. In the case of physical illnesses such as pneumonia and allergy, the body's defensive processes actually become more pathogenic than the original causative agents. The same is true in the case of mental disorders. Psychological defenses that were originally survival oriented can later become a threat to survival. These defenses constitute negative elements within the personality that limit and can even destroy an individual's life.

4 Brief Review of Psychoanalytic and Cognitive Approaches to Suicide

I could not sleep, although tired, and lay feeling my nerves shaved to pain & the groaning inner voice: oh, you can't teach, can't do anything. Can't write, can't think. And I lay under the negative icy flood of denial, thinking that voice was all my own, a part of me, and it must somehow conquer me and leave me with my worst visions: having had the chance to battle it & win day by day, and having failed. . . . I have a good self, that loves skies, hills, ideas, tasty meals, bright colors. My demon would murder this self by demanding that it be a paragon, and saying it should run away if it is anything less.

> "Letter to a Demon" by Sylvia Plath
> (Hughes & McCullough, 1982, pp. 176-177)

Whenever it is a damp, drizzly November in my soul, . . . then, I account it high time to get to sea as soon as I can. This is my substitute for pistol and ball. With a philosophical flourish Cato throws himself upon the sword; I quietly take to the ship.

> Herman Melville (1851/1943, p. 3), *Moby Dick*

What Is Suicide?

Is there a common, agreed-upon definition of *suicide*? Throughout history, the word has had a variety of meanings, from the French Academy's official definition in 1762 as "the murder of oneself" (Soubrier, 1993, p. 35), to Freud (1910/1967), who declared suicide to be "nothing else than a [sort of] exit, an action, an end to psychic conflicts" (pp. 504-505), to Edwin Shneidman (1985), who wrote, "Suicide is a conscious act of self-inflicted cessation" (p. 206). About suicidal thoughts and fantasies, the philosopher Nietzsche (1886/1966) said, "The thought of suicide is a powerful comfort: it helps one through many a dreadful night" (p. 91).

In his book *Definition of Suicide,* Shneidman (1985) argued that

> the definitions of suicide that we see in textbooks, use in clinical reports, read in newspapers, and hear in everyday talk are just not good enough to permit us to understand the events we wish to change. The basic need . . . is for a radical reconceptualization of the phenomenon of suicide. (p. 4)

Jean-Pierre Soubrier (1993) gave a traditional psychoanalytic definition of suicide as "a final act of despair of which the result is not known, occurring after a battle between an unconscious death wish and a desire to live better, to love and be loved" (p. 37). I conceptualize suicide as a triumph of the antiself—the self-destructive aspect of the personality.

"Mental Illness" and Suicide

The suicidologist Edwin Shneidman (1989) also emphasized that suicide is not an illness; rather, it is

> a human, psychological orientation toward life, not a biological, medical disease. . . . Suicide is a human malaise tied to what is "on the mind," including one's view of the value of life at that moment. It is essentially hopeless unhappiness and psychological hurt—and that is not a medical condition. (p. 9)

In this context, Menninger's (1938) view of psychosis deserves special attention. He conceived of schizophrenia as a method of self-destruction:

> This departure from reality standards enables the psychotic person to destroy himself in a unique way not available to anyone else. He can imagine himself dead; or, he can imagine a part of himself to be dead or destroyed. This fantasied self-destruction, partial or complete, corresponds in its motives to actual self-mutilation and suicide. (p. 187)

As noted in Chapter 2, I conceptualize the various forms of "mental illness" as disordered lifestyles based on each individual's choice of defense. As such, emotional problems represent limitations in living, a restrictive, self-destructive posture toward life that ultimately leads to the formation of neurotic or psychotic symptoms. I support the view that mental illness is an illusion or myth, as stated by a number of theorists and clinicians (Laing & Esterson, 1964/1970; Szasz, 1961, 1963, 1978). Szasz (1963) suggested that "mental illnesses . . . be regarded as the expressions of man's struggle with the problem of *how* he should live" (p. 16). In attacking the "myth of mental illness," Szasz faulted the careless use of language for perpetuating beliefs about psychological distress that are as archaic as the belief in witchcraft.

In their writing, the suicidologists Kalle Achte (1980) and Norman Farberow (1980b) described indirect suicidal manifestations in nonmedical terms, that is, as the methods people use to sabotage their own success, seemingly preferring to live miserable, restricted lives. Indeed, the syndromes or "symptoms" and behavioral peculiarities manifested in so-called neuroses represent a self-protective way of living—or, actually, *non*living—one's life.

In this chapter and the next, I briefly review a number of perspectives on suicide: (a) psychoanalytic and object-relations approaches, (b) cognitive approaches, (c) the interrelatedness of self-destructive behaviors, (d) the epidemiology of suicide, and (e) methods used by researchers and clinicians to assess suicide risk.

Psychoanalytic/Object-Relations Approaches

The Basic Split in the Personality

Psychoanalytically oriented theorists, including Sigmund Freud, Anna Freud, Guntrip, Fairbairn, Ferenczi, Klein, Winnicott, Balint, Grotstein, and others, have addressed the negative side of the split that exists within each individual and its relationship to depression and suicide. Freud (1921/1955) connected this split or division with depression in his description of melancholia:

> Another such instance of introjection of the object has been provided by the analysis of melancholia. . . . A leading characteristic of these cases is a cruel self-depreciation of the ego combined with relentless self-criticism and bitter self-reproaches. . . .
> But these melancholias also show us something else. . . . They show us the ego divided, fallen apart into two pieces, one of which rages against the second. (p. 109)

Anna Freud (1966) explained that the negative aspect of self resulted from the child's identification with the aggressor, a defense mechanism first described by Ferenczi (1933/1955). Fairbairn and Guntrip elaborated on the concept of this "internal saboteur," referring to it as an antilibidinal ego. In Guntrip's (1969) analysis of Fairbairn's theory of "ego-psychology," he used the terms *libidinal ego* and *antilibidinal ego* to delineate parts of the split ego: "Inevitably the libidinal ego is hated and persecuted by the antilibidinal ego as well as by the rejecting object, so that the infant has now become divided against himself" (p. 72). Guntrip linked the punishing ego function of the antilibidinal ego to depression and suicide: "The degree of self-hate and self-persecution going on in the unconscious determines the degree of the illness, and in severe cases the person can become hopeless, panic-stricken, and be driven to suicide as a way out" (p. 190).

In a review of the English school of object relations regarding the concepts of splitting and projective identification, Grotstein (1981) described an individual's compulsion to act out this split-off aspect of self in the form of self-destructive behavior:

> The significance of defensive splitting lies in the experience of confronting alienated aspects of oneself. "Split-off" really means that a part of one's being has undergone alienation, mystification, mythification, and re-personification—in effect, has become someone else, an alien presence within. The terms "impulse," "drive," and "part of self" are all inadequate to express the profundity of this experience. (p. 11)

In his treatment of suicidal patients, John Maltsberger (1986) found them to have parents who are unusually critical or hostile. Most had been deprived of consistent empathic contact and had suffered considerable neglect and abuse. Maltsberger stated that what once was experienced as criticism from outside became criticism from inside in the form of an aggressive, critical superego, frequently taking on "ogre-like" proportions. Introjection of parental attitudes has resulted in a severe and markedly sadistic superego: "The critical activities of the superego . . . [are] experienced subjectively like an interior demon, revealing its origins in the parents from which it sprang" (p. 13).

Cognitive Approaches

Albert Ellis (1973) developed a logical approach to the analysis of cognitive processes known as Rational Emotive Therapy in which he challenged "irrational beliefs." According to Ellis, such beliefs lead to self-defeating behaviors evidenced in depressed patients. In a number of research studies, cognitive therapists (Abramson, Metalsky, & Alloy, 1989; Hamilton & Abramson,

1983; Rose, Abramson, Hodulik, Halberstadt, & Leff, 1994) investigated the relationship between cognitive style and depression. Studies by Miranda and Persons (1988) demonstrated that latent dysfunctional schemas can be activated during the asymptomatic period in cases of depression. In other words, these negative thoughts were elicited even at times when the patients were not actively depressed.

Aaron Beck (1976), Victor Raimy (1975), and Gershen Kaufman and Lev Raphael (1984) have described negative thoughts toward self and others. Beck's descriptions of "automatic thoughts" as "specific, discrete, relatively autonomous" thoughts that "occurred in a kind of shorthand" closely correspond to my observations of the hostile thought patterns elicited through the procedures of Voice Therapy. According to Beck (1976), specific schemas that the client has developed are the basis for molding data into cognitions. "The cognitive triad (negative views of self, future, and the world), specific thinking errors deficient in logic, and the existence of hypervalent schemas form the cornerstones of this model" (Rush & Beck, 1978, p. 217). As depression worsens, the client's thinking becomes increasingly dominated by negative beliefs.

Cognitive Processes in
Severe Depressive States

In an article describing 40 depressed patients, Arieti and Bemporad (1980) elaborated the particular types of childhood experiences that inevitably lead to the patient's developing "beliefs about himself and others that are, to a large extent, unconscious but that determine much of his behavior" (p. 1364). They went on to say that these distortions are maintained in the adult's cognitive processes and are the basis of the "depressive personality."

> The depressive adult still rigidly adheres to his unconscious cognitive system for structuring his social and inner world. It is this continuation of childhood social-cognitive patterns which ultimately predisposes one for depressive illness and forms the basis of depressive personality organization. (pp. 1364-1365)

John Bowlby (1980), in his definitive work *Loss: Sadness and Depression,* discussed childhood experiences that are most likely to contribute to serious depressive disorders in adulthood. He enumerated the particular beliefs engendered in the child (in the form of object representations) through the following experiences:

a. He [the child] is likely to have had the bitter experience of never having attained a stable and secure relationship with his parents despite having made repeated efforts to do so. . . . [Later he may develop] a strong bias to interpret any loss . . . as yet another of his failures. . . .

b. He may have been told repeatedly how unlovable, and/or how inadequate and/or how incompetent he is. . . . [This] would result in his developing a model of himself as unlovable and unwanted. . . .

c. He is more likely than others to have experienced actual loss of a parent during childhood. (pp. 247-248)

Bowlby's formulations correspond to Heckler's (1994) recent findings in 50 individuals who made serious suicide attempts:

> At least one of three kinds of loss appears in every story. They are the most common precursors to suicide, and the most ruinous. They include: traumatic loss, extreme family dysfunction, and alienation. . . .
> For some, the losses are concrete: the sudden death of a parent, the unexpected or unwanted dissolution of a family or a relationship, or the loss of one's physical health. Also included here are cases of extreme family dysfunction, such as spousal and child abuse. . . .
> Most often, current suffering is compounded and rendered more complex by previous sorrow. Like a long string of dominoes falling, the cascading sequence of loss becomes frightening and enervating, and eventually leads to an attempt. (pp. 11-12)

Arieti and Bemporad (1980) differentiated between mild or neurotic depression and severe or psychotic depression. They conceptualized depressed states as existing on a continuum in terms of the extent to which the individual actually believes or accepts his distorted pathological conceptions of himself and others. Studies conducted by Beck, Rush, Shaw, and Emery (1979) have resulted in the construction of a new model of depressed states:

> The *personal* paradigm of the patient when he is in a depressed state produces a distorted view of himself and his world. His negative ideas and beliefs appear to be a veridical representation of reality to him even though they appear farfetched to other people and also to himself when he is not depressed. (p. 21)

My conceptualizations about the thought process in depressed states are generally in accord with Beck's cognitive therapy of depression. In my estimation, depressed patients perceive their negative, hostile views as part of themselves and no longer move between their own viewpoint and that of the voice. For whatever reason, whether because of overwhelming frustration, a deep sense of loss, or a positive event beyond their level of tolerance at this point, depressed patients are now more against themselves than for themselves.

Cognitive Constriction in Suicidal States

As the voice asserts complete control over the depressed individual's thinking process, there is a constriction of thought and diminution of genuine affect. The operations of the voice, which are primarily cerebral, act more and more as an antifeeling agent. The patient becomes totally focused on his or her own inner ruminations and, as a result, eventually becomes completely cut off from feeling for him- or herself and others. Shneidman (1985) recognized the severity of this constriction of rational thought and affect characteristic of the suicidal patient. In writing about the common cognitive state in suicide, Shneidman stated, "I believe that it [suicide] is much more accurately seen as a more or less transient psychological constriction of affect and intellect" (p. 138).

Shneidman went on to enumerate four psychological features that seem to be necessary for a lethal suicidal event to occur. These are (a) acute perturbation, (b) heightened inimicality and self-hatred, (c) a sharp and almost sudden increase of constriction of intellectual focus, and (d) the idea of cessation, "the insight that it is possible to put an end to suffering by stopping the unbearable flow of consciousness" (p. 36). The most important characteristic of severe depression and suicidal ideation appears to be the individual's profound feeling of being cut off or isolated from him- or herself or, in Freudian terms, from the ego (Litman, 1967).

The Interrelatedness of Self-Destructive Behavior

A number of prominent suicidologists (Farberow, 1980b; Menninger, 1938; Shneidman, 1966) have conceptualized suicidal behavior as existing on a continuum ranging from "partial" suicidal behavior to actual suicide. Durkheim (1897/1951), the French sociologist, was one of the first to recognize an essential continuity of self-destructive behaviors. In his pioneering text *Suicide: A Study in Sociology*, he declared,

Suicides do not form, as might be thought, a wholly distinctive group, an isolated class of monstrous phenomena, unrelated to other forms of conduct, but rather are related to them by a continuous series of intermediate cases. They are merely the exaggerated form of common practices. (p. 45)

Edwin Shneidman (1966) presented a similar conceptual model in his description of "inimical patterns of living." He described these "unfriendly" behavioral responses as the "multitudinous ways in which an individual can reduce, truncate, demean, narrow or shorten, or destroy his own life" (p. 199). He warned against perceiving these as "substituted suicides" and instead viewed them as a range of behaviors in which completed suicide is but the most extreme example.

Menninger (1938), in *Man Against Himself*, used the term *partial suicide* to signify a variety of self-destructive lifestyles that amount to suicide on a continuing, alienated basis. Menninger declared, "In the end each man kills himself in his own selected way, fast or slow, soon or late" (p. vii). Farberow (1980b) described certain areas of everyday activities, such as "eating, taking medication, social drinking, social gambling, driving and risk-taking sports" (p. 2), that can involve indirect suicidal behavior. Farberow (1980a) differentiated indirect self-destructive behavior (ISDB) from direct self-destructive behavior (DSDB), and suicide along two dimensions, time and awareness, stating, "The effect [of ISDB] is long-range and the behavior may span years; the person is usually unaware of or doesn't care about the effects of his behavior, nor does he consider himself a suicide" (p. 17). Beck et al. (1979) have also conceptualized an individual's degree of suicidal intent as a point on a continuum. Marsha Linehan (1981), in her description in "A Social-Behavioral Analysis of Suicide and Parasuicide," used the term *parasuicide* (Endnote 1) to describe suicide attempts that did not result in death. In his chapter "Definitions of Suicide," Soubrier (1993) described my concept of *microsuicide*, which includes behavioral patterns of progressive self-denial, withholding, destructive dependency bonds, and harmful lifestyles that are mediated by negative thought processes and function as a defense against separation and death anxiety (Firestone & Seiden, 1987, 1990b).

Summary

In summary, most psychoanalytic and cognitive theorists postulate that feelings of hostility, guilt, and a need for self-punishment become attached to internalized parental prohibitions and directives, and these dynamics play a strong role in depression and suicide. I feel that whether or not these feelings and cognitions are contained within the boundaries of a hypothetical super-ego, antilibidinal ego, or split ego is not as important as the fact that they are *retained in the form of destructive voices* within the adult personality. The voice process, in turn, plays a major role in precipitating the patient's depressive state. In Voice Therapy sessions, it becomes obvious that the voice is not merely a hypothetical construct but can be observed almost as a living "entity," and the behaviors it directs can be clearly discerned in the everyday lives of "normal," neurotic, and psychotic individuals.

Voice Therapy methodology is more deeply rooted in the psychoanalytic approach than in a cognitive-behavioral model. My theoretical focus is on understanding the psychodynamics of the patient's functional disturbance in the present, and the methods are based on an underlying theory of personality that emphasizes a primary defensive process (Firestone, 1988, 1990c).

Endnote

1. The term *parasuicide* was suggested by Kreitman, Philip, Greer, and Bagley (1969) and includes all categories of suicide attempts. Kreitman (1977) defined parasuicide as a "non-fatal act in which an individual deliberately causes self-injury or ingests a substance in excess of any prescribed or generally recognized therapeutic dosage" (p. 3).

5 The Epidemiology of Suicide and Brief History of Methods for Assessing Risk

Demographic Factors for Suicide in the United States

Suicide is a problem of considerable magnitude in the United States. In 1993, there were 31,102 suicides—one suicide every 16.9 minutes, 85.1 per day—with 12.1 of every 100,000 Americans killing themselves (National Center for Health Statistics, 1996). Currently, individuals in the "baby-boomer" population are approaching their middle and older years (the age group with the highest risk of suicide) and their offspring are reaching the adolescent years (the second highest at-risk group). The increase in suicides in both these age groups could well result in an unprecedented epidemic of suicides over the next decade.

White males account for 73%, and white females for 18%, of all suicide deaths (Kachur, Potter, James, & Powell, 1995). Men complete suicide at 4 times the rate of females; however, females are more likely to attempt suicide than males (Kachur et al., 1995) (see Figure 5.1). Dorpat and Ripley (1967) reported that 10% of suicide attempters go on to kill themselves at a later date.

In commenting on this trend, Maris (1992) stated, "Overall, men choose relatively few, highly lethal methods to commit suicide; women use a much greater variety of methods, many of which are of relatively low lethality" (p. 12). Firearms are the preferred means for 65% of the males committing suicide and for 42% of the females (Kachur et al., 1995) (see Table 5.1).

Alcoholism and depression are the leading diagnostic risk factors in suicide. Miles (1977) reported an estimated rate of 230 people per 100,000 for patients with depression and 270 per 100,000 for alcoholism. Goldring and Fieve (1984) noted that the bipolar type II group of affective disorders

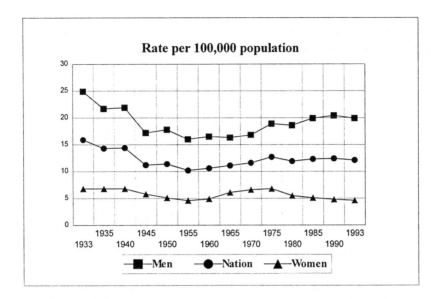

Figure 5.1. Trends in the United States: Rates by Sex
SOURCE: Data are from the American Association of Suicidology.

Table 5.1. Sex/Gender Suicide Methods

	Men		Women	
Firearms and explosives	65.6%	(16,395)	42.0%	(2,559)
Hanging, strangulation				
(suffocation)	15.3%	(3,824)	13.2%	(803)
Gas poisons	6.4%	(1,609)	7.9%	(483)
Solid and liquid poisons	6.2%	(1,552)	26.7%	(1,627)
All other methods	6.5%	(1,627)	10.2%	(623)
Total number	25,007		6,095	

NOTE: Firearms are the leading method for both men and women.

was the category most frequently associated with suicide. Research has shown that a high level of perturbation, as manifested in panic disorders, is also a danger sign of suicide (Weissman, Klerman, Markowitz, & Ouellette, 1989). Other risk factors, such as a diagnosis of personality disorder, living alone, being unmarried, being unemployed, having significant physical illness, and a history of a prior attempt, compound the risk for suicide in depressed and alcoholic patients. Miles (1977) has estimated that 10% of schizophrenic patients eventually kill themselves.

Suicide Among Women

Research has shown that women's patterns of suicidal behavior differ from those of men. A survey of suicidal feelings in the general population conducted by Paykel, Myers, Lindenthal, and Tanner (1974) demonstrated that suicidal ideation is more prevalent among women than among men. An analysis by Canetto (1992-1993) showed that suicidal behavior in women is typically nonfatal. Women outnumber men in rates of nonfatal suicidal behavior by an average of 2:1 in all industrialized countries except Poland and India.

Reviews of the literature on factors associated with suicidal behavior in women by Canetto and her colleagues found recurring themes of socioeconomic disadvantage, unemployment, hostile relationships, and a history of suicidal behavior among family and friends. A number of studies showed, for example, that "unemployment enhances the risk for nonfatal suicidal behavior in women" (Canetto, 1994, p. 517) (Endnote 1). In *Women and Depression: Risk Factors and Treatment Issues,* McGrath, Keita, Strickland, and Russo (1990) noted that "women are at higher risk for most types of depression" than are men (p. 1).

Suicide Among Children

According to the Centers for Disease Control, the rate of suicide among children aged 10 to 14 years increased by 120% between 1980 and 1992 (Kachur et al., 1995). In a study of 30 suicidal children, Shaffer (1974) found that the most common precipitating event for brief suicidal episodes in children was in relation to a crisis in discipline. Pfeffer (1986) reported that these "children were both expecting and receiving punishment from school or their parents" (p. 52). She noted that "children use jumping from heights as the most common suicidal method but rarely use firearms" (pp. 48-49).

Family stresses are far more prominent in the histories of suicidal children than in nonsuicidal youngsters. In describing the features of the family system of the suicidal child, Pfeffer (1986) included (a) a lack of generational boundaries; (b) a severe, inflexible spouse relationship with marked ambivalence, intense anger, and threats of separation; (c) a projection of conscious and unconscious parental feelings onto the child; (d) a symbiotic parent-child relationship, usually between the mother and the child; and (e) family rigidity, secretiveness, lack of communication, hostile interactions, and intolerance of change.

Pfeffer (1986) observed that suicidal children's conceptualizations of death vary; at one time they may acknowledge death as final whereas at other times they believe death is reversible. These fluctuations tend to occur in relation to the intensity of stress or trauma currently encountered by the child.

In his work, Orbach (1988) has also called attention to

> a "deadly message" that family members broadcast to the potential victim. This message is part of an unconscious plan to rid the family of an unwanted or scapegoated child. The goal of this plan is to resolve internal conflict or unbearable family conditions. (p. 139)

Regression to a previous developmental phase and primitive defensive processes such as ego-splitting are among the precursors or signs of suicidal behavior in young children. Pfeffer (1985) saw splitting mechanisms as one of the "last resorts" adopted by the child before suicidal action takes place. Orbach (1989) also discussed intrapsychic splits in suicidal children and adolescents that can be observed in many areas of functioning: in their perceptions, attitudes toward life and death, attitudes toward the body, toward physical pain, and in positive and negative views of the self.

Children's Verbalization of Negative Parental Introjects

The findings described by Pfeffer and Orbach agree in many respects with my own clinical findings (Endnote 2). It appears that the split in the psyche occurs at a relatively young age and can be inferred from a variety of behavioral, affective, and cognitive manifestations in disturbed and "normal" children.

Unfortunately, by the time most children are 4 or 5 years old, they have developed destructive thought patterns or voices that criticize, demean, and malign them. To illustrate, in a pilot study investigating negative thought patterns with a group of "normal," relatively high-functioning children where rapport had been established, my associates and I found that each child had developed self-critical thoughts and attitudes that, in most cases, had no basis in reality. We found that not only do children depreciate and berate themselves, but their self-attacks are resistant to change in spite of the fact that they lack objectivity.

In one discussion group, several children and adolescents, ages 6 to 15, expressed their negative thoughts about themselves as well as their problems at school, in peer relationships, and in competitive situations. Two of the youngsters verbalized thoughts related to self-destructive impulses and feelings of worthlessness. For example, at one point in the discussion, Mark, a 6-year-old boy, blurted out: "I have voices that tell me I don't deserve to live." Coincidentally, in an earlier parenting group, the boy's father had described the trauma he experienced early in life growing up with a severely disturbed mother and a cold, indifferent father:

> I remember wanting to kill myself. I thought of taking a knife from the kitchen and stabbing myself in the stomach. I was so confused by my mother's behavior, either building me up crazily, telling me how great I was, or totally ignoring me, and I was dying inside. I felt that killing myself would be the only way I could let her know how I felt.

Although Mark had no previous knowledge of these specific details related to his father's childhood, nonetheless it appeared that he had assimilated, on a nonverbal level, his father's self-destructive attitudes in the form of a self-accusatory thought process. Another youngster, Ricky, 10, who participated in the children's discussion, said, "Lots of times I have voices saying things to me like, 'You're no good. You're a jerk. You're not worth living. Nobody cares about you and you don't care about anybody but yourself!' " Later in the discussion, he answered back to this attacking voice from his own point of view, saying,

> I feel like saying back: "Leave me alone! It's not true. I'm not like that. I'm a good person. You're wrong. (Sad) That's just the way you think I am. I'm not like that! (Angry) I'm not a jerk! You're a jerk! Don't talk to me like that!"

As described in Chapter 1, investigations of the voice process demonstrated that individuals made direct connections between their self-attacks and negative experiences within the family. My associates and I have found confirmation of this process in our work with children. Furthermore, there has been a good deal of collaborative evidence from family members supporting the children's insights about the origins of their destructive thought processes. Clinical data from this longitudinal study of the voice process have contributed to the hypothesis that the origins of negative parental introjects or voices can be traced to the deficiencies and abuses of childhood. As the degree of trauma experienced in childhood increases, the level of intensity of voice attacks parallels this progression, and there are increasingly angry, vicious attacks on the self. In conjecturing about the voice, I suggest that the assimilation of parents' attitudes and defenses may be very closely related to a primitive biological survival mechanism. This protective mechanism is akin to the phenomenon observed in young animals, who instinctively pick up the parents' fears and act quickly to avoid imminent danger.

Multicultural Issues in Suicide

Sociocultural factors are clearly influential in determining suicide rates (Endnote 3). Hawkins (1990) raised questions concerning what specific variables of ethnic and racial differences appear to be associated with differential rates of violence and suicide. A cursory analysis of social risk factors such as unemployment, poverty, and drug abuse provides only a partial answer. Racism and discrimination place some groups at higher risk for violence than others.

The three groups briefly examined here—African Americans, U.S. Latinos, and Native Americans—have suicide rates that differ significantly from those of white Americans. All three groups share a "common experience of exploitation and oppression in this country . . . [and] all have a disproportionately higher experience of violence [either homicide or suicide] than Whites" (Hill, Soriano, Chen, & LaFromboise, 1994, p. 61) (see Figures 5.2 and 5.3).

African Americans

In 1992, the suicide rate for African American males was 12.0 per 100,000, slightly lower than the U.S. general population. Kachur et al. (1995) reported, however, that the suicide rate for black males ages 15 to 19 has increased dramatically, from 5.6 per 100,000 in 1980 to 14.8 per 100,000 in 1992. Suicide rates for black females remain low, at 2 per 100,000 (Kachur et al., 1995).

Baker (1989) emphasized that "Black males have a 'double risk of death' owing to their high rates of death from homicide and suicide" (p. 187). Homicide is the number one cause of death among African American youth (Fingerhut, Ingram, & Feldman, 1992). In elderly black males, for whom the suicide rate after age 80 is 22.3 per 100,000, hopelessness and despair are more prominent than violent behavior.

Theories explaining the factors that contribute to suicide among African Americans include those that call attention to "interpersonal conflicts,

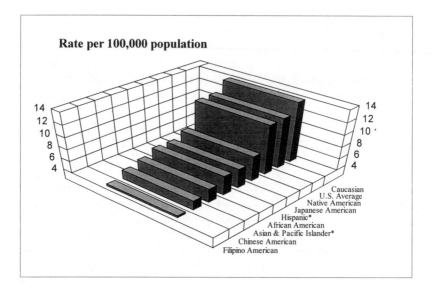

Figure 5.2. U.S. Suicide and Ethnicity: Suicide Rates for 1989-1991
SOURCE: Data are for 1993 from the American Association of Suicidology.
*Hispanic data may be for any group within the category and are available only for a few states. Asian and
  Pacific Islander data include those for Japanese, Chinese, and Filipinos.

familial discord, financial concerns, and the impact of poverty and racism
upon the individual and the family" (Baker, 1989, p. 188). Baker has provided
evidence, however, that contradicts the traditional "black family deficit theory," which he considers a biased perception. This distorted view "presents
the black family as being unable to meet the fundamental needs of its members
for survival, socialization and the transmission of a viable cultural heritage"
(p. 187), thereby placing family members at higher risk for violence and
suicide. Baker cited Lewis and Looney (1983), whose surveys showed that
many "working-class black families . . . are able to achieve patterns of
relationships that are associated with both a strong sense of connectedness
and high levels of individual autonomy" (p. 161).

U.S. Hispanics

In 1990, the suicide rate among Hispanic males was 12.3 and among
females, 2.3 per 100,000. In Hispanic young people ages 20 to 24 years, the

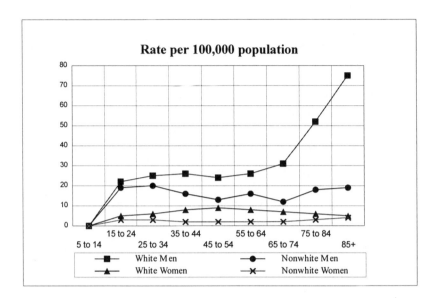

Figure 5.3. U.S. Suicide Rates by Age, Sex, and Race
SOURCE: Data are for 1993 from the American Association of Suicidology.
NOTE: Males are at higher risk at all ages. Age patterns differ by race.

rate of suicide is 17.8; suicides accomplished by guns are 11.0 per 100,000 (Kachur et al., 1995).

A study by Soriano and Ramirez (1991) found that "a Chicano who works in an unequal social power and influence environment scored higher on Anxiety . . . , lower on Self-Esteem . . . , and higher on Depression . . . compared to Chicanos in a more equal environment" (p. 396). Others have emphasized that Hispanic youths may be significantly affected by racism especially in a school system where Hispanic teachers are few. Thus appropriate models are unavailable to mitigate racism's effect. For example, Hispanic teachers represent only 2.9% of public and 2.8% of private school teachers in this country (De La Rosa & Maw, 1990).

Native Americans

In 1990, the suicide rate for Native American males was 21.1 per 100,000. In young males ages 20 to 24, the rate was 62.6 (Kachur et al., 1995). Suicide rates for "American Indians and Alaska Natives ages 10-14, 15-19, and 20-24 are higher than national averages; specifically 2.8, 2.4, and 2.3 times greater than the respective age groups for their non-Indian counterparts" (Dick, Beals, Manson, & Bechtold, 1992, p. 103). Although the suicide rate varies widely among reservations, this rate has been unusually high throughout the twentieth century and has increased markedly since about 1970. Reasons for this are unclear to date (Elliott, Kral, & Wilson, 1990).

The lowest suicide rates occur in Native American communities with the greatest number of intact traditional religions, clans, and extended family structures. In contrast, tribes described as "transitional or acculturated" tend to have the highest rates of alcoholism, homicide, unemployment, and physical and sexual abuse, as well as the highest rate of suicide and suicide attempts. One potential risk factor noted by Berlin (1986) was that "sixty percent of suicides attended boarding school before the ninth grade, compared with 27.5% of controls" (p. 1). According to Berlin, "the lack of effective adults to identify with and unemployment rates of 50% to 90% make the adolescents' future a hopeless one" (p. 1).

Psychodynamic Perspective on Suicide and Violence in Ethnic Minorities

As noted above, the majority of epidemiological studies of violence and suicide among ethnic minorities have focused on the influence of social forces such as racism, discrimination, poverty, and inequality on both destructive and self-destructive behavior. These factors are crucial precisely because any event, condition, or circumstance that causes an individual to feel persecuted and abused tends to intensify voice processes that predispose self-destructive behavior. On a societal level, whenever there is prejudice and discrimination as a predominant cultural pattern, members of the minority group tend to act out the negative stereotypes that are projected on them and, as a consequence, turn against themselves. This phenomenon was tragically demonstrated in Los Angeles in the 1992 riots that occurred within the inner-city communities, where minority people ultimately destroyed many of their own businesses as well as burning businesses owned by "outsiders." Rather than carry their attack to businesses located outside the perimeter of South Central Los Angeles, to those that were more representative of the oppressive power structure, they ended up damaging their own local resource base by destroying stores, businesses, and neighborhoods within the community.

In a society characterized by an unjust power structure and the presence of a disenfranchised group or groups, minority individuals incorporate the aggression that is directed toward them. When this internalized rage is activated (as it was following the judgment in the Rodney King case), they turn their rage against themselves. People living in an oppressive, inequitable society tend to direct their aggression against themselves rather than against the power structure for two reasons: (a) Their fear of the majority group and its retaliatory powers prevents them from attacking the aggressor, and (b), even more important, people have a strong propensity to identify with the more powerful, punishing figure, as was elucidated in our discussion of identification with the aggressor in Chapter 2.

The conditions that prevailed preceding the 1992 riots are analogous to the inequalities existing within dysfunctional families in which the power structure is hostile, rejecting, or emotionally inadequate for child rearing. Under conditions of extreme stress and punishment, children identify with the attacking parents and take on the hostile attitudes that are directed toward them. Later, there is a tendency to turn that anger and aggression against the self rather than against the family. The child takes on the image attributed to him or her of being the "bad" child and tends to behave accordingly.

In a sense, members of minority groups are traitors to themselves insofar as they live out the stereotypes that are imposed on them rather than experience and cope with the underlying powerlessness, hurt, fear, and disillusionment. Most remain unaware of their prejudice toward themselves and the corresponding self-destructive tendencies yet act out these attitudes at their own expense. A social system that makes unreasonable demands on a particular group within that system inevitably increases the aggression of that particular group. Unfortunately, as is evident in the grim statistics on suicide and homicide for minority groups in our country, that aggression is internalized and turned against oneself and one's own group.

In this section, I have discussed only a few of the many variables affecting suicide rates in terms of various populations including women and children and among ethnic groups. Population studies, including the demographic data on suicide as manifested in majority and minority groups, are informative only up to a point. Familiarity with the psychological risk factors in suicidal individuals combined with a knowledge of demographic factors is necessary in attempting to determine the seriousness or potential lethality of a client's suicidal intent.

The depressed or suicidal individual has tendencies in common with other people as well as specific and unique personality traits. In assessing suicide risk in a particular client, it is well to remember that most or all suicidal individuals, no matter what ethnic group or nationality they represent, seem to be preoccupied with perceived loss, rejection, or other aspects of the painful precipitating event. Shneidman's (1985) belief that "each individual tends to die as he or she has lived, especially as he or she has previously reacted in the periods of threat, stress, failure, challenge, shock and loss" (p. 201) is crucial in understanding the suicidal individual.

A Brief History of Methods
Used to Assess Suicide Risk

It is imperative that the assessment of suicidal risk combine clinical intuition and understanding with the application of objective measures and self-report instruments. An effective assessment model should be based on a larger conceptual framework or theory of suicidal phenomena from which relevant questions would be derived. The clinician must also depend upon his or her observations and perceptions of the patient.

Cull and Gill (1988) described three major approaches that have been directed toward the problem of predicting suicide. The first is the identification of risk factors such as sociodemographic characteristics. For example, adolescents and the elderly are at greater risk for attempting suicide than other age groups. However, Hatton, Valente, and Rink (1977) contended that applying this information to individual clients has not proved helpful because many individuals in the "high-risk" groups are not at risk for suicide; that is, there is substantial within-group variability.

The second approach involves the use of clinical signs and symptoms as indicators of suicide potential (Murphy, 1984; Pokorny, 1960; Shneidman & Farberow, 1957). These signs have been derived from "psychological autopsies" performed on persons who have completed suicide. The key factors that have been identified are verbal threats, a lethal suicide plan, availability of means, poorer physical health, previous suicide attempts, diminished mental status, recent negative life events, and a lack of social support.

The third approach has been the use of psychological tests. Mental health professionals have attempted to predict suicide through the use of a wide variety of psychological tests assessing personality traits or states assumed to be associated with suicidal behavior. Overall, the results have been discouraging, regardless of which psychological tests were used. For example, Neuringer (1974) concluded that the Rorschach is an ineffective technique for assessing suicide potential (Endnote 4).

Lester (1970) suggested that perhaps more appropriate tests for assessing suicide potential would be those specifically designed for that purpose; he recommended a shift away from using general tests of personality and toward the development of instruments focusing directly on the problem of suicide, suicidal ideation, and other relevant variables.

Results from research studies investigating the correlation between suicidal ideation and suicidal risk support a strong relationship between the two. For example, Miller, Chiles, and Barnes (1982) reported, "As with adult attempters, suicidal ideation and depression explained the greatest proportion of the variance in adolescent suicidal behavior; the more serious the suicidal ideation, the more likely was the adolescent to have attempted suicide" (p. 496).

Suicide Risk Assessment Scales
Currently Used in Clinical Practice

The most thorough research in the area of assessing suicidal risk to date has been conducted by Aaron Beck and his colleagues. Bedrosian and Beck (1979) established that suicidal ideation is a precursor to suicidal action (Endnote 5). Beck has developed scales that are relevant to suicide: the Beck Depression Inventory (Beck, 1978a), the Beck Suicide Inventory (Beck, 1991), and the Beck Hopelessness Scale (Beck, 1978b). A follow-up study (of 5 to 10 years) by Beck, Steer, Kovacs, and Garrison (1985) of 207 patients hospitalized for suicidal ideation showed that "only the Beck Hopelessness Scale and the pessimism item on the Beck Depression Inventory predicted the eventual suicides [of 14 patients]" (p. 559).

Linehan and Nielsen (1981) investigated the reasons people use to stay alive when they feel like killing themselves. Their Reasons for Living Inventory (RFL) (Linehan, Goodstein, Nielsen, & Chiles, 1983) taps cognitive abilities including the ability to sustain hope for the future and to visualize change. The Suicide Probability Scale (SPS) was developed by Cull and Gill (1988) as a brief self-report measure inquiring into the individual's feelings of anomie, introjected rage, lethality, and impulsivity, all of which have been found to be important factors contributing to suicide potential. The authors caution that the SPS is only an adjunct to a clinical interview and should never be used as a replacement.

Recently, the Firestone Assessment of Self-Destructive Thoughts (FAST) (Firestone & Firestone, 1996) was added to the repertoire of instruments for assessing suicide risk. Studies investigating the reliability and validity of the FAST demonstrated that the scale discriminated suicide attempters from nonattempters more accurately than other scales currently used in clinical practice (see Chapter 13).

Pfeffer, Conte, Plutchik, and Jerrett (1980) developed a battery of scales that have been useful in studying suicidal behavior in children. These scales are used in semistructured interviews with the child and the family. Reynolds (1985) has developed the Suicide Ideation Questionnaire in two forms, the SIQ for senior high school students and the SIQ-JR for junior high school students, to predict self-destructive trends. Suicide intent should be assessed by asking the patient about suicidal ideation, plans, methods under considera-tion, precautions against discovery, and past suicide attempts (see Chapter 14).

Conclusion

To conclude our discussion, it is important to note a significant dynamic often overlooked or underemphasized in both demographic studies and psychologi-cal profiles of the suicidal person. I have found that serious voice attacks are activated by unusual positive events as well as by negative events or circum-stances. Failure, loss, rejection, and other negative experiences tend to pre-cipitate voice attacks and feelings of self-hatred; however, it is very important to note that atypical positive events can also trigger the voice, causing regressive trends, self-destructive behavior, and, in extreme cases, suicide. Seiden (1984b) identified this factor in a number of demographic studies of suicidal young people. I discuss these dynamics in depth in Chapter 10.

Completed suicides have been found to correspond to an individual's *upward* mobility as well as his or her downward social mobility. Thus a *bipolar causality* must be taken into consideration. Both positive and negative factors affect suicidal behavior. Furthermore, we must establish the relation-ship between those positive events and the ensuing anxiety that precipitates regressive moods and accentuates self-attacks. Clinical and empirical research that my colleagues and I have conducted has led to a better understanding of these factors and has elucidated their causal relationship to actual suicide.

Endnotes

1. For reviews of this literature, see Canetto (1992-1993), Canetto and Feldman (1993), Cloward and Piven (1979), and Kushner (1985).

2. I have observed an important phenomenon in psychotherapy sessions with children who suffered emotional disorders When young patients were encouraged to make positive statements about themselves with feeling, they manifested strong reactions of sadness and deep sobbing. It was conjectured that verbalizing positive self-statements brought up pain because it countered the children's negative attitudes about themselves.

3. In my work, I have referred to cultural patterns and social mores as representing a pooling of individual psychological defenses. Social institutions and sanctions act back on each individual in the form of negative social pressure, that is, implicit and explicit value systems, that perpetuate the very destructiveness they were originally set up to control (Firestone, 1985).

4. Neuringer's (1974) research was supported by a number of investigations including those of Kendra (1979) and Exner and Wylie (1977). Clopton and Baucom (1979) found that the Minnesota Multiphasic Personality Inventory (MMPI) also was not a useful instrument for identifying potentially suicidal individuals. The Thematic Apperception Test, the Psychiatric Rating Scale, and the Bender-Gestalt, among others, have been found to be ineffective in predicting suicide (Eisenthal, 1974; Murray, 1943; Osgood, Suci, & Tannenbaum, 1957).

5. A significant correlation between suicidal ideation and suicidal risk was demonstrated in the studies of Bonner and Rich (1987), Linehan (1981), Rich, Bonner, and Reimold (1986), and Shafii, Carrigan, Whittinghill, and Derrick (1985).

6   Suicide Among Adolescents

She could have died when she overdosed
Luckily not me
She thought she was pregnant a couple of times
Luckily not me
She was into drugs and booze and sex and fights
Luckily not me. . . .
She was deserted more than once
She can't be me, she can't be me.

Diana, from *Teenagers Talk About Suicide*
(Marion Crook, 1989, p. 79)

This chapter contains an analysis of underlying cognitive processes that were found to strongly influence teenagers' movement toward self-destruction. Clinical material from a discussion with several adolescents illustrates significant warning signs of suicide; their self-disclosures provide a comprehensive view of suicidal tendencies in young people.

On March 11, 1987, four teenagers in New Jersey pulled their car into a garage, closed the garage door, and left the engine running. Thirty minutes later, they were all dead from carbon monoxide poisoning. A few days later, in Alsip, Illinois, two other adolescents killed themselves using identical means.

The latest official figures show that in 1992 in the United States, 4,693 adolescents and young adults in the age range of 15 to 24 years took their own lives (Kachur et al., 1995). Between 1950 and 1990, the suicide rate for young people in this age range has almost tripled—from 4.5 to 13.2 per 100,000 (Centers for Disease Control, 1994). Although the rate has leveled off since the late 1970s, suicide is still the third leading cause of death for 15- to

AUTHOR'S NOTE: Portions of this chapter were taken from "Psychodynamics in Adolescent Suicide," *Journal of College Student Psychotherapy, 4,* pp. 101-123 (Firestone & Seiden, 1990a). Used with permission.

24-year-olds (see Figure 6.1). Reports show that anywhere from 7 to 50 attempts are made for every actual suicide during adolescence (Dublin, 1963). This means that youthful suicide attempts can be estimated as numbering somewhere between 30,000 and 240,000 cases annually.

According to Hawton (1986), guns are the most popular method for committing suicide among 15- to 24-year-olds and are used in one half of the suicides committed by 10- to 14-year-olds. As is true with adult suicides, this is apparently a reflection of the ready availability of firearms in this country. Indeed, gun suicides in this age group have increased in tandem with gun ownership (Endnote 1).

A review of the literature on youth suicide demonstrates that there is "an almost bewildering array of conditions that have been cited as contributing to suicide risk" (Felner, Adan, & Silverman, 1992). Suicide experts have identified several important primary indicators of suicidal intent in adolescents and young adults, including use of substances, isolation, low self-esteem, a sense of despair, guilt reactions, psychological pain, and a progressive withdrawal from relationships and activities. Many of these symptoms are endemic to the lifestyle of teenagers in our country. Most adolescents are not involved in useful work and are left alone with a large amount of idle time on their hands. They are rarely asked to participate in activities that are functional or adaptive to survival. They are relegated to such mundane tasks as taking out the garbage, doing the dishes, and so on—chores against which they usually rebel. This pattern of neglecting the resources of our children and youth diminishes their self-esteem and leaves them feeling incompetent and inadequate.

These symptoms are prevalent in teenagers of every race, culture, religion, and class designation. They occur in both broken homes and intact homes. They do not result from a breakdown in "family values." The reverse is true. Family values break down as a result of dysfunctional family life. Indeed, to a certain extent, the nuclear family in our culture has evolved into a destructive institution. It is questionable whether the nuclear family is the optimal arrangement for the mental health of its members. Evolutionary psychologists and anthropologists have concluded that the open social organization of most primitive cultures was more effective for enhancing the survival potential of individuals than is the social organization in most modern societies (Endnote 2).

Many teenagers today are alienated from their parents and cynical about life. They are angry and often violent. Rap music and heavy metal lyrics about abuses in childhood address their sentiments. The language and themes of this music deserve our attention; they extend far beyond the subcultures from

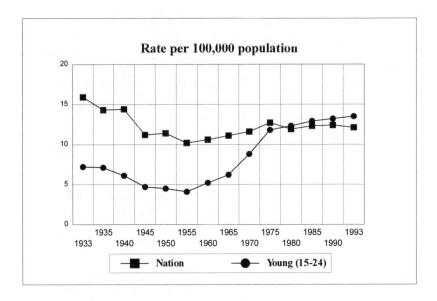

Figure 6.1 U.S. Trends: Youth Suicide
SOURCE: Data are for 1993 from the American Association of Suicidology.
NOTE: Youth suicides increased through the late 1970s and have remained mostly stable since that time. For 15- to 24-year-olds in 1993, there were 4,849 suicides. Comparatively, in 1993, for youth (15-24) there were 13.5 suicides per 100,000, but for the nation as a whole there were 12.1 per 100,000. This is a *238% increase for youth from 1956 (4.0) to 1993 (13.5).*

which they originated and permeate the lives of most young people in our country. Teenagers everywhere respond to this music because they too have been disenfranchised from power, in this case, by their families. The rage and disillusionment voiced in this music offer an insight into the alarming increase in teenage suicide. The discussion with adolescents that follows will reveal some of the meanings behind these trends.

Adolescents' Discussion About Suicide

After hearing about the rash of teenage suicides in 1987, I had the idea of asking several teenagers to contribute their ideas on the subject. The video-taped discussion (Parr, 1987b) began with the teenagers describing the danger signs of suicide they had observed in friends. As the conversation progressed,

Suicide Among Adolescents

they disclosed deep-seated problems in their own lives that had been troubling them, and thereby they shed light on general attitudes and conditions conducive to the increase in adolescent suicide rates (Endnote 3).

> *Jackie:* A friend I know at school talks a lot about how she's really unhappy with her situation. She sounds like she's given up trying to make her life okay. She has a certain religion and can't do what she wants. But it scares me when she talks. She says things like, "There's nothing else I can do." She told me that she's attempted suicide before. That seems like a warning, if someone sounds like they're going to give up.
>
> *Dr. F.:* It certainly does. That is one of the most serious kinds of precursors to suicide, actually giving off signals of that sort and stating the intention or even making attempts to do away with oneself.

Substance Abuse and Eating Disorders

Alice, 18, described changes in her emotional state that appeared to be related to her concern with her weight and dieting. She had been suffering from a serious eating disorder (bulimia) for approximately a year prior to the discussion. She revealed that her pattern of binging and purging became more serious after she became aware that her close friend, Anna, had developed symptoms of an eating disorder.

> *Alice:* I've been having a weight problem for a long time. I stopped caring about how I look, even though I feel bad when I look in the mirror. But I don't care at the time I'm eating.
>
> I remember feeling better last year when I was closer friends with Anna at school. But I started to hate you [Anna] for what you were giving up, for how you were living. I got into trouble, because I became cynical. I knew you were getting fat and that you didn't care about it.
>
> *Dr. F.:* It does seem to be connected in some way to the time Anna began to feel bad. I think as Anna regressed, you started to feel more angry at her, and yet started to indulge the same kinds of behavior, started to overeat. That's when you said you really started to hate yourself.
>
> *Anna:* About the same time that Alice started to feel bad toward me, I started to see myself as a bad person, and that I was making people feel bad. I felt I should just go away somewhere. I started putting on even more weight around that time.
>
> *Dr. F.:* The subject of contagion is significant. Basically teenagers affect one another in their choice of behavior. Usually when somebody behaves self-

> destructively, it tends to affect other people, like those kids who made suicide
> pacts. What do you think about that, in your life?
>
> *Alice:* I think that's really true. Even the people I see at school, some of the
> teenagers are always together, like they're one person. They hold on to each
> other, they won't do anything separate from each other. They're very imitative
> of each other. They have all the same classes, all the same work, they do
> everything together.
>
> *Dr. F.:* It's a little like that with you and Anna. You've grown up together, you've
> always tended to do the same things, and now you're still keying off each
> other.

Both Alice and Anna were struggling with eating disorders, using food in an attempt to satisfy primal hunger. As they turned inward and away from people, their guilt and self-hatred increased. Their addiction to substances was part of a regressive trend and a self-perpetuating cycle of self-destructiveness.

Eating disorders and excessive use of drugs and alcohol are significant signs of suicide potential in teenagers. The following are some of the psychosocial factors affecting the significant rise of substance abuse and suicide among our youth.

Factors Contributing to Adolescent Suicide

The social and psychological factors contributing to the epidemic of youth suicide are diverse and varied, and prediction remains complex and problematic despite the recent surge in research. From a sociological perspective, several trends in contemporary society can be assumed to have had an impact on the rising rate of teenage suicide that occurred between 1950 and 1980. Holinger and Offer (1982) suggested that overpopulation results in worse economic conditions for the subpopulation of adolescents. Cantor (1989) noted that "the increase in the absolute number of adolescents in society" may well have been one of the predisposing factors related to the increased suicide rate. She also pointed out two areas that need to be investigated with respect to social and familial factors affecting the suicide rate among teenagers: "the cultural pervasiveness of violence, and the negative social factors of neglect and stress" (p. 285). Richman (1984) observed "suicide-specific" features in families with a suicidal member. He described a double bind situation wherein the suicidal adolescent is isolated within the family "while intimacies with persons outside are forbidden" (p. 396).

Depressive disorder and conduct disorder are significant factors that correlate with completed suicides in adolescent and young adults (Berman &

Jobes, 1991). In light of the fact that a tendency toward isolation is an important factor or sign of suicidal intent, it is important to note that suicide among 15-to 24-year-olds is most prevalent in the western United States, particularly in the intermountain region—in areas of extremely low population density (Seiden, 1984a).

Among college students, it is often the academically superior student who kills him- or herself. Those who teach and counsel students are impressed with students' observations that it is the higher achieving students who are the most self-critical, the most critical of others, and the most relentless at self-attack (Harvey, 1984; Seiden, 1966). In commenting on this trend, Cantor (1989) noted that "suicide rates are high in societies where achievement is a major priority" (p. 286) as, for example, in Japan and Sweden. Recently, the tragic suicide of Vincent Foster was analyzed and demonstrated that perfectionism is a strong indicator of suicide risk in adults as well as adolescents (Blatt, 1995) (Endnote 4).

From a psychodynamic perspective, Shneidman (1985) concluded that "the vast majority (about 80%) of suicides have a recognizable presuicidal phase" (p. 39). My theoretical model suggests a powerful approach to understanding the precursors of suicide in both adult and adolescent individuals. The approach is based on my investigations into negative thought processes that regulate maladaptive and self-destructive behavior (Firestone, 1988). Findings from other studies (Beck, Steer, & Brown, 1993; Rose & Abramson, 1992) of cognitive processes known to be associated with presuicidal and suicidal states tend to support my conceptual framework. In my opinion, a combination of epidemiologic data on youth suicide and the psychodynamic/cognitive paradigm described here can help clinicians in their efforts to discriminate between the suicidal adolescent and the nonsuicidal adolescent. In this chapter, I have two goals: (a) to identify the specific behaviors manifested by young people who may be at high risk for suicide or who are in the presuicidal phase and (b) to identify specific underlying thought patterns influencing these behaviors.

Continuation of Adolescents' Discussion

In attempting to numb feelings of being unlovable and insecure, Alice and Anna found it necessary to increase their self-abusive pattern of binging and purging. These patterns led to feelings of shame and the need for punishment, and eventually to other forms of maladaptive behavior, such as the careless actions and accident-proneness reported below by Alice.

Alice: Sometimes when I'm feeling really bad, I'll get in the car to go somewhere and I'll purposely not put on my seat belt. I know it's dangerous, but I don't want to wear it. I'm much more spaced out when I feel like this. I was cooking last night and I burned myself three times, just being careless.

Intergenerational Transmission of Addictive Tendencies

Dr. F.: Both of you treat overeating as though you're bad, you're a bad person. How did you connect it to being bad, so that you hate yourselves for it? Why is that?

At this point, Alice's sister, Jackie, makes an important observation when she describes their self-destructive behaviors as an imitation of their parents.

Jackie: I think that we learned it, because that was our mom's attitude, when we were really young. Food and eating were such issues with her. She always had a weight problem; she was always nervous about dieting and overeating.

Dr. F.: I know that your mother judged herself as good or bad; life was wonderful or horrible, depending on whether she was dieting or not.

Alice: I'm like that. First I overeat, then I gain weight and feel terrible from it. But I don't feel like I can just lose it the next day, I think, "Oh, God, you're going to gain three pounds because you ate so much." Then I feel like I have to make myself throw up or I'm going to feel bad the next day.

Isolation

Alice talks about her tendency to put distance between herself and her friends. She reveals voice attacks that appear to control her behavior and influence her to isolate herself.

Alice: Recently I've been feeling more and more like giving up things. One of the biggest things I do is I stay away from my friends a lot more than I used to. I feel like I'm bothering my friends and I feel uncomfortable around them.

If I'm by myself or driving around, I start thinking: "You're a terrible person. People don't like you. You should stay away from them. You cause your family trouble all the time. You're not nice. You don't add anything to anybody's life. You're just making people feel bad. You should go away. You should *really* go away!"

The guilt, shame, and self-degradation that Alice experienced in relation to her self-abusive behavior finally culminated in her running away and living for some weeks as a "street person" in a distant city. In effect, she took action that was directly influenced by the destructive voice process. Fortunately, at a certain point during this crisis, she became frightened and concerned about her physical safety and welfare. Returning home, she entered a treatment program for eating disorders and has shown significant improvement.

Perfectionism

As noted earlier, attention has been focused on the perfectionistic standards manifested by some parents as having a strong negative influence on their adolescent offspring. These standards appear to be correlated with suicide in high-performing adolescents. Ken, 17, discloses that he feels under constant pressure to perform at an unrealistically high level, both in school and in competitive sports.

> *Ken:* I thought about how I've always been hard on myself and how I put so much pressure on myself. When I was in elementary school, I made almost all A's. But I was always terrified that I might get a B.
>
> If I'm playing baseball and I make an error, I just tear into myself. I think I'm such an idiot. I just sit there and call myself an idiot a hundred times. It's like I'm screaming at myself inside my head.

Ken's father was extremely hypercritical. He admitted putting similar pressure on himself at work. In a voice therapy session, he reported constantly telling himself, "You'd better be right" (angrily). "You'd better get it right! If you can't be right, you'd better not say anything! You'd better shut up!"

Jackie talks about a similar pattern in her own life.

> *Jackie:* I feel like I'm really hard on myself a lot. I pick on myself, but I feel like I was picked on as a really little child. I can remember being picked on by my parents. I feel like there's such pressure from my dad. I feel like he wanted me to do things right! "You'd better not mess up. You'd better show that you're good!"
>
> But it wasn't for me, it was for him. I have to be perfect in everything. If we're playing a sport and I'm doing okay, he still wants me to get it perfect.
>
> When I was a baby, I could feel from my mother that she didn't want me there, that I was a bother. I was someone she had to use her energy up to watch over. I felt bad for making her have to take care of me. I felt like she was sorry

she had me. And now if I'm feeling really bad, I feel like I shouldn't be here. I feel that my friends have the same feeling toward me that she had.

Dr. F.: You think that they're thinking the same things that you thought your mother thought.

Jackie: Yeah, and when I feel really bad, like I'm a bad person, I want to get alone. I just go into a room and I'm alone, and I just sit in that room and tell myself that I'm bad and prove to myself that my mother was right, that I shouldn't be here, that I'm just bothering people, that I'm a burden to her and I'm a burden to my friends.

Dr. F.: What Jackie is getting at is so important. These attitudes didn't come out of nowhere. You had these kind of feelings directed toward you, the way you experienced things in your life. Your way of talking to yourself, treating yourself, punishing yourself, or running yourself down does have some relationship to the way you were treated. It's not just an abstraction that you made up.

Several of the teenagers reported experiencing a deep sense of despair and hopelessness especially when under pressure to achieve or perform. Jason, 18, talks about how his overriding need to be perfect leaves him vulnerable to vicious self-attacks, feelings of futility, and thoughts of suicide.

Jason: I always feel like I'm a disappointment to people and it's hard to ask for anything because I'm not perfect. The person who I try to perform like, I can never be. And unless I'm that person, I don't deserve anything. I barely deserve friends, money, life, anything.

For a while, I was having a hard time in school and right around grading time, I would just get so afraid that I wouldn't be perfect. And I never was. It would just snowball down to where I'd just think life would be so much easier if I just killed myself. And it was very logical. Life would be simple. There would be no life and I wouldn't have to worry about grades or anything.

Negative Spiral of Guilt Feelings

Anna describes feelings of worthlessness and guilt that were intensified by her pattern of habitual lying.

Anna: I know that I've always felt bad. There are a lot of times when I'll do things that I know are bad for me, but instead of just thinking that they make me feel bad or unhappy, I think that I'm bad for doing them, and then I don't ever talk about them or I lie about them.

Dr. F.: That's the trouble with self-destructive signs and behaviors; they feed on each other. First you do something to isolate yourself and something even self-destructive like overeating. Then you hate yourself for it and you go further into more self-destructive behavior. It's a cycle. There is also guilt about choosing self-destructive modes of operation in relation to other people and in relation to yourself.

You'll let yourself have an accident, you'll be careless, hurt yourself, like you said, and then you punish yourself. You say, "See, you really are crazy! You really are a bad person. Look what you did. Now look, you went and burned yourself." This is how it builds on itself. I think this is what happens to many teenagers. They become progressively more guilty and act more self-destructively, hate themselves for it, and then repeat the pattern.

Psychodynamics

Profound feelings of being "bad" or undeserving were reported by each of the adolescents. During the course of the meeting, the young people traced these pervasive attitudes of worthlessness, inadequacy, and incompetency to earlier interactions in their families. Anna had considerable insight into the connection between the lack of clear-cut signs of suicidal crisis in young people and the fact that their feelings of being unlovable and bad are of long duration, probably originating in early childhood.

Anna: The reason there aren't definite signs is because it doesn't happen over-night—it happens their whole life. They feel bad their whole life. They always feel bad toward themselves. They always think that they're bad.

In the months prior to the meeting, Anna had gradually retreated from a close relationship with her boyfriend. Moreover, her apparent lack of interest in her studies and career plans had become of serious concern to family and friends. Here she investigates the origins of her lack of motivation and her diminished emotional investment in school activities and friendships.

Anna: I don't remember specific incidents from my childhood, but I just remem-ber feeling hated, just like a coldness, like it didn't matter that I was there. I feel like she hated me because I had needs. She would have rather had a doll that she could just dress and carry around with her and show off to people, that would make her proud, but that wouldn't need anything.

Dr. F.: Did you start to feel bad for wanting things?

Anna: Yeah, 1 didn't want anything, and whenever I did, I felt like I was mean, and I still feel that way.

Jackie identified strongly with Anna's statements and went on to explain:

Jackie: I have a voice and it feels like it comes directly from my mother: "Want anything? How could you want anything? You should be happy to be here. You're lucky that you're here. Look at all the trouble I had to go through just to bring you into the world!" And I feel a lot like Jason, that there's somebody, a perfect person, that I can't be.

Dr. F.: That you can never live up to.

Jackie: Yeah, that I'll never live up to. I think I idealize my friends and think that they're that perfect person, but I'm not and I'll never be. And if things are going really hard, if school is going bad, or if I feel like my friends hate me, I feel like, "Why go through all this trouble? If you just weren't here, you wouldn't have to go through all these feelings."

I don't feel like I'm going to kill myself, but there's a voice or a feeling inside: "Look at all this trouble you have to go through, look at all the trouble you're causing. If you just ended it, there would be no trouble. If you were dead, there would be nothing. You wouldn't be bad, because you wouldn't be!"

Although she was surprised at the maliciousness of the self-attacks she expressed, Jackie was able to recognize her own rational point of view, which is diametrically opposed to the voice. Because of her ego strength, good impulse control, and stable relationships, her suicidal ideation was not as alarming as it might have been in another, more seriously disturbed teenager.

David, 16, discloses ambivalent attitudes toward himself and toward suicide.

David: I usually don't have a feeling of really wanting to kill myself, but I get to a point where I'll start to feel bad or discouraged at school or at home and I'll run it through my head 500 times and at the end of it, I'm feeling worse and worse. It seems like if there's not someone around to snap me out of it, I don't know what would happen. I get to a point where I get so low, just from running it through my head over and over and seeing every little thing I did wrong in that instance. Then sometimes it will just turn around. I'll feel happy and I don't understand why all of a sudden it could switch, either way. Bad or good.

Dr. F.: Yes, it definitely can switch, and thank goodness it has a positive side. There's a part of you that obviously wants to live and there's a part of you that wants to destroy everything, to run you down, to pick you apart.

Although the adolescents who took part in this discussion are highly articulate and relatively high functioning in many areas, it is clear, nevertheless, that they are also in considerable pain psychologically. The source of their pain and poor self-image is evident in the stories they recount about the damage they sustained during their formative years. The young people were able to trace the roots of their self-critical thoughts to incidents of physical and emotional mistreatment or to an all-pervasive atmosphere of indifference and hostility that characterized their early environments. In many cases, they verbalized the contents of a negative thought process or voice that they had incorporated during harsh or punitive interactions with their parents.

Data from other sources tend to substantiate the experiences and feelings of the teenagers who participated in our videotaped group meeting. In interviews with 30 adolescents from various areas across Canada, Marion Crook (1989) uncovered similar problems. The concerns of the Canadian youth ranged from low self-esteem, grief over significant losses, pressures to "look happy," lack of supportive family relationships, and high family expectations about achievement. In describing these teens, Crook wrote (addressing teenagers):

> Many suicide attempts never get reported. Some of you told me I was the only one who knew. You aren't part of those statistics. (p. 20)

> Most of you suffered verbal abuse. You were yelled at, degraded, criticized, told you were incompetent, a loser, a misfit in the family. Sometimes you were told that your birth had wrecked the family, that your parents wished you'd leave. Under these conditions many of you had low self-esteem and considered suicide as a permanent way of leaving. (p. 28)

Several teenagers confided that they had experienced voices instructing them to kill themselves. For example, a 12-year-old recalled the first time she tried to kill herself with an overdose of 38 Tylenol tablets:

> Once you try suicide, then you think about it. It's easier to do the next time . . . like a habit . . . like, "Try it, see if it works." But I didn't really want it to work. . . .
> Once you have the idea in your head, it's something you can't get out. When you see a bottle of pills, you think, "Why don't you take them? It'll all be over. It'll all vanish." (pp. 63-64)

In substance, Crook's clinical study of teenagers in Canada coincides with the data in our clinical examples. Cantor (1989) has also delineated a number of predisposing factors in teenage suicide in the United States. Several of these factors reflect the experiences of Crook's interviewees: the disappearance of the extended family; the pressures put on kids to grow up too quickly; the special sensitivity of many kids to social isolation; the lack of socially acceptable ways for youngsters to express anger; a high level of social and academic competition and pressure; and the violence that children and ado lescents are exposed to, that is, real violence such as rape, murder, and child abuse as well as created violence in the media.

In addition, in cases of adolescent suicide, the phenomenon of cluster suicide is a dangerous trend. Youth suicides not only instigate self-destructive action in others, they have a kind of domino effect, causing incredible pain within the entire relationship constellation around the deceased young person. In instances of teenage suicide, whole schools often are affected, and many youngsters are at serious risk (Poland, 1989).

Interview About Adolescent Suicide[1]

In a discussion between the suicidologist Dr. Richard Seiden and the author in a postscript to the film (Parr, 1987a), Dr. Seiden made the following points regarding the epidemiology of suicide and related psychosocial factors, and I expanded on the issues that he introduced.

> *Dr. Richard Seiden:* One statistic that has not been fully acknowledged is the fact that the homicide rate among teenagers has risen faster than the suicide rate. So a lot of this anger is turned outward.

> *Dr. Robert Firestone:* Absolutely. My associates and I found when we were investigating self-destructive thought processes that the hostility was directed not only toward oneself but also outward toward the people one cares about. When a person is running down other people, feeling cynical toward them, feeling hostile and suspicious of others, that in itself is a sign of suicidal potential.

Social Factors

> *Dr. S.:* Not only is there a flurry of publicity about teenage suicides, the rates have actually tripled since the end of World War II. Do you have any ideas why? Is it more difficult to grow up these days, or are there other stresses?

> *Dr. F.:* In a culture where people are moving away from feeling and toward painkilling and/or mood-altering drugs, where the media make teenagers

---

1. This discussion was excerpted from a videotaped interview conducted by Richard H. Seiden, Ph.D. (Parr, 1987a).

immediately aware of tragic events in every part of the world, and where the threat of nuclear war reminds them of the impermanence of life, our young people develop cynical feelings about the world, themselves, and others. Simply being aware of the potential menace to life from a nuclear threat intensifies a person's self-destructive urges and sense of futility.

I think the primary reason the suicide rate has gone up dramatically for adolescents is that more and more families are dysfunctional in the sense that they do not meet the emotional needs of their offspring. Feeling alone and isolated, children turn inward toward passive recreation, such as addictive television viewing and computer game playing. They're tuned into the media and are familiar with the hostile state of the world and the tragic implications of man's destructiveness. If they turn on the radio, they hear about a 50-million gallon oil spill threatening wildlife, water supplies, and beaches, bomb blasts in London, foreign tourists gunned down in Miami, and a convicted killer choosing death by firing squad. They are vulnerable to the impact of these stresses at an earlier age than were adolescents in previous generations. Anything that creates a sense of despair and futility makes one feel cynical and triggers voices such as "What's the point of living anyway? Look what happens. You're only going to die in the end." Negative stimulation along these lines tends to influence the self-destructive process of not caring and not investing in life.

The point is that if a person lives closely with someone who manipulates the environment by either warding off people or by provoking aggression in them, it causes that person to suffer, and he or she will tend to turn against him- or herself. On the other hand, the more a person can maintain positive feelings, for example, if a child is allowed to feel loving feelings toward a parent, he or she will be less likely to develop an extensive self-destructive negative thought process.

The Suicidal Spiral

Dr. S.: You've said that everyone is influenced to some degree by this negative thought process or voice, and your investigations seem to bear that out. What happens to a person to take him along the road from indirect suicide to actually physically committing suicide?

Dr. F.: Obviously, these things are a matter of degree and intensity. The more disturbed the child's environment, the more likely he is to be damaged in self-esteem and the more he experiences increased guilt and an intolerance for feelings, the more the individual is headed in this direction. But what actually leads to this transformation? It's a cycle. For example, as the child suffers painful experiences in growing up, there's a tendency to rely increasingly on defensive mechanisms. They predispose a kind of withdrawal from personal activities or feelings, a kind of going against his or her wants and desires. All these movements are progressive as life's conditions worsen. The hurt person responds defensively and therefore becomes more maladaptive to environmental circumstances.

In other words, it's a spiral. The more frustration, the more the tendency to adopt a defensive posture. The guilt about withdrawing from personal relationships and the use of substances and fantasy for gratification fosters a spiral of self-depreciation and self-attack, which leads to more self-destructive actions.

One can become aware of this spiral effect if one takes a serious interest in the child, adolescent, or adult patient. For example, I would be worried if a teenager suddenly gave up a hobby or sport that had thrilled and excited him or if he became disinterested and cynical toward his close friends. I would be disturbed if he talked as though there were no future. Someone who was recently involved in a number of accidents or who had actually made attempts at self-harm would concern me no matter what the rationale. I would also be disturbed to see a young person cut off from feeling, with shallow affect and a monotone style of talking. In a sense, all the signs of suicide intent described by the experts fit the typical influences of a destructive thought process or voice. There is a tremendous overlap between what negative thoughts or "voices" are telling an adolescent about him- or herself and the signs recognized by suicidologists as predictors of a suicidal act.

Parenting Practices That Can Predispose a Suicidal State

Dr. S.: I watched the young people being interviewed yesterday, and I know that on balance they're relatively well-adjusted compared to many teenagers. Yet they all had problems. It's not that they were unloved, but in many cases, the love was conditional. It was not unconditionally given, but was given on the condition that you achieve, that you excel, that you compete and you win. Otherwise you don't merit love. The feeling of not living up to parents' expectations seemed to be strong and very corrosive and something they carry with them, even in spite of success.

Dr. F.: You're right. There's even a danger of overly praising or building up your child and making too much of his or her achievements. It creates a sense of vanity in children that they have to live up to, which only makes a mockery out of their real performance. The type of parent who exploits the child's good qualities, who lives through the child, who makes demands, who can't give love but only gives praise for the beauty or superiority of the child, damages the child's feelings of competency. Since the child's real achievements never measure up, he is left with a sense of being inadequate or bad, which increases his negative feelings toward himself and toward others.

Ambivalence

Dr. S.: You use the term *siding with the negative thought process* as if there were different sides, as if there were a contest or battle going on inside one's mind or one's thoughts, as if there were ambivalence. This seems to be a very strong factor in suicidal behavior, from my experience.

Dr. F.: There is ambivalence in suicidal individuals, both adolescents and adults, all the way to the final act. It is ironic but a person who is suicidal will be afraid of getting in an accident on the way to his destination where he plans to commit suicide. So there is ambivalence throughout. There's a constant struggle within an individual, to live, to feel, to be involved with people, to care, and at the same time, a negative thought process to obliterate that caring process.

Suicidal impulses in young people have to be taken seriously because, when the negative aspect is dominant, the person can be destroyed, whereas the next day, he or she might have felt okay again. There are forces in each young person that want to live and forces in them that want to die. It's very complex. Each person has a mixture of these feelings toward themselves, but most people downplay their importance. In addition, there is a tendency to deny the emotional pain that teenagers are in. We know that young people suffer because of the way they feel about themselves, within themselves. It has practically nothing to do with their outward circumstances. You can have ideal circumstances, a beautiful home, new car, wonderful community, but they won't affect the teenager who has bitter feelings toward him- or herself.

Three teenagers I know who lived in Malibu during the 1970s are a case in point. I was acquainted with their parents and thought they were fortunate in being able to bring up their children in this ideal community. I was mistaken. In this idyllic setting bordered by ocean and wooded mountains and with a school system reputed to be the best in southern California, the young people isolated themselves in their parents' beach houses, drank, smoked pot, and became addicted to dangerous drugs. My friends' children barely survived the emotional damage sustained in their family, and one made a serious suicide attempt. Many close friends of the teenagers I knew failed to survive their teen years; many died by overdose, suicide, or in motorcycle and car accidents. In one tragic case, a 16-year-old shot and killed his 10-year-old sister during an LSD flashback.

Guilt Related to Self-Destructive Habit Patterns

Dr. S.: When I was working with alcoholic patients, the kind of pattern I found fit into your conceptions about the voice. They would drink to begin with because they felt bad about themselves. They were constantly getting on their backs: carping self-attacks. By drinking, they blotted it out momentarily. But then they had the problem of getting on themselves for the drinking.

Dr. F.: Substance abuse interferes with adolescents' adjustment, with the pursuit of goals, with the life process, so now they hate themselves for damaging that. They're hurting other people incidentally. There is a lot of guilt about hurting others because a person senses as they go about their own self-destruction that they're worrying other people, they're making them afraid. They realize that other people are hurt by the fact that they're indulging in these defenses, so that compounds their guilt. Anything that makes them feel more guilty also makes them feel worse.

Preventive Child Rearing

Dr. S.: What can we do about all of this?

Dr. F.: Efforts can be directed toward education and toward parent training methods that would help parents become more aware of destructive elements they may be contributing to their child's development. For example, it's important for parents to understand that a hostile point of view toward self will predispose movement in the direction of self-destruction, whereas anything that makes the child or adolescent feel worthwhile, valuable, lovable, will tend to make him care about himself. In general, children should be discouraged from the type of activities that have a negative effect on their future development. I think that parents should be educated about the signs of problems. In this way, many of these self-destructive and suicidal patterns might potentially be averted. (See Chapter 16.)

Sexuality and Suicide in Adolescence

Sexual problems have been cited as important factors in the etiology of suicidal behavior among adolescents and young adults (Holinger, Offer, Barter, & Bell, 1994; Pfeffer, 1989; Plutchik & van Praag, 1990). Exploration of sexual behavior, sexual identity, and new relationships are among the major tasks of adolescent development. Orbach, Lotem-Peleg, and Kedem (1995) noted a number of environmental factors that negatively affect the child's emerging sexuality and his or her attitudes toward the body during the early years that lead to problems in this area, which can increase the risk for depression and suicide for many teenagers.

Sexual Child Abuse

Finkelhor and his associates (1986) summarized the prevalence of sexual abuse in this country and reported rates ranging "from 6% to 62% for females and from 3% to 31% for males" (p. 19). Findings from numerous studies have demonstrated a relationship between prior sexual abuse and adolescent suicide (Endnote 5). I contend that acts of a sexual nature, especially instances of physically aggressive sexual behavior, are tremendously damaging to the child. The consequences of these acts are exacerbated in a social structure where sexuality is distorted and where dishonesty and secrecy take precedence over genuine concern for the child. It is obvious that although sexual abuse of children is in itself a serious social issue, cultural views of sex contribute to and complicate this psychological problem. In fact, sexual abuse is partially induced by societal distortions and the restrictions placed on people's natural sexual development.

Disturbances in Sexual Orientation

In 1989, a U.S. Department of Health and Human Services report stated that "gay youth are 2 to 3 times more likely to attempt suicide than other young people" (Gibson, 1989, p. 110). The report estimated that gay and lesbian youth may constitute up to 30% of completed youth suicides annually. Findings from a number of other studies, however, have failed to support the prevalence rates reported by Gibson and others (Moscicki, 1995).

In considering the psychodynamics of suicide among gay and bisexual youths, D'Augelli and Dark (1994) conjectured that adolescents who become aware of their homosexual orientation and who choose to reveal their orientation to others usually experience emotional conflict at home, at school, and in their peer relationships. Hendin (1982) observed that the histories of the suicidal homosexual students were far more traumatic than those of nonsuicidal homosexuals and were characterized by "overt rejection, or the loss of a parent through death, and the parental desire for a lifeless child" (p. 122). The subjects in his sample were extremely vulnerable to separation anxiety "produced by maternal rejection or abandonment" (p. 123).

Psychodynamics

It is my view that problems associated with sexual functioning, including confused sexual orientation and long-term effects of sexual child abuse, are among the major factors influencing self-destructive behavior in adolescents.

During the teenage years, young people are faced with new and unfamiliar feelings aroused by their emerging sexuality. At the same time, they are dealing with their own emotional reactions to their moves toward indepen dence and separation from the family as part of the individuation process.

The crises in sexual orientation and problems in sexual relating experienced by many adolescents are closely associated with the voice process. In fact, nowhere are "voices" closer to the surface or more directly connected with behavior than in the area of sexuality. Adolescents have "voices" criticizing their appearance, their bodies—especially the sexual and genital regions—and their sexual behavior. Based on extensive clinical data, I suggest that the source of these hostile thought patterns and negative attitudes about sex can be found in internalized parental attitudes. These defensive and distorted views are transmitted intergenerationally and form the basis of sexual stereotyping.

Voice attacks occur far in advance of a sexual experience. They are activated on a fundamental level in relation to teenagers' basic feelings about themselves and their sexual identity. Many young people, for example, tell themselves not to become "too involved" whenever they consider dating a new person or when thinking of committing more seriously to a love relationship. They tell themselves: "Don't get too hooked on him (her). What if he (she) decides to break up with you later on? Why go through all those torturous feelings for a few short weeks of excitement?"

Teenagers have reported cynical thoughts that stifle their enthusiasm upon first meeting a potential new partner, such as the following: "Why should he (she) like you? Why would he (she) want to go out with you? You're not interesting. You're not popular. You're not attractive." The developing adolescent is influenced by the family's sexual inhibitions and negative attitudes toward the body that foster these types of self-attacks and cause him or her to feel abnormally ashamed of natural feelings of attraction toward members of the opposite sex.

With the advent of AIDS, some adolescents who were considering a sexual relationship disclosed "voices" warning them about the possibility of contracting the disease or another sexually transmitted disease. These negative thoughts, although seemingly protective of the teenager's life and health, nonetheless lead to feelings of distrust and hostility: "What if he (she) is not telling you the truth about being safe? How do you know you can trust him (her)?"

Self-destructive and cynical thoughts tend to leave young men and women confused about their sexuality. In particular, many adolescent males have indicated an insecurity about their masculinity. At the same time, they have a strong need to have their manhood validated.

> A 19-year-old adolescent entered therapy suffering from suicidal thoughts and a severe depression of several months' duration. His girlfriend of 2 years found a new boyfriend and suddenly rejected him, precipitating symptoms of anxiety and self-recrimination. In exploring his reactions to the loss, the young man discovered that it wasn't the rejection itself that had devastated him. It turned out that in the couple's last argument, his girlfriend said she was ending the relationship because she found him unsatisfying as a lover.
>
> The negative evaluation of his sexuality reinforced his inner doubts about his manhood and sexual performance. His real suffering and torture centered on the theme of sexual inadequacy; his girlfriend's criticism served to activate his own destructive thought processes, internal voices that attacked his manhood.
>
> Further investigation revealed that these voices were related to identification and incorporation of his father's defenses. In addition, he was fussed over by his mother, whose seductive attitude put pressure on his developing sexuality. (A seductive relationship with the mother often stimulates intense Oedipal rivalry and leads to powerful feelings of inadequacy for the growing boy.)
>
> Incidentally, several months later, the patient met another young woman and started a new relationship. His depression seemed to disappear overnight. He felt elated; he told me he felt "great." He said, "My girlfriend told me that I was the nicest man she had ever been with sexually."
>
> It was obvious that the young man took this new evaluation to mean that now he was "okay" sexually. His reactions indicated that he still sought definition and a buildup from a woman to cover up his self-doubts. I felt that he was still extremely vulnerable to depression as long as he needed reassurance from his girlfriend about his sexual performance.

In dealing with feelings of inadequacy, suppression and compensation are always ineffectual. They end up preserving, rather than relieving, the adolescent's doubts and fears. Only by exposing and working through the underlying dynamics can young people develop strength and self-confidence in interpersonal relationships.

Role Reversal in the Parents' Relationship

I have speculated that problems of sexual orientation and doubts about sexual adequacy originate in families where the parents have reversed gender roles. Because most individuals in our culture are still attempting to live up to socially constructed stereotypes of men and women, that is, the strong, dominant male and the weaker, emotionally compliant female, this type of role reversal is contradictory or diametrically opposed to traditional role expectations. Within a relationship constellation characterized by role reversal, that is, in which the woman has assumed a more domineering or controlling role and the man has become more compliant and passive, considerable confusion is created in offspring regarding gender role identification. For example, many young men grow up feeling that they have no ally or protector in their fathers. Boys tend to closely observe and incorporate the father's style of relating to the mother; they notice when the father sells out, is intimidated by her tears, or gives in to her control. They also observe and identify with their father's underlying hostile and defensive attitudes toward women. A fathers' weakness as a role model poses a serious limitation on the development of a strong sense of identity and maleness. Overall, men are in a state of transition and are generally dissatisfied with, and uncertain about, their roles and their relationships. Balswick (1982) asserted that many young boys feel intense anxiety, almost panic, if they are observed doing anything that might be considered feminine or "sissylike" by their peers. As a result, they try to stifle behavioral responses of tenderness, affection, or kindness.

Many adolescent girls experience separation anxiety and fear of the mother's envy or vindictiveness at crucial points in their sexual development, particularly upon entering adolescence. The psychoanalyst Dorothy Bloch (1978) and the psychiatrist Joseph Rheingold (1964, 1967) conjectured that some girls fear retribution or even annihilation at the hands of the mother, just for being a female.

Finally, adolescents who developed an image of being unlovable during their formative years face new challenges in attempting to relate on a more intimate level with a person of the opposite sex. The dating situation involves taking more chances in interpersonal relationships, which exacerbates teenagers' original feelings of inadequacy. They feel anxiety related to their ability to give and receive love, and have fears about physical touch and intimacy. For many, there is a resurgence of a deep sense of feeling unlovable. Without the foundation of positive emotional experiences during the pre-Oedipal and Oedipal stages of development, adolescents are limited, to varying degrees, in their ability to relate to others closely, and they tend to avoid potentially gratifying relationships. If they do reach out and take a chance, rejection or loss of their first love relationship can precipitate intense self-attacking voices, feelings of demoralization, depression, and, at times, suicidal behavior.

Endnotes

1. Berman and Schwartz (1990) reported that almost one in four adolescents who attempted suicide "reported that their families continued to have a firearm with ammunition in the home following the suicide attempt" (p. 310). Maris (1992) has persuasively argued that "suicide prevention is often gun control. If one can remove the gun or limit access to guns, the risk of suicide plummets" (p. 12).

2. Findings from recent research in the field of evolutionary psychology have shown that small kinship groups, similar to an extended family structure, characterized the social organization of many primitive cultures. Anthropologists who study these sites have noted that child abuse was rare in these societies. The more people lived socially, the less there was child abuse (Wright, 1995).

3. The young people participating in this discussion have been friends for many years. They have talked with Dr. Firestone and a number of his colleagues and friends in other discussion groups over an extended period of time and are accustomed to sharing their thoughts and feelings in a group setting.

4. Hewitt, Flett, and Weber (1994) studied two groups of subjects (91 psychiatric patients and 160 college students) and found that (a) perfectionism was significantly correlated with suicidal ideation, even after controlling for the influence of depression and hopelessness, and (b) two perfectionism dimensions interacted with life stress to predict suicidal ideation.

5. Studies indicating a connection between childhood traumas, including physical and sexual abuse, and the development of suicidal thoughts and behaviors during later childhood, adolescence, and adulthood have been conducted by Briere and Runtz (1987), Deykin, Alpert, and McNamarra (1985), and Sansonnet-Hayden, Haley, Marriage, and Fine (1987).

7   Suicide Among Older People

> Death by one's own hand is premature at *any* age and the premature deaths of older adults constitute a loss of talent and resources that no society can accept.
>
> John L. McIntosh (1995, p. 190)

In this country, the elderly have the highest suicide rate of any age group. In 1992, individuals between the age of 80 and 84 had a suicide rate of 24.6 per 100,000 population. In 1990, white males in that age group had a rate of 68.4 per 100,000, as compared with the overall suicide rate of 12.4 (Kachur et al., 1995) (see Figures 7.1 and 7.2).

In a survey conducted by McIntosh, Hubbard, and Santos (1985), it was found that whenever the subject of suicide came up, it was more likely to be associated with young people than with older adults. This common perception of risk is inaccurate. Although the number of young people who commit suicide is larger, suicide among the elderly is disproportionate to their numbers (McIntosh, 1995).

Unfortunately, older people tend to be more "successful" when they try to kill themselves. This trend is evident in the ratio of attempted to completed suicides in the elderly, which is estimated to be approximately 4:1 or even lower (Stenback, 1980). This low figure stands in contrast to the ratio of attempted to completed suicide in the general population, which is from 8:1 to 20:1, and in young people, where it is as high as 300:1. McIntosh (1995) cautioned physicians and mental health practitioners that it is even more crucial to take seriously any threats of suicide on the part of older patients because their efforts to take their own lives so often have a fatal outcome. The future is uncertain with respect to the rates and numbers of suicide among the elderly. McIntosh (1995) predicted that "even if suicide rates remain stable

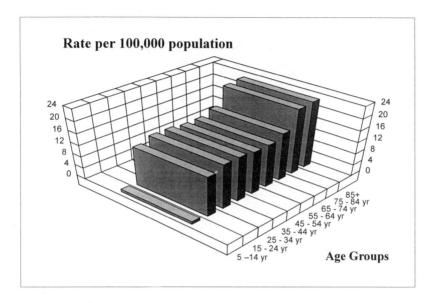

Figure 7.1. U.S. Suicide by Age
SOURCE: Data are for 1993 from the American Association of Suicidology.
NOTE: Rates generally increase with age, and peak in late life.

beyond the year 2000 . . . the larger size of the elderly population will increase the number of older adult suicides compared to today's figures" (p. 182).

Psychological Factors Associated With Suicide Among the Elderly

A number of danger signs, both demographic and experiential, have been found to be reliable indicators of suicide potential in older adults. Maris (1995) stressed that the psychological factors contributing to suicide risk in the elderly represent a gradual accumulation of many factors rather than a single event, loss, or other stressor. Shneidman's (1993) descriptive term *psychache,* which he emphasized as an important factor in suicide, is especially relevant in understanding self-destructive behavior and suicide in older adults. The amount of psychological pain experienced by an elderly person in relation to a single stressful event may exceed a level that he or she perceives

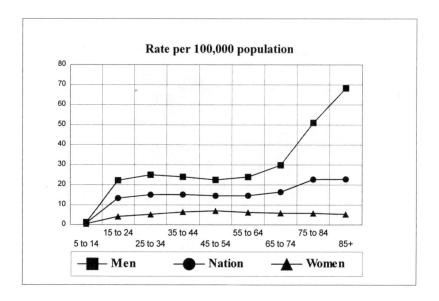

Figure 7.2. U.S. Suicide by Age and Sex
SOURCE: Data are for 1993 from the American Association of Suicidology.
NOTE: There are different age patterns for men and women.

as tolerable or bearable. For another elderly individual, however, the threshold of pain may be much higher, and he or she may be able to deal with a number of stressful events or losses without feeling overwhelmed.

The suicidologist Joseph Richman (1993) delineated and categorized important signs of suicidality in the elderly. A number of these are described below (Endnote 1). Any combination or interaction between these factors can create and/or augment psychological pain or "psychache" in the older individual: (a) ego-weakening factors including major mental, physical, and neurological illness, depression, paranoia or a paranoid attitude, alcoholism or heavy drinking, and intractable, unremitting mental or physical pain; (b) social isolation, for example, living alone, living in the inner city or a socially disorganized area, few or no friends, and isolation or social withdrawal of a couple (Endnote 2); (c) psychodynamic factors including a major loss such as the death of a spouse, a family history of suicide, major crises or transitions such as retirement or imminent entry into a nursing home, blows to self-esteem such as loss of income or loss of meaningful activities, and factors that limit one's independence, when feelings of dependence are unacceptable to the person; and (d) attitudinal and communication factors including rejection of help; a suspicious and hostile attitude toward helpers and society; increased irritability and poor judgment; direct or indirect expression of *suicidal idea-tion; expression of feeling unnecessary, useless, and devalued; expression of belief that one is a burden, in the way, or harmful to others; expression of the belief that one is in an insoluble and hopeless situation; feelings of being trapped with no way out, and finished with life; and acceptance of suicide as a solution.* I have added italics to indicate those factors that include beliefs, thoughts, and feelings that patients and subjects who were identified as at risk for suicide verbalized in the form of "voice" statements and endorsed as items on the Firestone Assessment of Self-Destructive Thoughts (FAST) (Firestone & Firestone, 1996).

Many of the factors delineated by Richman are commonplace experi-ences for older people (Endnote 3). Nonetheless, they are capable of generat-ing unbearable perturbation and psychological pain in vulnerable indivi-duals. This pain, in turn, leads to defensive responses that can become life-threatening. I contend that the degree of vulnerability in terms of the amount of psychological pain that an older person can tolerate is closely related to the extent to which he or she has used self-destructive defense mechanisms to cope with pain and stress throughout the life cycle.

A number of suicidologists, among them Shneidman (1985), Maris (1981), Clark (1993), and McIntosh (1995), have indicated that there are lifelong maladaptive patterns, that is, ways of trying to cope with life, that characterize the suicidal person. Elderly individuals who manifest these specific defense patterns and ineffective coping mechanisms can be identified as being more vulnerable to problems in old age and consequently more at risk for suicide. In his discussion of "suicidal careers," Maris (1995) empha-sized the fact that "every [elderly] suicide is chronic in the sense that the etiologies develop over about 40 to 50 years" (pp. 173-174).

My point of view regarding the dynamics of suicide in the elderly individual essentially agrees with many of the findings noted above. In my clinical experience, I have found that as people age, death anxiety becomes a more serious issue in their lives. The habitual methods they have used to defend themselves against the dread of death and interpersonal stress have become embedded in their character structure. An inward, self-protective posture and the associated defensive behaviors that have been used by indi-viduals since early childhood are increasingly relied upon as they attempt to cope with the social and psychological stressors of old age. Each dimension of the inward process—withholding patterns that cause problems in relationships, restriction of feeling, social isolation, habitual use of substances to soothe pain, cynical attitudes toward self and others, and lack of direction or transcendent goals—come to exert more and more influence over the older person's life. As time passes, there is increased demoralization. Elements of the antiself system become progressively more ascendant in the personality, while the positive elements and resources that make up the ego or self system diminish as a result of years spent in defensive, inward living. If actual suicide is not the result, psychological suicide, the obliteration of the personality, can be the outcome, as people face the difficulties of old age and the fact of their impending death.

Contrary to popular opinion, other studies (Clark & Clark, 1992) have shown that suicide in the elderly is not necessarily related to physical illness and social isolation but is related to the fact that the deceased had reached a crisis in which their vanity and illusions were breaking down (Endnote 4). My conception of "vanity" refers to a fantasized positive image of the self that people use to compensate for deep-seated feelings of inadequacy and inferiority. It represents remnants of the child's imagined invincibility, omnipotence, and invulnerability that live on in the psyche, available as an imagined survival mechanism at times of great stress or when the person becomes too conscious of the fallibility of his or her physical nature and the impermanence of life. In some sense, vanity expresses itself in the universal belief that death happens to someone else, never to oneself (Firestone, 1994).

The inevitable deterioration of physical strength and perceived attractiveness that occurs in the later years attacks a person's sense of power and image. One can no longer avoid one's face in the mirror. The eradication of vanity and important social roles that had served as symbols of immortality for the elderly subjects of the Clarks' study were major factors in the suicides. The customary methods of denial the subjects had depended on were being disrupted, and they had to face the fact that they were mortal. Researchers in the field of suicidology have consistently found the high suicide rate in elderly white males to be significantly correlated with their loss of status, role, power, and money. I believe that the reason for this high rate is related to the fact that male vanity centers on all aspects of achievement and performance, but on sexual potency in particular. When a man experiences a decline in any of the above, there is an increase in depression and self-attack. Incidentally, men tend to blame themselves for any sexual difficulty regardless of the fact that it is often precipitated by attitudes and defenses that may be operant in the women in their lives.

Developmental Crises in Adulthood That
Contribute to Hopelessness and Despair

> Suicide can be thought of as the ultimate in developmental
> stagnation.
>
> Ronald Maris (1995, p. 173)

An individual's development from early childhood through midlife sets the stage for his or her emotional health and sense of well-being during old age. Developmental crises that occur even prior to midlife also affect adult individuals and have long-term consequences. People experience separation anxiety at every stage of individuation and movement toward adult autonomy. How they cope with this anxiety will determine their degree of emotional well-being in interpersonal relationships and careers.

One major developmental crisis takes place at the point when men and women start families of their own. When new parents first observe themselves acting out destructive behavior in interactions with their children that they know damaged them as youngsters, they lose respect for themselves and become depressed and guilty. Most attempt to suppress this painful awareness through denial; they tend to minimize the impact that these negative responses have on their children while denying that as children they suffered similar mistreatment. This defensive denial is not entirely effective; on some level, there is an awareness of these damaging responses and a sense of demoralization.

One woman patient, in challenging her patterns of denial, began to gain insight into the origins of her faulty child-rearing practices. She described her experience of parenthood in the following terms:

> Before I was married, I would sometimes feel lonely and depressed, but I didn't know what depression really was until after Danny was born. When he was a few months old, I found myself being just like my mother in taking care of him. After that, I was a goner. I felt as though I had run into a brick wall. There was nothing I could do to relieve my depression. I became more depressed and self-hating the more I tried to pretend everything was all right.

Another crisis faced by people in their middle years occurs when they lose their parents through death. The death of one's parent is easily understood as a moving of the clock in relation to one's own demise. Intensified feelings of death anxiety at this point generate a movement toward defensive living as people try to protect themselves against the pain and anxiety of the separation associated with their parent's death.

In coping with this form of separation anxiety, many middle-aged people try to preserve an idealized image of the deceased parent. However, one cannot idealize one's parents without a correspondent demeaning of self. Building up or denying parents' faults leads to self-blame and supports a negative view of the self. As people age, there is a tendency to give up one's own identity or unique aspects of self. In retreating from themselves, people become progressively more hopeless because of their failure to live out their own destinies.

In examining the impact of critical events during adult development, two themes that Edwin Shneidman (1985) discussed in *Definition of Suicide* come to mind, themes that, although not necessarily characteristic of all suicidal episodes, are found in most of them:

> 1. A common psychodynamic thread—probably ubiquitous in cases in which a parent of the suicidal person has committed suicide—is the problem of *negative identification.* Negative identification has to do with the powerful unconscious emulation, patterning, modeling or copying of "negative" or generally undesirable traits or features in the person who is being copied. (p. 237)

> 2. If there are common psychodynamic themes in suicide, they probably relate to omnipotence and loss. . . . At the moment of committing suicide, the individual may feel he controls the world—and by his death can bring it down. At least he controls his own destiny. (pp. 237-238)

In my own work, I have emphasized the importance of these same themes in the development of suicidal ideation, depression, and self-destructive behavior. It is necessary to consider both perspectives, the psychoanalytic view of negative identification and denial and the existential issues related to death anxiety, to better understand the factors that predispose suicide and self-destructive actions.

The Psychodynamics of Elderly Suicide and Indirect Self-Destructive Behavior

Progressive Self-Denial

> The common denominator of all negative ways of dealing with anxiety is a shrinking of the area of awareness and or activity. . . . We are afraid to die,

and therefore we are afraid to live, or, as Tillich puts it, we avoid nonbeing by avoiding being. The avoidance of anxiety then means a kind of death in life. (Rheingold, 1967, pp. 204-205)

A particularly insidious defense against death anxiety is that of achieving control over death by committing small suicides on a daily basis. This universal propensity to become self-denying and self-destructive is not due to a death instinct; rather, it represents a powerful defense against the fear of death. People do not have instinctive death wishes toward self, yet they do try to protect themselves when faced with the specter of death. The anticipation of losing one's life and losing all consciousness through death can be so torturous that giving up provides relief from the anguish.

Otto Rank (1936/1972) wrote extensively about this process:

The freeing of instinct from repressions causes fear because life and experience increase the fear of death. (p. 133)

[Man] seeks in his own way to buy himself free from his guilt. He does this through a constant restriction of life (restraint through fear); that is, he refuses the loan (life) in order thus to escape the payment of the debt (death). (p. 126)

As people approach middle age, with all that it implies, and anticipate the next stage of development, old age, with its prospect of illness, infirmity, and death, many become fearful and apprehensive. During this phase, the voice takes increasing precedence over the self system. Negative parental prescriptions become more dominant and exert more influence by first encouraging and then rationalizing self-denying behaviors. The tendency to give up interest in and excitement about life is incorporated into an individual's defensive posture and can often be observed early in his or her life. Most people develop habit patterns of self-denial as a reaction to their guilt about having so-called selfish wants or desires. They prematurely narrow their lives or put limits on their experiences even prior to middle age.

As individuals adjust their behavior according to the dictates of the voice, they begin to reduce their activity levels. They remain unaware that they are acting against their own best interests; they fail to question their loss of enthusiasm for the more invigorating pursuits they enjoyed when they were younger. They justify and explain their inactivity with clichés such as the following: "Slow down, relax, and enjoy your retirement years, you've earned it." "You should act dignified, act your age." In deadening themselves emotionally in advance, people scarcely notice this transition from living to dying.

Voices Underlying Progressive Self-Denial
and Other Defenses Against Death Anxiety

The voice plays a central role in regulating self-denial by predicting negative outcomes, cautioning the individual to reject positive experiences over which he has no control, and steering him toward negative consequences that are more under his control. People are able to gain an illusory sense of control over death by holding back their emotional involvement in life itself in the same way that they try to protect themselves against potential rejection in personal relationships by withdrawing their interest and affect.

An analysis of destructive thought processes in the older adult indicates that the majority of the voice's injunctions and rationalizations are attempts to limit life by persuading the individual to gradually eliminate exciting and spontaneous pursuits. These negative thoughts or voices provide people with explanations for relinquishing interest in their favorite activities or sports— for example, "You're crazy to still play baseball at your age." or "Whoever heard of falling in love at 75? What a fool you are!" or "Why bother to start building that new house at your age? You may not be around to enjoy it when it's finished." In obeying these voices, people are still able to preserve their physical life, yet on an everyday basis, they are committing psychological suicide as they steadily, almost imperceptibly, narrow their world, trivialize their experiences, and fade into the background.

Poor health and illness also tend to activate self-critical thoughts about one's bodily integrity. This is especially true for the elderly. Perceived bodily weaknesses and a deterioration in physical fitness become the target of their self-depreciating thoughts. People who suffer from chronic illness frequently attack themselves as malingerers or see themselves as contaminating. Even older people who are in good health, in anticipating a routine checkup, are likely to torment themselves with such thoughts as these: "The doctor is going to discover something really wrong with you this time. You probably have a terminal illness and he'll have to break the news to you. Why go, anyway? It's better not to know."

The depression and irritability that accompany ill health in older adults are intensified, or may be directly caused, by negative cognitions: "You're always sick." "You're always complaining about your aches and pains." "Nobody wants to be around a sick person like you." Illness can also arouse morbid ruminations about death, thereby increasing one's feelings of resignation and futility about life.

People generally follow the dictates of the voice as they progress through the life span. Destructive patterns of behavior regulated by the voice that have gone unchallenged throughout life have done their dirty work, so to speak, by the time a person reaches the middle years. During the final stages in the developmental sequence, the defended individual is plagued by painful existential guilt about a life unfulfilled, a life not really lived. When people can no longer deny the emptiness of their lives, these feelings of existential guilt, in the form of self-recriminations by the voice, erupt into consciousness. The cycle of despair and hopelessness that follows can lead to the various forms of microsuicide or indirect self-destructive behavior originally described by Farberow (1980b). As a person exhibits more microsuicidal behavior, the pattern can shift to an actual suicidal crisis.

Societal Influences on Suicidal Tendencies in Middle-Aged and Older Individuals

Microsuicidal attitudes and behavior as well as self-destructive patterns and lifestyles are indicative of a broader pattern in the larger society and are actually supported by its institutions and mores (Endnote 5). Virtually all societies and social structures are restrictive of individuality and personal expression in the face of existential anxiety. To some extent, all cultural patterns represent a form of adaptation to people's fear of death. Increased submission to the defensive process of conformity reflects a movement toward a suicidal process and the destruction of all that is human. Despite the fact that each family or group has its own unique lifestyle, there are generalized negative attitudes, behaviors, roles, and routines in society that most of us accept uncritically. These socially approved patterns of behavior and points of view reflect a compilation of individual defenses. In other words, *"a society represents a pooling of the individual defense systems [of its members]"* (Firestone & Catlett, 1989, p. 29).

Progressive self-denial is reinforced by social mores that define age-appropriate roles and behaviors in a severely restrictive manner. In our culture, it is often considered a sign of "maturity" to withdraw from certain activities as one grows older. In spite of our professed beliefs in the value of staying vital and lively and remaining youthful, our concept of "maturity" often implies a gradual retreat from energetic activities as we grow older.

Examples of this disengagement from life can be found in every area of human endeavor. Each withdrawal is supported by social sanctions, institutions, and popular opinion: early retirement, limited participation in sports and other physical activities, a waning interest in sex and diminished sexual activity, loss of contact with old friends, and a dwindling social life. At the same time, there may be an increase in sedentary or self-nourishing activities, and people frequently become plagued with a sense of boredom and stagnation.

In light of the above discussion, the prejudice against the elderly in contemporary society, deplorable as it may be, makes a kind of logical sense. Basically, defended individuals and families don't want to be around those who remind them of their own mortality. In describing the devaluation of older people in advertisements, television, and other media, McIntosh (1995) remarked that "the old tend to be viewed as expendable, as having lived long enough and, perhaps, as having outlived their usefulness" (p. 190). Richman (1993) noted the prevalence of social beliefs that perceive old age "purely as a time of decline, illness, sexual impotence, physical weakness, mental senility and approaching death" (p. 81).

Treatment of the Suicidal Elderly

> As a society we must improve our attitudes toward the elderly
> and aging and change our stigmatizing beliefs surrounding mental
> health problems and the receiving of mental health services.
>
>   John L. McIntosh (1990, p. 307)

It's tragic but true that the majority of elderly people who commit suicide have seen a physician within a month of their death. Conwell, Henderson, Flannery, and Caine (1991) indicated that most of the individuals who had consulted a medical doctor prior to completing suicide were suffering from a treatable depression. Because physicians are the primary gatekeepers for the suicidal elderly, it seems imperative that they be educated in the indicators of suicidal risk and how to respond to these signs empathically and effectively when they observe them in their patients.

The depressed or suicidal older person is usually treated by interventions that differ from those administered to his or her younger counterpart. For example, the types of interventions recommended for the suicidal young adult include a psychodynamic, interpersonal, or cognitive approach along with the necessary medication. For the elderly suicidal person, the typical treatments recommended are electric shock therapy, medication alone (without psychotherapy), institutionalization, or placement in a senior center. These treatment strategies appear to be based on the prejudices described above by Richman and McIntosh. Richman also commented on the social pressure and bias against treating elderly patients on the part of many psychotherapists. He explained this bias as a continuation of Freud's (1937/1964) own counter-transference, which Freud had made explicit in his statement that older people could not change and therefore were not amenable to the therapeutic process. Freud declared, "But with the patients I here have in mind, all the mental processes, relationships and distributions of force are unchangeable, fixed and rigid. One finds the same thing in very old people" (p. 242).

Richman (1993) recommended family therapy as the intervention of choice in cases of elderly suicide and suggested group therapy as a possible new type of treatment strategy. His choice of the latter, group treatment, was influenced by his own and others' clinical experience. Richman suggested that "there is a life-affirming power in groups of people who have problems in common, i.e., homogeneous groups . . . [whereas] two suicidal people together instigate each other to self-destructive behavior" (p. 136).

In a treatment format based on the "narcissistic vulnerability" model, Maltsberger (1991) recommended that treatment be essentially supportive and provide the elderly patient with the functions he or she cannot perform alone. Smith and Eyman (1988) have discussed the Menninger "ego vulnerability" model that differentiates mild and serious suicide attempters. Richman reported that this treatment model emphasizes the importance of "helping patients become aware of their self destructive and self punitive wishes" (p. 149).

My treatment methods involve identifying the destructive thought processes underlying the client's suicidal state and encouraging the expression of angry affect that often accompanies the verbalization of internal voices. Voice Therapy in a group context is the treatment of choice for the reason noted by Richman (1993). My associates and I found that within a group setting, people cannot help but identify with the individual who is verbalizing his or her self-attacks. The quality and tone of these negative voices strike familiar chords in each person, regardless of age, gender, or background. It is important for older clients to find out what they are telling themselves, in the negative sense, about the process of aging, the loss of a significant social role, the death of a spouse or friend, or a chronic or terminal illness. Voice Therapy methods are used to separate these attitudes of pessimism and hopelessness from a more realistic, hopeful, and optimistic viewpoint regarding old age.

In addition, any inclination on the client's part to move toward more participation in life or affiliation with others needs to be supported by the clinician. Activities and friendships that arouse any sign of interest or excitement in the depressed individual should be reinforced. Collaborative interventions that bring about positive change in the client's everyday life are also a vital aspect of treatment. Both clinician and client participate in a discussion to identify specific self-destructive or addictive behaviors that are regulated by the voice, and to formulate ideas about altering these habitual patterns of behavior. Corrective suggestions for addressing problem areas and for expanding the client's range of experiences are generated through this collaborative effort in accord with the client's personal goals and interests.

In terms of future prevention and intervention efforts, McIntosh (1995) has recommended a number of "possible changes that might improve the delivery and nature of intervention resources" for the elderly. He has described a nontraditional "buddy system" format consisting of phone calls and visits to "achieve early identification and referral of the potentially suicidal" (p. 186) in which crisis intervention workers would travel to the home of the person in crisis. Fournier, Motto, Osgood, and Fitzpatrick (1991) have expressed a sentiment shared by all those who work to help older people combat stagnation and loss of meaning: "Hopefully, through receptivity and through active companionship with others, older adults may reduce their vulnerability to suicide and integrate and fulfill their life, even unto death" (p. 8).

The Right to Die Controversy

Before concluding this chapter, it must be emphasized that suicidal thinking is not only due to underlying psychological conflict and anguish; sometimes the agony and pain of physical ailments reach unbearable proportions. One day I was walking in the mountains and experienced severe cramps that were so intense that I could not imagine living with them. It was the first time in my life that I had experienced a degree of pain that I realized would be unbearable to live with if it were a permanent condition instead of a passing episode. I was reminded of a colleague of mine who had been severely burned and was in constant agony. It would be difficult to deny the right to die to patients who suffer from intractable pain or who are tortured by a terminal illness. In my opinion, however, only in these extreme instances would physician-assisted suicide be valid (Endnote 6). This statement applies in particular to cases of emotional stress and depressive states that are often transitional but have the illusion of permanence (Endnote 7). It would be tragic to take one's life during this phase, when the next day or week or several weeks later one might feel very different.

There are cases in which physician-assisted suicide has been abused. In reporting his observations of what he considered such abuses in the Netherlands, Hendin (1995) argued that the Dutch experience illustrates how legal sanction promotes a culture that transforms suicide into assisted suicide and euthanasia and encourages patients and doctors to see choosing death as a preferred way of dealing with serious or terminal illness. The extension of the right to euthanasia to those who are not physically ill further complicates the problems. (p. 193) (Endnote 8)

C. Everett Koop (1976), in *The Right to Live, the Right to Die,* cautioned that acceptance of euthanasia will foster abuse: "Once any group of human beings is considered fair game in the arena of the right to life," wrote Koop, "where does it stop?" (p. 122).

Books that help provide the means for self-destructive actions and suicide are dangerous, if not immoral. Teaching people the actual methods for committing suicide in books such as *Final Exit* by Derek Humphry (1991) and the French manual *Suicide Mode d'Emploi* (How to Commit Suicide) by LeBonniec and Guillon (1982) lead to very serious consequences. In 1987, the French legislature, influenced by Dr. Jean-Pierre Soubrier, a prominent suicidologist, while allowing publication of the section stating philosophical views on the "right to die," banned the instructional section of *Suicide Mode d'Emploi.* For those in our country at risk for suicide, the continuing availability of *Final Exit,* including detailed explanations of lethal dosages and other methods, is no different from putting a loaded gun into the hands of a depressed person.

At the same time, one must take into consideration Thomas Szasz's views on the inherent right of an individual to commit suicide. Szasz (1987) strongly opposed legislation restricting or prescribing people's behaviors in relation to their own bodies, their use of drugs, and their decisions about life and death (suicide); he perceived these laws as a fundamental violation of human rights and personal freedoms. Szasz also objected to "psychiatric coercion," that is, mental health professionals doing something to patients that the patients don't want done. Szasz perceived these coercive forms of treatment, which are often justified as "psychiatric emergencies," as unjustifiable infringements on people's rights (Endnote 9).

Szasz also made an important point about social forces that have a denigrating view of people's power and choice to live their own lives. An overly protective view or posture toward individuals, particularly on the part of institutions and government, is a violation of their basic rights. Yet, in cases where people are overwhelmed by psychological pain and compulsively involved in a suicidal trance state, it may become incumbent, in those extreme instances, to intrude on the person's acting-out behavior,

especially because suicide and suicidal attitudes reflect such dramatic ambivalence.

Although Szasz's position is important and logical, it does neglect the
obvious fact that in suicide, the basic rights of other human beings are being
violated. The suicide of a loved one, especially a parent, seriously damages
the psyches of the survivors, which leads to a social pressure to harm oneself.
Studies have also shown that the loss of a parent through suicide in early
childhood is devastating, arousing tremendous "survivor guilt" in the child
for simply being alive (Endnote 10). In his book *Children Who Don't Want to
Live,* Orbach (1988) declared,

> Parental suicide is one type of desertion that has no emotional parallel in its
> destructive force . . . . [The child is] bombarded by the forces of guilt, shame,
> self-punishment, and depression. Moreover, the act of suicide points out to
> the child the deadly means for coping with this maelstrom of emotions. (p. 87)

Conclusion

In understanding suicide among the elderly, one must be cognizant of each
individual's essential mood of meaninglessness, purposelessness, or emptiness, or, as the suicidologists Fournier et al. (1991) described it, "essentially
spirit-less or without satisfaction" (p. 8).

In relation to this understanding, and on a more personal note, when I was
a boy, my grandfather shared my bedroom. I remember lying in bed at night
listening to him struggling to catch his breath between paroxysms of cough-
ing. He was old, and I sensed that he would die soon.

My grandfather had lived with me all my life and so I knew him very
well. Having spent his life in a kind of half-miserable, yet somewhat comfortable daze, he was nearing the end. I was aware that he had no sense of
his impending death. I dreaded the probability that one morning he might
suddenly wake up as from a sleep and realize that he was at the end, that only
yesterday he had been a boy like me and that he had spent the intervening years not really living. I was terrified that he would know that he had
wasted his life in complaints, family feuds, and long hours at a job he
couldn't stand. He would realize that it was too late—there was no time left
to live.

In my mind, this would be the most horrible thing that could happen to
my grandfather. I hoped so much that he would not "wake up" but would just
die peacefully without this unbearable realization. The years passed and he

died, which left me with a lasting impression of a man who had missed his own life.

From this experience came a strong motivation on my part to try to live my life differently than my grandfather. I never wanted to be faced with the kind of final realization that I had dreaded for him. I wanted to experience all the facets of my life, the good and the bad, the painful and joyful events.

Otto Rank (1936/1972) wrote that anxiety could not be entirely overcome therapeutically—that it is impossible to face the truth of human existence without anxiety. However, when this anxiety is experienced, the choice is clear: whether to restrict and numb our feelings in an attempt to escape the terror or to live fully, with humility, meaningful activity, and compassion for oneself and others.

* * *

In conclusion, it should be noted that "on 16 December 1991 the United Nations General Assembly adopted resolution 46/91." The resolution contained the United Nations Principles for Older Persons "to add life to the years that have been added to life" by assuring them independence, participation, care, self-fulfillment, and dignity (United Nations Department of Public Information, 1992, p. 1).

Endnotes

1. These factors and others are based on Richman's (1993) book *Preventing Elderly Suicide,* p. 5. Used with permission.

2. Richman (1993) emphasized that social isolation as a couple can be equally as deadly as isolation for an individual. In his discussion of the dangers of symbiotic partnerships, he declared, "The problem in suicide is not only separation, but the wish to merge, to become one with the person who is lost or unavailable" (p. 106).

3. Another significant phenomenon noted by Richman (1993) in his discussion of danger signs was the frequency of suicide pact ideation in elderly suicidal patients who are married.

4. In one study, Clark and Clark (1992) conducted psychological autopsies of 73 cases of suicide by men and women aged 65 and over occurring in Cook County during the first 10 months of 1990. They found that "only 14% had been terminally ill, 23% had a severe chronic medical illness; yet two-thirds of the sample had not been exposed to unusual kinds or degrees of acute life stress" (p. 235). In addition, the majority of subjects were not living alone nor were they isolated from friends or family; "83% of the subjects [would have been diagnosed with] major depression in the weeks preceding death" (p. 235). In his interpretation of these findings, Clark (1992) proposed that many older individuals who kill themselves have a "lifelong character fault that may well remain invisible until aging life-changes force the issue into the open." The fault or

weakness, according to Clark, lies in "a fundamental adaptational capacity to adapt to irrefutable evidence of the aging process" (p. 237).

5. In considering the impact of social beliefs and mores on suicide in the elderly, one should also take into account social and economic conditions that may influence changes in suicide rates. For example, Richman (1993) noted that the rate decreased with the onset of Social Security during the 1930s and fell even further with the inception of Medicare. He pointed out that during the 1980s, the elderly suicide rate increased and "appeared to be correlated with threats to such services as Social Security and Medicare and the gradual, though covert, rationing of health care" (p. 13).

6. The reader is referred to Boldt's (1989) chapter, "Defining Suicide: Implications for Suicidal Behavior and for Suicide Prevention," in *Suicide and Its Prevention: The Role of Attitude and Imitation.* Boldt asserted,

> It is illogical to advocate, as some have done, for the right to suicide, on grounds that it promotes human dignity. Does a dead man experience dignity? Suicide may offer an *escape from* the *indignity* of an unendurable or degrading life; but, where is the dignity in suicide? Human dignity is rooted in a good life, a sense of community, a positive sense of self-worth, and so on. We promote human dignity when we provide these life conditions; not by guaranteeing the right to suicide. (p. 7)

7. Often the elderly patient is suffering from emotional distress or dysfunctional beliefs that are temporary in nature rather than from chronic physical pain. For example, a study in Washington State found that 75% of people seeking physician-assisted death cited "fear of being a burden," while only 35% gave "experiencing severe pain" as a reason (Shapiro, 1996).

8. Hendin (1995), in commenting on the "Dutch Experience," described a case in which a grieving mother who was not terminally ill was assisted in taking her life. The case "was seen as a triumph by euthanasia advocates since it legally established mental suffering as a basis for euthanasia" (p. 200).

9. Szasz (1987), in discussing psychiatric emergencies that demand coercive treatment such as in the last stages of anorexia or during a suicidal crisis, made an important distinction between "psychiatric coercion" and a compassionate method for preventing such life-threatening crises well in advance of the dangerous situation:

> I am distinguishing between concern, compassion and coercion. I think there is no need to coerce people if you show enough compassion and spend enough time. . . . A psychiatric emergency is justification for psychiatric coercion and no one can deny it. . . . "Desperate situations make for desperate measures." So the thing to do is to avoid desperate situations. (pp. 428-429)

10. A particular form of guilt associated with separation and death anxiety, "death guilt," was described by Lifton and Olson (1976) in "The Human Meaning of Total Disaster." According to these authors, death guilt is "the survivor's sense of painful self-condemnation over having lived while others died" (p. 3). They suggested that when an individual suppresses these painful feelings of guilt, the result is a kind of *"psychic numbing*—a diminished capacity for feeling of all kinds—in the form of various manifestations of apathy, withdrawal, depression, and overall constriction in living" (p. 5).

PART II

INDIRECT SUICIDE

8 Microsuicide[1]

> Now I know (Dr. D. told me) that the voice is me, Elizabeth. I
> am not having auditory hallucinations. . . . The voice comes out
> of my head. I don't argue with him. Of course the voice comes
> out of my head, but the voice isn't me. Oh, no, not me, not in a
> million years. Nobody understands this. But I know now that
> the voice is a separate entity that happens to reside in my head.
>
> Elizabeth Ikiru (1985, pp. 37-38),
> *The Voice Inside Me*[2]

This description was written by a highly intelligent woman diagnosed with a bipolar disorder. For over 10 years, she was tormented by a voice demanding that she inflict physical punishment on herself. Her pattern of self-mutilation, which was followed by temporary respite from the insistent voice, represents an extreme manifestation of "microsuicidal behavior." Although clinicians have investigated certain aspects of the dynamics operating in self-harm behavior, much remains to be understood about the negative thought process that regulates this and other, less dangerous forms of self-destructive actions and lifestyles.

Microsuicide encompasses behaviors, communications, attitudes, or lifestyles that are self-induced and threatening to an individual's physical health, emotional well-being, or personal goals. Examples of microsuicidal behavior include patterns of progressive self-denial described in the previous chapter, inwardness, withholding, destructive dependency bonds, and physically harmful actions and lifestyles (Firestone & Seiden, 1987, 1990b). In this chapter, we will focus on these self-destructive behaviors, which, although not actually life-threatening, are so common that we refer to them as the "microsuicides of everyday life."

1. Portions of this chapter were taken from "Microsuicide and Suicidal Threats of Everyday Life," *Psychotherapy, 24,* pp 31-39 (Firestone & Seiden, 1987). Used with permission.
2. Reprinted from "The Voice Inside Me," by Elizabeth Ikiru. Reprinted by permission of Zoë Hammond.

Since Durkheim (1897/1951) published his sociological study of suicide, the theorists and suicidologists Karl Menninger, Kalle Achte, Norman Far-berow, and Robert Litman, among others, have acknowledged that there are self-defeating behaviors and patterns that are not necessarily undertaken for the purpose of total self-destruction. They have been termed *indirect suicide, partial suicide, installment-plan suicide, slow suicide, inimical patterns of behavior, embryonic suicide, masked suicide, hidden suicide, parasuicide,* and *chronic suicide.* Although there are minor distinctions between these terms, they all describe lifestyles of gradual self-destruction. In *The Many Faces of Suicide,* Farberow (1980b) enumerated specific self-destructive behaviors that

> by their very familiarity and frequency of occurrence . . . must merge into the normal, acceptable end of the continuum of behavior. On the other hand, if they can be so self-destructive or self-injurious, they must merge into the pathological end of the continuum represented by overt suicidal activity. (p. 2)

My objective is to examine the myriad self-destructive behaviors that are so prevalent in our culture that we often fail to acknowledge their diagnostic importance or appreciate their negative effects on individual lives. In addition, I will examine the negative thought process or voice that mediates these actions and lifestyles. If we are to modify or change this type of behavior, we must first be able to identify and isolate the thought patterns that control it.

Separation Anxiety and Death Anxiety

Microsuicidal behaviors and the negative thought processes that mediate self-destructive behavior can be understood in terms of their role as a defense, first, against psychological pain and separation anxiety and, later, against death anxiety.

Separation Anxiety

Otto Rank became the first object-relations theorist when he conceptual-ized that pre Oedipal dynamics were the principal cause of the neuroses, and that internalized object representations of the mother led to transference distortions in later object relationships. Although he stayed within the psy-choanalytic framework, he was ostracized for rejecting Freud's view that the

Oedipal conflict was primary. Rank was aware of the significance of the child's relationship to the mother as the primary caretaker and her central role in determining the child's subsequent reactions to separation experiences. A secure and satisfying relationship with the mother predisposed a healthy resolution of the conflict between assertion and dependence.

In *The Trauma of Birth,* Rank (1923/1929) emphasized that life was a succession of weaning and separation experiences, culminating in death, the ultimate separation or castration experience. He noted that each phase of development was characterized by internal conflict between separation and individuation, on the one hand, and a defensive process that attempted to deny or cover up the fracture. Children first become aware of separation from the breast, and then later separation from the mother, father, and family, as they pass through the developmental phases. They must face losses at every level, and they gradually become aware of the fact that their parents will die and eventually they themselves will cease to exist. Painful trauma such as neglectful or emotionally impoverished parenting further complicates separation experiences and leads to even greater anxiety. The more rejected the child, the more he or she resists individuation and clings to the disturbing parental atmosphere. Even if a child experienced little or no interpersonal stress, he or she would develop a defensive process in relation to the human condition, that is, the painful realities of war, economic stresses, sickness, aging, aloneness, and, finally, death anxiety. Because defenses predispose voices, no child, indeed no person, is completely free of voice attacks.

Death Anxiety

> Everything that man does in his symbolic world is an attempt to
> deny and overcome his grotesque fate. He literally drives himself
> into a blind obliviousness with social games, psychological tricks,
> personal preoccupations so far removed from the reality of his
> situation that they are forms of madness—agreed madness, shared
> madness, disguised and dignified madness, but madness all the
> same.
>
> Ernest Becker (1973, p. 27)

A certain degree of alienation from oneself is inevitable in relation to death anxiety because direct contemplation of death's finality is too painful to face without defending or cutting off some amount of feeling for oneself (Endnote 1). As noted in the previous chapter, most people commit small suicides on a daily basis in an effort to accommodate the anxiety and dread surrounding the existential awareness of death. In an attempt to exert some power over their fate, they give up aspects of their lives through self-denial and self-defeating habit patterns, thereby creating a false sense of omnipotence.

The "normal" individual is not unlike the prisoner on death row who takes his own life in an effort to have some measure of control over death rather than live with the agony of knowing the exact time of execution. Why invest feelings in a life that one most certainly will lose? From this perspective, we can say that all people have the potential for suicide; it is only the idiosyncratic style and strength of the movement toward self-obliteration that varies. Through the process of progressive self-denial and other forms of microsuicide, the fear of death is converted into a fear of living, that is, of becoming too involved in or attached to life.

The Interrelatedness of Self-Destructive Behavior

All self-destructive behaviors are related, that is, they differ only in quantity, nature, and degree. Although the great majority of suicide attempters will not proceed to kill themselves in the future, a few will. According to Dorwart and Chartock (1989), "the best predictor for subsequent suicide attempts and completions is previous suicide attempts" (p. 41).

The Dynamics of Microsuicide

People's defenses correspond to the frequency and intensity of their negative cognitions. Self-limiting and self-destructive behaviors are based on powerful feelings of self-hatred and negative attitudes toward self incorporated by the child during the formative years. Self-critical attitudes, feelings of hopelessness, and the erratic mood swings that characterize certain types of depressive states are strongly influenced by internalized negative thoughts or "voices." Clinical data obtained from preliminary investigations indicate that the majority of these thoughts originate in family interactions. They are isolated phrases from a well-integrated system of destructive attitudes toward the self. As demonstrated earlier, these hostile thoughts can be identified and brought directly into consciousness through use of Voice Therapy procedures. The action of uncritically "listening to" or "obeying" voices predisposes one toward self-limiting and self-destructive behavior.

The Continuum of Self-Destructive Thoughts and Behaviors

Our clinical research has shown that negative thought patterns vary along a continuum of intensity from mild self-criticisms to malicious self-accusations and suicidal thoughts. Similarly, microsuicidal behavior exists on a continuum ranging from asceticism or self-denial to accident-proneness, substance abuse, and other self-defeating behaviors, culminating in self-mutilating acts and actual suicide. Often individuals who are accident-prone or who engage in risk-taking activities are considering suicide as an option. The 6-year-old who runs into the street may be one example of the wish to die or be killed (see Figure 8.1, "Continuum of Self-Destructive Thoughts and Behavior").

Microsuicides of Everyday Life

For didactic purposes, microsuicidal behavior can be divided into two categories: (a) behaviors predisposed by voices directed against the self and (b) behaviors predisposed by voices directed against others. Both predispose alienation from other people.

Behaviors Predisposed by Voices Directed Against the Self

Voices that predispose low self-esteem, self-denial, and isolation. Virtually all people are aware of self-critical thoughts; most are cognizant of an internal dialogue[2]: "You're going to make a fool of yourself." "You always make mistakes." "You're a failure." "You don't make enough money." "You're so awkward and unattractive, why would he (she) be attracted to you?" "You just don't fit in; you're different than other people." (All subjects tested on the Firestone Assessment of Self-Destructive Thoughts [FAST] endorsed this last item.) Negative comparisons with rivals are common. Many men tell themselves: "He's better-looking, smarter, and more interesting than you. You're boring and unappealing." Women run themselves down with thoughts like the following: "She's prettier than you. She's got a great body, but look at you. Men don't go for women like you."

Self-Critical Thoughts That Lead to Low Self-Esteem and Self-Denial

1. Self-depreciating thoughts of everyday life.

2. Thoughts rationalizing self-denial; that is, thoughts discouraging the person from engaging in pleasurable activities.

3. Cynical attitudes toward others leading to alienation and distancing.

4. Thoughts influencing isolation and nonproductive time spent alone where voices predominate.

Voices That Regulate the Cycle of Addiction

5. Thoughts that support substance abuse—food, drugs, alcohol—followed by self-attacks for indulging.

6. Thoughts that support compulsive habit patterns, deadening routines, compulsive overworking, and so on.

7. Thoughts that influence addictive relationships.

8. Thoughts that predispose eating disorders: anorexia nervosa and bulimia.

9. Thoughts that predispose accident-proneness.

Self-Annihilating Thoughts That Lead to Suicide

10. Thoughts influencing a person to give up priorities and favored activities (relinquishing points of identity).

11. Thoughts contributing to a sense of hopelessness, urging withdrawal or removal or getting rid of oneself.

12. Self-contempt; vicious self-abusive thoughts and accusations (accompanied by intense anger affect).

13. Injunctions to inflict self-harm at an action level; intense rage against self.

14. Thoughts planning the actual details of suicide (calm, rational, and often obsessive) indicating complete loss of feeling for the self.

15. Injunctions to carry out the suicidal plan; thoughts baiting the person to take the last step.

Figure 8.1. Continuum of Self-Destructive Thoughts and Behavior

Even when these self-critical attitudes have little basis in reality, they have a profound effect on behavior. Disparaging voices increase performance anxiety, particularly in sexual situations and in public speaking. They interrupt the ongoing pursuit of goals by generating painful feelings of shyness, self-consciousness, and humiliation, and precipitate withdrawal from interpersonal relationships. (Incidentally, fear of public speaking was designated as the number one fear of people in a recent survey.)

Our clinical data have demonstrated that self-denial on a behavioral level parallels voice attacks, and that seemingly innocuous patterns of self-denial often lead to more serious regressive behavior. Attitudes and thoughts that govern self-denial are almost ubiquitous in the general population. For example, a person who loves adventure and travel may rationalize his or her decision to stay home during a vacation: "You've taken a lot of trips. You could take it easy at home. Traveling is so expensive anyway. Look at all the money you save by staying home." As described in Chapter 7, progressive self-denial is part of an insidious process that becomes more pronounced as people go through the life span. As they retreat from seeking gratification in the external world, they become increasingly indifferent to life and find it easier to give up activities they once found pleasurable and meaningful.

Beverly, 38, an executive secretary, exemplifies this pattern. The story she told revealed that she had gradually restricted her life over the last 10 years "for no apparent reason." She realized that she had not only withdrawn from her relationship with a man who cared deeply for her but had steadily removed herself from the activities she loved the most. Although she and her boyfriend had been very close, she had powerful voices that attacked his loving feelings. "He doesn't really love you. Can't you see that he's just taking advantage of you? Who needs a man in their life?" The voice went on to predict a negative outcome that eventually became a self-fulfilling prophecy: "This isn't going to last. No one would want to stay with you."

She rationalized her withdrawal with such thoughts as the following: "Why go out with him tonight? It's more important to get caught up with your work." In the process, she developed a pattern of postponing gratification, putting things off to the future, telling herself, "You can wait to have fun this weekend (on your vacation, at the end of the year) and so on." As time passed, she explained away her lack of interest in sex: "You're getting too old for sex. Most women your age don't have sex anymore. They focus on other, more important things in life."

Becoming aware of these voices made sense to Beverly; however, she still faced a rough road to get her life back on track. She would find it difficult to change patterns that had been deeply rooted for the past 10 years. In countering her compulsive self-denial, she must face a good deal of anxiety. Seeking gratification would make her feel painfully vulnerable again. It would take courage to attempt to reestablish her life, and there would be setbacks. For example, she had alienated her boyfriend to such an extent that when she approached him to talk about renewing the relationship, he was somewhat distant and cool in his response.

In the early stages of withdrawal and self-denial, movement toward isolation cannot be distinguished from constructive time spent alone for concentrated or creative work. Later, defensive rationalizations break down, and it becomes obvious that a person is really ruining his or her life. Following the dictates of apparently self-protective voices is a form of microsuicide. Thoughts such as "Your life has been too hectic lately" or "You need some time alone" or "You need your own space" often mask self-destructive motives in people who are actually seeking isolation from others and are gradually retreating from gratification in the interpersonal environment. Extended periods of time away from social contact can be conducive to depressive reactions and progressive withdrawal, patterns that are detrimental to mental health in general.

Voices that encourage and perpetuate the cycle of addiction. As people go about the business of life, they tend to use more painkillers and involve themselves in progressively more activities that cut off feeling. They may end up overworking, overeating, smoking or drinking too much, and imperceptibly drift more and more deeply into passivity and self-indulgent habits and routines. Seemingly friendly voices suggest that they give themselves rewards: "Have a cigarette. It'll relax you." "You can have another snack after you finish this assignment." Although initially egosyntonic, when these habits become compulsive or addictive, they have serious consequences that foster considerable guilt reactions. Voices are perverse in that they persuade people to indulge their addictive habits, then berate them for their indulgences. This self-condemnation leads to painful feelings of shame and self-hatred, which in turn increase the need for relief in the form of more painkillers.

Bulimia nervosa, anorexia nervosa, and binge-eating disorders are representative of addictive, suicidal trends in the personality that at times reach life-threatening proportions. Anorexia is diagnosed in approximately .5% to 1% of females in the United States; between 5% and 20% of patients die as a result of complications of this disorder. Bulimia has been found in 1% to 3% of females. Kaplan (1984) emphasized that these pathological syndromes are the result of the person's struggle to individuate. She noted that "with the anorectic, asceticism takes over. . . . She listens only to the voices . . . which demand a narrowing of roles, renunciation, sacrifice" (pp. 263-264).

According to Kaplan, these young women typically report feeling that they are not acting on their own volition. One girl revealed: "There is another self, a dictator who dominates me. . . . A little man screams at me when I think of eating" (p. 269). In analyzing a large number of cases, Kaplan concluded, "The parental prohibitions and commandments then will continue to be experienced as coming from outside the self, or as alien inner voices" (p. 269). Sandbek (1993) also described voices reported by bulimic patients that controlled the cycle of binging and purging.

Routine habit patterns such as working compulsively to the point of exhaustion are obvious manifestations of self-destructive tendencies that have been studied by clinicians for many years (Farberow, 1980b; Nelson & Farberow, 1982). These behaviors represent direct assaults against the individual's physical health and emotional well-being, and lead to gradual deterioration.

In one case, Raymond, an attorney, found that he was spending an inordinate amount of time at work, at the expense of leisure time spent with his family and friends. He reported angry thoughts toward himself about working: "You'd better get to work." "You've got to win this case." "You've got a great record and your career is on the line!" He recognized that his typical routine of spending 18 hours a day preparing for a trial was having a detrimental effect on his state of mind and physical health. In a group discussion, he recalled childhood events that he connected to this destructive pattern, and began to question some of the functions his career has served.

> My father had no social life of any sort. He was very cynical about social life and he was cynical about women. He worked all the time. Basically, work was the only thing that absorbed him.
>
> On the other hand, my mother treated me like a show dog, a trained show dog. She even had a whistle when I was a kid that she would blow to summon me when I was out playing. I had no freedom. She would nag at me about everything I did so I had no life of my own. I was trained to perform.
>
> So now even though I'm a successful trial lawyer, I perform. That's the main part of the job. I have my own firm and I use it to duplicate the demanding situation in my childhood. I have somewhat more of a life than my father did, but I have so much less than is available to me. The things that I enjoy doing, I never do, generally because of work. I tell myself, "You should be at work where you belong."
>
> I love driving a power boat, but I haven't driven a power boat in months. I realize that the way I use my business has turned out to be so much like my mother. It actually treats me like my mother did in a lot of ways. It absorbs all my time. It controls me. It summons me all the time. Even though there are certain things about which I'm proud of myself as a lawyer, I get very little satisfaction out of it because I feel like I'm always performing for her still.

Raymond treated himself as an object in much the same way his mother had treated him. His indifference to himself as a feeling person allowed him to casually give up the activities and friendships he especially enjoyed. Because many people disregard themselves and their wants, they are capable of confining and limiting themselves while failing to notice that they are giving up broad areas of functioning in their lives.

Addictive personal relationships. An addictive attachment or *fantasy bond* is an illusion of connection formed by many couples to defend against separation and death anxiety (Chapter 12). It is addictive in the sense that both partners are primarily using each other to relieve feelings of anxiety and insecurity. This misuse of the other leads to a deterioration of the original feelings. One woman defined the fantasy bond intuitively in the most succinct terms: "I knew I was terrified of being alone, and I also knew that I was afraid to be close to a man. I found the perfect solution in my marriage. My husband is physically there, but I can relate to him somewhat distantly." In developing a chronic unfeeling attachment to a man who exhibited the same defense, this woman colluded with her partner to maintain a fantasy of closeness in the absence of in-depth feeling.

Many men and women develop fantasy bonds in an effort to compensate for feelings of inadequacy and hostile voice attacks. The more rejection or deprivation they experienced during the formative years, the more they seek security and a sense of wholeness through a fantasized connection with another person. A progressive loss of identity and individuality is symptomatic of the mutual self-destructiveness inherent in a fantasy bond. In some cases, there is observable physical deterioration or illness directly attributable to the negative, disrespectful style of interacting that characterizes many marriages. As the relationship degenerates in actuality, each partner may become more involved in a fantasy of being connected. Both give up broad areas of independent functioning to cling to this fantasized merger.

Within a fantasy bond, people come to depend on repetitive, habitual contact without much feeling. As they give up their real lives for an illusion of connection, they find life gradually becoming more hollow and empty. Yet they are reluctant to tamper with this defensive, addictive mode of relating. They are fearful of arousing a heightened state of anxiety and voice attacks that are immediately below the surface.

In our investigations, we found that the choice of a partner based on opposite or complementary characteristics represented an attempt to compensate for voices about perceived deficiencies. For example, a passive person may find an active partner; a quiet person may latch on to an outward, talkative person; an indecisive individual may be attracted to a person who is parental and controlling. In many instances, the respective partners reported reciprocal voice attacks. One insecure young man verbalized the following voice about a young woman he had recently become involved with:

"You should take care of her. Give her things, show her how much you care about her. Don't you realize how lucky you are to have her? Who else would have you? Nobody! So you'd better not let her get away. Hang on to her, buddy!"

The woman involved with this man also exhibited a poor self-image and strong feelings of worthlessness. Here she articulates the contents of a negative voice that incidentally represented her mother's point of view about men and relationships in general:

"You've got to hold on to this one. You may never get another chance. He's generous and buys you things, so don't ever let him down. If you play your cards right, he'll be happy to take care of you. That's what men are for, to take care of women.

"If he leaves, you'll never find anyone else. You've never found it easy to attract men, so don't make any mistakes with this one, or you'll end up alone!"

This woman's lack of a sense of self compelled her to seek out someone to define her, in an effort to fill the void that she felt existed in her personality. The neediness and insecurity of both partners were the basis of the intensity of their initial sexual attraction and later led to conflict and the dissolution of the relationship.

The selection of partners with opposite character traits in an attempt to compensate for one's limitations is rarely successful. The polarization that inevitably follows will lead to disillusionment. The very qualities people are attracted to originally are the same traits they begin to find extremely unpleasant and eventually come to hate. I conjecture that an intense sexual attraction may disguise underlying needs based on feelings of emotional hunger and desperation. The effort to become a whole person through connecting with another is doomed to fail, even though the relationship may endure.

In another case, a CPA who was cynical about relationships and who had for years lived a life devoid of romantic involvement, suddenly formed a deep attachment to a depressed, childlike woman considerably younger than himself. He quickly took on the role of therapist/parent and became consumed in the relationship. As he spent more and more time trying to breathe life into his new girlfriend, he lost considerable energy and vitality. His friends observed that at times his speech was actually slurred and he appeared drugged. The association with her seemed to drain the very life from this man. The effects could be discerned in all areas of his life. His work performance suffered and, indeed, over the next 2 years, his business failed and he was forced to declare bankruptcy. In time, he came to treat her with a certain disrespect, ordering her about in an authoritarian manner in spite of his protestations of love. Although it was clear that this man had essentially re-created his father's distant and condescending relationship with his infantile mother, he clung to it with the tenacity of a true addict.

The only way to judge the quality of a personal relationship is to observe the mental state and degree of aliveness of the individuals involved. If, during the course of the association, both partners have become more vital, energetic, and successful in their individual pursuits as well as having maintained feelings of attraction and friendship, the relationship would be evaluated as satisfying or positive. If, on the other hand, the people involved are miserable, emotionally deadened, or progressively malfunctional, it becomes necessary to face up to the negative aspect of the fantasy bond in the couple.

In studying the resistance to challenging the status quo of obviously destructive ties, I have discovered that people do not fear rejection or loss of their partner as much as they fear the intensity of the self-attacks that will be precipitated by their failure to achieve a "successful relationship." They live in terror of arousing malicious voices or even suicidal thoughts and often hold on to negative or abusive relationships in which they progressively give up their sense of identity and, in effect, lose their real lives.

Self-annihilating thoughts that lead to suicide. At a certain point on the continuum, angry, vindictive voices assault the individual, telling him or her that he or she no longer matters to anyone, that his or her absence would improve the lives of family and friends rather than diminish their lives and cause them grief. This crucial shift in thinking transforms suicide from an "immoral" act (in the sense that at least six people are profoundly affected by a suicide) into a moral act in the mind of the person bent on destroying him- or herself (Endnote 3). "Look at all the problems you're causing your family. If you just killed yourself, they'd be free of you once and for all!" or "Do them a favor, get rid of yourself." These are common voices reported by individuals who were interviewed after surviving a serious suicide attempt.

The insidious results of progressive self-denial are also evident at this level. Angry self-attacks and obsessive ruminations further deplete the vitality of those who have denied their wants and desires over a prolonged period of time and now feel they have nothing left to live for: "Nothing matters anymore. There's nothing to look forward to. Your life will never get better. Why keep on living?"

The culmination of renouncing basic wants and favored activities is illustrated in the play *'Night, Mother* by Marsha Norman (1983). In the course of preparing for her suicide, the main character confides to her mother that she can think of absolutely no reason to go on living. The mother tries to entice her by offering to make her favorite dessert, rice pudding. She responds that she no longer even likes rice pudding.

Malicious self-attacks, intense self-hatred, and murderous rage toward self escalate as a person moves closer to suicide. The severity of these voices is related to the degree of anger turned against the self, which naturally would have been directed outward against the source of frustration or punishment. Children who experience a frightening home environment cannot escape from the situation and must turn for security to the very people who mistreat them and arouse their anger. It is this unresolvable conflict between the reactive desire to murder one's oppressor and the fear of being murdered that leads children to turn their rage against themselves.

Voices that express the most vicious self-attacking posture are made up of angry, name-calling diatribes and bitter self-recriminations: "You're disgusting!" "You're nothing but a slut!" "You fat cow!" "Look at you! You deserve nothing!" In our clinical studies, we observed that apparently high-functioning subjects sometimes engaged in behaviors that were potentially dangerous to their physical health. One man, a construction worker who drove heavy tractors and bulldozers, reported a voice that taunted him when he worked overtime. "Watch out, you're tired. One mistake and this rig could flip over on you," then with anger, "Speed it up, buddy! See if you can drive it up that slope without losing control! C'mon, give it the gas!" When this voice was expressed in a session, the accompanying affect was shocking in its intensity.

Actual self-harm in the form of serious addictive disorders, accident-proneness, and other risk-taking behavior are more likely to be acted out when people withdraw their interest and emotional investment in themselves and avoid pursuing important personal goals. One woman who tended to be somewhat dazed and inwardly preoccupied was involved in three car accidents within a period of 6 months. After the third mishap, she remembered that immediately preceding the collision, she had experienced a brief thought that disconcerted and alarmed her, "Why don't you just drive over the center divider?" Even in so-called normal individuals, unexpected suicidal impulses or ideation sometimes erupt into conscious awareness. These thoughts are indications of the potential destructiveness of the negative thought process existing within every person.

As the voice gains in ascendance over rational thought processes, the individual becomes increasingly cut off from feeling and dissociated from him- or herself. Dire predictions by the voice about the self, others, and the future are accepted by the person as totally accurate statements and, as a consequence, suicidal ideation increases dramatically. In these circumstances, microsuicidal behavior has a lethal potential as one approaches the extreme end of the continuum.

In Chapter 2, I described the cold, calculating contemplation of suicide in the final phase when the person withdraws from interactions with others and listens more and more to voice attacks. These calculations lead to strategies regarding the specific time, place, and method of self-destruction, followed by commands to actually commit the final act.

Behaviors Predisposed by Hostile Thoughts Toward Others

Cynical, hostile thoughts toward others tend to occur in conjunction with self-critical thoughts. When people are suspicious and attacking of others based on negative, irrational beliefs, they tend to distance themselves and avoid close involvement. "Why would you want to go out with him? He's a real jerk," or "Why get involved with her? She'll just end up rejecting you like all the other women have." Feelings of anger and distrust are aroused when people listen to voices telling them that others don't really care. "*They* never take your feelings into consideration. Who do they think they are?" Or, more generally, "People just don't give a damn."

The voice uses popular stereotypical views of men and women to create distance in couple relationships. "Men are all alike. They don't want to commit to a relationship." Or "Women are so childish, emotional, and erratic. If you get involved, you're in for big trouble." Thoughts such as these create a basic distrust between men and women, which leads them to avoid intimate relationships with the opposite sex.

Members of minority groups have reported seeing themselves in a derogatory light that conforms to the prejudicial views prevalent in our society. If they try to break away from stereotypical voices, new voices attack them as "uppity" or traitorous. One African American disclosed a voice that taunted him angrily for socializing with his white colleagues: "What are you doing with these people? You don't belong there! What are you trying to do, be better than the rest of us?"

The voice also contributes to feelings of victimization and paranoia by promoting a state of passivity. The passive person tends to project angry, self-critical thoughts onto other people and perceives them as critical or hostile. Instead of taking action to change an unhappy situation, he or she will complain about the "injustice of it all." The voice constantly reminds the victimized individual: "It's not fair. This shouldn't be happening to you." "What did you ever do to deserve such treatment?"

In the workplace, people have angry hostile attitudes based on voices telling them they are being exploited:

> "Your boss is a real jerk. Who does she think she is?"
>
> "People seem friendly, but they all have an angle."
>
> "Nobody sees how much you contribute. No one appreciates you. So just forget them!"
>
> "Why does he always get all the breaks?"

Reacting to events as a victim leads to a buildup of internal hostility with a corresponding decrease in one's ability to cope effectively with negative circumstances. The accumulation of aggression can precipitate angry outbursts that go well beyond the reality of the stimulus situation.

Thoughts that predict rejection or other negative outcomes serve to protect the defense system. "Don't get too attached, you'll get screwed." The voice persuades people to avoid the risk of being vulnerable and tells them never to trust anyone. When maneuvers used by a passive, self-protective person to distance him- or herself become acutely paranoid, there is a buildup of corresponding rage. In some instances, the buildup of anger can become serious enough to erupt into violent, explosive behavior that may even lead to homicide. Extreme negative voices toward and about others are at the core of all forms of criminal and explosive behavior. Men and women who act out violent impulses justify their actions as being rightfully deserved by their victims. A mode of thinking that rationalizes revengeful action is also characteristic of perpetrators of domestic violence:

> "She had it coming to her. She knew what she was doing. She knew which buttons to push to make me explode."
>
> "I'll get even with that bastard. He thought he could get away with it. Maybe next time he'll think twice before he fools around."

The Manipulative Aspects
of Microsuicidal Behavior

To varying degrees, all microsuicidal behavior has a manipulative component. Self-defeating, self-destructive actions tend to induce feelings of fear, anger, guilt, or alarm in others. It is difficult to avoid struggling with a self-destructive person one cares about; indeed, all self-denying, self-limiting, and/or dangerous, risk-taking behaviors have a compelling element that demands a response. Most of us are acutely sensitive to covert or nonverbal suicide threats, even though the manifest behavior may not be suicidal.

Clinicians and other professionals often *overestimate* the manipulative motivations underlying suicidal acts because they mistake manipulative effects for manipulative intention. Although microsuicidal behavior is definitely coercive, this effect is usually of secondary importance compared with the more basic motive to withhold commitment to a life process that is temporal and limited in nature. It is clear that the closer one moves toward acting out actual suicidal behavior, the greater the hostility or malice toward oneself, whatever other factors are involved.

Family members and friends who are closely involved with a person chronically engaged in self-harm behaviors also experience emotional turmoil and stress. Their loved one's behavior is intimidating for two principal reasons: (a) because of the fear of actual object loss, loss of the fantasy bond, or breakup of the relationship, and (b) because of the guilt inherent in feeling that one is responsible for another person's life or death. Intense feelings of guilt stem from a fear of feeling this heavy responsibility of being implicated somehow in the destruction of another person.

Families in which one parent is an alcoholic, a drug abuser, or severely self-destructive are recognized as being dysfunctional. However, any family in which one parent is self-denying or feels martyred is also dysfunctional. Manipulations on the part of a self-sacrificing parent or parents restrict communication in the family and interfere with the development of autonomy and self-reliance in the children.

Summary

Patterns of microsuicidal behavior are not necessarily confined to serious addictions, depressed states, or risk-taking actions; they are representative of the norm in our culture. Deadening routines, self-denial, antagonistic attitudes toward self, and prejudicial biases toward others are not exceptional phenomena; they are all too common. They disrupt personal relationships and cause disharmony and misery on a pervasive scale in everyday life. The manipulative threats implicit in alcoholism, drug addiction, and serious neglect of health inevitably affect close friends or family members by arousing anger, fear, and guilt.

It is important to recognize that any combination of behaviors listed in Figure 8.1 can eventually culminate in serious suicidal action. Most particularly, thoughts promoting isolation, ideation about removing oneself from people's lives, beliefs that one has a destructive effect on others, voices urging one to give up favorite activities, malevolent, angry self-attacks, and, of course, voices urging self-injury or actual suicide are all indications of high suicide risk.

Patients may remain stabilized for long periods at lower (subclinical) levels of adjustment, pursuing, for example, an ascetic existence and rationalizing self-denial. However, any movement toward successive levels should be taken very seriously as a potential indicator that the patient is embarking on a regressive trend that could eventuate in destructive acting-out behavior. A downward-spiraling movement along the continuum of microsuicidal behaviors is a sign of suicidal risk. Herein lies the *predictive* value of eliciting and identifying the content of patients' negative thought processes and evaluating the intensity of their aggression toward self. In planning interventions with people identified as potentially suicidal, clinicians can focus their attention on exposing and understanding cognitive patterns that dictate microsuicidal behavior and on helping prevent the patient from acting out the commands in a suicide attempt.

Endnotes

1. This does not deny or rule out man's capacity to respond to the existential challenge and find meaning and significance in life. Faced with the realization of death, one might choose to enhance rather than curtail one's involvement in life experience.

2. Participants in our clinical studies found it natural to verbalize their self-critical thoughts as statements spoken in the second person, as though talking to themselves, *"You're* this or that," rather than "I'm this or that." Patients often adopt this format spontaneously without instruction or suggestion from the therapist.

3. Shneidman (1972) estimated the number of survivors created by the suicide of one individual by the following method: "If there are about 50,000 committed suicides in the United States each year . . . then there are at least 200,000 survivor-victims created each year whose lives are ever after benighted by that event" (p. x).

9   The Relationship Between Guilt and the Suicidal Process

We "murder" ourselves when we invoke self-hating devices and when we annihilate our potential for enjoying life's realistic good offerings. . . . These self-hating activities often have the special characteristics of being passed off as virtue. The victim rationalizes . . . guilt as a high sense of responsibility and morality. . . . [But guilt has] a depleting, fatiguing, constricting effect and . . . [is] ultimately destructive to self-esteem and to one's actual person.

Theodore Rubin (1975, pp. 72-73)

Guilt reactions are prominent in all forms of depressive and self-destructive ideology and are evident in every psyche (Endnote 1). All people experience restrictive training procedures in the course of being socialized, but qualitative differences in parental attitudes determine the amount of guilt that is engendered. A certain measure of control and regulation of impulses is necessary for people to lead a civilized existence among their fellow human beings. However, excessive constraints, rules, and regulations are detrimental to human development, and there is no place for critical, harsh, and sadistic treatment of children in the name of discipline. In general, the fewer rules and restrictions and the more they are enforced in a compassionate manner, the more likely they will result in the best guidelines for optimal socialization of young people. Unfortunately, this is not usually the case in today's nuclear family due to ignorance, toxic parental personality characteristics, and a failure to perceive children as feeling individuals. Inappropriate training and discipline combined with parental aggression and defensiveness cause a tremendous amount of unnecessary suffering.

The Relationship Between
Guilt and Religious Training

Religion plays an important role in establishing social order and allaying our insecurity in relation to death. However, exaggerated or fanatic religious practices have a significant negative effect on people's guilt reactions. Unnecessarily moralistic child-rearing practices often lead to increased aggression and hostile acting-out behavior that contradicts the original moral intent. For example, overly restrictive sexual prohibitions lead to greater frustration and a correspondent rise in aggressive impulses. Judgmental, distorted attitudes regarding sexuality play an important part in the development of sexual abnormalities that lead to perversion, rape, and, in some cases, domestic violence.

Religious ideologies that emphasize people's essential badness—that is, "original sin"—foster negative internal attitudes toward self. Based on material obtained from Voice Therapy sessions and feeling release therapy, it is clear that the majority of men and women in our society harbor feelings that they are bad or unlovable. Any influence that supports this voice process and defines people as "bad" is detrimental to mental health because it leads to self-hatred and antipathy toward self that predispose a great deal of psychological pain. Promoting feelings of guilt and badness does not lead to a moral approach to life. On the contrary, children who are defined by their parents as "bad" later go on to act out behaviors that coincide with these negative projections.

Religious dogma equating thoughts with deeds often interferes with psychological development. When aggressive thought patterns are suppressed, aggressive impulses are less under the individual's control. In addition, these impulses are often internalized or turned against the self, resulting in increased voice attacks and self-destructive manifestations.

As a psychotherapist, I have spent considerable time helping people to distinguish between thoughts and feeling processes that one must learn to experience in a nonjudgmental context, on the one hand, and actions that must be scrutinized and evaluated in relation to a moral context and adaptive function, on the other hand. No thought, no matter how mean, cruel, or savage, can be considered immoral in that it has no consequences, whereas a simple act of inconsiderateness, sarcasm, or intrusiveness that hurts other people *can* be thought of as inappropriate or immoral. Freud remarked that a thought murder a day keeps the doctor away. He meant that it is psychologically healthy to have an uncritical awareness of one's thoughts and feelings (Endnote 2). A person who accepts him- or herself is less likely to behave in a manner that is insensitive to others.

The Relationship Between
Death Anxiety and Guilt

Throughout history, faced with death's inevitability, people have attempted to defend themselves against painful anxiety states regarding their fundamental insecurity. There are myriad defenses against death anxiety; among them, religious beliefs concerning the meaning of life and death are primary. As described earlier, to a certain extent, all cultural patterns and social practices represent some form of adaptation to the fear of death. Much of people's destructiveness toward themselves and others can be attributed to the fact that they conspire with one another to create cultural imperatives and institutions that deny the fact of mortality. Later, they attack other people, groups, or nations who subscribe to different belief systems. Becker's (1973) views concerning the incidental destructiveness of defenses and their projection into society are closely aligned with my own thinking. Becker (1973) stated,

> If we had to offer the briefest explanation of all the evil that men have wreaked upon themselves and upon their world since the beginnings of time right up until tomorrow, it would be not in terms of man's animal heredity, his instincts and his evolution: it would be simply in *the toll that his pretense of sanity takes,* as he tries to deny his true condition. (pp. 29-30)

One might hypothesize that when overwhelmed by the specter of death, early (primeval) man postulated a soul that could survive. In their efforts to achieve the promise of an afterlife, people turned against the body because they knew that the body ceased to exist in time. This defense led to a significant trade-off in which people turned their backs on their physical nature and sexuality. Subsequently, everything associated with the body or bodily functions took on a negative, shameful, or sinful connotation.

The Garden of Eden myth has been distorted along these lines by theologians of various faiths. Originally the myth was a simple legend, an allegory about mankind's loss of innocence in the ascent to maturity, the necessary renunciation of childhood and blissful existence in the garden, and the confrontation with all the suffering of the ical world. Scholars have written extensively about St. Augustine's misinterpretation of this creation myth, which led to the establishment of a nonhumanistic view of man's nature that was, as Elaine Pagels (1988) asserted, "utterly antithetical to scientific naturalism" (p. 130) (Endnote 3). According to this thinking, death has been conceptualized as a punishment for Adam's act of disobedience, which was to eat from the forbidden tree of knowledge. Man is condemned for (a) seeking knowledge, especially self-knowledge that implies an adult and autonomous posture, and (b) natural sexuality. (Immediately after Adam took fruit from the tree of knowledge, "the eyes of both of them were opened, and they knew that they were naked" [Genesis 3:7].)

Many of the voice attacks reported by individuals correspond to religious and secular themes of selflessness, self-sacrifice, denial of one's physical nature, and perceptions of sexuality as animalistic and culpable. Religious dogma acts to instill a sense of shame and guilt in individuals, then offers expiation through various forms of confession and ritualized atonement. Fanatic or fundamentalist ministers rail at their congregations because of their so-called sinful nature. Their accusations and denunciations are acceptable to the members due to their own sense of guilt and need for punishment. Like the Garden of Eden myth, people feel confused and pained to have been offered the gift of life only to have it taken back. They experience the painful reality of death as a trick or punishment imposed on them because they are unworthy. After the realization that life is temporal, children are anxious, uncertain, and more susceptible to various forms of criticism or attack. Unfortunately, their guilt generalizes to other areas of psychological functioning and plays a destructive role in thinking processes that are self-limiting and demoralizing.

My commentary does not deny or minimize positive aspects of a religious orientation toward life, nor is it an angry diatribe against organized religion. I am merely trying to illustrate the relationship between severe forms of suppression and internalized negative voices that have an adverse effect on each person's sense of self-worth and foster cynicism and critical attitudes toward others.

The Voice and the Two Modes of Guilt Reactions

Human beings exist within a narrow range of choice or experience bounded by neurotic guilt related to individuation and movement toward self-affirmation, on the one hand, and by existential guilt related to giving up one's priorities and withdrawing from life, on the other. If one acts on the former, one is susceptible to the latter. In this section, I describe the two modes of guilt reactions and the voices that precipitate them—phenomena that clinicians and crisis workers need to be aware of in treating suicidal patients. The suicidal client clearly manifests an abundance of neurotic guilt feelings; however, existential guilt is also operant in relation to his or her sense of despair and hopelessness.

Guilt reactions are mediated by the voice process and as such contribute to the psychological pain experienced by the suicidal client. Feelings of shame and contrition are part of a pervasive process of self-limitation and self-hatred that can become severely restrictive. Out of a sense of guilt, people withhold happiness and pleasure from themselves, develop a variety of self-defeating habit patterns, sabotage their relationships, and become self-destructive or even suicidal.

Neurotic guilt (Endnote 4) can be defined as "unnecessary" guilt in that it represents an abnormal internalized value system that diverges from a humanistic view of human beings. It comprises feelings of self-consciousness, self-recrimination, or self-attack for seeking independence, moving toward special goals, and pursuing the satisfaction of wants and needs in the interpersonal environment. This type of guilt is closely related to parental prohibitions and faulty training practices in childhood.

Ernest Becker (1964) conceptualized neurotic guilt as "the action-bind that reaches out of the past to limit new experiences, to block the possibility of broader choices" (p. 186). Freud (1923/1961) noted that conscious guilt is "the expression of a condemnation of the ego by its critical agency" (p. 51). He also described unconscious guilt reactions that generally operate below an individual's awareness: "As far as the patient is concerned this sense of guilt is dumb; it does not tell him he is guilty; he does not feel guilty, he feels ill" (pp. 49-50).

The second type of guilt, *existential or ontological guilt,* is aroused when individuals turn their backs on important goals, withdraw from positive relationships, seek gratification in fantasy or addictive substances, or engage in other self-destructive behaviors. Maslow (1968) emphasized that guilt and self-hatred are precipitated when people move toward security and homeostasis rather than striving for self-actualization:

> If this essential core of the person is denied or suppressed, he gets sick sometimes in obvious ways, sometimes in subtle ways.... Every falling away

... [from our center] every crime against one's own nature ... records itself in our unconscious and makes us despise ourselves (pp. 4-5).

My conceptualization of existential guilt is in agreement with Maslow's views. When people act on the dictates of the voice in ways that are opposed to their unique priorities, they face serious consequences. These behaviors involve a withdrawal of feeling and energy from the self and external objects that initiates a progressive movement toward self-annihilation or actual suicide.

Neurotic Guilt

Guilt about individuation and independence. "And Jesus said to his disciples: I am come to set a man at variance against his father, and the daughter against her mother. ... He that loveth father or mother more than me is not worthy of me" (Matthew 10:35-37). In this passage from the Bible, Jesus proposed that an individual must throw off the shackles of past parental influences to achieve enlightenment. In modern words, a person must break with his or her programming to lead an independent quest for psychological and spiritual development. One must challenge authority figures and dependency bonds to find one's true calling.

Family systems theorists have emphasized the guilt inherent in differentiating oneself from the family system. Guilt feelings about separation or the evolution of the self are represented in the psyche by the internalized parent or voice process. Voices restrict, regulate, and control all aspects of psychological functioning throughout one's life. Indeed, it is much easier to become independent of one's parents in actuality than to break with parental prescriptions that are manifested in introjected voices.

Epidemiologists have puzzled over the causes of suicide in college students, especially among those who are leaving home for the first time. One important factor operating in many of these cases is the guilt involved in the students' attempts to become independent of their families. If we are to help prevent these suicides, we first must be able to identify and understand the inimical thought patterns that regulate this form of neurotic guilt.

I have come to understand the role that neurotic guilt plays in restricting the pursuit of autonomy and corresponding differentiation from family. Attempts to separate from the fantasy bond with one's family predispose anxiety and intense guilt reactions. Victims of dysfunctional family practices and of emotionally hungry family members feel imprisoned by guilt and almost paralyzed in their efforts to pursue their personal freedom. In their magical thinking, they equate their emancipation with destroying the lives of other family members.

My views are congenial with those of Otto Rank (1936/1972), who wrote about guilt in relation to separation and individuation experiences:

> The problem of the neurosis itself is a separation problem and as such a blocking of the human life principle, the conscious ability to endure release and separation, first from the biological power represented by parents, and finally from the lived out parts of the self which this power represents, and which obstruct the development of the individual personality. It is at this point that the neurotic comes to grief, where, instead of living, of overcoming the past through the present, he becomes conscious that he dare not, cannot, loose himself because he is bound by guilt. (pp. 73-74)

"The biological power represented by parents" referred to by Rank can be thought of as a transcendental hope that parents hold out to their children and themselves, that is, the possibility of surviving death through an illusion of fusion. This fantasized connection is costly because, as Rank puts it, the child, upon attaining adulthood, is too guilty to "loose himself" from his bonds.

Most parents have children for "the wrong reason" with respect to their children's lives and futures, namely, as a defense against death anxiety. They perceive their children as extensions of themselves and imagine somehow living on through them and their progeny. However, the more the child is *different* from his or her parents, the more he or she disturbs this illusion of immortality. Indeed, many parents categorize nonconformity or individuation as bad, and submission or obedience as good. Although they may be disappointed, dissatisfied, or unhappy with their own lives, they feel a sacred obligation to impose the same standards and beliefs on their children. Most children, having been "properly brought up" in this style, give up their autonomy early in life, and their insecurity and guilt feelings prevent them from breaking the fantasy bond with their parents. They find it difficult to live their own lives and develop their own values and beliefs separate from detrimental family and societal influences (Milgram, 1974).

When parents are immature, frightened, or hostile, the family system often manifests the qualities of a cult or fanatic religious sect that practices subtle forms of thought control. Powerful forces are operating that act to control other family members, "brainwash" them with a specific philosophical outlook, and manipulate them through guilt and a sense of obligation.

Voices attacking individuation. Subjects in our clinical investigations have verbalized self-attacks that reflect guilt about individuating or simply living differently from their parents. The most common voices include the following statements: "You think you're better than us?" "What makes you think you can be different?" "Who do you think you are?" "The way you're living is like a slap in our face." "After all we've done for you, how could you do this to us?"

Many parents feel they must prevail on their adult children's sense of guilt to get them to call or visit: "Why don't you ever write to us?" "Wait until you have children of your own, then you'll understand what you're putting us through." These guilt-inducing manipulations are internalized by their off-spring, who then accuse themselves of being mean and experience tremendous guilt. The following are examples of their internalized voices: "You're so selfish and inconsiderate for not calling." "You'll break their hearts if you don't come for Christmas." "What kind of an ungrateful person are you?" "It's such a small sacrifice to make them happy." "You're depriving them of their grandchildren." Television commercials exploit this form of guilt: "With our long-distance rates, you can make the call your mother is waiting for," and so on. It is important to answer the question: Why don't adult children desire to communicate with or enjoy visiting their parents? If the family dynamics were positive and supportive, adult children would naturally seek out the companionship of their parents.

Many people have disclosed self-attacks linking them by association to negative characteristics of one or both parents. "You're just like your father." "You're crazy like the rest of your family." "It's in the genes." In addition to activating feelings of guilt and remorse, the voice undermines people's efforts to change undesirable behaviors in a direction that diverges from the negative patterns manifested by parents and siblings: "What makes you think you can change? You were born this way (angry, rebellious, bad, and so on). That's just the way you are." Voices based on guilt predict that the person lacks the tenacity or strength of character to change and live a freer, more fruitful life: "You think you can be self-reliant? You're just fooling yourself. You can't make it on your own. You're a born loser." When patients fail to question or challenge these self-attacks, they give up broad areas of functioning related to living a full life.

Leah, a 35-year-old woman, manifested a regressive pattern based on voices many years after a successful psychotherapy. Her history showed that at the age of 17, she suffered a schizophrenic breakdown and had been committed to a mental hospital. After her release, she had decided to leave home and live with her aunt on the West Coast. The guilt she experienced in separating from her family was intense at times, causing her considerable perturbation. For many months, she practiced obsessive acts of atonement in an attempt to relieve these painful feelings. Nevertheless, she made progress in therapy and began a career as a fashion consultant, which brought her a sense of fulfillment. Later, when her obsessive symptoms abated, she made an excellent recovery, married, and started a family.

Her life seemed in good order with a good deal of personal satisfaction. However, sustained contact with her family over the years began to take a toll on her independence and feelings of worth. First gradually and then with greater momentum, she systematically withdrew from the activities and friendships that she had come to value in the new life she had created. Eventually, she undermined most of her gains and led a very restricted life. As she gave up gratifications in important relationships, she became more and more wretched. Virtually the only activity open to her was her work, and she developed a compulsive work neurosis. In a Voice Therapy group, Leah verbalized angry voices that were directing her withdrawal and self-denial:

> I feel very nervous when I hear anyone who has an angry tone of voice or who is critical of me. The voice that goes along with this feeling is: "Who do you think you are? (sarcastic) Just who do you think you are? What makes you think you can have *anything*? Look at you. You thought you could just move off and have your cute little life. (snide) What about us? You never think of anybody but yourself. Well, just try it. Go ahead. Try to have your nice little life. See, you can't have it. You're never going to have it. I'm not going to let you have anything (louder, angrier voice).
>
> "You don't deserve happiness. You don't deserve anything after what you did to us. You've never thought about anybody but yourself your whole life. Do you hear what I'm telling you? You're not going to have anything because you don't deserve a thing" (enraged, embittered tone).
>
> (Pause) I know that it's my mother's voice telling me these things.

The most interesting aspect of this case is that after verbalizing her self-attacks, Leah felt a sense of relief from the guilt she had harbored for so many years. Her face and demeanor expressed a new vitality and energy, and she once again began to pursue long-neglected interests and relationships.

Serious examples of self-limitation based on guilt reactions associated with differentiation from and disruption of the bond with one's family can escalate to suicidal states. Joseph Richman (1986) described what he conceived to be an important factor contributing to suicide attempts in young people. According to Richman's studies, tormenting feelings of guilt often have their basis in the family's damaging interpretation of separation. The suicidal patient's family often misperceives the adolescent's moves toward independence, especially the development of peer relationships outside the family, as being threatening to family cohesiveness or survival of the family system. Richman depicted this type of maladaptive alliance between family members as a "symbiotic bond" wherein "the development of uniqueness or individuality in a key member opens up the threat of separation and must therefore be opposed or 'corrected' " (p. 19).

Guilt in relation to career choice. Guilt reactions are intensified when young people move away from the identity assigned to them by their family or fail to follow the destiny envisioned for them. Usually children uncritically accept the labels imposed on them, those of being the "smart" one, the "bad" one, the "plain" one, the "troublemaker," and so on. I found that the child who is categorized as bad is induced into acting bad and feels self-loathing and self-disgust for acting out undesirable or antisocial behaviors.

R. D. Laing (1969/1972) elucidated the theme of parental labels and attributions and the power they hold over children's lives:

> A naughty child is a role in a particular family drama. Such a drama is a continuous production. His parents tell him he is naughty, because he does not do what they tell him. What they tell him he *is, by induction, is far more potent than what they tell him to do.* (p. 80)

Laing drew an analogy between these "induced attributions" and hypnosis when he asked, "How much of who we are, is what we have been hypnotized to be?" (p. 79). When people make progress and move away from these labels or categorizations, they face increased voice attacks and elevated feelings of guilt.

Parents employ a wide variety of techniques in their attempts to persuade their offspring to conform to the parents' likes, dislikes, choice of career, religious beliefs, and political orientation. They expect compliance. For example, parents who are staunch Democrats would be horrified to learn that one of their adult children had joined the Republican Party. Often parents try to foist their own personal and vocational interests on their children and then take vicarious pride in their children's successes. As the child moves away from these choices, considerable pressure is brought to bear.

The 21-year-old son of an old friend of mine tried to step out of the family tradition by choosing a career other than medicine, which had been the profession of every male in his family for several generations. I had known the boy's father since he was a child, and it seemed to me that my friend had always been destined to be a doctor. As an adult, he fulfilled this prophecy, set up a successful medical practice, married, and had two sons. It was assumed that both sons would follow in their father's and grandfather's footsteps.

When he was in college, however, the older son decided to change his major and pursue a different career, one that reflected a special interest close to his heart. He told his parents that he planned to study economics and eventually start a business of his own. Both parents were shocked and prevailed upon him to change his mind—his mother through tears and his father through criticism and expressions of disappointment. After enduring several weeks of manipulation and "silent treatment," the son capitulated and changed his major back to premed.

He became a physician and married a woman similar to his mother in manipulative style. After completing medical school, he established his practice in a distant state. Today, at 32, he has fulfilled his destiny as a practicing physician but suffers from feelings of emptiness, unhappiness, and recurring bouts of depression. Recently he exhibited a reliance on Demerol and other painkilling drugs, a warning sign of potential suicidal intent.

When people move away from their priorities or are discouraged from activities or interests that excite them, there is a general decline in their capacity to feel for themselves, and depression often follows. A character in one of Andre Dubus's (1975) short stories illustrates this pattern. In the story, a young woman is dissuaded by her parents from having a baby she really wants, because the baby was conceived out of wedlock. Her boyfriend was willing to get married if she so desired, but her parents felt that the matrimonial solution would have a negative impact on their daughter's career. Out of weakness, her boyfriend succumbed to the parents' argument and accepted their solution. When she observed her boyfriend's passivity and lack of a strong will, the young woman lost respect for him and became disillusioned. Finally she herself yielded to her parents' advice to have an abortion. After submission to her parents' point of view, she turned against herself and never regained her vitality or interest in her life. From that point on, she was a lost soul, merely going through the motions of living.

Guilt about surpassing the parent of the same sex. Symbolically surpassing one's parent of the same sex in an educational or competency area or in an area of personal relationships in which that parent failed can lead to feelings of guilt, symptom formation, and self-destructive behavior. In competitive situations, guilt reactions are activated and are accompanied by self-destructive thoughts. People retreat before they become consciously ware of these self-attacks or suicidal voices. Instead, the aggression they feel toward themselves is projected onto new objects in their current situation.

One subject in our studies, a 30-year-old man, Michael, had achieved considerable success in his computer business but began to feel depressed and was tortured by paranoid feelings toward his coworkers. Several weeks prior to this, his father had approached him and asked for a loan to help avert bankruptcy in his real estate business. At the time, Michael was feeling exceptionally good but soon after was vaguely aware that he had begun to feel ashamed and guilty about his financial success. He realized that his father's misery and business failure had a pulling power that made him want to retreat from the positive movement in his own life. Michael recalled that he had felt worried that his father would suffer humiliation after borrowing money from him. As the months passed, Michael became progressively more discouraged, self-attacking, and paranoid and eventually experienced fleeting thoughts of suicide. In a voice session, he verbalized angry self-attacks related to his guilt and paranoia: "What are you trying to do, show me up? Just take your place. You simple shit. It's just luck that you're successful. You don't deserve anything. You don't deserve to be where you are."

As he continued, his anger increased in intensity, and his voice attacks escalated and contained actual injunctions to commit suicide: "You always stirred up trouble in our family. You should never have been born in the first place. You were an accident, an abortion. Get yourself off the earth. Go ahead, get a gun and blow your brains out."

In identifying the voice as connected with his father's angry feelings toward him, Michael developed insight into the source of his paranoid reactions and suicidal ideation. The guilt he originally experienced in relation to surpassing his father was transformed into a rage against himself as punishment for the imagined degradation of his parental authority figure.

Michael's father was immature and, throughout Michael's childhood, had resented the youngster and perceived him as a rival for his wife's attentions. He had death wishes toward the boy on an unconscious level. Michael's guilt about surpassing his father brought the internalized parental rage and associated suicidal ideation to the surface. When he projected this anger onto the men in his current life and distorted their responses to him, he began to feel persecuted.

Guilt after contact with family members. Renewed contact with parents or family members serves to reinforce the voice process in most people. Many report increased guilt reactions after parental visits. This is particularly true of patients who have improved as a result of psychotherapy. The contact throws them back to feelings from earlier in their lives and makes them aware of a disturbance in their family system. Regression in schizophrenic and psychosomatic patients following parental hospital visits is indicative of the anxiety and guilt triggered by these contacts. These effects have been observed in psychotic patients who, after showing a modicum of progress in therapy, regress after spending only an hour or two in a seemingly innocuous visit with family members. This manifestation of guilt is a common experience in residential treatment centers and mental hospitals (Lidz, 1969/1972).

At the National Jewish Center for Immunology and Respiratory Medicine, my colleagues and I observed the positive impact that separation from parents had on young patients suffering from intractable asthma. The children's symptoms improved considerably or virtually disappeared during a 2-year separation period or "parentectomy." However, patients manifested increased symptomatology preceding, during, and immediately following parental visits. In a large number of cases, when these children returned to their homes, asthmatic symptoms recurred (Seiden, 1965; Strunk, Mrazek, Fuhrmann, & LaBrecque, 1985).

Neurotic and normal individuals who live separately or are geographically isolated (from their parents) also display a rise in guilt feelings and heightened self-attacks after contact with parents or siblings. Clients often report deterioration in mood, mounting tension, and an increase in marital disputes after family visits. In my clinical experience, I have witnessed numerous cases where this has been a key dynamic. For example, one female patient, who had progressed in therapy and had recently become involved with a man she really cared for, received a phone call from her sister. When she told her sister of her new relationship and expressed optimism about the future, her sister remarked bitterly that her own personal life was terrible, her husband had just asked for a divorce, and she was drinking heavily "to drown out her misery." When the patient responded with concern and empathy, her sister rebuffed her and accused her of being "the mean-spirited one in the family. You never lifted a finger for anyone, so don't pretend you care now." Several weeks later, the woman terminated therapy and returned to her home town in an attempt to "rescue" her sister and prove to herself that she was not cold or heartless. Follow-up showed that she had become dispirited, had rejected her romantic interest, and was currently living alone in an apartment near her sister.

Guilt about betraying "family secrets" in therapy. As patients progress in psychotherapy and experience memories of traumatic incidents, they have considerable guilt about revealing "family secrets" to the therapist. This guilt is especially pervasive after recovering memories about incidents of physical and sexual abuse. In some cases, the guilt is so intense that patients subsequently invalidate their insights and revert to self-destructive patterns over which they had recently gained control or mastered. This sequence was evident in the case of Teresa.

While attending college, Teresa sought help from a counselor for symptoms of depression. Her father, who had agreed to pay for the sessions, later called the counselor to find out what his daughter was discussing in her sessions. When advised of the confidentiality of psychotherapy, he refused to pay the fee.

Some years later, after moving to another part of the country, Teresa entered long-term psychotherapy and significantly improved her life and relationships. At this point, she wrote to her parents telling them about her newfound happiness and the understanding she had gained during the course of her therapy. In the letter, she naively mentioned several childhood events that she felt had affected her in her adolescence and adult life.

At first, her parents failed to respond to her letter. When they eventually did, they were indignant and told her that she had distorted those events. Teresa experienced intense guilt feelings and began to second-guess her motives for sharing her insights with her parents. During the following period of time, her adjustment deteriorated, and she ultimately made a serious suicide attempt. Her parents were contacted, and when they arrived at the hospital, rather than inquiring about their daughter's condition, they nervously asked the doctor whether she had revealed anything of consequence while in her comatose state. It was painfully obvious to the doctor that Teresa's parents were more concerned with protecting the image of their family than with their daughter's survival.

Guilt in relation to anger. During the socialization process, children learn to suppress strong feelings of anger, sadness, excitement, even happiness. Parental admonitions such as the following act to stifle children's expression of emotions: "What's the big deal?" "Don't get so worked up." "Why are you so excited?" "Don't get your hopes up. You'll just be disappointed." This suppression of feelings contributes to an intensification of aggression, and when there is no acceptable outlet for these emotions in the family, the child turns his or her frustration and rage against him- or herself. Going inward with anger is fundamentally connected to self-destructive and suicidal tendencies.

People blame themselves for their psychological problems and tend to deny negative parental influences. The guilt about suppressed hostile impulses toward parents remains a limiting factor throughout an individual's life. In psychotherapy sessions, this guilt makes the expression of anger toward parents and parental introjects a problematic issue. In becoming aware of the damage they sustained in childhood, patients experience considerable pain and sadness as well as anger and outrage. In the omnipotent thinking of the unconscious mind, uncovering murderous rage toward their parents is symbolically equivalent to actually killing them. The anger activates intense guilt reactions, feelings of loss, and anxiety that can precipitate regression in the treatment process. Patients' guilt and fear cause them to turn the hostility toward themselves and take on the parental point of view. In many cases, they never fully resolve or work through this anger and the associated guilt feelings, and negative therapeutic reactions inevitably follow.

Sexual guilt. Sexual guilt is pervasive in our culture. The degree of limitation based on restrictive patterns amounts in itself to a kind of sexual abuse because it is so damaging. People have guilty reactions and voices about every aspect of their sexual lives. Generally speaking, people have both a natural, healthy, "clean" orientation toward sex and an acquired unhealthy, "dirty," or distorted view overlaid with guilt reactions. Guilt about sexuality and bodily functions is usually based on deep-seated conflicts from the patient's past and feelings of shame acquired early in childhood. Guilt reactions reflect the introjection of parents' inhibitions and rejecting attitudes toward the child's bodily needs, specifically his or her need for warmth, affectionate contact, and physical care. When these basic requirements are not met, children feel guilty for even possessing natural desires and needs, much less expressing them.

Children come to confuse sexual functions with anal functions. At the stage of toilet training, they assimilate verbal and nonverbal cues that communicate the disgust and displeasure that many parents feel about bodily emissions, odors, or functions. Later, because of this association, many children perceive sex as "dirty" and come to feel that everything below the waist is unacceptable. One manifestation of this distorted view is the degree of fastidiousness that pervades our society about smells or genital odors. As Mel Brooks's "2,000 Year-Old Man" quipped about modern life: "Look what they've done! They've even taken away our smells. Today everybody smells like a strawberry!" (Brooks & Reiner, 1973).

Early traumatic experiences of being "caught" by parents in the act of masturbating cause a great deal of shame. There is corresponding guilt about nudity and about sexual thoughts, fantasies, and impulses. Sexual feelings are a taboo subject in our society, and the resultant guilt generalizes to all manifestations of people's sexual nature.

Guilt about valuing one's life. Despite an overt emphasis on assertion and competitiveness in our culture, acts of self-interest take on a negative connotation and are generally condemned. When people are accused of being selfish or self-centered, there is a tendency to renounce one's selfhood. In actuality, when a person gives up being him- or herself, he or she has little to offer. Selflessness carried to its ultimate extreme actually implies the obliteration of self. By ridiculing children's desires, labeling them as selfish, and arbitrarily saying "no" to their requests, withholding parents make their children feel guilty, bad, and undeserving. These attitudes are incorporated as self-accusatory voices such as the following: "You only think of yourself." "Why can't you be happy with what you've got?" "You're so selfish and self-centered." "Why would anybody want to do anything for you?" "Don't ask, you're just an annoyance."

If a child was unwanted or born at an inconvenient time, he or she may develop feelings of being a burden to his or her parents or create fantasies of being adopted, of not really belonging to the family. As an adult, these individuals tend to feel that they have no rights, are undeserving of love, and on a deeper level may even feel guilty for being alive. In these cases, the voice attacks take the following form: "You don't deserve to live." "There's really no place for you here." "You're a misfit."

One 12-year-old girl, whose parents were cold and rejecting, expressed painful self-attacks about feeling unwanted and unloved:

> I have voices all the time that say, "Nobody likes you. Everybody hates you. Why should anybody be nice to you? You aren't nice to them. No one wants you around." (sad) "You shouldn't be on this earth. You never should have been born in the first place." (cries deeply)

Survivor guilt is a special type of neurotic guilt that is related to death anxiety. As noted in Chapter 7, Lifton and Olson (1976) have defined this guilt as a "painful self-condemnation over having lived while others died" (p. 3). This dynamic helps to explain the suicides of many survivors of German concentration camps. In his novel *Sophie's Choice,* William Styron (1979) portrays this type of guilt reaction. Sophie was the only member of her family to survive a concentration camp. While imprisoned, a sadistic SS guard threatened to execute her and her two children. He offered Sophie a choice:

Choose which of her two children should die and she could save herself and the remaining child (Endnote 5). Sophie sacrificed her daughter to save her own life and the life of her son. Years later, she was still agonized by guilt for her survival. In the end, Sophie sought relief from her torment by entering into a suicide pact with her psychotic lover.

The typical response to survivor guilt is to give up the very activities and relationships that imbue one's life with meaning. This insidious form of progressive self-denial, which is part of a suicidal process, diminishes the guilt about embracing and choosing life. However, it leads to the second type of guilt, existential guilt, which Becker (1973) described as "guilt [resulting] from the unused life, for 'the unlived in us' " (p. 180).

Existential Guilt

> A person may feel consciously guilty for not pleasing authorities, while unconsciously he feels guilty for not living up to his own expectations of himself.
>
>   Erich Fromm (1947, p. 165)

Clinicians are familiar with the neurotic guilt experienced by individuals as they attempt to overcome self-defeating patterns and pursue a better life. However, they understand less about the existential guilt aroused in their patients when they surrender their point of view and submit to their programming. People become depressed and demoralized when they act in a manner that goes against their own goals and priorities. They feel guilty when they withhold feelings for their loved ones and indulge in self-nurturing habits. Because they sense they are acting with self-destructive motives, patients in psychotherapy become the most defensive, stubborn, or hostile toward the therapist when they are confronted about using substances or addictive patterns to cut off emotions.

In addition to their guilt about harming themselves, people feel guilty about hurting those close to them. A number of patients reported experiencing self-hatred and guilt whenever they became remote or distant from their marital partners. They attacked themselves for sabotaging the close association and felt remorse about causing pain to their partners.

"You can never make a relationship work,"
"You're never going to have anybody in your life."

"The way you acted really hurt his feelings; you always drive people who love you away."

"They'd be better off without you."

Voices prevent people from maintaining loving relationships, and then criticize them for pulling away. These self-attacks prevent people from feeling compassionate toward themselves and their loved ones.

The pathological nature of regressive and self-destructive behavior, compounded by existential guilt and increased self-hatred, can be traced in studying the auditory hallucinations of schizophrenics (Endnote 6). It is apparent that voices, although not in hallucinated form, also exist in neurotic patients who act out self-mutilating behaviors as well as in normal patients who engage in less extreme self-destructive actions. In all of these situations, voices continually direct or coerce patients to act against themselves and subsequently castigate them for submitting to these hurtful impulses.

Similarly, less disturbed patients and "normal" individuals first experience neurotic guilt about directly pursuing their goals and priorities. Later they are caught in a double bind because if they succumb to this form of guilt and move toward fantasy, passivity, and self-nurturing behaviors, they experience more existential guilt. Whenever people become withholding and less adaptive, they feel ashamed of their failures and inadequacies. In attempting to cover up or disguise their inwardness, withholding, and withdrawal, most individuals rationalize their behavior and deceive themselves that they are still pursuing satisfying relationships and vocational goals. As a result, their communications become duplicitous, further complicating their lives and intensifying their guilt.

The customary response to neurotic guilt on the part of most individuals is to relinquish the activities and relationships that they most value. Feelings of hopelessness and despair accompany this form of progressive self-denial—a suicidal process that under certain conditions can precipitate a downward spiral to actual self-destruction. Existential guilt is an essential element in this process as people obsessively punish themselves for withdrawing from life.

Conclusion

Guilt reactions can predispose serious consequences and regressions and can be detrimental to an individual's development over extended periods of time. The range of each person's experience is delineated by the boundaries imposed by neurotic guilt, on the one hand, and existential guilt, on the other—and by the thought process that mediates guilt, the voice. However, by identifying this voice and bringing it into conscious awareness, people are able to cope more successfully with their self-limiting and self-destructive tendencies. I believe that this technique helps suicidal patients isolate these negative thoughts and become conscious of the dual nature of their guilt feelings. Furthermore, an understanding of how both forms of guilt affect the patient's ambivalence about living is vital for clinicians working in crisis intervention as well as in long-term therapy (see Chapter 15). By challenging the voice, patients who are recovering from a suicidal crisis become freer to pursue their lives, thereby minimizing regressive trends and the complex guilt feelings associated with self-betrayal.

Endnotes

1. An important distinction has been made in the literature between guilt and shame. Shame is associated with pre-Oedipal phases of development, whereas guilt is associated more with the Oedipal stage. I include both concepts when referring to the conflict between moving toward self-activation and away from infantile dependency sources, versus retreating from personal goal-directed activity into passivity, symbiosis, and fantasy processes. Both refer to an insidious process of self-limitation and self-hatred internalized during early childhood in the form of self-critical thoughts or voices. *Shame* is related to basic feelings of being bad, worthless, deficient, whereas *guilt* refers to feelings of self-recrimination about acts of commission or omission. *Existential guilt* is related to acts of omission and is aroused when one withholds behavioral responses that would have led to the fulfillment of one's personal and career goals.

2. According to Freud (1915/1957b),

> For strangers and for enemies we do acknowledge death, and consign them to it quite as readily and unhesitatingly as did primaeval man. . . . In our unconscious impulses we daily and hourly get rid of anyone who stands in our way, of anyone who has offended or injured us. (p. 297)

3. Elaine Pagels (1988) wrote,

> Augustine's theory . . . was a radical departure from previous Christian doctrine, and many Christians found it pernicious. Many traditional Christians believed that this theory of "original sin"—the idea that Adam's sin is directly transmitted to his progeny—repudiated the twin foundations of the Christian faith: the goodness of God's creation; and the freedom of the human will. (p. 131)

> In Augustine's version of the myth, Adam's disobedience led to Adam and Eve's banishment from the Garden of Eden, "lest he reach out his hand and eat of the tree of life and live forever" (Gen. 3:22, Modern Phrased Version), attaining eternal life along with knowledge (Pagels, 1995, p. 159).

4. It is important to distinguish "realistic" guilt from neurotic guilt. In discussing the profound negative effects of guilt on human beings, I am not implying that people should live a hedonistic, self-centered, amoral existence with no regard for others. To the contrary, it is altogether appropriate to feel contrite about real mistakes, failures to measure up to one's values or standards, or behaviors that one finds undesirable in oneself so that one can then go on to make the appropriate changes.

5. In his book *The Suicidal Mind,* Shneidman (1996) adapted this brief scene from *Sophie's Choice* and applied it to his "Psychological Pain Survey." The survey elicits the respondent's psychological needs that are being frustrated and attempts to measure his or her level of psychological pain through use of the "Sophie's Choice" incident as a comparison. (See pages 173-178 in Shneidman's Appendix A.)

6. See Sechehaye's (1951) book *Symbolic Realization,* a case history of a schizophrenic girl who was tortured by existential guilt and hallucinated voices in relation to her regressive, self-destructive behaviors.

10 Regression Precipitated by Positive Circumstances

The illness followed close upon the fulfilment of a wish and put an end to all enjoyment of it. . . .

At first sight there is something strange about this; but on closer consideration we shall reflect that it is not at all unusual for the ego to tolerate a wish as harmless so long as it exists in phantasy alone and seems remote from fulfilment, whereas the ego will defend itself hotly against such a wish as soon as it approaches fulfilment and threatens to become a reality.

Sigmund Freud (1916/1957c, pp. 317-318),
"Those Wrecked by Success"

Like Polycrates, the ego sacrifices success in order to avoid the evil of death, or at least to put it off.

Otto Rank (1936/1972, p. 188),
Will Therapy and Truth and Reality

The Bipolar Causality of Regression

The process of regression described in this chapter is related to the fundamental conflict between the drive toward assertion and separateness and the unresolved need to remain dependent and fused with another. Human beings have powerful strivings toward fulfilling their potential as unique and independent individuals, on the one hand, while, on the other hand, they have self-destructive and self-limiting tendencies and strong unconscious desires to be taken care of. People usually feel the best emotionally when they are

AUTHOR'S NOTE: The substance of this chapter was taken primarily from an article titled "The Bipolar Causality of Regression," *American Journal of Psychoanalysis, 50,* 121-135 (Firestone, 1990a). Used with permission.

experiencing a clear sense of self and personal identity, yet these occasions are often fraught with separation anxiety and consequently are of brief duration.

Clinicians have long recognized the importance of negative environmental influences and interpersonal stress as causative factors in regression and the various manifestations of self-destructive behavior that generally ensue; however, they tend to underestimate the importance of positive events. Unfortunate events such as financial loss, poverty, illness, divorce, or the death of a parent or loved one do contribute to regression; nonetheless, success—personal, professional, or financial—a satisfying love or sexual relationship, marriage, and parenthood are also primary factors in precipitating regressive trends manifested in childlike, maladaptive behaviors and addictive, self-destructive, or suicidal actions. Indeed, regressions characterized by personal setbacks in psychotherapy, failure experiences, and prolonged periods of anguish are more likely to have been activated originally by positive movement toward individuation than by negative occurrences. Reactions of this sort are often overlooked or misunderstood because at first glance they do not fit conventional logic.

Consider, for example, the following cases: A rock musician finally achieves fame and fortune when sales of his first album pass the 1 million mark. His use of drugs escalates, and 1 year later he is found dead from an overdose.

According to news reports, a 16-year-old honors student enrolled in college prep courses achieves new status among his peers when he sets up his own band. His growing popularity attracts the attention of a girl he has admired for many months and they begin dating. The boy is reported as being "really happy" about receiving his first paycheck from his first part-time job. Two months following their first date, the two teenagers are found dead at the foot of a cliff overlooking the ocean. Their suicide notes reveal their expectations of being united forever in death.

A young woman who as a child vowed she would never marry falls in love and gets married. Her life seems to have gone beyond her highest expectations. Months after the wedding, she begins drinking excessively on business trips and gradually develops a pattern of promiscuity. On an extended trip to the East Coast, she contracts hepatitis. She refuses to seek a second opinion when her doctor's prescription for sustained bed rest fails to arrest her symptoms. Two years after being married, she undergoes an unsuccessful liver transplant and dies.

In a less dramatic, but no less personally devastating story, an up-and-coming major league pitcher is offered an $8 million contract for 3 years. The following season, his performance falls off substantially and eventually he is retired to a farm team. The team physician reveals to reporters that the once exceptional pitcher is suffering from an acute depressive reaction that makes it impossible for him to play.

What combination of incidents or circumstances precipitated the regressive movement toward suicide, life-threatening behavior, or major depression in each of the above cases? In those cases where suicide was the outcome, would investigations using a "psychological autopsy" (Endnote 1) have revealed information that might further our understanding of the suicidal process?

My purpose in this chapter is to focus on the bipolar causality of regression and to delineate the crucial events in a person's life, both positive and negative, that tend to activate regressive trends and self-destructive behavior. I emphasize the importance of taking into account unusual or atypical positive incidents in patients' lives when examining the factors that can precipitate a suicidal crisis. As the therapist becomes acquainted with the specific conditions in each patient's life that have symbolic meaning relevant to the trauma of separation and death anxiety, he or she can begin to sort out the complex causality underlying patients' regressive responses to these events.

Regression as a Defense Mechanism

I conceive of regression as the defense mechanism that is used to heal the fracture in the original fantasy bond with the mother/parent caused by events, symbolic or real, that remind one of being separate and vulnerable to death. As such, regression represents an unconscious decision to return to a state of imaginary fusion with the mother/parent.

The tendency to regress starts early in life with the infant's dawning realization of its existence separate from the mother. As noted in Chapter 9, Rank's (1936/1972) theoretical approach is similar to my description of an individual's emotional response to progressive separations from the maternal figure. Rank believed that "the authentic meaning of the therapeutic process . . . comes to expression only in the end phase" (p. 195), that is, in the termination of therapy. He focused his attention on the dynamics of the ending phase because he believed that the patient's reactions to the anticipated separation from the therapist revealed the core neurotic conflict. Rank recognized that the patient tended to regress immediately prior to this crucial separation. He concluded that the patient's desire to remain ill and dependent on the therapist expressed itself in repeated efforts to prolong the therapeutic process by reverting to old symptomatology.

I concur that patients who are approaching termination in therapy revert to symptom formation because of their fear of ending the fusion inherent in the therapeutic relationship. In this sense, they are reacting adversely to the positive event of becoming healthy and happy and feeling in control of their lives. In the therapeutic situation, the patient's good feelings about change and improvement paradoxically lead to inevitable problems of separation. It is generally agreed that all psychotherapies promote regression in some form. The unique qualitative experience of being accepted and taken seriously by an interested person arouses separation anxiety from family and stirs up deep unresolved conflicts and repressed feelings from earlier developmental stages in the patient's life.

One measure resorted to by the regressed individual is to form a fantasy bond, a dependency relationship with a significant other, in which an illusion of connection and of being taken care of prevails. In his discussion of Hellmuth Kaiser's concept of a delusion of fusion, Louis B. Fierman (1965) stated,

> The individual blunts and distorts his own awareness of separateness, creates the illusion of fusion, and is precariously gratified on an imaginary basis in a fusion relationship with the other person. (p. 209)

> The universal psychopathology is defined as the attempt to create in real life by behavior and communication the illusion of fusion. (pp. 208-209)

The Split Ego in Regression

In his interpretation of Fairbairn (1952), Guntrip (1969) conceptualized regression as *"withdrawal from a bad external world, in search of security in an inner world . . .* , the deepest element in all psychopathological development" (pp. 55-56). He stated, *"The process of withdrawal in successive stages through fear emerges as a major case of what we have come to call 'ego-splitting,' the loss of unity of the self"* (p. 64).

Psychoanalysts, in general, have become increasingly aware that the split ego is alien or antithetical to the core self and serves a defensive function, and that its dominance in the personality leads to serious pathology and regressive trends.

My conceptualization of the voice process points out the sources of the self-punishing and self-parenting aspect of the split ego in the negative parental attitudes incorporated by the individual during childhood. When this thought process or destructive "voice" prevails over thoughts of rational self-interest, severe regression occurs, accompanied by strong self-destructive tendencies and, at times, suicidal ideation and behavior.

It is my hypothesis that the longing to merge with the parental figure (or its substitute) is an individual's most basic response to fear of separation and anxiety about death, and that this anxiety is aroused by both positive, gratify-ing experiences and negative, traumatic events. This tendency of human beings to revert to patterns of distorted thinking and immature behavior that support an illusion of connection is universal and occurs whenever the fear of separation, aloneness, and death overwhelms the ego.

To interrupt regressive trends and modify self-destructive behaviors in our patients, and possibly avert a suicidal crisis, we must understand the outward manifestations of the fantasy bond that are at the core of these phenomena. Furthermore, it is important to identify the stages through which an individual passes in his or her retreat from positive circumstances and success.

Early Regression Related
to Separation Anxiety

The original bond or fantasized fusion with the mother is formed as a response to infantile frustration, the all-encompassing pain and fear of anni-hilation experienced by the infant at times of stress and during separation experiences. The primitive illusion of connectedness alleviates pain and anxiety by providing partial gratification of the infant's emotional or physical hunger and acts to protect the child against an awareness of being separate and alone.

Even during very early stages of development, the child's fears are partly relieved as he or she becomes more adept at calling up an image of mother whenever he or she feels threatened (Mahler, 1961/1979; Winnicott, 1958a). The primary fantasy bond, together with primitive, self-nourishing behaviors such as thumb-sucking, rubbing, stroking a blanket or special toy, and later masturbation, help the child cope with anxiety reactions. The more depriva-tion there is in the infant's immediate surroundings, the more dependency there is on this imagined connection. This sense of being at one with the mother leads to feelings of omnipotence and a posture of pseudoindependence in the growing child ("I don't need anyone; I can take care of myself"). The illusion of self-sufficiency, of being able to meet his or her own needs without going outside him- or herself, is actually a desperate attempt on the child's part to deny his or her true state of helplessness and vulnerability.

The Relationship Between Separation Anxiety and Fear of Death in Precipitating Regression

As noted in Chapter 8, at a certain stage in the developmental sequence, separation anxiety becomes associated with the knowledge and dread of death. My clinical experience has shown that children progress through several stages in their discovery of death. In the initial phase, they attempt to avoid the new threat to their security by regressing to an earlier stage of development, a level at which they were unaware of death. They reinstate the imagined connection with the mother and use the self-parenting process to reassure themselves that even in the event of the parent's death, they can take care of themselves (Endnote 2).

Still later, children become aware that they cannot sustain their own lives. Unable to bear the prospect of losing the self through death, they retreat to a previous level of development and reaffirm the fantasy bond with the parental image. The fear of death now becomes the driving force behind regressive behavior and the formation of dependency bonds. Thereafter, any negative event or reminder of death such as illness, rejection, or accident can precipitate regressive trends in an individual. In addition, any positive event or evidence that heightens a person's awareness of being separate, of being a free agent, can foster regression. Indeed, any experience that reminds the individual that she possesses strength, independence, personal power, or acknowledged value as a person will make her acutely conscious of her life and its eventual loss. In that sense, any development that breaks a fantasy bond or threatens an illusion of being connected to another can be perceived as a life-threatening situation.

In the face of this perceived threat, people give up mature pursuits, adult responses, and genuine relating for a more childlike orientation. They retreat into dependent, destructive bonds with significant others in their interpersonal relationships. Furthermore, as described earlier, whenever there is progression to a new stage of individuation brought about by crucial life events such as leaving home for college, getting married, setting up one's own home, starting one's own family, or achieving an important personal goal, an individual becomes acutely conscious of both existential issues—his or her basic aloneness and the temporary quality of his or her life. Whenever people become more invested in their lives, they experience a sharp and poignant awareness of the potential loss of themselves and loved ones through death. In this sense, neurotic regression connects to a very *realistic* fear: the terror and anxiety that surround a person's awareness of death.

Anxiety states generated by nightmares about death are common in both children and adults and can lead to regression (Endnote 3). This reminder of death appeared to be a precipitating factor in the regressive episode of a wealthy and successful businessman.

After a routine physical checkup, Cliff, 45, a hardworking CEO in a large corporation, was advised by his physician to take a brief vacation from work. He responded to the invitation of a close friend and his friend's wife to spend 2 weeks relaxing at their home in the country. There he enjoyed the congenial atmosphere, meaningful conversation, and companionship of the couple, their children, and other friends. As his vacation drew to a close, he enthusiastically declared that he had never felt happier or more "himself" in his entire life. His friends observed that Cliff had essentially come to life during the course of the visit.

Coincidentally, a small farm adjacent to his friend's country home was for sale, and Cliff began to make plans to purchase it to use as his own weekend retreat. He also planned to drastically cut back his work schedule. He remarked that he didn't want to jeopardize his newfound sense of freedom or the companionship of his friends by again submerging himself in his work. On the night before his departure to the city, Cliff had a terrifying nightmare in which he experienced an acute awareness of his imminent death. In the dream, he felt anguished about losing his life and leaving his friends. He awoke from the nightmare feeling groggy and strange. Returning to the city to arrange the details of his move to the country, he found himself again caught up in the pressures of business.

Months passed and Cliff never made the necessary arrangements for the move. Instead, he became almost totally involved in work. A year later when he visited his friends, they were appalled at his condition. He had gained weight, and his face was pale and tense. They found him to be remote and apathetic, in stark contrast to his previous warmth and drive to make changes in his life.

According to information gleaned from psychotherapy sessions, it became clear that when Cliff attempted to expand his life and seek more personal satisfactions, death anxiety came to the surface in the form of the repetitive nightmare that initially occurred during the period described above. As people choose life and move toward expanding their boundaries, many tend to experience increased death anxiety, as Cliff did. They regress so as to cut off these painful feelings and often give up their priorities in life. It is my contention that death anxiety increases with life's satisfactions and the pursuit of one's unique self, a point of view that is congenial with the thinking of Rank, Becker, and Maslow.

The Relationship Between Separation
and Guilt in Precipitating Regression

Each phase in an individual's development toward maturity is marked not only by guilt for leaving the parents behind but also by fear and anger at having to face the world alone. Many patients report that successes in therapy and in their personal lives made them aware of their parents' limitations and disturbed style of relating. Having a more realistic or objective view of their families triggered separation anxiety, fears of retaliation, and guilt reactions.

In one case, Scott, a good-looking man in his late twenties, was actively succeeding is life as a boat captain and business manager. He was an excellent athlete, popular with his friends, and attractive to women. Scott's father had always had trouble in his relationships with women, but when he was in his fifties, he took it particularly hard when a woman he was close to rejected him and he had to undergo knee replacement surgery. After this point, Scott's father seemed to give up and turn his back on life.

When his father became depressed, deteriorated in his physical health, and withdrew from relationships with the opposite sex, it had a huge impact on Scott. He became unsure of himself, found himself role-playing and officious in a manner similar to his father's style, and was moody and hypercritical of others; eventually his marriage broke up. His regression mirrored his father's retreat and his life deteriorated in all areas. He lost his sense of personal power, and he was constantly troubled by voices that criticized and undermined him.

Scott dated his regression to the time his father had to have the knee replacement surgery and reacted to the ensuing pain by becoming infantile, withdrawn, and practically comatose. Scott was horrified and deeply saddened by his father's loss of spirit. He alternately felt guilty and enraged and finally succumbed to a pathological identification with him.

Scott's background explains this negative trend. His mother was a paranoid schizophrenic who was in and out of mental institutions, and his father was away for extended periods, leaving Scott insecure and threatened. The anxious attachment to a disturbed mother led to an exaggerated fantasy bond with Scott's father. Subsequently, whenever his father retreated from life, Scott was pained and experienced a resurgence of being left alone and terrified. Unconsciously, he attempted to fuse with his father to heal the fracture and avoid psychological pain.

In general, surpassing one's parent of the same sex is fraught with separation anxiety, guilt, and increased voice attacks.

Stages in the Regressive Process
Following Positive Events

I have noted several stages in regressive episodes that are precipitated by positive events or circumstances.

Initial Reaction

After a significant accomplishment, an individual generally experiences feelings of excitement and a sense of personal achievement. There is an inner glow of satisfaction, a feeling of exhilaration, optimism, and a sense of expanded boundaries. There are feelings of appreciation and gratitude toward whoever contributed to one's success. The degree or intensity of an individual's initial excitement varies according to the personal meaning he or she attributes to the event and its implicit meaning about his or her identity.

However, immediately following a positive experience, there often is an exaggerated sensitivity to negative feedback or potentially adverse responses from others. In this state of acute awareness, a person tends to scan the interpersonal environment in search of the slightest sign of disapproval or censure. In this manner, one's perceptions and emotional reactions become highly attuned to the environment, and there may be powerful mood swings following an unusual success.

Self-Consciousness:
A Precursor to Guilt Reactions

Feelings of self-consciousness are aroused if the positive event is especially meaningful or represents the fulfillment of a lifelong fantasy. Unpleasant emotions may arise almost immediately (in stage 1) or may come about gradually. Moreover, extraordinary success generally arouses reactions of admiration, envy, or resentment from others. These ambivalent responses elicit painful feelings of self-consciousness in achievers, which alert them to differences between themselves and their peers. Minor criticisms or competitive remarks from rivals contribute to people's tendencies to observe themselves with unfriendly eyes, thereby enhancing their discomfort. Feelings of self-consciousness are exacerbated by public acknowledgment of one's success and by means of such symbols of accomplishment as advancement to a leadership position or a significant raise. As the individual continues to move toward success and greater accomplishment, he or she will experience guilt reactions in relation to symbolically leaving others behind, disrupting ties with the family, or surpassing a parent's level of achievement.

Anxiety and Fear of Loss

Anxiety reactions, due to a deep fear of object loss, become progressively more unpleasant and painful. As a person achieves increased personal power, separation anxiety is intensified because he or she is symbolically moving away from sources of security within the family and peer group. As there is movement toward individuality, there is a sense of increased ambiguity and uncertainty. The new events evoke fear reactions, and death anxiety tends to intensify; indeed, thoughts about the inevitability of death become increasingly unacceptable or disturbing as life becomes more precious and as the achiever recognizes his or her self-worth and value as a person. Patients often report having felt that life was "too good to be true" in enjoying the thrill of significant success or personal growth.

Paradoxically, achievement and increased fulfillment make people more aware of potential losses and of the inevitable loss of self through death. It is important to note that in most cases, the anxiety associated with separation from symbolic parental figures and fears of death do not actually reach conscious awareness. The individual may revert to childlike defenses almost automatically, with little or no awareness of unpleasant feelings of self-consciousness or anxiety.

Actual Retreat

Feelings of depression arise when anxiety and guilt reactions are translated into regressive, childlike behavior. The individual increasingly turns against personal goals, wants, and priorities as well as against the agents of his or her success. This stage is characterized by intense self-attacks as well as angry, cynical thoughts about the person or people who were supportive. Of interest, these self-hating and hostile ruminations appear to reduce painful feelings of anxiety, yet they invariably lead to disillusionment with self and to depressive reactions.

In addition, during this phase, many individuals tend to increase their reliance on drugs, alcohol, food, or other addictive habit patterns in an effort to relieve intense anxiety states. However, these indulgent, self-nourishing responses interfere with one's ability to cope and lead to existential guilt that has a profoundly demoralizing effect on the individual. An almost imperceptible retreat into dependent, immature functioning and self-defeating behavior commences as the person gradually withdraws from the position of power that he or she recently attained. Moreover, there is a concomitant failure to pursue other adult goals. Many people are largely unconscious of how much their energy and drive to achieve have diminished. Others rationalize their loss of enthusiasm and motivation by attributing it to external circumstances.

Regression to Fusion Relationships
and Self-Nourishing Habits

Regression is fully established as the patient retreats to a more primitive or less mature level of adjustment, thereby minimizing or eradicating his or her success or uniqueness. Efforts are directed toward reestablishing a sense of sameness with one's family and other significant figures in one's life. Self-nourishing and self-destructive behaviors become routine or habitual and function to limit or invalidate prior achievements so that recent positive changes in identity or self-image are drastically reduced.

Self-attacks increase in intensity and frequency, and suicidal thoughts often emerge in the patient's thinking. The patient adjusts his or her behavior according to the dictates of the voice and feels powerless to resist its injunctions as well as demoralized about his or her failure to do so. In some cases, patients have reported that they were unaware of self-critical thoughts at this point in the regression; by this stage, their behaviors represented a direct expression of the negative introjects, and the voices were stilled.

In general, the latest achievements and most profound changes in identity are the first to be renounced or sabotaged. As the regression becomes long term, the patient may retreat several stages in his or her development and become seriously disturbed and disoriented in diverse areas. Old defense mechanisms and childlike behaviors come to the foreground as the individual attempts to fuse with significant others to achieve a sense of security.

As previously noted, regressions are frequently misinterpreted as being adverse reactions to negative events. This is understandable when one considers the fact that a patient's retreat after success provokes rejection from significant figures in the interpersonal environment. For example, as a result of regressive, childish, or incompetent behavior, the individual actually may come to lose a personal relationship, a position of power, or his or her job. Often, the consequences are mistaken for the causes.

An understanding of the stages of regression is helpful in unraveling the complex factors contributing to adolescent suicide. In young people, as in adults, unusual achievements, breaking family traditions, or involvement in romantic or sexual relationships can precipitate serious regressive states manifested by increased risk-taking actions, excessive drug or alcohol use, or actual suicide. In cases of completed suicide, in which it appeared that the adolescent had everything to live for, one needs to closely examine both recent and past events in the teenager's life to determine the onset of the regressive trend.

Episodic Regression Due to Positive Events

Regression Following Unusual Career Successes

Long-term regression can occur in reasonably well-adjusted individuals when they experience an atypical success or achievement in their careers. Numerous examples of incompetency, inadequate performance, and the onset of self-destructive behavior following an important promotion, the assumption of an executive position, or public acknowledgment of an important achievement have been documented in the literature (Clance & Imes, 1978) (Endnote 4).

In one case, a woman received a new car as a special bonus for making a significant contribution to her company's financial success. Subsequently, she made a series of managerial errors. Her behavior was completely out of character and made her employers wish they had never given her the car. After being reprimanded a second time for mishandling affairs and warned that she had only one more chance to show improvement, she entered therapy. In analyzing the situation, it became apparent that she had reacted adversely to the tangible acknowledgment of her work by regressing. The positive acknowledgment created extreme anxiety, which led to the deterioration in performance. The generosity of the bonus contrasted with the emotional tightness she had experienced growing up and challenged the negative self-image she had developed in her family. Realizing this, she was able to gradually reverse the process and get back on track at work.

Case Study

The stages in the regressive process delineated above are evident in the following case.

Initially, Dr. S., a research scientist, attributed the cause of his depression and serious drinking problem to negative circumstances in his current situation, namely, his divorce and loss of prestige at work. As treatment progressed, the truth emerged that this was not the case.

Dr. S. entered therapy several months after his divorce. The diagnosis was major depressive episode with indications of a compulsive personality disorder. For a number of years prior to the onset of his depression, Dr. S. had served as a project leader in one of the country's most renowned "think tanks." On one project, he was in charge of over 50 scientists and systems analysts who had studied specific strategic positions and then arrived at a consensus. The project culminated in a proposal that Dr. S. presented to the Joint Chiefs of Staff in Washington, D.C.

According to the patient, his reception at the initial meeting was extremely positive, and he was acknowledged for making an important contribution to the country's overall defense program. In Dr. S.'s words, the enthusiastic responses "really shook me up." He recalled being very agitated and unable to sleep that night. The next day, Dr. S. summarized his ideas at a larger gathering of important officials. Again, the reaction was overwhelmingly positive, but there was one ranking officer who voiced some reservations. A meeting at which a final decision would be made was scheduled for several months in the future. Returning to Chicago, Dr. S. feverishly set about correcting what he now considered to be errors in his project. His exaggerated, peculiar focus on the minor criticism expressed during the second meeting, in spite of the overall positive reactions, was symptomatic of the early phase in his regressive pattern.

Dr. S. began to have doubts about his proposal achieving final acceptance. He worked long hours locked in his office, compulsively poring over the details of the next position paper he was to present in Washington. During this period, he spent more evenings and weekends away from his family and increased his consumption of alcohol. His relationship with his wife deteriorated as he began to make neurotic demands upon her to provide him with reassurance and support during the pseudodramatic crisis.

Several months later, the project was shelved due to delays in Dr. S.'s presentations as well as outside budgetary considerations. At about the same time, his wife decided to leave him. The combination of events at work and the separation from his wife threw him into a state of agitated depression and confusion. It was at this point that he sought professional help.

In his therapy sessions, Dr. S. recognized that the first signs of his retreat from power had occurred immediately following the public acknowledgment of his leadership abilities, his influence over a major policy decision, and his competence as a scientist. These symbols of power were indications of a separation from the negative self-image and feelings of inferiority Dr. S. had incorporated in his early interactions with his family.

During the course of therapy, the patient recalled numerous degrading labels and negative traits attributed to him by both parents. He remembered his father predicting that he would "never amount to anything" and referring to him as a "bum," "ditch-digger," and "stupid shit." Dr. S.'s mother, although not overtly degrading, nonetheless had focused on the patient's physical health, with constant reminders that he was too "sick" or "weak" to function as well as other youngsters. Achieving success had activated voice attacks similar to the labels his father had assigned him. Dr. S. reported self-depreciating thoughts such as the following: "You can't keep up this high level of work." "You're way out of your league." "You're just a simple country boy. Stop acting like somebody you're not!"

Furthermore, being recognized as an authority in an important area of endeavor effectively placed the patient in a position far superior to that of his father, who had failed repeatedly in business and who was not admired in the community. Dr. S.'s significant success triggered a severe state of anxiety, resulting at first in sleeplessness and gradually escalating into a paranoid state. He focused his attention on the minor criticism voiced by one individual and mistakenly believed this was responsible for his subsequent regression and misery.

In part, Dr. S.'s regression represented an unconscious imitation of and identification with his father's pattern. On a deep level, it cemented his bond with his family. In therapy, Dr. S. began to understand how this connection with his father affected his life. He recalled his father's paranoia toward other men, particularly authority figures. As Dr. S. developed awareness of the origin of his depression and compulsive work patterns, his depression eased. He gradually regained a sense of dignity and self-respect and gave up his excessive use of alcohol.

Severe episodic regressions, such as the one reported above, are not unusual for individuals who reach high levels of achievement, attain leadership positions, or pass specific milestones in their professional lives. Many people, like Dr. S., attribute their anxiety and the source of their troubles to outside forces and experiences rather than recognizing the propensities for self-destructiveness within themselves. In the case of Dr. S., months of working through the underlying causes of his regression were required before he could assimilate, on an emotional level, the effects of his retreat from power and, from there, begin his slow recovery.

Regression Precipitated by Dependency of Others

Emotionally healthy individuals who develop personal power in terms of leadership qualities, ego strength, and self-confidence arouse feelings of dependency in others who then turn to them for support and guidance. The increased responsibility and emotional load that accompany the assumption of a leadership position exert pressure on the individual while at the same time, on a personal level, he or she is challenging his or her own dependency on parental figures. Voices related to separation anxiety and loss of support are prominent in these cases: "Now you're the one responsible for the entire division." "What are you going to do when you really come up against it?" "Who are you going to turn to for advice?" Numerous other comparable self-attacks and self-doubts can be reduced to a general overriding theme: "Who is going to take care of you?"

Furthermore, passive, dependent people tend to be paranoid toward a powerful, authoritative person. Their distortions and negative reactions are confusing, provoking, and demoralizing. As individuals develop leadership qualities or become powerful and effective in a particular field of endeavor, their motives are often misunderstood or perceived as exploitative. This form of paranoia contributes to a negative social pressure that has an insidious impact on business and political leaders and can trigger a regression to less effective and nonfunctional styles of management.

Regression Precipitated by Positive
Events in One's Personal Life

There are a number of incidents in one's personal life that are capable of precipitating regression. Individuals who begin a romantic love affair are risking a great deal emotionally. Their sense of being vulnerable arouses considerable anxiety and can induce a return to a more isolated, pseudoindependent posture. Reaching sexual maturity can also trigger regressive reactions. For example, a woman who is able to experience orgasm after years of suffering with problems in that area may revert to immature behavior in other areas of her life.

The decision to make a commitment to a long-term relationship or marriage can precipitate regressive trends in both men and women. The concept of marriage has a different symbolic significance for men and women. For men, a satisfying marriage symbolizes the fulfillment of their desire for close, affectionate contact with the mother they have longed for since early childhood. For women, movement toward sexual intimacy and closeness with a man threatens the emotional tie or fantasy bond with the mother. It implies a step away from the mother and a loss of the hope of ever satisfying their longing for maternal love.

Both extensions of the fantasy bond with the mother are indicative of regressive trends. Men who turn away from genuine closeness with the woman in their lives and form a bond tend to become either desperate, dependent, and possessive of their mates or distant and uncommunicative. Others develop compensatory feelings of vanity and demand a buildup from their partners. Women tend to sacrifice their sexuality to hold on to the imagined union with the mother, particularly if she was self-denying and asexual. To relieve unconscious fears of punishment and separation anxiety, women take on a sameness with the mother that makes them hate themselves, thereby exacerbating the regression.

Joseph Rheingold (1964), in his book *The Fear of Being a Woman,* declared, "Marriage is a crisis for the woman . . . because it represents two bold acts of self-assertion: assuming the status of the married woman and entering into a publicly announced heterosexual relationship" (p. 437). Many women who profess goals of marriage and family become disturbed at the actual prospect of becoming involved in an intimate relationship with a man or of having a child. Several subjects in our studies reported having angry responses to acknowledgments of love from the men in their lives. For example, one woman revealed that she had responded coolly to a marriage proposal. When her boyfriend declared his love and commitment to the relationship, she condescendingly replied, "Oh, really!" After the couple married and had children, the woman became increasingly hostile and with-holding toward her husband. Her initial sarcastic remark had been a portent of her subsequent regression and foretold an unhappy marriage.

Rather than dealing with the separation anxiety involved in the step toward further individuation implied by marriage, many women experience a renewed involvement (either actual or symbolic) with their mothers following the wedding ceremony. Nancy Friday (1977) noted this "reunion" in her book *My Mother/My Self.* Based on interviews that she conducted with over 200 men and women, Friday reported that the majority of the women imitated their mothers' style of relating in the relationships with their husbands.

Regression in Women
Precipitated by Motherhood

For many women, having a child is the ultimate fulfillment of woman-hood. However, because it symbolizes a separation from one's own mother, this significant step can also arouse considerable anxiety. Starting a new family effectively signals the end of childhood and causes many women to regress and revert to helpless, childlike patterns of behavior during pregnancy and following the birth of the baby (Endnote 5). Traditional attitudes regarding women's weakness and need for protection tend to support a woman's return to dependency and self-indulgence during this critical period. Moreover, after delivery, there is a fundamental shift in the emotional climate, wherein the woman is now expected to take care of and nurture her baby. This drastic change from being taken care of to becoming a caretaker can foster regressive behavior, and it constitutes a significant factor in postpartum depression. In some cases, these depressive reactions reach psychotic proportions (Rosberg & Karon, 1959) (Endnote 6).

Symptoms of regression during pregnancy include anxiety about "unacceptable" aggressive fantasies in relation to the unborn infant and fears of giving birth to a defective baby (Endnote 7). In observing over 2,500 cases of pregnant women treated during a 10-year experimental study, Rheingold (1967) found that women's ambivalence about having a baby tended to continue long after the child was born, although the more negative aspects were either completely forgotten or partially repressed.

Conclusion

Regression caused by unusual positive events becomes more understandable when viewed as a reaction to the trauma of separation—the original separation from the parent at weaning and later the anticipation of the final separation from the self that occurs at death. Positive or especially fortunate circumstances—success, the attainment of mature love, and sexuality—disrupt dependency bonds and make us acutely aware of valuing our lives. Good feelings and good times are frequently accompanied by moments of clarity and an unusual awareness of separateness and limitation in time. Positive experiences in real life as compared with fantasy gratification threaten the illusion that we are, somehow, immortal. Negative events, on the other hand, followed by demoralization, fit into general regression theory. Their causal relationship to regression, self-destructive behavior, and suicide has always been more predictable and straightforward.

Most people live within a narrow range of experiences bounded by debilitating emotional responses to negative incidents and failures, on the one hand, and by adverse reactions to atypical positive events, on the other. Successful psychotherapy broadens this range by helping patients minimize and cope with negative events and increase their tolerance for positive, fulfilling experiences.

Endnotes

1. According to Jacobs and Klein (1993), Edwin Shneidman coined the term *psychological autopsy* to refer to a procedure used to classify equivocal death through the use of interviews with the deceased's relatives, friends, physicians, and so on.

2. In a number of studies of suicidal children and adolescents, it was found that fantasies of merging with a parent or returning to the bliss of an earlier imagined fused relationship with the mother were prominent features. The fusion fantasies were symptomatic of a severe regressive state that resulted in the attempted or completed suicide (Pfeffer, 1986).

3. Studies have shown that adults who experienced the demise of relatives or close friends in their early years, especially before the age of 10, have significantly more nightmares involving themes of death (Feldman & Hersen, 1967).

4. Ellis and Allen (1961), in *Traitor Within: Our Suicide Problem,* stated, "Strangely, a rapid rise up the economic ladder can cause some people to end their lives" (p. 24).

5. Developmental psychologists, pediatricians, and psychiatrists have written extensively about this "maturational crisis" in the lives of women (Benedek, 1970; Brazelton & Cramer, 1990; Elmer, 1967; Klaus & Kennell, 1976; Rheingold, 1964, 1967). Benedek (1970) contended that regression to the oral phase of development is inherent in pregnancy.

6. In some cases, infanticide followed by the mother's (or father's) suicide are the outcomes of severe postpartum disturbance or psychosis (Resnick, 1969).

7. Klaus and Kennell (1976) stated, "The production of a normal child is a major goal of most women. Yet most pregnant women have hidden fears that the infant may be abnormal or reveal some of their own secret inner weaknesses" (p. 42).

PART III

THEORY OF

DEFENSE FORMATION

11 The Voice Process and the Fantasy Bond

No one ever becomes completely emancipated from the state of infantile dependence . . . and there is no one who has completely escaped the necessity of incorporating his early objects.

W. R. D. Fairbairn (1941/1952, p. 56)

The relation of the ego to the object is twofold . . . because of the child's original idea of the mother as both *good* (vouchsafing) and *bad* (depriving) object. . . .

Every object relation nevertheless holds destructive elements within it, since the deposit of overcome and renounced ego phases always involves a breaking up and reorganization of the ego structure, which we know and fear as the destructive side of love.

Otto Rank (from a 1926 lecture, "The Genesis of Object Relation," cited by Kramer, 1995, p. 315)

For the past 39 years, I have devoted my life's work to the study of resistance in psychotherapy and human beings' fundamental resistance to a "better life." My search has led me from studies of psychopathology to the investigation of the core conflict for "normal" individuals in everyday life. In spite of my own resistance and idealization of the family, I reluctantly traced the development of defended lifestyles to basic destructive dynamics in the nuclear family. Later I came to understand how existential issues affect and solidify the defenses formed in the earliest years.

Initially I worked with schizophrenic patients in a residential treatment community (Endnote 1), later with psychosomatic disturbances in a hospital setting, and for the next 22 years, I was fully engaged in the private practice of psychotherapy with a wide range of patients. Finally, in 1979, I was asked to participate in an ongoing study of normal individuals interested in pursuing an open and honest lifestyle. Because of this community's commitment to forthright and direct communication, I saw an unusual opportunity to match internal dynamics, exposed through honest self-disclosure, with a longitudinal study of personal relationships. This unique psychological laboratory would enable me to extend my insight into problems of everyday living, psychopathology, and human suffering (Endnote 2).

This chapter represents a synthesis of my theoretical viewpoint as expressed in articles, books, and filmed documentaries (Endnote 3). In my work, I emphasize the exposure of destructive fantasy bonds as externalized in interpersonal relationships or internalized in the form of object representation (parental introjects). Dissolution of these bonds and movement toward separation and individuation is essential for the realization of one's destiny as a fully autonomous human being. Separation as conceptualized here is very different than isolation, defense, or retreat; rather, it involves the maintenance of a strong identity and distinct boundaries at close quarters with others. Indeed, without a well-developed self system or personal identity, people find it necessary to distort, lash out at, or withdraw from intimacy in interpersonal relationships.

A defended life characterized by imagined fusion with another or others acts to limit a person's capacity for self-expression and self-fulfillment (Firestone, 1984; Kaiser, 1955/1965; Karpel, 1976; Laing, 1961; Wexler & Steidl, 1978; Willi, 1975/1982). A merged identity or diminished sense of self is a microsuicidal or even suicidal manifestation, as one no longer lives a committed, feelingful existence. Without a strong sense of self, life seems empty, meaningless, and without direction.

Given this premise, what are the threats to an individual's sense of identity? What are the sources of pain and anxiety that disturb the individuation process and diminish one's sense of self and essential humanness?

Origins of Psychological Pain

As noted in Chapter 1, there are two major sources of psychological pain and anxiety: (a) deprivation, rejection, and overt or covert aggression on the part of parents, family members, and significant others, particularly during the formative years, and (b) basic existential problems of aloneness, aging, illness, death, and other facts of existence that have a negative effect on a person's life experience: social pressure, crime, economic fluctuations, political tyranny, and the threat of nuclear holocaust. *Interpersonal pain* refers to the frustration, aggression, and abuse one experiences in relationships, whereas issues of being, aloneness, and the fact of death fall into the *existential* category.

It is important to integrate both systems of thought, psychoanalytic and existential, to achieve a better understanding of the conflict between the life-affirming propensities and self-destructive tendencies operating within each individual. One must consider both the "down and dirty" issues dealt with by the psychoanalysts as well as the "higher level" or ontological concerns of the existentialists. To develop a complete picture of a human being's struggle, one must understand that defenses formed in early childhood are critically reinforced as the child develops a growing awareness of death.

The Basic Defense System

The fantasy bond is the primary defense against separation anxiety and interpersonal pain (Firestone, 1984). The primary defense is the process of parenting oneself both internally in fantasy and externally by using objects and persons in one's environment. The result is a pseudoindependent posture of self-sufficiency—a fantasy that one can take care of oneself without needing others. The process of parenting oneself is made up of a self-feeding component as well as a component of self-condemnation and self-attack. Both aspects of self-parenting take on their unique character from the introjection and internalization of parental attitudes and responses in the process of growing up in a specific interpersonal environment (Firestone, 1984, 1985). Self-nourishing propensities persist into adult life in the form of praising and coddling oneself, vanity, eating disorders, addiction to cigarettes, alcohol, and other drugs, compulsive masturbation, and an impersonal, self-feeding, habitual style of sexual relating. Self-critical thoughts, guilt reactions, and attacks on self are examples of the disciplinary aspect of parental introjects. They represent the self-punishing element of the core defense.

The child experiences a false sense of self-sufficiency or omnipotence because he or she has introjected an image of the "good and powerful" mother or primary caretaker into the self. Unfortunately, at the same time, the child must also necessarily incorporate the accompanying parental attitudes of rejection. The introjected parental image takes on the significance of a survival mechanism in the child's mind.

The *fantasy bond,* originally an imagined fusion with the mother or primary parenting figure, is highly effective as a defense because the capacity of humans for imagination provides partial gratification of needs and reduces tension. However, the more an individual comes to rely on fantasy, the less he or she will seek or be able to accept gratification in real situations and relationships. When aspects of the self-parenting process are extended to others, they lead to addictive attachments as contrasted with genuine relating (Firestone, 1987a).

Fantasies of fusion and self-parenting systems act as painkillers to cut off feeling responses, which impedes the development of a true sense of self. The end product of this progressive dependence on self-nourishing patterns is a form of psychological equilibrium achieved at the expense of genuine object relationships. Defended individuals seek equilibrium over actualization; that is, they are willing to give up positive, goal-directed activity to maintain internal sources of gratification.

The *voice process* supports the defense system (Firestone, 1988). As described earlier, the voice may be conceptualized as a well-integrated, discrete, antiself system, an alien force that is an overlay on the personality at the core of an individual's maladaptive behavior. In the course of our investigations, my associates and I found that individuals were able to readily identify the content of their self-critical, self-destructive thoughts or "voices" when they verbalized them in the second person, that is, as though another person were addressing them, and in the form of statements *toward* themselves rather than statements about themselves.

In our pilot studies using this technique, (a) the extensiveness and intensity of our subjects' self-hatred and aggression toward themselves were surprising; (b) the majority of subjects had a clear-cut view of their childhood and a realization that the source of their negative voice attacks was related to interactions with parents and family members (Endnote 4); (c) subjects made spontaneous intellectual connections and were able to interpret their own material in the absence of a priori hypotheses; (d) subjects' voices dictated injunctions and prohibitions that were diametrically opposed to self-affirmation and goal-directed behavior; and (e) their voices not only were directed inward toward the self but also were focused on others. Our findings (Firestone, 1986, 1987b, 1988, 1990b) supported an evolving hypothesis that the voice represented the introjection of negative parental attitudes, defenses, and aggression that were incorporated in particular during times of stress. In addition, voices predisposed behavior imitative of parental defenses, supported parents' defended lifestyles, and influenced a choice to withdraw from life in the face of death anxiety.

The voice should not be confused with a conscience, superego, or value system. The voice alternately builds up and tears down the self and provides ostensibly rational reasons for self-denial, isolation, and avoidance of others.

The voice functions as an antifeeling, antibody process, comparable to obsessional thinking, wherein people live primarily in their heads, cut off from their emotions and bodily sensations. Even so-called positive voices of approval and seeming self-interest are indications that people are fragmented and removed from themselves. To fulfill their human potentiality, individuals must not relate to themselves as objects or products. They need to feel and be themselves in the living present.

On the basis of our data, I hypothesized that *thoughts* antithetical to the self vary along a continuum of intensity from self-critical or self-depreciating to angry recrimination and actual suicidal ideation. As described in Chapter 8, self-destructive behavior exists on a parallel continuum ranging from self-denial to accident-proneness, substance abuse, microsuicidal behavior, bodily harm, and actual suicide.

The Paradox of Defenses

There is a natural tendency for people to resort to psychological defenses to eliminate primal pain. The degree to which one defends oneself depends on the degree of trauma and deprivation suffered early in life. Ironically, defenses erected by children to protect themselves from a toxic environment as well as painful aspects of the human condition can eventually become more damaging than the original trauma.

A Developmental Perspective

Psychological defenses formed as a reaction to interpersonal pain precede the child's growing awareness of death. They represent an adaptation to the parental climate and act as a psychological survival mechanism to maintain equilibrium. The original defenses are extended and reinforced when the child first experiences death anxiety. Subsequently, defense mechanisms go beyond an individual's attempt at self-protection and the avoidance of personal hurt and rejection in relationships. Now, the core defense is directed at defending against death anxiety, and unpleasant or painful interactions with others may at times be preferred as a distraction.

In my clinical experience, I have noted that children progress through several stages of separation. As described in the previous chapter, these stages correspond to the successive steps they take in diffcrentiating themselves from the mother and later the father and the extended family. In early infancy (birth to 6 months), children feel utterly dependent on the mother and experience themselves as merged. Later (4 or 5 months to 2 years), there is a gradual accommodation to the reality of being separate from the mother (Mahler, Pine, & Bergman, 1975).

Separation anxiety is experienced at every phase of individuation and precipitates a fear of loss of self and a terror of annihilation (Bowlby, 1973; A. Freud, 1966/1989; A. Freud & Burlingham, 1944; Winnicott, 1941/1958b). To compensate, there is an imagined fusion with the mother or primary caretaker. This connection leads to an illusion of self-sufficiency—a desperate attempt on the child's part to deny his or her true state of aloneness, helplessness, and vulnerability. By the time children develop a structured concept of their own personal death, they have already established a complex system of defense against separation anxiety. Indeed, death symbolizes the ultimate separation.

Children's Reaction to
the Discovery of Death

At a critical point in the developmental sequence, sometime between the ages of 3 and 6, children become aware that people die, that their parents are vulnerable to death, and that they themselves cannot maintain their own lives. Their world, which they had experienced as permanent, is literally turned upside down by the dawning awareness of mortality (Firestone, 1985).

In learning about death, most children feel, on some level, that a terrible trick has been played on them. Many become angry or distant from their parents, while others exhibit an intensified clinging or dependency. In general, children try to ameliorate this final blow to their security by regressing to an earlier stage of development in which they were unaware of death. Remaining infantile or suspended in a childish state is a primary defense against death anxiety, as aging is associated with movement toward an impending death. As noted, faced with death anxiety, children attempt to reinstate and reinforce the imagined connection with parents and parental introjects. On a behavioral level, increased preoccupation with fantasy, acting out, nightmares, signs of depersonalization, and other regressive trends are common during this crucial phase (Endnote 5).

One apparently universal response to the knowledge of death is manifested in a basic paranoid orientation toward life; that is, the fact of death gives rise to a core paranoia that is then projected onto other situations. In some sense, paranoia is an appropriate reaction to existential realities, as powerful forces are operating on people that are beyond their control and that eliminate all chance of ultimate survival. Children generalize death anxiety to other objects and often develop fears of monsters, ghosts, and other imaginary dangers. Adult anxiety disorders, phobias, fear of intimacy—the fear of being drained or subsumed by another person or persons—are related to the basic paranoia (Endnote 6). Claustrophobia—fear of being imprisoned, confined, being unable to breathe—barely masks man's primitive fear of death.

In summary, the point in the developmental sequence when the child first discovers death is the critical juncture where his or her defense system crystallizes and shapes the future (Endnote 7). Thereafter, most people accommodate the fear of death through the withdrawal of energy and emotional investment in life-affirming activity and close, personal relationships. In renouncing real satisfaction, they rely increasingly on internal gratification, fantasies of fusion, and painkillers. The thought of losing one's life, losing all consciousness, losing all ego through death is so intolerable that the process of giving up offers relief from the anguish.

Defenses provide a method of escaping psychological pain at the expense of varying degrees of obliteration of personality and experience. Unfortunately, defenses cannot selectively cut out emotional pain without seriously interfering with other functions. They act to dull awareness, distort perceptions, deaden emotional responses, and eventually lead to an overall deterioration in the quality of life.

The Core Conflict

Human beings appear to exist in a "no-win" situation in relation to defenses. They must either experience primal pain or, in defending themselves, cut off their emotional responsiveness and basic human propensities. When defenses are operating, people may feel less anxious and temporarily more secure; nevertheless, the defended posture has negative consequences in a loss of freedom and a constricted life. Looking at the other side, the comparatively less defended individual experiences a good deal of sadness and pain yet feels integrated, experiences more fulfillment, has a stronger identity, a greater potential for intimacy, and tends to be more humane toward his or her fellow man.

All people exist in conflict between an active pursuit of goals in the real world and a defensive reliance on self-gratification. Retreat to an increasingly inward posture represents, in effect, a form of controlled destruction of the self. Anything that threatens to disturb an individual's solution to the core conflict arouses fear. Movement in any direction, that is, a retreat further into fantasy and self-parenting or movement toward external goal-directed behavior, is accompanied by anxiety. The rise in anxiety results in both aggressive and regressive reactions. This phenomenon can be observed in a wide range of situations. As discussed earlier, these dynamics explain perverse reactions to unusual achievement, positive acknowledgment, and satisfaction in a love relationship—reactions such as depression or retreat to a self-destructive lifestyle after success.

The choice to adopt defenses as a resolution of the basic conflict is determined, to a considerable degree, by the amount of pain experienced, the extent of confusion or mystification of reality, and the type of defense mechanism that works most effectively to cut off pain and anxiety at the time of crisis. In addition, the way a person chooses to handle pain determines the level of his or her suicidal potential.

Effects of Defenses on
Interpersonal Relationships

Human beings cannot be "innocently" defended. The choice to live defensively limits one's capacity for feeling and affiliating closely with others, and causes corresponding damage to loved ones, especially one's children. The adherence to a defended posture leads to unnecessary anguish in human relationships. Contrary to other, more superficial explanations regarding the causes of marital strife, most difficulties in marriage and child rearing are deeply affected by individual modes of defense. Indeed, men and women fight about and are deeply disturbed by their partner's psychological defenses and microsuicidal tendencies, and they act out in angry reactions to confrontation.

The lack of tolerance for feeling the closeness of another human being and a fear of rejection and potential loss are at the core of marital and family distress. Most couples appear to choose debilitating, conventional forms of security and "togetherness" yet reject genuine affection and companionship. More often than not, they re-create early painful experiences from childhood in their current relationships while maintaining a fantasy that they can somehow escape death through merging with another person. However, this use of a relationship for security, which depersonalizes interactions and obliterates real feeling, is tantamount to losing that relationship.

To summarize, overreliance on psychological defenses has the following negative consequences for the individual: (a) suppression and blockage of feeling, (b) the tendency to develop psychological and somatic symptom patterns caused by the repression of feeling, (c) a personal style of dishonesty and lack of integrity in communication and behavior (Endnote 8), (d) impaired ability to function and cope with life because of increased dependence on fantasy and addictive behavior, and (e) incidental damage to other people.

It is logical and understandable to defend against pain; however, one's defenses necessarily hurt others. This creates a moral dilemma for every individual. I contend that the impact of people defending themselves in regard to personal and existential issues is destructive to each succeeding generation.

The Universality of Child Abuse

> To grow up at all is to conceal the mass of
> internal scar tissue that throbs in our dreams.
>   Ernest Becker (1973, p. 29)

Emotional child abuse refers to the damage to the child's psychological development and emerging personal identity that is primarily caused by parents' (primary caretakers') immaturity, defended lifestyles, and conscious or unconscious aggression toward the child. We must consider it abuse when imprinting from early interactions with parents has long-term debilitating effects on a person's self-concept, impairs personal relationships, leads to unhappiness and pain in one's sexual life, and interferes with and stifles development of career and vocational pursuits (Endnote 9). Although personal deficiencies and limitations in adult functioning are at times related to biological or hereditary factors, in our experience they have most often been found to be closely related to, even overdetermined by, abuses suffered in the process of growing up.

I have been forced to face the fact that normative child-rearing practices in our society have pathogenic properties and effects (Endnote 10). Although emotional child abuse is present in virtually all traditional family constellations, the degree to which children are damaged varies considerably. The more parents are defended, retreat from valuing themselves, and minimize or avoid personal relationships, the greater the impairment of parental functions, regardless of parents' stated commitment to or concern for their children.

Reasons Parents Damage
Their Children

1. Parents have a fundamental ambivalence toward themselves and their children. They both love and hate themselves and naturally extend both feelings to their productions. Most parents admit their nurturing tendencies but suppress or deny their negative feelings or aggression. Because of this, they are often defensive about their child-rearing practices. Parents generally want to love their children and help them fulfill their potentialities. At the same time, the parents' behavior is often punitive, and they inadvertently stifle their children's excitement, cut off their emotional responses, and act out with hostility toward them.

2. Parents tend to dispose of their self-hatred and the traits they dislike in themselves by projecting them onto their children. In the process of projection, the child is basically used as a waste receptacle or dumping ground. In most cases, children accept parental attributions and take on the assigned negative identity while maintaining an idealized image of their parents.

3. Most parents are unable to sustain consistent loving relationships with their children because the aliveness, spontaneity, and spirit of the child threaten parents' defenses. Feeling deeply for the child revives painful primal feelings that were previously repressed from parents' own childhoods. Sensitive treatment of their children, particularly in areas where parents had been treated badly, arouses poignant, painful feelings that they attempt to avoid. It reminds them of the preciousness and fragility of life and tends to precipitate fears of potential loss. Consequently, parents maintain a certain distance and relate to the child primarily in terms of role-determined emotions and behaviors.

4. Parents mistake powerful feelings of desperation and emotional hunger for genuine love and concern for their children (Endnote 11). Immature parents tend to make demands for love, fulfillment, reassurance, and even parenting from their children rather than offering affection and love to them. The child growing up in this type of environment is depleted by physical contact with the emotionally hungry parent (Endnote 12).

5. The nature of traditional coupling fosters dependence and exclusivity in the parents' relationship that has a detrimental effect on the child. In forming a fantasy bond, each partner has been diminished in his or her vitality, individuality, and sense of self through use of the other for purposes of

security. Parents in this situation have very little energy to offer affection or direction to their children (Endnote 13).

The deterioration in the quality of relating occurring within the couple is covered by a pretense or fantasy of love and closeness. The discrepancy between parents' behavior toward each other and their words of love confuse the child and seriously distort his or her sense of reality. In addition, people in a fantasy bond often present a singular point of view, a united front, to the world and to their offspring. Parents suppress, either consciously or unconsciously, their children's reactions, communications, and perceptions that contradict the parents' belief systems or disrupt their illusion of closeness, which thereby creates a toxic atmosphere of secrecy and duplicity in the home.

6. One interesting existential issue often overlooked is that most parents have children as a defense against death anxiety, that is, a bid for immortality. To the extent that children closely resemble their parents in appearance, personality characteristics, behavior, and style of defense, they are the parents' legacy to be left in the world after the parents' death as evidence that their lives were meaningful. Parents imagine, on some level, that this "belonging" or merger imbues them with immortality. However, the more the child is different from the parents, the more he or she poses a threat to their illusion of immortality. Nonconformity and individuation are judged or perceived as "bad," while sameness with, or submission to, one's parents is seen as good.

7. In using the child as a symbol of immortality, parents feel both the need and the obligation to impose their own standards, beliefs, and value systems on their child. They feel duty-bound to teach their own self-protective coping mechanisms, even though these may be distorted, crippling, and maladaptive. They transmit their defenses, beliefs, and values to children both implicitly and explicitly, that is, by example and direct instruction. Having been thus "processed," most children grow up feeling alienated from themselves and feel that they have no inherent right to their own point of view as separate human beings.

The Effects of Emotional Abuse on the Child's Humanness

Emotional abuse often has a more profound impact on the child than physical abuse in terms of its overall effect on the psyche, the spirit, and the humanness of the individual. To fully understand the mistreatment of children, one must be cognizant of the qualities that are essentially human. Indeed, if we fail to give value to those aspects of individuals that are vital to their humanness, we cannot correctly evaluate the extent of damage incurred by the child in the nuclear family.

What are the characteristics that are uniquely human, that reflect more than the primary drives, that is, thirst, hunger, and sex? They include (a) the capability of giving and receiving love, (b) a sense of oneself and one's boundaries, (c) the ability to relate to or affiliate with others, (d) the development of a personal value system, (e) a capacity for symbolic thought, awareness, and reflection, (f) a sense of curiosity and creativity, and (g) a desire or passion to search for meaning in life. In addition, people need a transcending goal or cause, something higher than practical, everyday concerns, to give their lives a true sense of fulfillment.

If any of the human potentialities are fractured during the formative years, children are deprived of their intrinsic humanity. Tragically, within the traditional nuclear family, well-meaning parents often damage their children's capacity for excitement and spontaneity, their awareness of the world, and their ability to feel and care deeply for themselves and other human beings. Well-intentioned parents attempt to protect children from death anxiety and other negative, painful issues in life, which leads to denial and distortion of their sense of reality. Although their motives are benevolent, a good deal of harm may be done. For example, efforts to isolate children and prevent them from forming friendships outside the family represent a serious form of emotional maltreatment that can predispose subsequent self-destructive or suicidal behavior (Richman, 1986). Yet this restriction may be imposed by fearful parents who are attempting to protect their offspring from negative peer pressure and other "bad influences."

On a deep level, most parents sense that they are damaging their children by the manner in which they live and interact with them, yet when a choice must be made between parental defenses and the child, the child's well-being is expendable and parents' defenses are maintained. For this reason, parents suffer considerable guilt and remorse.

Parental guilt reactions serve no positive function in altering child-rearing practices; rather, these reactions complicate family interactions and lead to the parents' further alienation from their children. Indeed, to judge or blame mothers and fathers rather than have compassion about the reasons they damage their children compounds the problem and causes additional suffering. My approach stresses accounting for and understanding the roots of psychopathology, which is vastly different from focusing blame. Parents themselves were damaged in their upbringing and inadvertently pass on this damage to their children. In each case, both parent and child should be viewed with compassion.

The Voice and the Intergenerational Transmission
of Negative Parental Traits and Defenses

As noted, the repetition of child abuse through successive generations occurs despite parents' best intentions. In the course of examining manifestations of the voice process, my associates and I found that the effects of painful traumatic experiences in childhood are incorporated in the form of hostile thoughts toward ourselves. The majority of subjects in our 17-year clinical investigation into the voice process identified this self-critical thought process as statements and attitudes that one or both parents directed toward them during their formative years. Others remembered negative feelings they had picked up in their parents' tone of voice, body language, or other nonverbal cues that seemed to be directly related to the subjects' self-attacks. While verbalizing the voice in an abreactive manner, individuals had powerful insights that enabled them to understand the origins of their self-limiting behavior and self-hatred.

From the clinical data, my associates and I began to understand the connection between subjects' verbalizations of the voice and negative parental statements and attitudes assimilated by them as children. The part that the voice played in perpetuating the mistreatment of children through the generations became apparent to us. The following example illustrates a pattern of emotional abuse and the types of self-attacks generated by the original traumatic experiences.

Michelle, a young mother, revealed that she projected traits she hated in herself onto her 8-year-old son, Tom. Michelle's own parents had identified her as the troublemaker and the "weird one" in the family, an identity she found difficult to refute and move beyond. When she had a son, she experienced many self-doubts about her abilities as a mother. To relieve the painful feelings associated with the view she had of herself as a "bad" mother, she externalized her self-attacks and instead perceived her son as somewhat strange and different than other children. In a parenting group, she disclosed feelings she had previously been ashamed of in relation to her son.

> *Michelle:* I see Tommy as odd. There's something wrong with him. It's a deep feeling, like I would say to him, "There's something wrong with you." A strong attack on him—"Look right, straighten up! Sit up, look right, change that face." (cries, deep sobs)
>
> When I said that, I felt it switch from him to myself. "Change your face!" I know that was done to me in my own family. I was always told: "Don't let

it show." But really angry. "Just don't let anything show, don't let your feelings show. You're always bothering people, and stirring up trouble. Just keep quiet and keep your feelings to yourself!" I realize now that I have an image of Tommy as miserable and a misfit. I really see him as a misfit.

Michelle's son accepted these negative attributions and indeed saw himself as different from his friends. As a 6-year-old, he had been diagnosed with a learning disability and needed private tutoring. Now at 8, he was being incorporated into a new school setting, a class attended by many of his friends. His anxiety about the new experience was accompanied by self-critical thoughts about not fitting in.

> *Tom:* I hear voices all the time when I'm in school. They say that I'm stupid, that I'm a dumb person, that I can't do anything in school. I'm just a dumb person. If I didn't have these voices, I could do my school work way better.
>
> Other times when I'm not in school I have a voice that says, "You're a jerk. You don't belong here. You're not the kind of a person that should be in this class. You don't deserve to be here. You don't deserve your friends. You don't deserve to have any fun. You don't deserve any of that."

Resistance

Resistance goes beyond the therapy process and is an integral part of a defended lifestyle characterized by personal limitation. Although defenses against personal and existential pain have profound effects on an individual's life, people have it within their power to alter destructive patterns. Indeed, there is no psychological problem or emotional malady (short of physical impairment) that is impervious to change, provided that a person has motivation, understanding, and the courage to take risks and alter behavior patterns.

Most individuals feel trapped in their defense system, are guilty and fearful of individuation, and tend to deny their power to change. At a crucial point in the therapy process when people have progressed and feel out on a limb, there is a tendency toward regression. When this occurs, they tend to project their desire for change onto the therapist and strengthen their resistance. When regression takes place based on the fear of therapeutic development or change, it becomes the central issue in the therapy process. Indeed, resistance is at the core of maladaptive living and affects every aspect of a person's lifestyle. In this sense, resistance is the essential "disease" or problem; it represents holding on to an imaginary connection to others or internalized objects, due to the dread of reexperiencing one's helplessness, aloneness, and vulnerability to death. Most people never reach an optimal level of differentiation, individuation, or separateness because they stubbornly refuse to step beyond their customary defenses.

Summary and Goals of the Therapeutic Approach

The ultimate goal of psychotherapy is to help the individual establish a free and independent existence, attain personal satisfaction, remain open to experience, and respond with appropriate feeling to both positive and negative events in his or her life. My goal is not to change people but to offer each person the maximum possibility for growth consistent with their desires or motivations. My therapy techniques do not represent an onslaught on defenses or an attack on the way people choose to live; rather, they imply a sensitive interrelationship characterized by respect for the individual and his or her right to make choices, even when that choice is to be defended.

I recognize the pervasiveness and essential destructiveness of defenses while, at the same time, I understand that people come by their defenses honestly as events in their early lives led to the necessary adaptation for psychological survival. Insight into the dynamics of defense has helped me to approach each individual with compassion and a heightened sensitivity to patterns of defense. Although I have pointed out what I considered to be significant blocks to a person's overall development, I have always respected the fact that the ultimate decision to challenge or disrupt fantasies of fusion, addictive habits, and attachments rests with each individual.

Endnotes

1. From 1956 to 1957, I conducted psychotherapy with schizophrenic patients under the auspices of John N. Rosen (1953, *Direct Analysis*).

2. Fruitful clinical research and theory formation requires a unique window or vantage point from which to observe human experience (e.g., Freud, 1893/1955, free association; Janov, 1970, primals). For the past 17 years, my associates and I have had a special opportunity to observe participants' interactions with their original families, their mates, and their children. Thus we were exposed to key dynamics of interpersonal relationships over three generations (Firestone, 1985). I am greatly indebted to these people for opening their lives to me in this intimate setting.

3. The reader interested in an expanded version of these ideas and their application to a wide range of concerns in the field of mental health can find the appropriate references in the reference list and in a compendium in *Combating Destructive Thought Processes: Voice Therapy and Separation Theory* (Firestone, 1997).

4. When expressing negative thoughts toward self in the second person as noted above, it was clear in many cases that subjects' accents resembled the style and intonation of one or another parent or family member (most typically, but not exclusively, the parent of the same sex).

5. Nagy (1948/1959), Anthony (1971), Rochlin (1967), and Kastenbaum (1974) have attempted to document children's reactions to the knowledge of death. In my experience, children who were supported rather than discouraged from expressing their views on this subject frequently brought up their fears and anxiety about dying. It was clear that their moods and behavior were deeply affected by their concerns. I believe that further research is needed in this area because of its developmental significance.

6. People fear the unknown. Contemplating a finite existence or even a never-ending life is terrifying. Defenses against death anxiety or denial of death—such as the conceptualization of life after death (heaven, the second world), the philosophy of reincarnation, the postulation of a soul that survives—never offer complete security. There are always flaws in the defense system. For example, there would have been no need for religious wars throughout history if people felt secure in their own defenses against death anxiety.

7. With respect to the significant period in a child's defensive posture or retreat from life, it is interesting to note that the "primal scene" or "primal phantasies" described by Freud (1915/1957a) referred to the child's witnessing and misperceiving the parent's sex act as a form of violence, while for Janov (1970) it represented a culmination of primal pain in a symbolic traumatic event where the child shuts down and completely gives up. I contend that the "primal scene" in an individual's development occurs when there is a full realization of death's inevitability.

8. It is virtually impossible to have truthful verbal communication when people retreat from their priorities and personal goals to protect a posture of denial or avoidance. If their behavior contradicts their expressed goals, they are dishonest and send mixed signals. On the other hand, if they recognize their paradoxical behavior and say they don't want what they truly want or desire, they are still not telling the truth. Honesty is possible only if individuals pursue their unique priorities and assert themselves. Then, and only then, will their behavior match stated goals, and they will not confuse or mislead others.

9. The prevalence and extent of child abuse of all forms has been minimized in our society because of an idealized image of the nuclear family. The widespread use of drugs among our youth to kill the emotional pain they are in, however, is one indication of the high incidence of neglect and destructive parenting practices. As noted, substance abuse and diagnosis of a psychiatric disorder are two major risk factors in suicide.

Clinical observation using intense feeling release therapy also supported the hypothesis regarding the universality of childhood trauma (Firestone, 1985). In a population of over 200 individuals, we found that, without exception, every subject expressed deep-seated pain that he or she had previously suppressed. We agree with Janov (1970) that people maintain a defensive posture and arrange their lives in a manner to avoid the recurrence of painful feelings of sadness associated with early trauma.

10. R. D. Laing (1969/1972), Alice Miller (1980/1984), Leonard Shengold (1989), and James Garbarino (Garbarino & Gilliam, 1980; Garbarino et al., 1986), among others, have emphasized the pervasiveness of emotional mistreatment of children in our culture. They stress that many of these abuses would be considered to be normal practices.

11. One cannot consider parental love separate from loving operations or behaviors. Criteria such as genuine warmth, tenderness, and physical affection, pleasure in the child's company, respect for the child's boundaries, responsible and sensitive care, and a willingness to be a real person with the child rather than simply act the role of "mother" or "father" define the operations of love. When parental actions contradict these criteria and are disrespectful, overprotective,

intrusive, neglectful, or outright hostile, one must consider these actions as abusive or hateful rather than manifestations of love, regardless of the subjective inner feeling described by parents. Parents' actions must coincide with their internal feeling state for their "love" to be valid or have a beneficial effect on the child.

My distinction between emotional hunger and love, two very different parental emotional states and behaviors, explains the dynamics underlying patterns of anxious attachment as compared with those of secure attachment described by Bowlby (1973) and Ainsworth, Blehar, Walters, and Wall (1978).

12. Parents very often tend to compensate for the damage they sense they are causing by choosing to spend more time with their child. However, increased contact with a hungry, immature parent increases the damage to the child.

13. Parents must be able to provide both love and the necessary controls to meet the child's basic needs. I have referred to this product as "love-food" (Firestone, 1957), which implies both the capacity and the desire to provide for the need gratification of the infant and young child. The absence of either component, either affection or control, seriously interferes with the child's development.

12 Couple and Family Relationships

I do not know . . . when my mother and father began their long, dispiriting war against each other. Most of their skirmishes were like games of ringolevio, with the souls of their children serving as the ruined captured flags in their campaign of attrition. Neither considered the potential damage when struggling over something as fragile and unformed as a child's life. . . .

As with many parents, their love proved to be the most lethal thing about them.

Pat Conroy (1986, p. 3), *The Prince of Tides*

Personality theorists are accustomed to thinking of bonds as constructive attachments typified by long-lasting love and devotion or in terms of the positive bonding that occurs between mother and infant. This chapter focuses on *fantasies of connection or destructive ties* that damage marital and family relationships and enter into psychological disturbance. So powerful are these ties in couple and family relationships that when they are broken, they are the most prominent cause of personal distress and potential suicide. Indeed, the loss of objects has been noted by suicidologists and clinicians as one of the most significant factors in suicide (Heckler, 1994; Richman, 1986). According to Litman and Farberow (1983), a majority of calls to crisis hot lines involve issues of rejection, abandonment, or loss of a significant relationship.

Psychodynamics of the Fantasy Bond: Brief Review of the Literature

Manifestations of a fantasy bond can be observed in those behaviors that lend support to an illusion of being connected or of belonging to another person.

As noted in Chapter 10, Hellmuth Kaiser (1955/1965) was an astute observer of this symptomatology in a wide range of patients. In "The Problem of Responsibility in Psychotherapy," he developed his concept of a "delusion of fusion":

> He [the neurotic patient] wants either to incorporate himself into the other person and lose his own personality, or to incorporate the other person and destroy the other person's personality. When an opportunity for such fusion or identification seems to be offered, every function is drawn into the service of the desire for closeness, in the regressive sense. (p. 4)

A Developmental Perspective

A number of psychoanalytic theorists have referred to fantasies of connection in their writing. For example, Blanck and Blanck (1974), in their review of Margaret Mahler's and Edith Jacobson's contributions to developmental theories about symbiotic states, wrote, "[Mahler and Jacobson describe] the tendency, traces of which remain throughout life . . .to merge with the object in search of the gratifying experiences which emanate from her" (p. 64). In her discussion of the separation/individuation phase of development in psychotic children, Mahler (1974) concluded,

> We became more and more convinced that the "basic fault" in the psychotic was his inability to perceive the self and the mother as separate entities, and thus to use the mother as a "beacon of orientation in the world of reality," as his "external ego." (p. 91)

Mahler also observed behavioral manifestations of what she conceptualized as an imagined state in "normal" toddlers. Kohut (1971) emphasized the pseudoindependent function of this symbiotic merger in his analysis of "transmuting internalizations." "The internal structure, in other words, now performs the functions which the object [mother] used to perform for the child" (p. 50).

The Fantasy Bond in the Adult

Fantasy bond is used here to describe both the original imaginary connection formed during childhood and the repetitive efforts of the adult to continue to make connections in intimate associations. The fantasized connection may be conceptualized as an addictive process, similar to the use of habit-forming drugs. Initially formed to compensate for what was lacking in the early environment, it later becomes habit forming, with many negative side effects. Once this illusion of connectedness with another person has been formed, experiences of real love and intimacy interfere with its defensive function, whereas symbols of togetherness and images of love strengthen the illusion.

Wexler and Steidl (1978) concluded that many individuals in marital relationships avoid experiences that threaten to disrupt their illusions of oneness. They described an undifferentiated state where couples regress to an earlier symbiosis "in the face of separation anxiety." In their analysis, they wrote, "Adults who seek to fuse with their mates are in many respects like the toddler who seeks to fuse with his mothering person" (p. 72).

By contrast, Boszormenyi-Nagy (1965) described mature relationships as those in which "the act of mutually trusting the Other is an important structural requisite of the dialogue" (p. 56). In commenting on Nagy's analysis of mature modes of relating, Karpel (1976) cautioned, "But features that characterize less mature forms of relationship [pure fusion and ambivalent fusion, among others] will always be present to varying degrees at varying moments" (p. 81).

A substantial body of empirical research on adult romantic attachments developed by Phillip Shaver and his colleagues tends to support the psychoanalytic formulations described above. These studies show that defensive patterns of anxious/ambivalent and avoidant attachment formed in infancy are maintained throughout the life span by mental representations or "internal working models" of self and attachment figures and are manifested in adulthood through differential styles of relating. Citing a study conducted by Feeney and Noller (1990), who analyzed differences in attachment styles, Shaver and Hazan (1993) described ambivalently-anxiously attached adult individuals as follows: "[These] subjects were characterized by 'neurotic love' (preoccupation, mania, dependence, idealization, and addictive reliance on a partner)" (p. 37) (Endnote 1).

Fantasy bonds exist as implicit defensive pacts between individuals. Members of the couple or family conspire both to live with and to protect each other's defended lifestyle. Both collaborate to preserve a fantasy of love. R. D. Laing (1961) demonstrated how "collusion" is an important relationship dynamic:

> Two people in relation may confirm each other or genuinely complement each other. Still, to disclose oneself to the other is hard without confidence in oneself and trust in the other. Desire for confirmation from each is present in

both, but each is caught between trust and mistrust, confidence and despair, and both settle for counterfeit acts of confirmation on the basis of pretense. To do so both must play the game of collusion. (pp. 108-109)

Laing's analysis of the development of collusion is similar to my conceptualization of the process of fantasy bond formation in the couple. Individuals who have been damaged in their earliest experiences are reluctant to reveal themselves in new relationships. They are resistant to taking a chance on being hurt again. The tragedy of people's retreat from their original emotional investment with each other is compounded by mutual self-deception.

The Fantasy Bond in Marital Relationships

Destructive fantasy bonds exist in the large majority of couple relationships and are present to some extent in most families. The process of forming destructive bonds greatly reduces the chance of achieving a successful marriage. Most men and women are unaware, however, of their strong propensity for giving up their individuality to become one half of a couple or to merge themselves with another person for purposes of security. In growing up, the more rejected the child, the more desperately he or she clings to the mother and forms a fantasy bond with her.

In a sense, the rejected child cannot leave home, cannot develop an independent life, and transfers this abnormal dependency to new objects. Consequently, as an adult, he or she avoids or rejects any experience or person that is not a repetition of the early experience.

People attempt to re-create the original conditions within the family through three major modes of defense: selection, distortion, and provocation. (a) They tend to choose and marry a person who is similar to a parent or family member because their own defenses are compatible with this type of personality. (b) Their perceptions of new objects are distorted in a direction that corresponds more closely to the members of the original family. (c) If these maneuvers fail to protect them, they tend to behave in ways to *provoke* familiar reactions in their loved ones.

Cases where one or both partners behave in a manner that is inflaming can lead to strong aggressive reactions toward oneself as well as one's partner. This phenomenon is an important dynamic in domestic abuse. One patient, Phil, a truck driver for a large beer distribution company, was married to an extraordinarily provoking woman. He was constantly annoyed by his wife, who was withholding and accusatory and played the victim. Her behavior aroused strong hostile feelings in this otherwise mild-mannered man. When he evinced signs of anger, she whimpered and cowered as though he were going to hit her. Her victimized posture and tearful accusations that he was a terrible person for expressing even mild annoyance with her further enraged him and validated his own view of himself as harsh and mean. Each time, he would resolve not to be drawn into an altercation with her, yet within minutes of their being together, she would succeed in antagonizing him. Her manipulative behavior finally caused Phil to feel murderous rage toward her and actually triggered an urge to hit her. Although he resisted this impulse, he nonetheless experienced tremendous guilt.

As a result of these types of interactions, Phil thought he was a terrible person and felt increasingly demoralized. He revealed that for the first time in his life, he had thoughts about killing himself. Simply experiencing the violent impulses toward his wife was enough to seriously compromise his adjustment. Phil's progressive deterioration and the compulsive patterns of incitement in this couple demonstrate a suicidal and potentially homicidal process that pervades many couple relationships.

Using selection, distortion, and provocation and a wide range of other manipulations, people are able to externalize the fantasy bond, thereby re-creating negative aspects of the family with new attachments. The process of forming these new connections effectively undermines real relationships and damages the individuals involved. The fantasy bond is an addictive attachment, similar to other addictions, and is part of an inward process. This style of relating cuts off genuine feeling and functions to deaden each partner. When either partner moves away from the fantasy bond toward independence or autonomy, symptoms similar to those manifested in withdrawal from chemical dependency are aroused in the other. These symptoms include feelings of emotional hunger, disorientation, debilitating anxiety states, depression, and intensified voice attacks.

The fantasy bond as manifested within the couple represents the externalization of the self-parenting process onto one's partner. For example, a man or woman may alternately act out either the nurturing, punitive parent or the helpless, needy child. People misinterpret emotional hunger as love and act out the dependency that is predisposed by their feelings of emptiness. Their desperation to hold on to the fantasy of love is based on their fear of rejection or object loss. They are not only apprehensive about losing the love object but fear that the rejection will support the internal voice process and self-destructive impulses. Individuals in a fantasy bond tend to project their voices onto each other or induce their mates to verbally attack them. Once close and loving, they later become intimate enemies.

Early Symptoms

The condition of feeling or being in love is volatile and unstable at the inception of a new love relationship. Fear of loss or abandonment, a dread of being rejected, together with the poignancy and sadness evoked by positive emotions, frequently become intolerable, particularly for those individuals who have suffered from a lack of love and affectionate contact in their early lives. Because they are afraid of feeling vulnerable, most men and women retreat from being close and gradually, albeit imperceptibly, give up the most valued aspects of their relationships.

As a couple's relationship unfolds, symptoms of the fantasy bond become more apparent. Couples who at the beginning spent hours in conversation start to lose interest in both talking and listening. Spontaneity and playfulness gradually wane, and their sex life frequently becomes routine or mechanical. As the partners begin to withhold the desirable qualities in themselves that attracted the other, they tend to experience feelings of guilt and remorse. Consequently, both begin to act out of a sense of obligation and responsibility instead of a genuine desire to be together.

Another symptom of deterioration is a lack of direct eye contact. People who once gazed lovingly at each other now avert their glance. This symptom of diminished relating is indicative of an increasingly impersonal mode of interaction. The style of communication becomes dishonest and misleading. Couples make small talk, speak for the other, bicker, interrupt, and come to talk as a unit, referring to themselves as "we" instead of "I." They manipulate each other, make their mate feel guilty, and often provoke angry or parental responses. They are critical when their spouses fail to live up to their expectations.

When I have seen troubled couples for conjoint therapy sessions, each is hypercritical of the other's traits, assigns blame to his or her mate for deficiencies in the relationship, and manifests considerable hostility. Yet in spite of their stated attacks, on another level, they attempt to maintain an idealized image of the partner.

In a typical interaction, the husband complains about his wife's withholding, dependency, and childishness, while the wife in turn attacks her husband's coldness and uncommunicativeness. Each enumerates the other's nasty behaviors, unpleasant habits, and various other shortcomings. It is apparent that they are accurate in their descriptions of each other's behavior. They *do* really know each other. However, when asked why they stay together, the usual response is "because we really love each other." It is difficult to believe this pronouncement of love once habitually destructive patterns are established.

Although there is a reduction in real affect or feeling in a fantasy bond, dramatic emotional reactions to imagined losses or threats to the bond are common. This emotionality and desperation are often mistaken for real caring about the relationship. As the process of deterioration continues, the couple's emotional responses to one another become progressively less appropriate to the real situation and contain elements and distortions based on the frustrations and pains of their respective childhoods. Now each individual implements the other's neurosis and strives to preserve the fantasized connection.

It is commonly thought that marital relationships deteriorate because of the familiarity and routine of married life—"familiarity breeds contempt." The real source of the problem is the fact that both partners have personal defense systems that act against intimacy. As the relationship becomes more problematic, they attempt to deny the alienation and form a fantasy bond as a security mechanism. Yet the formation of this connection in fantasy militates against preserving the excitement and vitality that characterized the early phases of the relationship.

A Couple

When Paul and Miranda met, they were very attracted to each other. Paul was divorced and had been living on his own for 2 years. In his marriage and in previous relationships, he had always sought definition from a woman. Since his divorce, he had developed a sense of identity and a feeling for his independence.

Miranda had recently left her native country to travel in the United States. She had had a pattern of promiscuity and a series of casual relationships with immature men. Both Paul and Miranda felt different in this relationship than they ever had before. He felt confident and strong, and she felt equal and adult. They were each interested in the other and felt respect for one another. In trusting Paul, Miranda was able to overcome sexual limitations and develop feeling for herself as a woman.

Early in the relationship, there were incidents in which Miranda tried to manipulate Paul and exert control over him as she had in other relationships. She was especially jealous and possessive and would fly into rages whenever Paul acted independently of her. At first, Paul refused to submit and the relationship continued to be equal and respectful, but as Miranda became more important to him, he became afraid of losing her and gradually gave in to her manipulations. The more Paul yielded to Miranda's control, the weaker and more desperate he felt. Miranda was consequently less attracted to Paul and in general felt childish and depressed. Her outbursts were always followed by remorse and resolutions to be different but, inevitably, she could not resist acting out her explosive anger. In therapy, she realized that this acting out was a replication of her mother's behavior.

> *Miranda:* After my mother got divorced and was with her boyfriend, the way she acted was so victimized, angry, and childish about him doing other things with his kids or with his friends or anything that didn't include her. I was sick of it by the time I left home. But it's interesting to me that now I sometimes act that way. I actually picture myself looking just like how I saw my mother. It's almost like I was trained to be that way, because I knew nothing better. And now when that happens, I feel terrible and I can't stand to be like her.
>
> Right now in my relationship with Paul, I'm struggling to change the way I see him, which is exactly the way my mother sees men. She thinks things like "a man doesn't care, they have better things to do than be tender, loving, and sweet to a woman. They don't see what a woman's talking about. If a woman feels bad, they don't care about that at all. Basically they're assholes." That's definitely my mother's viewpoint, and when I'm not myself, it's unfortunately mine.

In spite of Miranda's insights, the abusive incidents continued; Paul grew more alienated and finally revealed that he no longer felt close to Miranda. Nevertheless, Miranda tenaciously maintained her illusion of having a perfect love.

This is a sad, yet unfortunately not unusual, story about what happens in a relationship. Originally these two people were ideally suited for each other. There was nothing essentially wrong with the relationship, except for the defensive attitudes and weaknesses that existed within each individual. In our study of couple relationships, my associates and I found that the lifestyle of each partner directly followed his or her specific voice attacks or parental prescriptions, as was evident in Miranda's case. Other clinicians have noted similar phenomena in their work (Kaplan, 1979).

Form Versus Substance in Marital Bonds

When people form destructive ties, they are unable to accept the reality of their diminished feeling and increased emotional distance from their loved ones. They feel deeply ashamed of no longer feeling as attracted or interested in one another as they were during the early phases of the relationship. Unable to live with the truth, they attempt to cover up their lack of feeling with a fantasy of enduring love. They begin to substitute *form,* routine, role-determined behavior, and conventional machinations of "togetherness" for the real *substance* of the relationship and are cut off from feeling genuine love, respect, and affection.

Once a fantasy bond has been formed, any change in either of the individuals disturbs the equilibrium within the couple. Members of a couple tend to hold each other back, stifling the other's independence and development. It would be ideal if people evolved at similar rates, but, unfortunately, they do not. Any attempt on the part of one partner to disrupt this pattern can lead to tremendous guilt and pain. The loss of this fantasized connection figures more significantly in depressive reactions than does the loss of the real relationship (real object loss).

Patterns of Collusion Within the Fantasy Bond

Couple relationships can be as detrimental as any other addiction to an individual's mental health. When one partner assumes the "progressive" position and attempts to take care of, "feed," or sustain the life of the regressive partner, there is a decline in the overall quality of relating and deterioration in the partners. Both partners tend to play a part in maintaining the collusive pattern of parental caretaker and dependent child.

When Russ and Eileen first met, they immediately liked each other and their relationship quickly developed. Russ became disturbed that Eileen had other friendships with men and grew insecure. In an attempt to assure himself of fidelity, he asked her to marry him. After the wedding, Russ assumed the role of parent and Eileen became less independent and more immature in her responses. She gave up her job, made monetary demands on Russ, and put on a great deal of weight. As she regressed, Russ lectured her about spending money and complained about her weight gain. Meanwhile, he took care of her completely, even paying her tuition at an expensive private college. After 2 years of marriage, Eileen felt increasingly criticized and unhappy. To reassure herself that she was still appealing to men, she entered into a relationship with a professor at her college. When Russ became suspicious of Eileen's unexplained absences from home, he confronted her and flew into a jealous rage when she admitted to the affair. Some months later, when the couple separated, Eileen became agitated and depressed and eventually made a serious suicide attempt.

Some fantasy bonds take a sadomasochistic form in which there is a pattern of mistreatment that gratifies both the victim and the perpetrator. One case, taken from a short story in my collection of actual therapy cases, involved a man whose relationship with his wife potentially could have resulted in a homicide or a double tragedy involving homicide and suicide.

The patient, a 31-year-old man named Arnold Rocco, was built like a middleweight prizefighter. When he came for therapy, I couldn't exactly figure out his motives for seeking psychological help. He was of a savage disposition and lived his life on the edge of an explosive reaction. The patient was a self-made businessman whose success in the tire business was based on an aggressive attempt to compensate for deep-seated feelings of inferiority. Mr. Rocco (I'll call him Arnold) acted tough and superior and was suspicious, distrustful, and mean. It was hard to find anything likable about this man and virtually impossible to feel sympathy for him. His angry eyes, seething manner, and hostile body language aroused fear in me, and my fear caused me to dislike him.

The patient had married his high school sweetheart, a pretty blond girl, when they were both 18. The couple had two children, a 12-year-old boy and a girl of 11. It was an unhappy family, completely dominated by this insensitive, tyrannical individual.

In the second session, Arnold confessed that he was seriously considering murdering his wife. He had avidly followed a murder trial in which a prominent individual had devised a clever scheme to rid himself of his mate, and ever since Arnold had been obsessed and morbidly preoccupied with working out the details of a similar crime. While he lay on the couch talking about his hatred of his wife, his muscles would flex and he would practically convulse with rage. He looked particularly menacing at those times, as if he might flail out crazily and act out violence on me. At other times, he appeared quite cool and would meticulously work out nefarious schemes to do away with his spouse without getting caught. He was resistant to exploring his motives for wanting to kill her and preferred discussing his plans with me. He took pleasure in the idea of outwitting the law enforcement officers who he imagined would eventually try to solve the mystery of his wife's demise.

The patient's disclosure placed me in a dilemma. According to the code of our profession, a psychotherapist has a duty to society and must warn any possible victim of a patient's violent intent if the psychotherapist considers the patient to be dangerous. However, if I notified his wife, she would probably do something that was likely to trigger her husband's rage. She would probably push him over the edge to action. If I informed the police, he would deny everything and their hands would be tied. There was no real way that they could help, and my patient would be outraged at me and break off therapy, which would leave no possibility of his getting help. My instincts told me that I could get him through without a violent outcome, but I stood on shaky ground. If I had been wrong, I don't know how I would have dealt with my own emotions, much less the possible negative consequences for my professional life.

Arnold warned me that he might have to kill me because I knew too much about his wife's possible murder. I told him, tongue in cheek, that I had discussed his case with all of my associates and he would have to kill them too. He smiled.

The patient also told me that he enjoyed hurting people. One day he talked about holding his kids' heads underwater in his pool until they thought they were going to drown. Only when they writhed around in a last desperate struggle against suffocation and impending death did he release them. I couldn't listen to this sadistic story without registering strong disapproval: "Look, Arnold, you're going to have to cut out this sadistic crap if you expect me to continue working with you."

He was angry and accused me of losing my therapeutic cool. He told me that he expected me to be objective and analytical, and criticized me for my unprofessional outburst. I told him, "I don't give a shit what you think of me, I won't accept this type of behavior."

The incident passed, but I had made a major statement about limits and he had, on some level, implicitly agreed to play by my rules. I felt that he was starting to like me. That was the beginning of genuine therapeutic progress. The strength of our relationship acted to support his weakened ego, thereby averting destructive action. The subsequent control permitted us to get at his underlying depression and work on the basic conflict. We were able to trace the roots of his hatred to the frustration he experienced as a young child with a cruel, emotionally frozen mother and weak father who refused to defend him from her insults or protect him from her wrath.

There is one twist to the story that reveals a powerful truth about human nature and the collusion between members of a couple. Arnold's wife had stuck it out for many years, accepting his abuses. When asked about why she put up with the mistreatment, she would cling to him in desperation and proclaim a strong and everlasting love for him. Yet when Arnold developed in therapy, improved in his treatment of the family, and showed feeling for her, she left him.

Problems With Intimacy and Genuine Love

Most people find it difficult to accept love and to maintain an intimate relationship. Once a fantasy bond is formed, an individual comes to prefer fantasy gratification to real satisfaction and love from others. Anything that arouses an awareness of separateness or a nonbonded existence is anxiety provoking and often leads to hostility. There is often animosity toward the very people and circumstances that offer a person the most satisfaction. This anger is frequently experienced in the form of voice attacks against one's partner; at the same time, hostility is often experienced against oneself.

Most men and women have discordant voices about themselves and the opposite sex that interfere with closeness and intimacy. These attitudes are made up of sexual stereotypes as well as negative parental prescriptions about how to respond in a relationship: "Don't let your feelings show. Don't let her know that you really care. Play it cool." "Why get so involved? You'll only be rejected in the end." "Don't get too happy from being with him, or you'll really be disappointed." Or "Don't disagree with her. Don't cross her or she will be angry and get rid of you." "You've got to build up a man, make him think he's really important." "You've got to put up with a lot to stay involved with a woman, so just be patient. Don't be mean like those other men."

Paradoxically, at times, a satisfying sexual relationship can be a major disruption to the fantasy bond, or the illusion of being connected. The sex act itself is a real, but temporary, physical connection followed by a real separation. Similarly, affection is intimate contact with subsequent separation. Real communication involves a sharing of thoughts and feelings followed by a distinct awareness of boundaries. In a fantasy bond, all of the above situations are avoided; the moving in and out of contact, which is a natural condition of a close relationship between two people, is intolerable to those who have come to depend upon repetitive, habitual contact to avoid feeling. Many couples shy away from interpersonal communication because expressing their views implies that each of them is an independent entity. This awareness stimulates the fear of separateness and aloneness.

Genuine love and intimacy challenge the fantasy bond of connection and arouse an acute awareness of mortality. People avoid intimacy and closeness because of their fear of potential rejection or object loss. The fear of object loss becomes emotionally equated with loss of self. I have concluded that most people avoid mature sexuality, physical intimacy, and honest communication because they are reluctant to face the fact that each of these transactions has an ending and necessitates a letting go. Each small ending can remind them that everything eventually ends, in death—the ultimate separation.

To preserve a loving, intimate relationship, individuals must be willing to face the threats to the defense system that positive treatment evokes. To be able to accept genuine affection and love, they must be willing to challenge their negative voices, alter the image of themselves formed in the family, and give up long-established defenses that they often feel too threatened to relinquish. In addition, they must face the fact that someone sees them as unique and desirable, an awareness that connects them to feelings about their personal worth. The process of valuing oneself and one's experience increases existential concerns and arouses a poignant, painful feeling about the fragility and preciousness of life itself.

Family Bonds

The emotional climate into which a child is born is largely determined by the nature of the parents' relationship. By the time the child is born, the fantasy bond in the couple is generally already well established. The paradox of the family in conventional society is that it serves the function of nurturing and protecting the physical lives of its members while at the same time distorting their sense of reality and stifling all but social role-determined feelings. When parents are defended, they necessarily, albeit unconsciously, suppress the aliveness and spontaneity of their offspring to protect themselves from unwanted stimulation of repressed feelings.

Although close family interactions could well serve to encourage family members to grow psychologically and develop their individuality, generally this is not the case. To the degree that parents are defended, children incorporate their parents' illusions and neurotic behavior patterns. Through the process of imitation, they learn to adopt defenses that isolate one person from the other and to cover up any indication that family members are not close. They learn to distort their real perceptions and deny the reality that their parents are defended.

Murray Bowen (1978) has discussed "undifferentiated" parents as individuals who have grown up "as dependent appendages of their parents, following which they seek other equally dependent relationships" (p. 400). He contended that the child born to their union is also expected to meet his or her parents' emotional needs. In the resulting dysfunctional family, the child is excluded from his or her parents' bond with each other or, at other times, is himself merged with one or the other parent.

Restrictions on Communication
in the Family Bond

Because of the dishonesty and pretense involved in maintaining the fantasy bond, interpersonal communication within a couple and in most families is customarily duplicitous and manipulative. Freedom of speech is curtailed, as certain topics are forbidden. In general, any communication that threatens to disrupt the fantasy bond or interrupt the illusion of enduring love between family members is not permitted. Any suggestion that a parent might be inadequate or weak, any hint that maternal love is not an inherent feminine quality, any indication that a husband is not preferred at all times by his wife, any sign of unfaithfulness or sexual infidelity in either partner threatens the imagined connection.

Realistic perceptions of children frequently are also taboo. Adults continually view children as angels and innocent long after the youngsters have developed undesirable and offensive character traits. Adults also fail to realize that children are capable and far less helpless and incompetent than they may act. Having a more accurate view of children, that is, seeing their positive and negative qualities rather than a fantasized family picture, would tend to disrupt the parent's sense of having proprietary rights over them. Similarly, any notion that one's family is not superior to those of one's friends and neighbors is not tolerated because it would destroy the image of the family as special, that is, the superior attitude that "we eat the right food, wear the right clothes, drive the right car, or raise our children the right way."

Within many families, children are afraid to speak their minds out of fear of retaliation, fear of causing pain and regression in their parents, or fear of loss of the parents' love. As in couple relationships, real communication between family members involves an intimate sharing of thoughts and feelings that makes one aware of one's separateness and the distinct boundaries of the other person.

When communication is limited or restricted, the resulting hostility and resentment create a toxic environment for the developing child. However, the child must not show his or her pain or unhappiness, because this would betray the destructiveness of the family and break the fantasy bond. Perceptions and feeling responses that would disrupt the illusion of closeness are suppressed, which increases the child's tendency toward inwardness and cynicism. Studies have shown that being forced to go inward with one's perceptions in a defended family structure is a primary causative factor in psychological disturbances. The greater the discrepancy between what is communicated and what is acted upon, the greater the potential for mental illness (Bateson, Jackson, Haley, & Weakland, 1956/1972; Laing & Esterson, 1964/1970; Satir, 1972, 1983; Watzlawick, Bavelas, & Jackson, 1967; Weakland, 1974/1977; Wynne, Ryckoff, Day, & Hirsch, 1958).

Restrictions on communication are fairly common in family constellations. For example, Beavers (1977) reported findings from a large sampling of families that were studied in relation to their styles of communication and "encouragement of autonomy." He stated,

> Severely dysfunctional families invade and attempt to distort individual reality. Midrange families believe in external absolutes and attempt to control by intimidation and coercion. Only the optimal families showed any areas free from efforts at thought control. (p. 147)

Beavers defined the midrange family as approaching the norm. He wrote, "A third definition of normality is statistical: It is the average. With this orientation, midrange families would probably be closer to the normal than . . . [healthy families]" (p. 124)(Endnote 2).

Thus, in many so-called normal families, it appears that children frequently receive conflicting messages. Similarly, restrictions of free speech in these families can lead an individual to be distrustful and defended in his or her adult relationships, which, in turn, sets the pattern for the new family.

One of the most discouraging patterns in family life occurs when parents act out abuses on their children. Parents who have suffered abuse and deprivation in their own childhoods cannot help but pass on this damage to their offspring, despite their best intentions and efforts to love and nurture them. In attempting to preserve an idealized image of their own parents and maintain the self-parenting process, they are compelled to mistreat their children in much the same way they were mistreated. As noted in Chapter 7, when parents do act out these abuses, they experience extreme guilt as well as feelings of demoralization, depression, and hopelessness.

Friendship and Love Relationships

In contrast to the fantasy bond, real friendship and loving relationships are characterized by freedom and genuine relating. In a friendship, a person acts out of choice, whereas in a fantasy bond, he or she acts out of obligation. Therefore, friendship has therapeutic value, whereas the types of bonds described here are antitherapeutic in nature. People cannot be coerced into feeling the right or correct emotion, and when they attempt to make their emotions conform to a standard, their affect becomes shallow and inappropriate and they lose vitality.

Men and women can remain close friends if manifestations of the fantasy bond are understood and relinquished. Healthy relationships are characterized by each partner's independent striving for personal development and self-realization. In a loving relationship, open expression of physical and verbal affection are evident. Acting out of choice leads to a feeling of joy and happiness while diminishing one's self-hatred. Hostility and anger are not acted out but disclosed in the couple's ongoing dialogue. Negative perceptions, disappointments, and hurt feelings can be dealt with, without holding grudges. In the type of relationship that is growth enhancing, partners refrain from exerting proprietary rights over one another. Each is respectful of the other's boundaries, separate point of view, goals, and aspirations.

The fact that many people prefer to pursue relationships in fantasy and reject genuine friendship and actual love accounts for a great deal of their seemingly perverse or irrational behavior. An individual's fantasy source of gratification is threatened by genuinely satisfying experiences. For this reason, people's actions are often directly contrary to their own best interests. Understanding the dynamics of the fantasy bond helps explain self-limiting and self-destructive behavior that interrupts the flow of goal-directed activity.

Therapeutic Approaches

A major problem with many psychotherapies is that both the therapist and the patient refuse to challenge the core defense—the fantasy bond. Intense reactions and strong resistance are inevitable when separating from illusory connections with one's family or mate. For this reason, the therapist is often afraid of retaliation from family members. Further, therapists may conform to standard beliefs about the sanctity of the family as protection against seeing the destructive processes within their own families.

Once a fantasy bond is formed, many patients erroneously equate breaking the bond with terminating the relationship itself. In actuality, exposing destructive ties opens up the possibility of a renewed and better relationship. In this context, it is important for patients to recognize that, for the most part, divorce or rejection of the other may represent a step backward into an inward, unfeeling, or self-denying life. Despite the many rationalizations offered for breaking up or leaving a long-standing relationship, in the majority of situations, patients are preserving their defensive structure rather than moving toward a positive life choice.

Unless manifestations of the fantasy bond are identified and consistently challenged, there will be no sustained therapeutic progress. Therefore, in an effective psychotherapy, destructive bonds are exposed and understood in the context of an individual's fears and anxieties. This approach assists the couple in relating to each other on a more positive basis and frees them to experience genuine loving feelings.

Conclusion

Human beings desire freedom and individuality, but paradoxically they fight stubbornly against change and progress. Ernest Becker (1964) attempted an explanation for this dilemma:

> It is barely imaginable that one should struggle so hard, except against the relinquishment of real basic inner drives, of irrevocable natural urges [instincts]. . . . But this is to fail to understand human action: the patient is not struggling against himself, against forces within his animal nature. He is struggling rather against the loss of his world, of the whole range of action and objects that he so laboriously and painfully fashioned during his early training. (p. 170)

I suggest that the concept of the fantasy bond—the illusion of connection to the mother or primary caretaker—and all the subsequent actions, thought processes, and involvement with others in addictive attachments are a dynamic formulation of the primitive defensive inner world that Becker wrote about. Anxiety arises whenever this inner world is intruded upon, whenever the fantasy bond is threatened. Anxiety is also aroused whenever there is an awareness of one's separateness and mortality, whenever the fantasy bond is broken. The patient's resistance functions to protect him or her from experiencing anxiety states that arise from threats to the defensive solution, that is, the person's unique resolution of the conflict between dependency on inner fantasy for gratification versus his or her desire for real gratification in the interpersonal environment.

As humans, we are torn between pursuing an assertive goal-directed, independent life and fused relationships characterized by passivity and dependence. How we resolve this basic conflict determines whether we have a free-flowing, changing existence or a static, rigid, defensive posture that can, under certain circumstances, lead to self-destructive or even suicidal behavior.

Endnotes

1. Included in the body of work on adult attachment styles are articles by Bartholomew (1990), Brennan and Shaver (1993), Feeney and Noller (1990), and Rothbard and Shaver (1994), among others.

2. "Srole [Srole, Langner, Michael, & Opler, 1962] and his coworkers suggested that there are more individuals who are emotionally disturbed than are asymptomatic: If this be so, then this midrange group is probably larger than any other group, including healthy families, no matter how generously defined" (Beavers, 1977, p. 83).

PART IV

ASSESSMENT

AND TREATMENT

13 Identification of the Suicidal Individual

The Development of the Firestone Assessment of Self-Destructive Thoughts

> Suicide does not always occur on a given occasion, with explosive suddenness; often it also appears as the result of chronic melancholic depression, during the course of which *suicidal ideas force themselves again and again upon the person's mind* [italics added].
>
> David Ernst Oppenheim, Vienna Psychoanalytic Society,
> April 1910 (cited by Nunberg & Federn, 1967, p. 485)

It is difficult to reduce the complex results of an empirical study to their essentials; however, in this chapter I will attempt to elucidate the history of the development of the Firestone Assessment of Self-Destructive Thoughts (FAST) (Firestone & Firestone, 1996) and report interesting findings obtained in the course of testing the instrument with outpatient and inpatient samples.

Background of the Study

Part of the inspiration for developing the scale originated in a suggestion by Dr. C. Everett Koop, who was U.S. surgeon general at the time. Frank Tobe, a political consultant and close friend of mine, was on an airplane flying to a

AUTHOR'S NOTE: Portions of this chapter are taken from *The Firestone Voice Scale for Self-Destructive Behavior: Investigating the Scale's Validity and Reliability,* Doctoral dissertation, California School of Professional Psychology (Lisa Firestone, 1991); and from the *Firestone Assessment of Self-Destructive Thoughts* manual by R. W. Firestone and Lisa Firestone, copyright © 1996 The Psychological Corporation. Used with permission. All rights reserved.

business conference in Washington, D.C. He found himself sitting beside Surgeon General Koop and began talking about my ideas in relation to suicide. Koop responded with interest but emphasized the importance of rigorous scientific research to bear on the subject.

When Frank told me about his encounter, I immediately decided to pursue a research methodology based on Voice Therapy theory. I had two motives. First, I felt that a voice scale to determine self-destructive and suicide potential could save lives, and, second, I thought that a scientific study using this type of scale would offer empirical validation to the underlying theory. My assumption was that a scale of negative voice attacks on the self would parallel destructive acting-out behavior, and that if a person scored very high on these items, he or she would be more likely to injure him- or herself. My associates and I began to gather items for the new scale from the negative self-attacks of colleagues and patients (Endnote 1).

Description of the Scale

Most individuals who seek psychological services experience self-defeating and self-destructive thought processes that can be conceptualized as an internal dialogue or "voice." The FAST is based on Voice Therapy theory, a comprehensive approach to psychopathology and corresponding model of mental health. The instrument was derived from 20 years of clinical research into self-attacking attitudes or introjects that restrict or impair an individual's psychological development. I believed that it was logical to use these negative thought patterns to predict increasingly aggressive cognition and affect toward the self that are closely related to self-destructive behavior and actual suicide (Firestone, 1986, 1988).

The FAST is a self-report questionnaire consisting of 84 items drawn from 11 levels of progressively self-destructive thoughts. Clients endorse the items on a 5-point, Likert-type scale from "Never" to "Most of the time." The scale includes items drawn from each level of the "Continuum of Negative Thought Patterns" (see Figure 13.1). The scale is used to assess a patient's suicide potential and to identify the aspects of self-destructive behavior and psychological functioning in which the patient has experienced the greatest degree of difficulty.

The Need for a Reliable Instrument
to Assess Suicide Risk

The suicidologist Ronald Bonner (1990) wrote that suicide is one of the ultimate tragedies faced by the mental health treatment community. The risk

Levels of Increasing Suicidal Intention	Content of Voice Statements
Thoughts that lead to low self-esteem or inwardness (self-defeating thoughts):	
1. Self-depreciating thoughts of everyday life	*You're incompetent, stupid. You're not very attractive. You're going to make a fool of yourself.*
2. Thoughts rationalizing self-denial; thoughts discouraging the person from engaging in pleasurable activities	*You're too young (old) and inexperienced to apply for this job. You're too shy to make any new friends,* or *Why go on this trip? It'll be such a hassle. You'll save money by staying home.*
3. Cynical attitudes toward others, leading to alienation and distancing	*Why go out with her (him)? She's cold, unreliable; she'll reject you. She wouldn't go out with you anyway. You can't trust men (women).*
4. Thoughts influencing isolation; rationalizations for time alone, but using time to become more negative toward oneself	*Just be by yourself. You're miserable company anyway; who'd want to be with you? Just stay in the background, out of view.*
5. Self-contempt; vicious self-abusive thoughts and accusations (accompanied by intense angry affect)	*You idiot! You bitch! You creep! You stupid shit! You don't deserve anything; you're worthless.*
Thoughts that support the cycle of addiction (addictions):	
6. Thoughts urging use of substances or food followed by self-criticisms (weakens inhibitions against self-destructive actions, while increasing guilt and self-recrimination following acting out)	*It's okay to do drugs, you'll be more relaxed. Go ahead and have a drink, you deserve it. (Later) You weak-willed jerk! You're nothing but a drugged-out drunken freak.*
Thoughts that lead to suicide (self-annihilating thoughts):	
7. Thoughts contributing to a sense of hopelessness, urging withdrawal or removal of oneself completely from the lives of people closest	*See how bad you make your family (friends) feel. They'd be better off without you. It's the only decent thing to do–just stay away and stop bothering them.*
8. Thoughts influencing a person to give up priorities and favored activities (points of identity)	*What's the use? Your work doesn't matter anymore. Why bother even trying? Nothing matters anyway.*
9. Injunctions to inflict self-harm at an action level; intense rage against self	*Why don't you just drive across the center divider? Just shove your hand under that power saw!*
10 Thoughts planning details of suicide (calm, rational, often obsessive, indicating complete loss of feeling for the self)	*You have to get hold of some pills, then go to a hotel, etc.*
11. Injunctions to carry out suicide plans; thoughts baiting the person to commit suicide (extreme thought constriction)	*You've thought about this long enough. Just get it over with. It's the only way out!*

Any combination of the voice attacks listed above can lead to serious suicidal intent. Thoughts leading to isolation, ideation about removing oneself from people's lives, beliefs that one is a bad influence or has a destructive effect on others, voices urging one to give up special activities, vicious self-abusive thoughts accompanied by strong anger, voices urging self-injury and a suicide attempt are all indications of high suicide potential or risk.

Figure 13.1 Continuum of Negative Thought Patterns

of suicide, including attempts and completions, is high among mental health clients already in treatment. According to Maltsberger and Buie (1989), therapists tend to rely almost exclusively on their intuitive sense to determine the dangerousness of suicidal crisis. Most clinicians have rarely experienced in their personal lives the profound sense of loneliness, devastating shame, unworthiness, and vicious self-recriminations that suicidal individuals feel. This lack of direct personal experience in some cases leads to defensive denial and faulty judgment. Slaby (1994) has asserted that "although a number of scales have been devised to predict suicide, their value has been limited" (p. 417). Therefore, clinicians need an easy-to-administer and thorough clinical assessment strategy for evaluating suicidal risk as well as a conceptual model for understanding the self-destructive individual.

Scale Construction

The items for the FAST were derived from the actual statements of clinical outpatients and normal (nonclinical) individuals. Patients and participants in clinical research into the voice process verbalized their self-attacks in the second person format as though they were being addressed by another person. For example, "*You're* worthless." "Who could love *you*?" "*You* don't deserve to live." Both research subjects and patients closely identify with this format. The most actively suicidal thoughts were gathered from individuals who had made serious suicide attempts or were currently suicidal (Endnote 2).

The initial version of the scale consisted of 10 items from each of the 11 levels on the "Continuum of Negative Thought Patterns." The continuum depicts levels of increasing self-destructiveness. It delineates specific negative thoughts, attitudes, and beliefs typically reported by nonclinical individuals and a broad spectrum of clinical patients, including substance abusers, self-mutilators, suicide ideators, and suicide attempters. The FAST was constructed to assess the full continuum of self-destructive thoughts, from self-depreciating thoughts of everyday life (Level 1) to the more severe, self-annihilating thoughts that culminate in injunctions to carry out a suicidal plan (Level 11).

The scale incorporates a unique approach: Instead of the client being asked to report symptoms, the client is asked to endorse how frequently he or she is experiencing various negative thoughts directed toward him- or herself. In other words, clients are not asked about beliefs or symptoms they may be experiencing; rather, they are asked to estimate the frequency and severity of their self-critical (self-depreciating) thoughts in the Voice Therapy second person format. When items are presented in this format, they bring to light elements of a self-destructive process that may have been partially or completely unconscious.

Theoretical Basis of the Study

As noted, the FAST is based on Voice Therapy theory (Firestone, 1988, 1990c), and items on the FAST were gathered during clinical investigations into negative thought processes or voices. On a clinical level, I observed that the extent to which individuals acted according to these voices (their early programming) determined the degree to which they behaved in ways that were antagonistic to their major goals and priorities. My associates and I noted that the voice process was particularly significant in relation to all varieties of self-destructive behavior. Therefore, we thought that it was reasonable to use these negative thought patterns to construct a scale to predict self-destructive behavior and actual suicide by identifying the associated aggressive cognition and affect toward self.

I postulated four hypotheses regarding the relationship between the voice process and self-destructive behavior and suicide: (a) A conflict exists within each individual between life-affirming propensities to actively pursue goals in the real world, and self-denying, self-protective, and self-destructive tendencies that are related to seeking gratification primarily through fantasy processes; (b) thoughts antithetical to the self vary along a continuum of intensity from mild self-reproach to strong self-attack and actual suicidal thoughts; (c) self-destructive behavior exists on a continuum from self-denial and self-limitation to isolation, drug abuse, and other self-defeating behaviors, culminating in actual bodily harm; and (d) both processes, behavioral and cognitive, parallel each other, and suicide represents the acting out of the extreme end of the continuum.

The Initial Study

The "rational approach" (Jackson, 1970) to scale construction was adopted from the beginning of the development of the scale. Items were retained or deleted on the basis of their distributions and correlations with hypothesized constructs (Endnote 3). Initial research on the FAST focused on establishing the statistical significance of the original 220-item pool of self-report items. The original participants were 21 volunteers. Nine of these subjects had a previous history of serious suicide attempts, and the remainder engaged in less extreme forms of self-defeating and self-destructive behavior such as self-denial, isolation, substance abuse, and eating disorders.

The responses of individuals with a history of suicide attempts were compared with those of the control group (persons without a history of suicide attempts). The suicide attempters were asked to respond as though they were in the same frame of mind as when they made the suicide attempt. The rationale for this comparison was based on the fact that there is a relationship between a history of suicide attempts and actual suicide potential. Differences between groups were evaluated, and items found to significantly discriminate between attempters and nonattempters were retained.

Methodology

The purpose of the outpatient study was to investigate the reliability and validity of the FAST. To accomplish this, the FAST was administered to the very population it was designed to address—subjects with a large cross-section of psychological problems and self-destructive behavior. It was predicted that the scale would be able to discriminate between individuals with a past history of suicide and those without such a history, and therefore would be closely related to self-destructive behavior and actual suicide (Endnote 4). It was also hypothesized that the scale would identify where an individual falls on a continuum of self-destructive potential, because the items on the scale include the entire range of self-destructive thought patterns.

A total of 507 respondents who were currently in treatment (the majority in outpatient psychotherapy) were recruited for the first main study. The subjects were drawn from a variety of mental health settings to represent a range of disorders and self-destructive behavior patterns (see Research Note 1). All subjects were administered a testing packet consisting of a Subject Consent Form, a face sheet for socioeconomic information, and 10 instruments, including the FAST, presented in random order. The therapists of these subjects each filled out a therapist packet consisting of a Therapist Consent Form, a Therapist Information Form developed for this study, and, if the patient had made a previous suicide attempt, the Suicide Intent Scale (Beck, Schuyler, & Herman, 1974).

In addition to socioeconomic information, the face sheet asked for a mental health history on the subject's family of origin. Subjects were also asked to indicate whether they had engaged in self-harm or suicide attempts, or if anyone in their immediate families had demonstrated these behaviors (including completed suicide for family members). Subjects were asked to complete nine other self-report questionnaires, including the Beck Hopelessness Scale (Beck, 1978b) and the Suicide Probability Scale (Cull & Gill, 1988) (see Research Note 2). If the client had a past history of suicide attempts, he or she was asked to complete the Suicide Intent Scale in relation to the attempt or attempts. The subjects' therapists also completed a questionnaire, rating each client on the 11 levels of self-destructive behavior on the "Continuum of Negative Thought Patterns."

The subjects were administered the battery of tests in a private setting with the main researcher or a research assistant present. These researchers were available to answer questions and to communicate with subjects who might become disturbed by feelings aroused during the testing. As a precaution, if subjects appeared to be upset, the researcher notified the therapist to schedule an extra session for the subject shortly after testing. Following testing, the Beck Hopelessness Scale and the Suicide Probability Scale were scored immediately, and the therapist was informed within 24 hours if any of the scores was in a range of concern.

Results of Initial Study[1]

Validity. The sample consisted of 93 subjects who had made suicide attempts and 414 who had not. Of the 93 attempters, 76% were women and 24% men. The validity for the FAST was evaluated by comparing subjects' scores with their reports of previous suicide attempts. The FAST was found to have higher correlations with the prior suicide attempts than any of the other measures included in the study. A subsequent analysis revealed that the total score on the FAST added significantly to our ability to identify those individuals who made prior suicide attempts and who, by inference, represent a greater potential threat of actual suicide.

Other findings. An unexpected yet crucial finding of the research regards the subjects' reporting of past suicide attempts. Results indicated that of the 93 cases where subjects reported a history of suicide attempts, only 38 therapists were aware of this fact. In other words, for over half the subjects with this serious indication of future suicide potential, the therapist had apparently not asked this important question. Subjects were explicitly aware (having signed releases) that the testing information would be shared with

---

1. The most technical results are reserved for Research Notes 3 and 4 at the end of the chapter, and one can turn to that detailed analysis for further information.

their therapist, which implied that they were willing to tell the therapist about these prior suicide attempts.

Several interesting findings obtained in the course of the study are important to note here. One discovery was that respondents reported it was easy to identify with the negative thoughts as stated in the second person format on the FAST. A number of subjects disclosed that they felt they knew themselves better as a result of answering the questions. Statements such as "I see my pattern is to be inward and isolated," or "I did not realize I was talking to myself so much," frequently occurred. Therapists reported that in the weeks following testing, clients often expressed more emotions and brought up new material and topics not previously mentioned, including patterns of substance abuse and self-mutilation. Several revealed that while reading the items on the FAST, they had a feeling of being understood in a way they had not felt prior to the testing (Endnote 5).

Findings From Inpatient Study

In a second study, inpatients from selected groups representing various diagnostic categories were administered the FAST and six other instruments (Research Note 5). The study included 479 inpatients diagnosed with schizophrenia, depression, and bipolar disorder. The FAST distinguished suicide ideators from nonideators in each of the diagnostic categories. In comparing 296 depressed inpatients with 162 anxiety-disordered outpatients, suicide ideators diagnosed with depression received higher scores on the Beck Anxiety Inventory (an average of 27.8) than did suicide ideators diagnosed with anxiety disorders, who received an average score of 26.6 (Goldenberg, 1995). This finding points out the importance of assessing patients who are diagnosed with depression for elevated anxiety states. Patients manifesting this combination of depression and extreme perturbation are at high risk for suicide (Endnote 6).

Clinical Findings Supported
by Exploratory Factor Analysis

An exploratory factor analysis was conducted to investigate the structure of the FAST. Using data from the initial (outpatient) study, the analysis revealed three factors of increasing self-destructiveness: the "Self-Defeating Compos-ite," the "Addictions Composite," and the "Self-Annihilating Composite." The factor structure remained constant using data from the second (inpatient) study, which confirmed the three factor composites for the FAST.

The results from both factor analyses appeared to support our findings regarding the levels of increasing intensity of voice attacks experienced by subjects in my clinical studies. In laboratory procedures (Voice Therapy) during which subjects verbalized their self-critical thoughts, my associates and I were able to identify three levels of the voice in terms of intensity and content: (a) at the first level, we discovered that every individual was able to identify a self-critical thought process or internal dialogue; (b) when subjects verbalized their self-attacks in a dramatic or cathartic manner, they often launched into an angry diatribe against themselves that was shocking in its intensity; (c) on a deeper level, we observed an extraordinary rage toward the self expressed as actual suicidal impulses or commands to injure oneself (Firestone, 1986).

The three levels correspond to different aspects or functions of the voice that progressively influence maladaptive behaviors along the continuum of self-destructiveness. There are two essential modes of operation. The first refers to thought processes that lead to self-denial, that is, attitudes that are restrictive or limiting of life experience, while the second, self-attack, refers to self-destructive propensities and actions. Some overlap clearly exists between these two aspects of the voice; however, the self-denying, prohibitive quality appears to be based on the child's imitation of and adaptation to the parental defense system, while the self-attacking, malicious aspect of the thought process is more closely related to repressed or overt parental aggres-sion. The restrictive quality of the voice functions to limit one's experience and stifle one's enthusiasm, spontaneity, spirit, and sense of adventure. These self-attacks restrain or completely block an individual's wants and desires before they can be translated into action. Negative thoughts provide seem-ingly rational reasons for self-denial, isolation, and alienation from other people.

The malicious aspect of the inimical thought process issues directives to mutilate the self emotionally and/or physically (Firestone, 1988). These thought patterns are accompanied by intense anger and even rage against the self. As described earlier, when verbalized out loud in the second per-son, voices made up of vicious, degrading self-accusations and injunctions to injure oneself are intensely powerful and dramatic. It is important to emphasize that in almost every case, emotional catharsis appeared to decrease the need for action. Facing up to the enemy within acted to relieve the pressure, and individuals gained a measure of control over self-destructive impulses.

Empirical Findings Related to
Increasing Levels of Self-Destructiveness

As noted, results of the two exploratory factor analyses mentioned above revealed three factors of increasing self-destructiveness.

Composite Factor 1 was labeled the "Self-Defeating Composite" and consisted of self-critical thoughts (for example, "You're a misfit, a failure"); self-denial ("You're too old [young] to take on this project"); cynical or hostile attitudes toward others ("You can't trust anybody"); gradual withdrawal into isolation ("You should try to get away for a while; you need some time alone to think about things"); and self-contempt ("You worthless piece of shit! You bitch! You're disgusting!"). The level of intense anger toward self associated with the thoughts at this last level appears to be an important step in the progression toward overt self-destructive acts because it leads to considerable perturbation and psychological pain.

Composite Factor 2 was labeled the "Addictions Composite." These are the types of thoughts that support the cycle of addictions, for example, "You've worked hard all week; you deserve a break. Have a drink and relax." "Wouldn't it feel good to get high tonight?" Later, subjects attack themselves with voices that punish them for indulging: "You broke your promise. You got drunk again. You're just a drunken bum. You have no willpower."

Composite Factor 3 was labeled the "Self-Annihilating Composite." These are thoughts that represent the full spectrum of self-annihilation, ranging from psychological suicide to actual physical suicide: hopelessness, or urging the removal of oneself from significant others (for example, "Everybody would be better off if you weren't around"); thoughts associated with giving up one's priorities and favored activities ("Nothing matters to you anymore; you'd just as well give up"); self-mutilation ("Go ahead and burn yourself; you'll be relieved"); suicidal plans ("You should get a gun"); and actual physical suicide ("Go on and get it over with, you coward!").

The "hopelessness" level of Composite 3 includes thoughts that influence the individual to give up points of identity and his or her investment in life by indicating that "nothing matters." This type of thought process (the divestment of energy or decathexis) leads to alienation from the self and extinction of the personality (psychological suicide).

The Suicide Intent Composite of the FAST

The 27-item Suicide Intent Composite is the FAST's best estimator of suicide risk. This composite is composed of those items that were found to be the most significant in distinguishing suicide ideators from nonideators, regardless of their status as outpatients or inpatients. These items represent thoughts that contribute to a sense of hopelessness, helplessness, and despair (Research Note 6).

The Total Score Composite of the FAST

The Total Score Composite of the FAST provides an overall assessment of the client's level of psychological pain, that is, the intensity of negative thoughts the client is experiencing. It is this barrage of negative thoughts that creates perturbation, emotional distress, and agitation in the client. This information is of clinical significance because heightened levels of psychological pain and anxiety increase the probability that the client will act out in an attempt to dull or numb painful emotions. This acting out is often manifested in addictive habit patterns, self-limiting behaviors, and aggressive actions against the self. For the depressed client, suicide is perceived as a final refuge; therefore, the client obtaining a high total score is at risk for acting out self-destructive behaviors including suicidal actions.

Discussion

The results of this study provide strong support for the reliability and validity of the Firestone Assessment of Self-Destructive Thoughts (FAST). Most important, the subjects' scores on the FAST were significantly correlated with past suicide attempts. This correlation was significantly higher than with all other instruments. Results from validity studies support the notion that the levels of the FAST may be used to evaluate self-destructive behavior along a continuum of negative thought patterns.

The scale identifies the level at which the client is experiencing the highest frequency (intensity) of self-destructive thoughts. Using this information, clinicians can direct their interventions toward the area where clients are experiencing psychological pain, thereby potentially averting the acting out of the corresponding self-destructive behavior. In addition, scores on the

FAST identify less extreme types of self-destructive thoughts so that they can be addressed by the clinician before they lead to or precipitate a suicidal crisis.

In using Voice Therapy as a laboratory procedure in the earlier clinical studies, I noted that the method of expressing the voice dramatically was an important part of our approach. The process of verbalizing destructive thoughts and expressing the intense angry affect represents a more direct pathway to deeply repressed material in the subject's unconscious. This method elicited unconscious or partly conscious thoughts that were directly related to maladaptive behaviors. At that point, I anticipated that this method of uncovering voices had potential as an important research tool with which to study the unconscious cognitive processes involved in depression, self-destructive behavior, and suicide. This expectation appears to have been validated in that the empirical research described here demonstrated that items on the FAST discriminated between individuals with a history of suicide attempts and those with no history of attempts better than other instruments. As noted, these items were gathered directly from "voice" statements verbalized by subjects in the original clinical investigations. It can be hypothesized that the FAST measures an important variable in suicide that other instruments do not measure, that is, the internal cognitive processes mediating or controlling self-destructive and suicidal behavior.

Application of the Concept of the Voice to the Assessment of Violence Potential

As noted in Chapter 8, in some individuals the tendency to distort others or to view them with suspicion is more prominent than attitudes of inferiority or low self-esteem. These people display a basic paranoid or victimized orientation toward life. A paranoid orientation stems from the projection of one's voice attacks onto another person or persons as well as the attribution of one's own negative qualities to others in the interpersonal environment.

In clinical practice, many patients have histories of suicidal behaviors as well as violence toward others. Holinger, Offer, and Ostrov (1987) and Farberow (1980b) have observed that homicide can sometimes be categorized as "victim precipitated" or self-inflicted in that, on those occasions, victims may provoke their own deaths. van Praag, Plutchik, and Apter (1990) have also cited numerous studies that demonstrated a significant correlation between violence and suicide.

Recently, a pilot study was undertaken to develop a new instrument, the Firestone Voice Scale for Violence (FVSV) for assessing violence potential for both criminal and family violence. The development of the new instrument is based on the same theory of psychopathology as the FAST. My associates and I conjectured that as the use of voices proved valuable in predicting suicide, the same methodology would be effective in predicting violence because the voice process attacks the self and others (see Research Note 7). Results from this initial study indicated that the FVSV significantly discriminated between violent and nonviolent subjects in the sample population studied. A related purpose of the study was to investigate the hypothesized relationship between suicidality and violence. Therefore, subjects were also administered the 84-item final version of the FAST. Results showed that subjects' scores on the FAST correctly classified 83% of the suicide attempters.

Conclusion

The findings documented in this chapter suggest that the Firestone Assessment of Self-Destructive Thoughts (FAST) is a significant diagnostic tool that provides insight into destructive voices that negatively influence important areas of an individual's life. Results from investigating the reliability as well as construct and criterion validity of the FAST tend to validate the theoretical constructs and hypotheses on which the scale was constructed; that is, they support the hypothesis that an individual's "voices" are directly related to self-destructive behavior in general and suicide in particular. Studies have also shown that voices can be deduced from an individual's specific actions and lifestyle, thereby providing clinicians with a method for helping those clients who may not be able to readily identify their voice attacks.

Suicidal individuals have reached a level on the continuum where the hostile, alien point of view represented by the voice has become accepted as their own point of view. They have adopted the prohibitions, directions, and injunctions of the voice as their own and believe the negative, depreciating statements about themselves and others. A progressive loss of contact with the real self, combined with seemingly hopeless estrangement from others, leads to a further submission to the voice. Increasingly aligned with the voice, the suicidal person reacts as if he or she were the incorporated other. I agree with Rosenbaum and Richman's (1970) statement indicating that if that other person or the parent wished the patient to be dead, the patient may well oblige by committing suicide.

The value of the FAST lies in its ability to identify, to a significant degree, the point on the continuum where the client's thinking currently resides.

Subsequently, the additional knowledge gained through accessing and identifying the partially unconscious thought processes driving a suicidal individual toward death can well be used to set into motion potentially life-saving interventions.

Research Notes

1. Testing sites included local mental health clinics (18%), a day treatment program (5%), several drug rehabilitation programs (5%), and outpatient psychotherapy practices (72%). Out of the total subjects, 169 were male (33%) and 338 were female (67%). Although a concerted effort was made to include minority participants, only 4% of respondents were black, 4% Hispanic, and 2% Asian.

2. The battery of questionnaires for the first (outpatient) study included the Suicide Probability Scale (SPS) (Cull & Gill, 1988); the Reasons for Living Inventory (RFL) (Linehan et al., 1983); the Beck Hopelessness Scale (BHS) (Beck 1978b); a two-question subset of the Survey on Self-Harm (SSH) (Favazza & Eppright, 1986); the Eating Disorder Inventory (EDI) (Garner & Olmsted, 1984); the Inventory of Feelings, Problems, and Family Experiences (IFPFE) (Cook, 1986, which consisted of three tests: the Internalized Shame Scale, the Problem History Scale, and the Family of Origin Scale); the Monitoring the Future Substance Use Battery (MTF) (Bachman & Johnston, 1978); an 11-item Socially Desirable Response Set Measure (Hays, Hayashi, & Stewart, 1989); and the CES-D Depression Scale (Radloff, 1977).

3. *Reliability studies—internal consistency:* In the initial (outpatient) study, alpha coefficients ranged from 0.78 for Level 2 (self-denial) to 0.97 for Level 11 (injunctions to commit suicide). The estimated internal consistency of the total score was very high (alpha = 0.98).

4. *Hierarchial construct validity:* A Guttman Scalogram Analysis (the microcomputer program SCALO by Gilpin & Hays, 1990) was conducted to examine the hierarchy of the self-destructive levels represented on the FAST. The level prevalence observed varied somewhat from prediction, with Level 4 (isolation) receiving a higher level of prevalence than any other level. In addition, Level 6 (addictions) and Level 10 (suicide plans) each had slightly lower levels of prevalence than predicted. However, the coefficient of reproducibility (CR) was 0.91, with a standard of 0.90 or higher considered acceptable. The coefficient of scalability (CS) for a slightly modified ordering

of the levels (i.e., by difficulty) was 0.66, with a CS of 0.60 as a standard for acceptability.

Construct validity: The FAST total score was significantly correlated with the SPS total score, $r = 0.77$ ($p < .05$); the BHS, $r = 0.60$ ($p < .05$); the EDI, $r = 0.62$ ($p < .05$); the CES-D, $r = 0.63$ ($p < .05$); and other measures. The FAST total score also correlated significantly with therapists' overall evaluation of the self-destructiveness of the clients, $r = .40$ ($p < .05$). However, the FAST total score and the Reasons for Living Inventory were not significantly correlated.

Criterion validity studies: Criterion validity was evaluated by comparing FAST scores with previous suicide attempts. Steiger t-ratios were calculated to estimate the significance of the difference between the correlations. The FAST correlation with the criterion variable was significantly higher than all other instruments except the SPS, where the difference was not significant. However, correlations for the FAST Level 10 (thoughts planning suicide) and Level 11 (injunctions to commit suicide) with the SPS total correlation self-reported suicide attempts were significantly larger than with this criterion. These "suicide" levels of the FAST demonstrate a significantly higher correlation with reports of past suicide attempts than any of the other measures administered.

Incremental validity analysis: A logistic regression coefficient was obtained using the following variables as predictors of past suicide attempts: SPS total score, BHS total score, age, income, gender, race, employment status, and marital status. Subsequently, with the FAST total score added, a logistic regression was run. The difference in resulting logic coefficients was compared χ^2 (1, $N = 383$) = 7.268 ($p < .05$) and revealed a significant difference.

5. Tests included in the second (inpatient) study were the Beck Depression Inventory (Beck, 1978a), the Beck Hopelessness Scale (Beck, 1978b), the Beck Suicide Inventory (Beck, 1991), the Beck Anxiety Inventory (Beck, 1987), the Substance Abuse Subtle Screening Inventory (Miller, 1985), and the Socially Desirable Response Set Measure (Hays et al., 1989).

6. *The Suicide Intent Composite:* Results from the inpatient study showed that the 27-item Suicide Intent Composite has high levels of sensitivity and specificity for distinguishing ideators from nonideators. In distinguishing ideators from a nonclinical group, the cutoff score of 50 had the highest sensitivity and specificity, accurately identifying 95.8% of the ideators and 89.2% of the nonideators. This cut point was chosen to maximize both sensitivity and specificity.

7. To construct the FVSV, an initial version (187 items) was administered to 916 subjects, including 491 incarcerated inmates, 88 parolees, 119 participants in anger management groups, 125 normals, 56 nonviolent outpatients, and 37 other subjects.

Endnotes

1. Lisa A. Firestone and Robert W. Firestone are coauthors of the FAST and the manual for the scale. "FAST" is a trademark of the Psychological Corporation.

2. Anton Leenaars, in a review of this book, wrote that he was "struck how voices are equal to statements in suicide notes."

3. Numerous small-scale studies preceded the larger standardization and validation studies. The organization of items into the 11 levels on the "Continuum of Negative Thought Patterns" was accomplished by using content experts. Two studies were conducted where judges (advanced graduate students and psychologists with training in Voice Therapy) were asked to classify the items according to the continuum levels. The items with the highest levels of agreement were retained for the 110-item scale.

4. Dorwart and Chartock (1989) unequivocally stated that the best predictor of subsequent suicide attempts and completions is having a history of previous attempts.

5. Often patients who bring up the subject of internal voices in sessions feel misunderstood because therapists have tended to perceive them as psychotic. These patients are aware that they are not hallucinating or "going crazy" but have been treated as though they were.

6. Weissman et al. (1989) surveyed 18,011 residents of five major U.S. cities and concluded that "panic disorder and attacks are associated with an increased risk of suicidal ideation and suicide attempts. Physicians working in general medical settings and emergency departments should be alert to this problem" (p. 1209).

14 Treatment Strategies and Malpractice Issues

Everything naturally loves itself and preserves itself in being;
suicide is against natural inclination and contrary to the charity
which a man ought to bear toward himself.

                                                    Thomas Aquinas

Case management of the suicidal patient involves dealing with specific problems that are often very different than issues encountered in psychotherapy with nonsuicidal individuals. Suicidal patients sometimes require intensified contact with the therapist for some period of time, so the therapist needs to ensure his or her availability to that patient. This may include taking actions that go beyond the boundaries and limits set for traditional psychotherapy. Proper case management coincides with taking the necessary precautions in relation to malpractice issues.

General Discussion

Prior to committing suicide, people usually indicate to one or more persons, in more or less overt ways, their intention to die. Bonner (1990) noted that most people who kill themselves have visited a health care professional in their last few months of life. Jobes and Berman (1993) reported that approximately 50% of those who complete suicide have had a previous experience with psychotherapy.

Dealing with potentially suicidal individuals who seek treatment has proven difficult for psychologists and psychiatrists. Surveys show that a suicidal crisis is the therapist's worst fear, often paralyzing the clinician emotionally and interfering with sound clinical judgment. Birtchnell (1983),

Hendin (1981), and Deutsch (1984) agree that a patient's statements about suicide create more stress in clinicians than any other behavior or communication.

A patient's suicide is a traumatic event for a therapist, and he or she may experience many of the same psychological reverberations as family member survivors. The therapist may suffer the loss of professional and personal self-esteem (Michalik, 1988), not to mention the fear of malpractice litigation and community scorn (Gable, 1983). In recent years, malpractice suits brought against psychologists for "wrongful death" in completed suicides are "the sixth most frequently claimed [and] the second most costly" (Jobes & Berman, 1993, p. 92).

The response an individual receives to his or her communication of suicidal intention or ideation can affect the outcome of a suicidal crisis. Dr. Milton Rosenbaum (cited in Roberts, 1975) asserted, "It is not to be forgotten that patients almost always cry out for help before attempting suicide. It is when the cry is unheeded that the likelihood of a suicide attempt is at its height" (p. 49). The patient's unremitting ambivalence in relation to killing him- or herself affirms our responsibility to appeal to and support the part of the person that still wants to live. Leonard (1967) summarized this sentiment in his statement: *"Their 'right' is not to commit suicide but to have their need for psychological assistance met so that they may enjoy a satisfying life among us"* (p. 223).

"How do clinicians treat suicidal people?" asked George Colt (1991), journalist and author of *The Enigma of Suicide* (p. 311). Colt referred to answers provided by Edwin Shneidman (1985) in *Definition of Suicide:* "The therapist should try to understand not only the hurt that the patient is feeling but, centrally, the 'problem' that the individual is trying to solve. . . . In part, the treatment of suicide is the satisfaction of the unmet needs" (p. 227).

Shneidman (personal communication, 1990) told the story of an honors student in engineering at UCLA who disclosed plans to kill himself that afternoon because he had received an A– in one of his courses. His grade point average was a perfect 4.0, and even though the A– would not have altered his perfect record, the young man was suffering extreme perturbation and distress, for unknown reasons, over the less than perfect grade. After assessing the lethality of the suicidal intent (the student possessed a gun) and acknowledging the deep meaning the grade held for the student, Shneidman appealed to the dean of students to reissue the grade and give the student an A rather than A–. The dean complied, the immediate crisis was averted, and the student was referred to the campus clinic for treatment.

Acceptable Standards of Care

A number of important clinical, legal, and ethical issues confront therapists working with suicidal patients. With the increased numbers of malpractice suits, it is essential that the clinician be familiar with the ethical and legal issues in treating high-risk patients—those who are dangerous to self or others. Stromberg et al. (1988) noted that practitioners are likely to be found liable in cases of completed suicide if "similarly situated practitioners would have provided more care or would have controlled the patient better" (p. 467) (Endnote 1).

The procedures described in this section have a dual purpose. The methods, if followed consistently, help protect both clinician and patient. They are excellent strategies to follow in terms of (a) offering one's patient good care and (b) protecting oneself against malpractice suits. By ensuring that they have taken care of the practical aspects of case management described below, clinicians will experience less anxiety, feel more confident in trusting their clinical intuition, and free themselves to focus on the psychodynamics of the patient and the actual treatment. Thus the discussion that follows is not meant to be a "paranoid" tactic to help psychotherapists defend themselves against potential lawsuits; it represents an effective treatment method in that it exemplifies appropriate concern for the patient and the seriousness of his or her condition (Endnote 2). The following discussion summarizes basic techniques of risk management that, when put into practice, will minimize the psychotherapist's risk of being found negligent in a malpractice action.

Definition of "Acceptable Standard of Care"

Although there are invariably differences of opinion regarding treatment strategies, and although it is clear that a patient's suicide is not always preventable, there are certain principles that define an acceptable standard of care for high-risk patients, both legally and ethically (Endnote 3). The courts have found negligence in cases where the evidence showed that

> the practitioner must have failed in some way to live up to the demands of acceptable practice. The breach of duty may involve overt actions, such as giving the wrong treatment, or may arise from omissions, such as failure to take precautions against suicide. (Meyer, Landis, & Hays, 1988, p. 15)

According to a recent court decision, the "acceptable practice" or standard of care required by a psychiatrist is as follows. "A psychiatrist owes his patient a duty to exercise that degree of care, skill, and diligence which a reasonably competent psychiatrist engaged in a similar practice and in a similar community would ordinarily have exercised in like circumstances" (*Naidu v. Laird,* 1988).

Based on recent court decisions, Bongar (1991) and Berman and Cohen-Sandler (1982) have described the following basic principles that the reasonably diligent clinician would use in assessing and treating suicidal patients.

Initial Intake Interview and Evaluation

The first decision that comes under scrutiny in the clinician's treatment plan is his or her determination of the appropriate treatment setting. This decision rests upon clinical judgment regarding the degree of the patient's suicidality, which, in turn, is based on information gleaned from the initial intake interview. See Figure 14.1, "Assessment and Management of the Suicidal Patient," which provides a structure for the evaluation process and includes the essential steps in case management (modeled on the flow chart developed by Fremouw, de Perczel, & Ellis, 1990).

Assessment of risk factors. The clinician should begin by assessing for the presence of risk factors—psychiatric, psychological, as well as social (Endnote 4). *Psychiatric* risk factors include (a) diagnosis of major depression, bipolar disorder, alcohol dependence, drug addiction, schizophrenia, organic psychosis, borderline or compulsive personality disorder; (b) past history of attempts or family history of attempts; and (c) poor physical health. *Psychological* risk factors include (a) recent losses and how they relate to past losses (such as loss of parent in childhood), (b) lack of a social support system, or loss of previous support, and (c) anniversary or important dates—markers of past tragedies. *Social* risk factors include (a) gender; (b) ethnicity; (c) age; (d) location (i.e., people in urban areas have a higher rate than nonurban residents); (e) marital status (being divorced, widowed, or single puts a person at higher risk); (f) income (the wealthy and the very poor have higher rates); and (g) religion (Protestants and atheists have slightly higher rates than Jews and Catholics).

Maltsberger (1988) emphasized that

> the clinician who [must decide] how much at risk for suicide an individual patient may be is in a quandary. The enormous amount of information available . . . on the psychological, psychodynamic, behavioral, epidemiological,

social-relational, and biological risk factors in attempted and completed suicide—as well as psychological tests and sophisticated suicide rating scales—are not adequate to allow one to adequately answer: "Is the patient, sitting here with me now, about to commit suicide?" (p. 47)

The clinical interview. For a comprehensive evaluation of suicide risk, the clinician should conduct a clinical interview to establish rapport and help the patient feel at ease, listened to, and cared about. A mental status examination should be performed, involving observations of the client's presentation, appearance, mood, expressed affect, intellectual functioning, thought processes, insight, judgment, and presence or absence of hallucinations or delusions.

Direct questions should be asked regarding the patient's thinking about suicide. In particular, the clinician needs to ask the following questions: Do you currently consider suicide an option? How suicidal do you see yourself as being now? Do you have a plan for committing suicide? Do you have the means to carry out your suicide plan? What is the time frame for your plan?

Clinicians often have some degree of trepidation about asking patients direct questions about suicide. It is important for them to explore these fears as well as any other personal issues that might interfere with their ability to manage their clients' suicidal crises. Patients frequently feel understood by the therapist's inquiries and regard these questions as permission to talk about painful, distressing thoughts and feelings. The clinician should investigate the meaning of the present crisis for the patient by asking about precipitating events that may be connected to it. How does the patient interpret the crisis? Does the patient perceive his or her situation realistically? Are cognitive distortions affecting his or her perceptions and interfering with his or her ability to cope?

Therapists must pay close attention to their own emotional reactions because suicidal patients often provoke feelings of dislike, aggression, discomfort, and even malice in therapists. Negative feelings that suicidal patients feel toward themselves are evoked in the therapist during sessions or interviews. Experiencing these reactions should alert the therapist that the patient may be at risk for suicide.

Collateral information. Past behavior is an important predictor of future behavior; thus the therapist needs to make a concerted effort, with the client's permission, to locate past psychiatric and psychotherapy records and obtain information on current medical status. Again, with the client's permission, the clinician should interview significant others such as family members and people close to the client to gather more information. The clinician's

(text continued on p. 240)

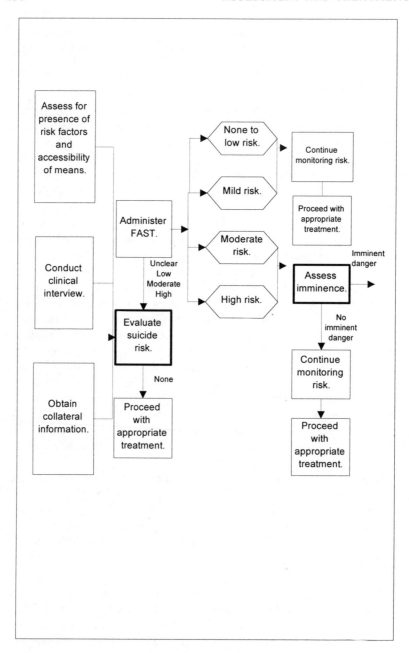

Figure 14.1. Assessment and Management of the Suicidal Patient
*Document each step in the decision process.

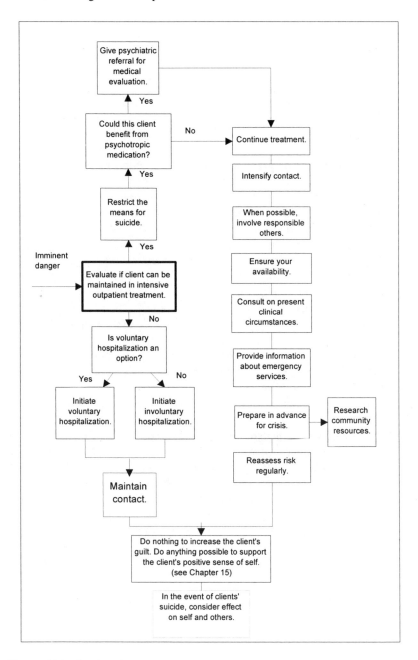

Figure 14.1. Continued

assessment of risk factors, his or her clinical judgment, and this collateral material must be combined with objective methods to properly evaluate the patient's risk of suicide.

Documentation and Consultation

Bongar (1991) emphasized that "[p]sychologists must be aware of the vital importance of the written case record. In cases of malpractice, courts and juries often have been observed to operate on the simplistic principle that 'if it isn't written down, it didn't happen.'. . . Defensive clinical notes, written after the fact, may help somewhat in damage control, but there is no substitute for a timely, thoughtful, and complete record that demonstrates (through clear and well-written assessment, review, and treatment notes) a knowledge of the epidemiology, risk factors, and treatment literature for the suicidal patient" (pp. 202-203). Case records and progress notes should contain a formal informed consent for treatment, assessment of competence, and explanation regarding the limitations of confidentiality conveyed to the patient at the onset of treatment. The clinician should have on record specific notes regarding all treatment plans, actions taken, and their effects on the patient's behavioral responses.

Bongar (1991) also stressed the importance of consultation: "Psychologists should routinely obtain consultation and/or supervision (or make referrals) on all cases where suicide risk is determined to be even moderate, and after a patient suicide or serious suicide attempt" (p. 203). It is obvious that the clinician should seek consultation with, or refer cases to, appropriately skilled professionals for patients who present problems that are outside his or her training, education, or experience. Psychologists should understand the therapeutic use and side effects of drugs in current use for depression and suicidality, and, in particular, seek medical consultation for the patient when they become aware of any signs of organic complications. If the clinician decides against the use of medication in the treatment program, he or she should document the reasoning for this decision in the written case record.

Involvement of the Family and Significant Others

Clinicians should warn the patient's family and significant others of the patient's potential for suicide and enlist their involvement in management and treatment, unless such involvement is clinically contraindicated due to toxic family interactions. Providing the family with information during the course of treatment can lead to active collaboration and help in monitoring the patient's and family's distress. In terms of the legal aspects of suicide, the family is less likely to bring suit against clinicians who have previously established good relations with them and demonstrated their concern for the patient (Endnote 5).

Hospitalization

On the basis of all available information, the therapist needs to determine the patient's level of risk. If the patient is perceived as being at mild to low risk, the therapist should proceed with appropriate treatment and continue to periodically monitor the level of risk. If there is evidence of imminent danger, the clinician should evaluate whether the patient can be maintained in intensive outpatient treatment or requires hospitalization. If the patient presents a clear danger to him- or herself or if his or her environment cannot be made safe—that is, through the removal of means, through the support of significant others, and so on—the client should be hospitalized. If there appears to be no immediate danger, the clinician should, of course, document the evidence for this conclusion.

Following hospitalization, whether voluntary or involuntary, it is essential that the clinician take the necessary steps to remain an integral part of the patient's ongoing treatment program. Of course, one can do this only to the extent to which it is feasible within the limitations of the institution. It is imperative that the clinician maintain contact with the patient and not abandon him or her at this crucial point. Careful follow-up is vital to a successful outcome. According to Friedman (1989), one of the highest risk periods for suicidal patients is upon release from the hospital. Thus intensive outpatient treatment should begin immediately upon release, and the risk element must be closely monitored.

Antisuicide Contracting

Clinicians should make judicious use of antisuicide contracts. These are written or verbal agreements in which the patient agrees not to kill him- or herself during the next period of time (decided upon by therapist and patient) and commits to contact the therapist at any time he or she feels unsure of his or her ability to resist suicidal impulses. The contract is conducive to establishing a therapeutic alliance and indicates the patient's motivation to improve; that is, it is a sign of the patient's acceptance of responsibility for the therapy program along with the clinician. Thus antisuicide contracts have a positive effect in partially relieving the clinician's anxiety regarding a negative outcome. The therapist, however, should not be lulled into a state of security that fails to appraise the ongoing risk situation.

Knowledge of Community Resources

Bongar (1991) noted that "[p]sychologists who see suicidal patients should have access to the full armamentarium of resources for voluntary and involuntary hospital admissions, day treatment, 24-hour emergency backup, and crisis centers" (p. 204). They should become familiar with these institutions and use them as necessary. The clinician can work directly with these institutions or develop an ongoing collaborative relationship with a psychologist or psychiatric colleague on his or her staff who has such a relationship.

Consideration of the Effect on Self and Others

In the case of a completed suicide or serious attempt, Bongar pointed out that "psycholgoists/clinicians should be aware (not only) of their legal responsibilities (e.g., they must notify their insurance carrier in a timely manner) but, more important, of the immediate clinical necessity of attending to both the needs of the bereaved survivors and to the psychologist's own emotional needs" (p. 204). After consulting with colleagues and an attorney, psychologists should provide assistance to the survivors as part of a sensitive and concerned treatment program.

Determination of Technical and Personal Competence

The treatment of suicidal patients requires training in a broad spectrum of psychotherapeutic approaches to depression and suicide as well as an understanding of the limitations and benefits of the various psychosocial and medical therapies. Clinicians should have sufficient knowledge of relevant clinical and research literature to allow them to determine when it is appropriate to request a consultation for psychotropic medication.

In his summary, Bongar stated that "psychologists must be cognizant of all of the standards above and take affirmative steps to ensure that they have the requisite knowledge, training, experience and clinical resources prior to accepting high-risk patients into their professional care. This requires that all of these mechanisms be in place before the onset of any suicidal crisis" (p.201). In addition, it is clear that therapists should not burden themselves with more of these serious cases than they can reasonably handle, given the amount of personal attention required by suicidal patients.

Common Errors

Obviously, the key "don'ts" in treating the suicidal patient would be the clinician's neglect of the "do's" listed above. A number of other "don'ts" can be found in an informative essay, "Ten Most Common Errors of Suicide Interventionists" (Neimeyer & Pfeiffer, 1994). Maltsberger and Buie (1989) also conducted an in-depth analysis of serious mistakes of commission and omission on the part of clinicians working with suicidal outpatients and inpatients. Two important and potentially dangerous errors noted in their essay deserve further discussion here: (a) "errors arising from countertransference" (p. 285) and (b) "errors arising from failure to take into account the sources and reliability of emotional support" (p. 291).

(a) As noted earlier, suicidal patients often evoke feelings of dislike and rejection in the therapist. The hate that is aroused, especially when it remains outside the therapist's awareness, tends to distort clinical judgment and can lead to unfortunate outcomes or even tragedy. Maltsberger and Buie described cases in which patients' self-destructive acting-out behavior eventually resulted in the therapist's issuing an ultimatum that "if such behavior is repeated the therapy will be terminated" (p. 286).

(b) Similar errors can be made when the clinician overestimates the support system available to suicidal patients upon their release from the hospital and underestimates the profound sense of loss they experience when they leave this protective environment. When patients improve during their hospital stay, and appear cheerful and optimistic, they may be discharged within a few days. This situation is particularly common today in light of managed health care and the limitations of insurance coverage. Many patients become severely depressed upon their return to the family or community. Their regression is often the result of loss of the supportive hospital milieu and, more specifically, the loss of specific supportive individuals within the hospital network. When this is compounded by a lack of available support in the patient's social environment, or by diminished involvement on the part of the treating clinician, a suicidal crisis can be precipitated.

Case Study

Dave, a 30-year-old single man, was referred to Dr. M. by his ex-girlfriend. She had become alarmed during a telephone conversation in which Dave became extremely upset over losing the relationship and expressed suicidal thoughts. After evaluating the patient's suicide intent and mental status, Dr. M. referred him for treatment to L. L., his female psychological assistant. Before instituting a treatment program, L. L. referred Dave to a psychiatrist for medical evaluation. Dave refused to take the referral or to consult any psychiatrist but appeared to form a positive attachment to the psych assistant.

Three months later, the psych assistant left on a previously scheduled vacation, and during her 3-week absence, Dr. M. assumed responsibility for the case. Dave agreed to a suicide contract with Dr. M., promising to call before taking any action to hurt himself. However, during L. L.'s absence, the patient became increasingly depressed and suicidal and then disappeared for 2 weeks without informing anyone of his whereabouts. When he returned, he phoned Dr. M. and revealed that he "just can't take it anymore" and admitted he had a gun.

Dr. M. dissuaded Dave from taking immediate action and hospitalized him (a voluntary commitment) in a private psychiatric hospital. At this point, Dr. M. decided to turn Dave's case over to a staff psychologist at the hospital. The plan was that the staff psychologist would continue to treat Dave upon his release from the hospital. Dr. M.'s psych assistant returned from vacation during Dave's hospitalization but did not reinvolve herself in the case.

Dave appeared to adjust well to the hospital setting, began a course of antidepressant medication, worked out daily in the gym, and responded appropriately in the therapy groups he attended. After a 3-week stay in the hospital, it was decided to grant the patient a day pass for a home visit.

Leaving the hospital that morning, Dave was able to obtain a gun on his way home (probably purchased at a pawn shop). He returned to the apartment he shared with his friend, Mark. He opened his mail and drank a cup of coffee, a common routine. Mark was concerned, however, because he sensed that Dave was "down." Later, Mark reported that he was unable to "even get him to crack a smile." After Mark left for work, Dave walked to a nearby park and shot himself in the head.

A number of case management errors are suggested in this example. The psych assistant's abandonment of the patient, Dr. M.'s decision to dispense with the case during and after hospitalization, the staff psychologist's failure to properly reassess the patient's suicidality before granting the pass, and his lack of knowledge about the inadequate support system of the patient's "home" environment are factors that in all probability contributed to the negative outcome.

Being bounced around the referral network probably exacerbated Dave's despair and sense of hopelessness. Discharge from the hospital, receiving a day or weekend pass, and an inappropriate referral to another therapist are but a few of the many events that can arouse intolerable feelings of loss and abandonment in a severely depressed or suicidal patient. Finally, even though some patients have family and friends who seem loving and supportive, the clinician must ascertain, through careful evaluation of the patient and his family, (a) whether the patient is willing or able to use the available resources and (b) whether these resources would, in fact, enhance the patient's life and help avert future suicide attempts.

Treatment Strategies
Based on Theoretical Models

Jacobs (1989) has observed that "because suicide cuts across the whole spectrum of psychiatric illness, a therapist should be familiar with several theories as part of developing a therapeutic strategy" (p. 329).

Cognitive-Behavioral Interventions

The primary goal of cognitive therapy in treating high-risk cases is to "widen the scope of view of the patient, so that the patient can see more options other than a suicide solution" (Litman, 1994, p. 276). According to Beck (1976), as depression worsens, the suicidal patient's thinking becomes increasingly constricted and dominated by negative beliefs. Beck's cognitive model of depression postulates the concept of the "cognitive triad," which includes (a) the client's negative view of self, (b) the tendency to interpret experiences in a negative manner, and (c) the client's negative view of the future. Cognitive therapy is based on the formulation that psychological problems are a result of "incorrect premises and a proneness to distorted imaginal experiences" (Beck, 1976, p. 19). The treatment approach consists of specific experiences designed to teach the patient methods for countering such thinking.

Linehan (1993) has developed Dialectic Behavior Therapy (DBT) specifically for the treatment of chronically suicidal patients, many of whom are diagnosed with borderline personality disorder. According to Briere (1996), who has adapted the DBT intervention model for treatment of sexual abuse survivors, Linehan emphasized that "affect regulation problems do not reflect a structural psychological defect . . . as much as insufficiently developed self-skills arising from distorted or disrupted childhood development" (p. 126). In Briere's modified DBT treatment, the focus is on identifying the "intrusive and repetitive cognitions that often trigger and feed overwhelming affect" (p. 127).

Psychodynamic-Psychoanalytic Approaches

Psychoanalytic treatment focuses on making the unconscious conscious to the suicidal patient. One significant impact that psychoanalysts have had on our understanding of suicide is implicit in their attempt to answer the question: "What is the real reason for this suicide?" Litman (1994) attempted to uncover the reasons that the patient believes he or she "has something worth dying for." Has the patient "suffered a loss, or the threat of a loss so serious that it threatens to destroy the patient's self-image?" (p. 277).

It is impossible to address the wide range of psychoanalytic treatment approaches; however, it is possible to comment on (a) the ways in which an objective assessment can affect a treatment program that is oriented toward early object relations and personality dynamics and (b) how important treatment issues such as transference and countertransference can be clarified through the use of such assessment.

1. The Firestone Assessment of Self-Destructive Thoughts (FAST) provides insight into partially unconscious thought processes by accessing clinical material similar to that gained through the technique of free association (Endnote 6). Identification of the patient's self-attacks or negative parental introjects as endorsed on the scale enhances the clinician's understanding of how these introjects are manifested in the patient's life. In particular, the effects of early object losses on the patient's current functioning can be understood and interpreted in the context of the items endorsed.

2. The specific content of these negative parental introjects are often expressed in the patient's transference and the therapist's countertransference reactions. For example, through the process of projective identification, a suicidal patient's malicious attitudes toward self may evoke corresponding feelings of strong dislike in the treating clinician. Using the FAST as an objective measure of these introjects, the clinician can monitor the types of countertransference responses most likely to be elicited by such a patient and diminish the probability of committing a serious error in treatment. For example, specific items on the FAST that predict rejection or negative outcomes may be endorsed with high frequency by patients manifesting negative transference reactions and/or eliciting negative countertransference in the clinician (Firestone & Firestone, 1996).

Existential Framework

As discussed in previous chapters, existential issues need to be considered in our thinking about the suicidal process. Lifton (1989) stressed this point and noted, "With suicide, there are questions about death equivalents—about separation, stasis and the fear of disintegration—and about death itself. It is amazing how often death can be left out of suicide in at least many of our constructs" (p. 463). Lifton went on to assert that, in many patients, "it is the element of despair that is central to suicide. . . . One kills the 'dead self' in order to break out of the despair" (p. 463).

Existential psychotherapists who treat depressed or suicidal patients tend to focus on events in patients' lives that have meaning in terms of arousing death anxiety and feelings of hopelessness, despair, and aloneness. As noted earlier, the arousal of death anxiety generally leads to an increased reliance on defensive behaviors, including progressive self-denial, return to addictive habit patterns, and existential guilt related to regression. All of these issues pertain to increased suicidal risk.

In the intake interview, the existential therapist would inquire about events, both positive and negative, in the patient's life that could have precipitated the acting out of self-destructive or suicidal behavior. In the closing phase of treatment, he or she would necessarily deal carefully with the issue of termination and the patient's feelings of aloneness as well as abandonment anxiety associated with the conclusion of therapy. The patient's reactions to termination can be conceptualized not only as a reaction to the positive event of improvement and separation from the therapist but also as a reflection of the symbolic meaning of termination, that is, a reminder of the ultimate separation from self and significant others at death.

Personality of the Therapist
Treating Suicidal Patients

Although the therapist's personal qualities are vital factors in determining the outcome of any therapeutic endeavor, they are especially significant in the treatment program of suicidal individuals. Empirical research on psychotherapy outcomes has shown that certain attributes of clinicians as well as specific characteristics of the therapist-patient relationship are likely to lead to a successful treatment (Beutler & Clarkin, 1990; Bongar & Beutler, 1995). Indeed, the personality of the therapist sets the tone and emotional quality of the therapy process and cannot be divorced from the interventions described above.

To offer real assistance to the depressed or suicidal individual, the therapist would ideally be a person of integrity and personal honesty. He or she would be uncompromising in his or her approach to defenses that limit the patient and, at the same time, sensitive to the patient's unique goals and priorities. The clinician's demeanor, behavior, and life outside the office setting would not be a basic departure from the qualities he or she exemplifies in the therapy setting. If therapists lack integrity or act out defensively in their personal lives, they will necessarily be limited in the amount of assistance they are able to offer their patients.

Effective therapists do not set themselves apart from their patients; rather, they function as role models, demonstrating through their responses and behavior how to struggle against destructive forces within the personality and how to live less defensively. Their therapeutic responses are authentic, direct, nonmanipulative, and sensitive to patients' innermost feelings and fantasies. They do not fit their patients into a theoretical system or model. Instead, they are willing to experience the painful truths their patients reveal during the course of treatment. They are nondefensive in recognizing therapeutic errors or "failures in empathy" (Kohut, 1977). Therapists who work with suicidal clients must remain human, that is, be interested, warm, caring, and empathic. Their interactions with patients should be characterized by equality, openness, and true compassion. Therapeutic interventions must be direct and responsive, and ideally the therapist would possess a good sense of humor (Endnote 7).

Dynamic Issues in Postvention

> The truth of suicide dies with the victim. The survivors can only
> guess. They must put the pieces of a life together to try to come up
> with reasons for an unreasonable death.
>
> Susan White-Bowden (1985, p. 12)

Each year in the United States, there are approximately 184,000 new survivors of suicide, that is, people who have lost a family member or friend by suicide. In her book *Survivors of Suicide,* Robinson (1989) wrote that "for everyone who commits suicide, their deed reaches out to touch dozens of acquaintances, friends, and family members" (p. xv).

In considering Szasz's (1987, 1989) point of view about the "right to die" issue discussed earlier, it is almost impossible for an individual not to be psychologically impaired by a loved one's suicide. The reasons are apparent. The self-inflicted death of a family member or close friend reinforces destructive thought processes in the survivors. Suicide strengthens the antiself system of those left behind; the act of self-destruction is almost always used in the survivors' defense system, which causes emotional damage.

Negative Identification in Survivors

Voices not only represent the internalization of negative parental attitudes, they also reflect an identification with parents' defense systems. Children and adolescents tend to follow the destiny or developmental pathway of their parents, especially that of the parent of the same sex. When a parent commits suicide, the identification can develop into a powerful compulsion to imitate this act of self-destruction. These dynamics were operating when Susan White-Bowden's son, a young man who had "everything to live for," killed himself when he was 19, using the same means his father had employed to kill himself when the son was 14. Tragically, no one informed this mother that her son was at risk for suicide following his father's suicide (White-Bowden, 1985).

It has been estimated that during the last 40 years, more than 1 million children have lost a parent or parents to suicide. Under normal circumstances, the loss of a parent has a tremendous impact on a child. However, in the case of suicide, I have found that the normal feelings of grief are complicated by guilt, anger, and an intensified pull to forfeit one's individuality and adopt the parent's identity and point of view. This weakened sense of self leaves the patient with a tendency to capitulate to others. Lesser threats of self-destruction, or microsuicidal behavior, will take a greater toll on an individual who has experienced this type of loss.

Typical Reactions

Shock. Suicides sometimes occur in the absence of any prior danger signs, and the shock to loved ones is profoundly shattering. The blow disrupts their equilibrium and leaves them feeling devastated, confused, and disoriented in trying to make sense of a seemingly senseless act. Suicide without warning can leave the survivors in a state of unresolved bewilderment. This is understandable when one considers the secretiveness and isolation sought by the inward, potentially suicidal person. These individuals go to enormous lengths to conceal their negative thoughts from those closest to them.

For example, I was familiar with a prominent pediatrician, 60, who killed himself without displaying any warning signs and did not leave a note. He lived in a beautiful home in the suburbs, was highly successful in his practice, and had ministered kindly and effectively to children for more than 30 years. In the aftermath of his death, feelings of shock, disbelief, and confusion overwhelmed family members, friends, and colleagues. As yet, no one has unraveled the mystery surrounding his suicide; his wife still wonders what was going on in her husband's mind that drove him to take his own life.

George Colt (1991), after interviewing family members who survived the suicide of a parent or child, concluded, "Although the pain is over for the one who died, and his problems, in their way, answered, the survivor is left only with questions" (p. 409).

Guilt. Survivors tend to blame themselves for the suicide of a family member or close friend. No matter what their rational point of view is, they feel a deep sense of guilt and torture themselves: How could I have prevented this? What could I have done differently that would have prevented the irreversible act of self-destruction? Why did it happen? What did I do wrong? These unanswerable questions continue to haunt people, sometimes for a lifetime. These feelings of guilt and self-recrimination are difficult to cope with because of the tendency to idealize someone after death, especially in the case of parents, spouses, and those with whom one has formed a close attachment. In the case of suicide, nothing is more important than to help survivors develop a more realistic view of the deceased and a rational approach to the causality of the self-destructive act.

Anger. Idealizing the qualities of the person who committed suicide compels survivors to deny the feelings of anger that are always aroused by this type of loss. Anger is a natural human response to both frustration and abandonment. Suicide in a family member intensifies abandonment anxiety in those remaining, which in turn generates anger and even rage. However, idealizing the dead person acts to suppress this anger and effectively eliminates the opportunity for a healthy outlet. The more survivors deny their outrage at being left, the more inward, self-critical, and self-hating they become. In turning their anger against themselves, they become progressively more debilitated.

Postvention Strategies

Ideally, postvention strategies will extend beyond the initial stage of shock to a more complete psychotherapy program (Endnote 8). In my postvention efforts with survivors, I try to help them accept and express both sad and angry feelings toward the deceased, which is a fundamental part of the grieving process. In treating children and adolescents who are going through the crisis of a parent's suicide, I sensitively help them develop a more objective perspective regarding the event. The manner in which children cope with the loss of a parent, even under normal circumstances, has major consequences in terms of their adjustment and well-being as adults. In child psychotherapy, it is vital to establish a strong transitional relationship to help them get through the suicidal crisis. It is imperative that we ameliorate the unnecessary suffering brought about by the suppression of their anger, the expression of which they rightly perceive as being socially unacceptable.

Therapists as Survivors

At some point in his or her professional life, a clinician may become a survivor (Endnote 9). Berman and Jobes (1991) have noted that "the personal and professional issues inherent in a patient's suicide provide a complex matrix of various manifestations and consequences for the treating clinician" (p. 258). Among the personal reactions are anger, denial, guilt, and shame. As professionals, therapists have fears about censure by colleagues, damage to reputation, and doubts regarding their adequacy or competence. Perhaps even more than nonprofessionals, they tend to wonder what they might have done to prevent the fatal outcome. It is appropriate for clinicians facing this type of stress to explore their own psychodynamics in consultation with other professionals. Facing the issues realistically and working through the feelings evoked by a patient suicide, can, under the best circumstances, transform a negative professional experience into a positive growth experience.

Conclusion

In his discussion of the limitations of crisis intervention, Leenaars (1994) concluded that "there is no universal formulation regarding how to respond to a highly lethal person. . . . Yet understandably yearning for universal suicidological laws persists" (p. 58). I agree with Leenaars and other suicidologists on a major point: namely, that psychotherapists working with suicidal clients should not work in isolation. In his work, Leenaars has stressed the following point of view:

> I do not believe, in principle, in the solely individual private practice of suicide intervention with highly lethal individuals. Suicide intervention is optimally practiced in cooperation with a number of colleagues, representing various disciplines, and even individuals outside the helping professions. (p. 58)

Finally, even in an excellent treatment program with a competent, knowledgeable therapist who adheres to the guidelines described above, the suicidal patient may ultimately choose to end his or her life. At that point, it is important for us to realize that, as clinicians, we are "neither omniscient nor omnipotent, and the law does not require that we be so. When our best efforts fail, we share with other survivors, a 'despair born of death too soon' " (Slawson, Flinn, & Schwartz, 1974, p. 63).

Endnotes

1. Sadoff's (1975) definition of liability includes the "Four Ds"; that is, a clinician may be held liable for wrongful death of a patient if it can be determined that there was dereliction of duty directly causing damages.

2. Gutheil (1980) commented that the prudent mental health practitioner can "use paranoia as a motivating force to make psychiatric records effective for forensic purposes, utilization review, and sound treatment planning" (p. 479).

3. There are specific guidelines for the treatment of patients who present an elevated risk for suicide. In our summary of risk management, we have cited the work of Bongar (1991, 1992) and Berman and Cohen-Sandler (1982), who summarized these techniques.

4. Adapted from the *Concise Guide to Consultation Psychiatry* (second edition) by Michael G. Wise and James R. Rundell (1988, p. 154).

5. Reporting an adolescent's suicidality to parents is mandatory for patients under 18 years of age and is a judgment decision for those over 18.

6. This discussion is taken from material in the *Firestone Assessment of Self-Destructive Thoughts (FAST) Manual* (Firestone & Firestone, 1996).

7. The suicidologist Joseph Richman (personal communication, 1988), well known in the field for his sense of humor, tells the story of a chronically suicidal elderly woman whom he had treated for several months and who refused to enter into an antisuicide contract. Severely depressed and anhedonic, she made repeated suicidal threats and attempts and was unable to conceptualize the future. One day, she announced to Dr. Richman that he should be relieved about her state of mind in relation to feeling hopeless about the future because she had just purchased groceries for the next day. Richman asked what she had bought, and the woman replied, "Fruit, some nice, ripe bananas." Richman quipped back: "I would be relieved if you had bought green bananas." The woman burst into laughter—the first time she had during a session with him. A therapeutic alliance was established in this interaction, and the patient began to show improvement.

8. Scott Poland (1989) has delineated postvention procedures for school counselors, teachers, and administrators to follow in case of a student suicide, including how to deal with the media. The reader is also referred to *Suicide and Its Aftermath*, edited by Dunne, McIntosh, and Dunne-Maxim (1987). The American Association of Suicidology lists over 120 support groups for survivors. Contact Elaine Sullivan, President of Survivors of Suicide, Idaho State University, 2411 S. University, Idaho Falls, ID 83404, for a list of available programs and their locations. A list of survivor groups is also included in Rita Robinson's (1989) book *Survivors of Suicide*.

9. Chemtob, Hamada, Bauer, Torigoe, and Kinney (1988) reported that "22% of psychologists have experienced a patient's suicide" (p. 416). Chemtob, Hamada, Bauer, Kinney, and Torigoe (1988) found that "51% of 259 psychiatrists sampled had had a patient who committed suicide" (p. 224).

15   Voice Therapy Methodology in the Treatment of the Suicidal Patient

What then is the "psychological soil" in which the suicidal mind malignantly flourishes?

Edwin Shneidman (1996, p. 162)

Voice Therapy is especially applicable to the treatment of depression and suicidal trends. In developing the methodology over the past 20 years, I have found that in no other mental condition are internalized voices more obvious to the patient or their self-attacks more uncritically accepted as real (Endnote 1). In this chapter, I set forth a systematic approach to psychotherapy with suicidal clients that challenges defenses at every level—cognitively, affectively, and behaviorally.

Two clinical uses of Voice Therapy can be elucidated: (a) in crisis intervention and (b) in long-term treatment for suicidal patients. In crisis intervention, Voice Therapy methods are valuable in ameliorating perturbation and lethality during the actual crisis and are conducive to quickly establishing the therapeutic relationship. The client's agitation and angry affect toward self are directly associated with the voice attacks typical of the "suicidal trance." Thus the therapist or crisis hot line worker who shows an understanding of "voices" has tremendous leverage in establishing the rapport necessary to continue the dialogue and possibly save the caller's life.

In the context of long-term treatment, Voice Therapy methods are used to help avert suicide attempts and regression to severely depressed states. By identifying the negative cognitions driving suicidal actions, patients gain a measure of control over all aspects of their self-destructive or suicidal behavior. They become cognizant that the way they negatively perceive or distort stressful events, not the events themselves, is the principal cause of their depression, dysphoria, or hopelessness. Patients are able to generalize the understanding they develop in Voice Therapy sessions to their everyday lives. In my clinical experience, I have found that if people simply recognize when they are attacking themselves, this awareness is, in itself, enormously therapeutic. Merely becoming conscious that one is thinking in terms opposed to one's self-interest enables one to begin to challenge the process of destructive, obsessive ruminations.

In more serious cases, the identification of the specific content of negative thinking and the release of associated feeling provides patients with tools to counter serious injunctions to harm themselves. They learn to deduce from their own behavior or change in mood that, on some level, they must be experiencing an onslaught of self-accusations. Subsequently, they can attempt to identify the specific voices motivating their behavior. Uncovering elements of negative thinking that have previously existed only on an unconscious level can interfere with further self-destructive acting out. This type of awareness is vital for patients who act out self-destructive behavior with little or no insight; it provides them with a sense of mastery over behaviors they previously perceived as being beyond their control. This understanding is especially valuable for suicidal patients who are subject to panic attacks and impulsivity, that is, those patients who studies have shown are the most likely to commit suicide.

Finally, Voice Therapy methods are fundamental to identifying and supporting the special wants, priorities, and interests of patients that give meaning to their lives. These unique predilections are factors that keep the patient's spirit alive; thus understanding these factors can help in crisis intervention. An understanding of the self and antiself systems focuses the therapist's attention on specific needs in the patient that were being frustrated and that may have precipitated the suicidal crisis. Shneidman (1985) contends that the "common stressors in both suicide and parasuicide are frustrated psychological needs" (p. 215) (Endnote 2). When the suicidal crisis is over and patients are on the upgrade, their personal goals become the primary focus of attention in the therapy.

Use of Voice Therapy Methodology in
Crisis Intervention and the Intake Interview

Model of Crisis Intervention

The goal in crisis intervention is, obviously, a simple one—that is, as Leenaars (1994) succinctly put it, to "keep the person alive" (p. 46). Leenaars described a model of crisis intervention that includes (a) establishing rapport, (b) exploring, (c) focusing, and (d) developing options and a plan of action. Although there is no single formula that can be applied to all patients, suicidologists have developed these and other guidelines for crisis intervention from which responses may be adapted as appropriate for the individual.

Establish rapport. The crisis hot line worker or clinician must be able to establish rapport quickly to reduce the level of lethality (the probability of the patient's killing him- or herself). A compassionate, nonevaluative attitude and an active, at times directive, intervention are necessary. Most important, as Leenaars (1994) states, "For rapport to be established, love must predominate over hate" (p. 49). The therapist or crisis worker should inquire about suicidal thoughts, fantasies, feelings, and plans to commit suicide; in cases when there is a plan, the crisis worker should inquire about the method. For example, the caseworker might ask, "What are the things you are telling yourself?" "What kinds of thoughts are you having about yourself?" "What are you telling yourself about that event (loss, rejection, public humiliation, and so on)?" Questions are asked concerning the accessibility of means of suicide. For example, does the person possess a gun? Where is it located? In dealing with calls on a crisis hot line, the interventionist asks about the whereabouts of the caller. Is he or she alone? Has he or she been drinking or taking drugs?

Explore. The suicidal crisis is defined by the patient's perception of the problems in his or her life that he or she feels can be escaped only by committing suicide. The therapist helps the patient redefine the problem through further exploration of the patient's thoughts, feelings, and conceptualization of the problem. Leenaars (1994) made the point that if therapists passively accept the patient's perspective—that is, "I can't live with this"—they are "tacitly colluding with the person's decision to die, and the patient cannot survive" (p. 50). Naive reassurances or judgmental statements about the patient's self-destructive thinking and behavior are particularly damaging.

Focus. Suicidal patients have difficulty concentrating on one subject because they are too disturbed and anxious. Questions that direct their attention to reality considerations in their lives—such as "What were you hoping to accomplish by calling?" or "What would be most helpful to you right now?"—allow the clinician to determine whether he or she can be of practical assistance. This focus and the obvious interest and concern on the part of the clinician can help reduce the patient's level of stress.

Develop options and constructive action. The main goal at this point is to help patients solve the problem or problems they face so that their pain is diminished to a tolerable level. In his model, Leenaars (1994) emphasized that "the person wants prompt relief. To save the person's life, the therapist has to do something!" (p. 52). Relief from intense perturbation comes when the patient can see options for action other than suicide. Shneidman (1981) has described a crisis technique that involves listing options (often over the patient's objections) other than suicide and ranking them in order of the patient's preference (Endnote 3). The crisis worker encourages the patient to communicate with others about his or her situation, involve friends and family members, get rid of the means for suicide, and make an appointment with a counselor. Once it is determined that the patient's lethality has been lowered and the pain is more bearable, traditional psychotherapy treatment can commence, or, in the case of emergency calls to a crisis line, the patient can be referred for psychotherapy or counseling.

Guilt and Crisis Intervention

Recognizing the role that guilt plays in the suicidal process is vital in dealing with patients in crisis intervention. The more the crisis worker understands about the various manifestations of guilt discussed throughout this book, the better equipped he or she will be to help people in a suicidal state. Given the ambivalence between the desire to live and the impulse to die that exists in the suicidal individual until the last moment of life, it is crucial to avoid any response that might play on the guilt of the patient. Such communication (evaluative or judgmental) strengthens the voice and tends to push the patient closer to suicidal action. Therapists may inadvertently precipitate these guilt reactions in a misguided effort to restrict a patient's acting out of self-destructive behavior. This may have been the case in an audiotaped suicide that is played at the beginning of the documentary film *Suicides* (Hubert & Addis, 1983). The following is a transcript of that call received by a Crime Prevention Center worker in a large city somewhere in the Midwest.

CALLER: Can I talk to somebody there from the crime prevention center?

WORKER: This is the Crime Prevention Center. How can I help you?

C: Sounds crazy, but I'm going to kill myself.

W: You're going to kill yourself?

C: Yes.

W: Why are you going to kill yourself?

C: I've got indebted and my wife don't love me anymore.

W: That's no reason to kill yourself, sir.

C: I don't see no reason for living no more.

W: What's your name?

C: (Gives name)

W: How old are you?

C: 39. I want to ask one of the officers if I do, could they deliver me to Los Angeles before you bury me?

W: You want to go to Los Angeles, to be buried in Los Angeles. Do you have relatives in Los Angeles?

C: Yes, my mom.

W: Your mom lives there?

C: Yes.

W: How are you going to kill yourself?

C: With my gun.

W: Do you have your gun there with you?

C: Yes, right beside my bed.

W: What kind of gun is it?

C: A 38 special.

W: Are you in bed right now?

C: Yes.

W: Have you been drinking?

C: Yes.

W: What's your address?

C: (Gives address)

W: Are you there now?

C: Yes.

W: What's your phone number?

C: (Gives phone number) I want to notify my mother before I kill myself.

W: Do you have any kids?

C. Yes.

W: How many kids do you have?

C: Four.

W: Don't you think they would want you to live? Don't you want to live for your kids?

The next sound on the tape is the blast of a gunshot, followed by loud yells of pain, and a second shot.

W: Is the ambulance on the way? (Pause) I think he's dead.

Although there was a delicate balance between this man's desire to live and his desire to destroy himself, attempting to develop an imperative or implicit demand in regard to his children may have triggered a particular blend of psychological pain and guilt about which we can only conjecture. This recording also demonstrates the anguish that people suffer in dealing with suicidal clients.

Judgmental parental attitudes on the part of clinicians or caseworkers that arouse either neurotic or existential guilt have a negative effect on the suicidal client. Indeed, any response that supports a person's self-attacks or negative voices is detrimental whereas any communication or behavior on the therapist's part that shows genuine feeling, support, and compassion can act to strengthen the self and support the patient's desire to live. On certain occasions, honest anger expressed directly as a concerned response on the part of a sensitive therapist will be experienced by the suicidal patient as supportive and can serve to circumvent a potential suicide. It is the sincere and personal expression of caring, without judgment, that is most likely to reach a person at risk.

In general, therapists need to support any investment in life regardless of the form it may take for a particular patient. This is important because significant interpersonal interactions can either turn people against themselves or make them feel more themselves, in a positive sense. The aim in psychotherapy is not to project one's values about what constitutes adjustment but to facilitate the patient's growth by strengthening his or her sense of self.

In concluding this section on the crisis intervention model, it is important to note that there are no foolproof or perfect procedures or responses to a person in a suicidal crisis. A great deal depends on the caseworker's or therapist's personal makeup and genuine emotional concern for the client's well-being. Of utmost importance is the value that the therapist places on life itself.

Procedures Used in the Clinical
Interview in Long-Term Intervention

During my 22 years of practicing psychotherapy, I used the intake interview to assess the suicidal potential, ego strength, and type and level of defenses of new patients, and to begin to establish the therapeutic relationship. I asked the patient, "How do you feel when you feel the most down?" and followed up with questions like these: "What's the lowest you ever felt?" "What are the worst attitudes you ever had toward yourself?" Later, I inquired directly about previous suicide attempts and asked whether they had ever experienced self-destructive or suicidal thoughts or fantasies. I asked them to estimate how depressed they were when they considered suicide or made the attempt. As the interview continued, I found it valuable to go into greater detail concerning their history of depression or suicide attempts. I requested information about the content of their thoughts and the intensity of the affect they experienced during their depression. My questions were an attempt to discern whether their suicidality was expressive of an action level or occurred only as thoughts. Finally, I asked of the patients who reported a history of depression or suicide attempts: "Are you currently in that frame of mind?"

Through these inquiries, asked in a spirit of genuine interest and consideration, I was generally able to glean most of the information I needed about patients' suicide potential. My questions also had the purpose of determining a particular patient's ability to withstand the highs and lows of the treatment itself. During the course of any therapeutic endeavor, regression and negative therapeutic reactions are bound to occur, and I needed to know how patients would handle the low points. Would they become suicidal during a therapeutic crisis? (With borderline patients, how would they handle the underlying depression?)

In using the concept of antisuicide contracting, I informed patients that they could call me at any time, day or night, whenever they felt overwhelmed by anxiety states, depressed affect, or suicidal thoughts or impulses. (Incidentally, not one of my patients has ever abused this privilege.) My conscientious regard for this agreement conveyed to patients my feeling that they should not suffer unnecessarily when help was available. I also wanted them to learn that being open about their feelings and communicating with a concerned person could help alleviate their pain. I was sensitive to any nuance of an attempt to break the traditional antisuicide contract and confronted them with the effects that disregarding the agreement could have on their condition and the outcome of the therapy. For example, if a patient told me he had gone through a particularly bad weekend and had not called me, I would be angry and respond with something like the following: "Look, we agreed to keep contact. If you felt terrible, you should have called. Even if you weren't close to actually hurting yourself, you should call before it gets too bad. Don't let the depression sink in. Discuss your voices before they get out of hand. Being outward about your self-destructive thoughts is the way out of this mess."

It is important to establish and adhere to this principle before patients enter the suicidal "trance" phase. By the time it reaches those proportions, the destructive voices often preclude any communication.

In general, the compassionate, feeling practitioner who is not afraid of suicidal clients will fare better than those who approach such clients without this distinctive balance of strength and warmth. Clinicians who take the precautions described in the previous chapter will also feel stronger and more self-assured about relying on their clinical intuition. In dealing with highly lethal patients, they will feel more confident about taking certain chances on being spontaneous, straightforward, and even confrontational in their responses. There are always risks, however, and it is the therapist's peace of mind that is often at stake.

To illustrate, in an intake interview several years ago, I became alarmed at a patient's self-destructive tendencies and allowed myself to angrily confront his defenses. This behavior was a sharp contrast to my usual therapeutic calm and neutrality. His appointment happened to occur on a Friday afternoon, and because of the man's depressed state, I scheduled our next meeting for Monday morning at 9:00 a.m. The patient dispiritedly and reluctantly agreed to my conditions of treatment, including the requirement that he call if things got too horrendous for him over the weekend. After he departed, I was afraid that my confrontational manner might have provoked a suicidal outcome rather than averting one. I spent the entire weekend with the problem always on the edge of my consciousness. On Monday morning as I approached the reception room door, I heard the sound of cheerful whistling and my doubts and fears were immediately allayed. I cursed myself for spoiling my days off. I realized that I had somehow done the right thing and that I'd better trust my intuition in the future. My thoughts were affirmed by the patient's opening words. "Gee, Doc, you hit me like a ton of bricks. On Friday when I walked in here, I thought my life was a goner. When you let me have it, oddly enough I began to see things in perspective. I didn't at first but by the time I got to my car, I noticed that I felt different. Your anger amused me, made me kind of laugh at my stupid mood. Funny thing, when you were pissed off, I felt like you really cared." I made the following response: "I'm glad that you could look at it that way, and I'm pleased that you feel better. Now it's important for us to get at the issues, to see how you got into trouble with yourself in the first place."

Use of an Objective Measure,
the FAST, in the Intake Interview

Determination of level of suicide risk. After the clinician has assessed for risk factors, conducted a comprehensive clinical interview, and collected collateral data, he or she should have reached a decision point: Does the patient appear to be at risk for suicide? If uncertain about the possibility of any risk, the therapist should administer an objective assessment instrument or battery of instruments. The FAST is one instrument that can provide important information regarding the patient's level and intensity of negative thoughts or voices. Administering the questionnaire provides the clinician with data about the specific thoughts that lead to a sense of hopelessness, the relinquishing of special interests and activities, giving up on oneself, self-harm, suicide plans, and actual injunctions to commit suicide. This aspect of the scale is particularly important in the case of a suicidal crisis, for which immediate, appropriate intervention may be lifesaving.

Use of the FAST in planning the treatment strategy. Using information about the items or levels that patients endorse as being experienced with higher than average frequency, clinicians can direct their interventions toward those areas in which their patients are experiencing psychological pain. This evaluation helps the clinician identify and address less extreme types of self-destructive thoughts before they are acted out behaviorally or precipitate a suicidal crisis. Clients receiving high scores on the Suicide Intent Composite (the 27-item brief screening instrument for suicidal intent) are experiencing the types of thoughts that can culminate in actual suicide. By comparing the scores obtained by a patient with those of the standardization group, clinicians can quickly ascertain if the patient's score or scores fall within a normal, nonrisk range with respect to the self-destructive behaviors under consideration (for example, substance abuse or self-harm behaviors) and can monitor changes in scores at various stages in the treatment process. Treatment strategies are directed toward counteracting the dictates of negative voices and behavior patterns that are outside of the normal range on the scale. Elevations in specific categories help determine the direction of the treatment program.

Use of Voice Therapy Methodology in Treatment[1]

My approach to psychotherapy has come to be known as "Voice Therapy"; it is a procedure for giving language or spoken words to the negative thought process that is at the core of an individual's self-destructive behavior. Its purpose is to separate and bring out into the open elements of the antiself system that originated in the internalization of negative parental attitudes and damaging childhood experiences.

Voice Therapy was originally a laboratory procedure used to understand personality dynamics and only secondarily evolved into a psychotherapeutic methodology. The clinical investigations revealed core dynamics that limited people's productivity and satisfactions in life and made them feel depressed and anxious. When used as a therapeutic procedure, the specialized techniques of Voice Therapy consist of three components: (a) the process of eliciting and identifying negative thought patterns, which makes them more accessible and susceptible to control; (b) the feeling release component, that is, recovering repressed emotions and releasing the affect associated with destructive thinking; and (c) the process of counteracting self-destructive behaviors regulated by the voice through the collaborative planning and application of appropriate corrective experiences.

It is important to emphasize that these components are not necessarily undertaken in the order delineated here. Even in the early phase of treatment, corrective suggestions may be used to facilitate release of feeling in sessions where patients verbalize the content of their negative thinking. Patients are encouraged to avoid the addictive substances, habits, and forms of acting-out behavior that they typically use to suppress feeling. Indeed, challenging addictive aspects of the personality is a fundamental part of Voice Therapy. When these outlets are blocked, there is an outpouring of emotion, followed by insight. During the phase when patients are involved with identifying internalized voices, they make their own choice to "defy" voice commands and alter behaviors. Voice Therapy is not interpretive or analytical given that

---

1. The material in this section was taken from "Prescription for Psychotherapy," *Psychotherapy*, *27*, pp. 627-635 (Firestone, 1990c). Used with permission.

patients form their own conclusions as to the sources of their destructive thinking.

Sessions in Which Patients Bring Internalized Voices to the Surface

In this phase of treatment, patients learn to verbalize their self-critical, self-destructive thoughts in the second person, as though another person were addressing them, that is, in the form of statements toward themselves rather than statements about themselves; for example, "You're worthless. You don't matter to anybody," rather than "I feel like I'm a worthless person. I really don't matter to anybody." Expressing the voice in this format facilitates the process of separating the depressed or suicidal patient's own point of view from alien, hostile thought patterns assimilated during the developmental stages. Patients frequently connect voices with parental attitudes and interactions that defined them and fit them into the family system either explicitly or implicitly.

The process of identifying the voice can be approached intellectually as an analytical or cognitive technique or, more dramatically, using cathartic methods (Endnote 4). In the latter technique, there is an emphasis on the release of the affect accompanying the self-attacks. In this abreactive mode, patients are asked to bring out their negative thoughts and express them more emotionally, with instructions such as the following: "Say it louder," or "Let go and say anything that comes to mind." Many patients voluntarily adopt an emotional style of expression when "saying" the voice. They often release intense feelings of anger and sadness as they reveal the self-derogatory thoughts that hold special meaning for them (Endnote 5).

The techniques break through the resistance with which the depressed patient is holding on to self-depreciating attitudes and ideologies. As noted previously, depressed patients have reported a unique familiarity with destructive voices, whether on a neurotic or a psychotic level (as auditory hallucinations), and feel considerably understood by therapists using Voice Therapy methods.

Intense Feeling Release Sessions

Prior to feeling release sessions, patients are asked to avoid painkillers, cigarettes, alcohol, and other self-feeding habits, and are encouraged to spend time in isolation and self-contemplation while developing a written case history (Endnote 6). This presession period generates anxiety, and the patient's feelings tend to surface. In the sessions, patients are encouraged to breathe deeply, to allow sounds to emerge as they exhale, and to verbalize any thoughts that come to mind. As powerful feelings are vented, patients are supported in amplifying this emotional expression, with the following types of instructions: "Really let go," or "Let out a louder sound."

After feelings are released in this manner, patients form their own insights and spontaneously relate irrational or primitive emotional responses, as well as present-day limitations, to early negative experiences within the family. Most individuals describe their memories with unusual clarity and lucidity and appear to genuinely relive events and feelings from early childhood. Patients generally interpret their own material and integrate it without assistance from the therapist; thus transference reactions tend to be minimal. The knowledge of self gained through feeling release sessions is unusually direct and pure. It is as though patients are able to envision their childhood situations and "see through" their present-day problems rather than intellectually "figuring them out" or analyzing them.

These two components—the identification of self-destructive thoughts and intense feeling release—are valuable and necessary for bringing to the surface unconscious elements of the personality that have caused patients severe distress and psychological pain, at times driving them toward depression or a suicidal state. Eliciting and identifying internalized voices provides access to negative parental introjects, the punishing parent part of the antiself system; whereas feeling release sessions uncover the vulnerable, hurt, child part of the split.

Corrective Suggestions

In this phase, therapists work with patients in an attempt to interrupt self-destructive habit patterns through collaborative planning and corrective suggestions in accord with each individual's personal motivation. Plans for behavioral change fall into two categories: (a) corrective suggestions that help control or interrupt self-feeding habits, disrupt fantasy bonds, and other addictive patterns; (b) corrective suggestions that expand the patient's world by encouraging him or her to take risks and thereby overcome fears related to pursuing wants and priorities.

First, patients formulate the unique values that give their lives special meaning. Second, they plan with the therapist means of supporting these goals. Last, as they move toward risk situations and a new level of vulnerability, they learn to tolerate the anxiety involved in positive change and individuation. The overall procedure has an experimental flavor and is undertaken in a cooperative spirit. Corrective suggestions, if consistently followed, bring about changes in the emotional atmosphere that lead to a corrective emotional experience. Patients report that often there are strong voice attacks after significant forward movement but that these self-attacks gradually diminish after they have maintained the new behavior over an extended period of time. The importance of teaching patients to "sweat out" major changes in their style of relating cannot be overestimated.

Corrective suggestions teach patients, on a deep emotional level, that by using self-discipline, they can gradually increase their freedom of choice and self-actualization without being overwhelmed by primitive fears, anxiety states, and self-destructive, suicidal thoughts.

The overall approach is *not* didactic, that is, there is no attempt to directly persuade people to think or behave rationally; rather, I help them discover what they are telling themselves about important situations and uncover the origins of their destructive, self-limiting voices as well as assisting them in exploring ways to move away from negative attitudes and restrictions.

Voice Therapy lends itself well to group interaction. We have observed that when a patient expresses self-attacks that reflect core issues in his or her life, strong feelings are often aroused in the other participants. They have empathy for the person going through the process as well as compassion for themselves. This is particularly evident when the abreactive technique is being used. In Voice Therapy groups, the voices expressed are similar in content— typically restrictive of personality functions—and usually sound so much alike that one person verbalizing his or her voice strikes a familiar chord with others in the group.

Application to Depressed and Suicidal Patients

With patients who are unusually depressed or facing a suicidal crisis, establishing a strong therapeutic relationship and trust is essential. Even then, appraisal of the patient's ego strength is necessary before considering which specific techniques will be used and in which order. Subsequently, the therapist can approach identifying the patient's self-destructive thoughts in sessions. With more seriously disturbed patients, the feeling release component is generally introduced at a later stage of treatment when the patient's ego is stronger and acting out is more under control. A note of caution: In attempting to counteract the effect of the voice on their lives, patients have a tendency to answer the voice dramatically with strong anger as in a dialogue. "Yelling back" even at *symbolic* parental figures unleashes feelings of hatred for which one may later feel tremendous guilt and anxiety. Responding angrily to their self-attacks from their own point of view and differentiating themselves from their parents, for example, "I'm not like you! I'm different!" often leads to increased voice attacks. Voicing angry, hostile feelings toward parents or parental substitutes in sessions tends to cut a person off from imagined or symbolic sources of security, and regressive trends may follow. Therefore, after these sessions, the patient's behavior must be carefully monitored.

In relation to the problem of how to respond to voice attacks, the most effective procedure to follow is a gradual, step-by-step collaborative planning of corrective actions that go against the dictates of the voice, rather than direct verbal confrontation. The part of the patient that is antithetical to his or her interests (the antiself system) cannot be eliminated by using dramatic techniques. Instead, the therapist helps the patient move slowly and consistently toward his or her personal goals, keeping in mind at all times the patient's ego strength and level of tolerance for anxiety states induced by changing behavior patterns. Because the methods of eliciting and identifying voices are relatively simple, easily applied, and immediately understood by the majority of patients, the techniques could be potentially harmful in the hands of an inadequately trained or personally immature therapist.

Voice Therapy Session With a Depressed Patient[2]

A 39-year-old woman, CS, requested an interview with me following a prolonged period of marked improvement in her life and relationships. Through the years, she had succeeded in breaking her addiction to drugs and later to binge eating. Recently, after hearing that her mother had terminal cancer, CS called her and an important conversation ensued. Within several weeks, CS had regressed to a depressed state characterized by symptoms of insomnia and obsessive thoughts of suicide. The suicidal ideation was reminiscent of patterns of thinking she had experienced prior to two serious suicide attempts in her early twenties (Endnote 7).

> *Dr. F.:* How are you today?
>
> *CS:* I haven't been feeling very good for about 3 weeks, but trying to, because it doesn't seem like anything is really happening. But I can feel myself getting more depressed. That's why I wanted to talk to you.
>
> *Dr. F.:* You say about 3 weeks ago?

2. This material is excerpted from a Voice Therapy training videotape. CS had already benefited from Voice Therapy sessions many years prior to this interview and was familiar with the techniques. Her "voice" statements appear in italics.

CS: There were a few things that happened. I talked to my son, who told me that my mother was sick, that she had cancer. When I first heard it, I realized that I had no desire to call her. I was sorry to hear that she was sick, but I didn't want to make any contact with her because she's been so abusive to me in my life that I didn't feel that need to make contact with her, which is very different for me.

But then a friend of mine said that they wondered if I'd feel bad if I didn't talk to her, which triggered tremendous guilt in me. I felt cold-hearted toward my mother. I started attacking myself right away. So I called her, but in the phone call she was vicious, as she usually is. But I sort of brushed it under the carpet and forgot about it, but I don't think I really forgot about it, because I started attacking myself and then I was susceptible to everything that happened after that. I didn't feel strong anymore.

Dr. F.: In other words, you were feeling in a really good state—

CS: A really good state.

Dr. F.: Until that phone call. And you made the phone call because you started to feel guilty. What were you telling yourself? Could you say it as a voice? You said something about being cold-hearted. Try to really say—

CS: Like, *Don't you care about anything? Don't you care about anybody? You never cared about anybody! You never cared about her!* (loud voice and crying) *You never cared about me! You cold-hearted bitch! You don't care about anybody. You think you care about people. You don't care about anything. You think you value your life so much. Look at how much you care! Look at how much you feel!* (pause)

I started believing that voice and acting out those feelings in my real life. I got so distant from my friends and so inward. I kept doing all the things I love to do, but they lost all the joy and all the feeling that I had before. I think I didn't believe that I cared about anything since then because I keep attacking myself. Every time someone says something nice to me, I feel like, "If they only knew, if they only knew."

Dr. F.: Say it as a voice.

CS: *If they only knew what you're really like. I know what you're really like. I lived with you.* (angry, furious) *You ruined our lives! It was your fault! We would have been better off without you.*

Dr. F.: What if you really let go and just let out this anger that you're expressing toward yourself, let it really go.

CS: It scares me to do that.

Dr. F.: You started to.

CS: *Just shut up! Just shut up and get out of the way.* (cries) It's painful to say this.

Dr. F.: Really let go. You might as well get it out.

CS: (Yelling, face set in grimace) *You ruined our lives! You ruined our lives. Just die! Just die, you little shit! Just keep away. Shut up! Just get out of here. Just stop bothering us. We don't care what you think. We don't care what you feel. You don't matter. You aren't important!* I just feel such rage in it.

Dr. F.: Let it out.

CS: I don't know how.

Dr. F.: You're doing fine.

CS: It's really fast, like: *Get back! Just shut up. Get out of here! Stay away! You don't feel anything, nothing matters to you. Don't act all feelingful.* (sarcastic)

Dr. F.: What does it say about your present life? What do they say about your present life?

CS: You think you're so different. You think you're so different from me. You don't feel anything either. You don't have anything in your life. You just make it look like you do. You think you have friends? You don't have anything. Are you married? You think you have children in your life. Are you nice to your own? You're a failure. You're a failure. You can barely tolerate having a boyfriend. You're a failure. And you're getting old. You're getting old and you're going to die a failure. I have voices saying, *You sound crazy, the way you sound screaming at who? Who are you screaming this to, you stupid bitch?* (pause)

Dr. F.: What are you feeling?

CS: One thing is I've always had this thing where I have this need to eat alone. It's been a big thing in my life. And over the last month, I've just decided that's one thing I wouldn't do, was eat alone. But the feeling is like now you have nothing, absolutely nothing. Even though I know it's not true, it's a very depressing feeling. Because whatever that isolation meant to me, it felt like I had something. It's something I've done ever since I was so little. It's hard to shake the feeling but that's a big source of why I have nothing. It's almost like, "You have nothing to live for now."

Dr. F.: Say it as a voice.

CS: What's the big deal? (snide) *Your new deal: you're not going to eat alone. What is that shit? Now what do you have? You have nothing to look forward to. Now you're just going to die. You're just going to die like me.* (loud, rageful expression) *A sick death! You're going to die of cancer. Just wait till you get it. Just wait! Get checked. Get checked because you're going to die just like me!* (deep sobs)

Dr. F.: It seems like that was the final attack. The final upper hand.

CS: Because that's what she said in the phone call.

Dr. F.: What happened in the phone call?

CS: I didn't even notice it, but I called her because I finally decided to and I felt very sad for her, just for a human being having something painful like that wrong with her. It was painful and I wanted to be nice to her.

Dr. F.: What did she say?

CS: She said, "It's my responsibility to tell you that I have colon cancer and that you'll probably get it, so have yourself checked right away so they can catch it early." I said, "If there's anything I can do for—" I didn't get the words out of my mouth before she said, "I don't need anything from you."

Dr. F.: How did she say it? What tone of voice?

CS: She said, "I don't need anything from you. I have people who love me. I'm beautiful. I'm a blonde now (and this is a woman who is fat, hugely fat), I'm thin." She said, "I have people who worship the ground I walk on. I have family." Her family was her brothers and sisters, it was never me. (sad) When I went to the doctor, my regular doctor, for an annual checkup and I told him about the conversation, he said, "She is so sadistic toward you. What's she doing, making a connection with you through death now? She needs to call you and tell you, you're going to die, too? Every time she gets sick." But I knew he was right. That's what hurt. She didn't want anything from me. She just wanted to tell me, "You're going to die too, you know." But I felt old after that whole thing. Before that I felt young, alive sexually, wanting more from my boyfriend and just happy with myself. And I was angry. I didn't want to go for that kind of checkup. I will go sometime of course, but I didn't have to do it right away. It's like, I'm not dying. It wasn't me.

Dr. F.: Say it.

CS: "I'm not dying! You are! (angry) I'm not miserable! You are! I like when people care about me. You don't! I don't have the kind of things in my life that you do. I have things in my life that make me feel good, not connections. I have simple friendships that mean more." It feels hard to say these kinds of things, I don't know why. (pause)

Dr. F.: Looking back at these past weeks, it seems like you gave up your life.

CS: I felt like giving up.

Dr. F.: You really gave up your life and feeling even though you went through the motions.

CS: Yes. I didn't feel happy. I felt tortured, so tortured, sleepless nights which I haven't had insomnia or anything like that in so many years. I couldn't feel good. And I've been so overemotional.

Dr. F.: It seems like there really were two parts to this: The traumatic attack that your mother made on you and her tone and feelings toward you reminded you of the feelings that you had growing up, through most of your life really. But at the same time, things were accentuated by the fact that you were giving up an addictive style of living, which was an attempt to help yourself. Giving up eating in that way and binges, patterns that would hurt you and make you feel bad about the way you look, made you exceptionally vulnerable at the time of the phone call.

Giving that up alone would have created a depression. Just changing an addictive pattern and not giving in to that pattern would have led to feeling sad or feeling hyperemotional. But the two things combined were an odd combination which created conditions for you to be really thrown back in to the other, old situation.

CS: Without the old defense.

Dr. F.: Yeah, without the old defense, right. So that's why you have been so tortured.

Later, CS discussed incidents from her childhood that she felt had contributed to her addictive patterns of overeating.

Dr. F.: Why do you think food became so important to you in the context of what we're talking about?

CS: Well, I know that I was starved as a child. My mother was very fat. She weighed 210 pounds and was about five foot two. And she always said, "I'm going to keep you thin no matter what." So she controlled everything I ate to the point where I couldn't sleep because I was so hungry. That led to a whole secret pattern of sneaking food and eating horrible food while hiding in my closet.

Dr. F.: So you're tampering with a lifelong pattern actually. It seems like you took on an awful lot at the same time. It was an unfortunate coincidence, it seems like. How do you feel now?

CS: I feel so much more relaxed. I can feel my size. It's weird. I haven't felt my size.

Dr. F.: Your size?

CS: Just feeling myself. I feel like a woman sitting here and I haven't felt like that in a while. I felt so physically awkward with my body, just trying to look right, you know. And relaxed. I feel so much more relaxed. I really appreciate talking to you so much.

Dr. F.: Thanks.

Discussion and Outcome

The process of identifying her self-attacks and releasing the associated angry affect in the session enabled CS to emerge from her depressed state and begin to enjoy her life again. The session gave her clarity about crucial events that had triggered her depression, and she made significant connections between early incidents in her life and her current situation and relationships.

CS experienced a decrease in self-critical thinking and guilty self-recriminations immediately after the session. She reported experiencing "no voices at all" for several weeks following the interview. After dealing with her reactions to giving up a lifelong addictive pattern, she was now more free to pursue gratification in the interpersonal environment. Later, as she expanded her boundaries and accepted more affection and love, she became aware of times when she would begin to attack herself. At this point, she was better able to counter these negative thoughts before they reached the point of undermining her good mood. Follow-up 1 year later indicated that CS's emotional state had remained stable, her relationship with the man in her life was a source of happiness to her, and she had continued to develop in other areas.

In analyzing the dynamics of this case, it becomes apparent that while in the process of dealing with the remnants of a serious addictive pattern, CS was negatively affected by the abusive conversation with her mother. This contact reactivated voices that had been prominent throughout CS's childhood and adolescence, injunctions that she should disappear or kill herself. Following the phone call, CS took on an alien point of view and was cut off from feeling for herself and from taking advantage of the gratifications in her life. Although in reality nothing had changed, she found herself descending into a depressed state.

This case exemplifies an important dynamic in suicide. In general, when individuals submit to the dictates of the voice, they become progressively alienated from themselves, even in the absence of conspicuously stressful events. It is the ascendance of the voice process that is primarily responsible for their depression, anxiety, and emotional pain. This is a significant point for the clinician to consider when treating chronically suicidal patients. It is also relevant in many cases of adolescent suicide where there appear to be no external precipitating factors.

As described in Chapter 10, the good-looking, popular honors student who suddenly commits suicide presents a puzzling phenomenon. In actuality, these young people kill themselves because they have gradually become overwhelmed by self-attacks and internalized rage toward self. Self-attacks of this sort are often precipitated by fear of separation induced by movement toward individuation and breaking bonds with one's parents, which leave the person with increased guilt and anxiety. As the voice process progressively takes precedence over their natural desire to live, they yield to its injunctions and ultimately act out death wishes.

These dynamics were clearly operating in CS's case. During her childhood, she had sensed her mother's hatred and aggression and had endured overt expressions of it in verbal abuse, beatings, and the sadistic application of a severe dietary regimen. This hostile behavior toward her was typical throughout CS's childhood. Her mother was an intrusive, self-nurturing woman, who attempted to make connections to CS in every interaction. For example, at CS's wedding, her mother reached into CS's dress, grabbed her breast, and was squeezing it, when CS protested, "What are you doing? Are you crazy?" Her mother replied, "What are you talking about? I'm your mother. I have a right. You belong to me." This intense enmeshment was played out in the phone conversation with her daughter, arousing internalized aggression in CS that manifested itself in malevolent voice attacks and injunctions to get rid of herself.

The session illustrates how Voice Therapy methods quickly uncover the core issues in an individual's life. This partially conscious material would have been more difficult to elicit in traditional therapy, and treatment would have taken considerably more time. A therapist's interpretation would not have had the impact on CS that Voice Therapy techniques did, that is, enabling her to identify and understand the source of her regression. Nor would it have provided the clinician with any indication of the power of the destructive voices that were holding sway over her life. Prior to the session, CS had been only slightly aware of some of her negative thinking. However, during the interview, she gave vent to voices that revealed the key issue—that, like her mother, she too was going to die. Her mother's warnings about cancer and death triggered the final triumph of the destructive ideation. In the session, CS could feel the death wishes that her mother had felt toward her throughout her childhood and in the bizarre connections her mother continued to make with her, as she had done in the phone call, with devastating effects.

Overview of Voice
Therapy Methodology

Although it is relatively easy to elicit the destructive voice process and bring it to the surface, Voice Therapy is not a short-term procedure or a simple cure-all. In fact, it is more theoretically oriented than technique oriented. It is impossible to conceive of "cure" without patients being able to change the fundamental aspects of the ways they are living out their defensive structure. Patients must devote themselves to identifying voices and changing their lifestyle by refusing to comply with internalized negative prescriptions (acting on the self versus the antiself system). There must be movement toward expanded choices in the direction of a wider, more satisfying range of living.

In the course of long-term treatment, clinicians have to confront core issues, of both interpersonal trauma and existential pain, with sensitivity and respect for each patient's idiosyncratic modes of defense. In addition, they must understand that not only suicidal patients but all individuals suffer from some degree of addiction that interferes with their living fully. In challenging these addictive or compulsive patterns, the therapist can be conceptualized as a "transitional object" in that he or she provides an *authentic* relationship for the patient during the transition from depending on self-nourishing processes to seeking and finding satisfaction in genuine relationships outside the office setting.

The therapist needs to understand the dynamics involved in suicide threats, gestures, and attempts when they are used as a method of control or manipulation. Self-destructive behavior does act as a manipulation that hurts others, but patients must learn that it is not worth the pain they must endure to make the manipulation work. Suicidal motives are multidetermined; however, it is always important for the clinician to bear in mind that suicidal attitudes, motives, and ideology, although not necessarily manipulative or a struggle for control, are largely interpersonal responses and must be understood and treated as such.

Therapists treating depressed or suicidal individuals must help them understand that abuse of oneself reflects anger turned inward and is never an acceptable alternative. It is not appropriate to attack oneself even when the self-criticism has some basis in reality. In my work, I attempt to show patients that it is maladaptive to punish or hate themselves for self-destructive actions or for possessing negative traits or personality characteristics. One's energy is better directed toward changing undesirable traits. I sometimes cite the example of a patient with a below-average IQ who berated and attacked himself, calling himself "stupid, an imbecile, a totally despicable person." His actual limitation did not merit his self-attack or account for the hostility toward himself. Indeed, people's self-attacks constitute a violation of their own human rights.

The therapist's primary goal is to help patients come to terms with the painful feelings and frustrations that caused them to retreat to inward, self-nurturing patterns and self-destructive machinations. The therapeutic task involves helping patients to become aware of their ongoing desires and needs and to use the therapeutic situation to ask directly for what they want. The limits to personal gratification inherent in the therapeutic relationship lead to frustration of the patient's wants, which in turn arouses anger. Patients come to realize, on an emotional level, that they can survive without the therapist gratifying their needs, and they gradually learn how to handle their angry responses. Dealing with anger is, of course, a central issue in the treatment of depressed or suicidal patients because of their strong propensity to turn their aggression against themselves.

Termination

Dealing with the termination phase and its meaning with respect to separation and individuation is a critical part of the therapeutic process. The clinician must understand depression occurring at this stage of treatment as related to separation anxiety. Often the patient will maintain symptoms and regress to try to hold on to the therapist. The only interpretation that is productive at this point will focus on the dynamics underlying the patient's attempt to maintain a fantasy bond with the therapist. In anticipation of the termination phase (and throughout the therapy), the effective therapist encourages the independent development of the patient's own point of view. The focus is on helping patients to be inner directed as opposed to outer directed, that is, living life according to their own beliefs and values rather than submitting to or defying the point of view of others.

In addition to separation anxiety, existential issues invariably affect the self system. As in CS's case, when the phone call with her mother served to remind her of her own mortality, a heightened awareness of separation, death, or loss often leads to a sense of despair and hopelessness. The sobering realities of aloneness and death tend to reinforce the defense system and play an important role in regression. It is difficult for most people to maintain a powerful investment in a life that they inevitably will lose. Therapy must help the individual rise to the challenge of making his or her life experience all the more meaningful in the face of certain death.

Conclusion

An understanding of Voice Therapy theory is more important than the specific methods used in the treatment of high-risk patients. The primary determinants of therapeutic success, however, are the personality of the therapist and his or her degree of maturity and capacity for feeling. The clinician who respects the necessity of defense formation and understands that the patient's symptomatology was necessitated by his or her circumstances will be better able to communicate this empathic understanding, thereby enhancing each person's feeling of compassion for him- or herself.

Voice Therapy is a serious approach, requiring a strong clinician—ideally, one relatively free of his or her own defenses or defensiveness. He or she would feel a strong conviction that if people address the issues involved in their self-destructive thinking and show courage in accepting corrective suggestions, they can alter any pattern of self-destructive behavior and change deep-seated character defenses. This optimistic outlook would not reflect an idealistic view of people but would take into account the fact that the capacity to change is dependent on one's willingness to suffer through the pain and anxiety inherent in making significant adjustments in one's identity and lifestyle. The patient must overcome the fundamental resistance to a better life characterized by autonomy and self-actualization.

The techniques outlined above, albeit governed by the patient's level of ego strength, allow for behavioral changes that often go beyond what is possible in many other therapeutic formats. Because individuals in Voice Therapy are engaged in breaking with powerful defenses that have limited and depleted their energy, it is vital that the therapeutic approach offer maximum opportunity for emancipation and expansion of personal boundaries.

Endnotes

1. For an in-depth explanation of Voice Therapy theory and methodology, the reader is referred to "Voice Therapy" in *What Is Psychotherapy? Contemporary Perspectives* (Firestone, 1990d), "Prescription for Psychotherapy" (Firestone, 1990c), *Voice Therapy: A Psychotherapeutic Approach to Self-Destructive Behavior* (Firestone, 1988), and *Combating Destructive Thought Processes: Voice Therapy and Separation Theory* (Firestone, 1997).

2. Shneidman (1985) cited Murray (1938) in constructing his categories of symbolic and real needs that "provide a possible useful taxonomy of suicidal behaviors" (p. 126).

3. This "case example, following a prototypical example (Shneidman, 1981), illustrates how the therapist can widen the number of options for the suicidal patient" (Leenaars, 1994, p. 54). A middle-aged suicidal businessman with high lethality declared that he simply "could not bear to live" because of the loss of his job, a prestigious position he had held for 18 years.

At that point, it seemed that *only* suicide was an alternative for him. Initially, the therapist did several things. For example, the therapist attempted to begin to "widen his blinders" and said something like, "Now let's see . . . you could look for another job." "I couldn't do that." (It is precisely the "can't" and "won't" and "have to" and "never" and "always" and "only" issues that are addressed with highly lethal individuals.) "You could hire a consulting firm to help you look for a job." "I couldn't do that."

Finally, after making a list, with the patient's cooperation, of a dozen or so alternatives, the therapist said:

"You can always commit suicide, but there is obviously no need to do that today." No response. "Now let's look at our ideas and rank them in order of your preference, keeping in mind that not one of them is perfect." . . . Within a few minutes, he [the patient] was less lethal. His emotions were less overpowering and his logic and perception were less constricted. What was important was that suicide was no longer ranked first.

4. *Clarification of specific techniques for verbalizing voices:* The patient presents a problem, for example, he or she complains about the onset of depression. The therapist might ask, "When did you start feeling this way?" The patient describes an event that he or she believes signaled the onset of the problem. The therapist inquires, "What do you think you were telling yourself about this event?" The patient discusses his or her thoughts related to the event. If, for example, the incident was a phone call in which a male patient asked for a date and was rejected, the therapist asks, "What were you telling yourself about being turned down?"

The patient at this point might say, "I was telling myself that I'm not very attractive. I'm not very interesting. Girls don't like me very much." The therapist then instructs the patient to say these thoughts in the second person, as a voice—for example, *"You're* not attractive. *You're* not interesting. No girl would like *you"*—statements made *to* himself, about himself. When the patient puts his thoughts in this form, strong feelings emerge and the whole affective tone of the verbalization is transformed from flat, matter-of-fact statements to an intense emotional outpouring. As patients express the voice in this format, they usually have their own steam and keep the words and feelings going on their own volition. The therapist simply offers encouragement with statements like, "Say it louder." "Don't hold back."

Another technique is illustrated in the following example. A patient discloses that he or she was hurt by a criticism from someone. The therapist in this instance would ask, "Why do you think you were so hurt? Is it true?" The patient discusses whether he or she thinks the criticism was fair or unfair and may emphasize that it really bothered him or her. In cases where people respond in a dramatically negative manner, it's not the truth that hurts, but the fact that the negative feedback happened to correspond to specific self-critical, self-attacking thoughts already existing. The therapist says, "What types of negative thoughts do you have about yourself?" After the patient relates the thoughts, the therapist says, "Now try to say these as statements being said to you." To understand the methodology used directly to help patients get into the "voice," the reader is referred to Chapters 9, 10, and 11 in *Combating Destructive Thought Processes: Voice Therapy and Separation Theory* (Firestone, 1997) and the videotape *Voice Therapy With Dr. Robert Firestone* (Parr, 1984).

5. The impact of the sessions cannot be described adequately in words; one must view videotaped sessions to appreciate the depth of pain and anger expressed both by relatively healthy individuals and by depressed patients. (See the list of Voice Therapy training videotapes in the Appendix.)

6. Although our overall treatment approach is very different than that of Arthur Janov (1970) and Primal Therapy, we have found his technique valuable for helping people get to their feelings. It is preferable to conduct the feeling release component for extended sessions with multiple sessions per week during the early phase.

PART V

CONCLUSION

16 Guidelines for Primary Prevention of Suicide and Summary

> No treatment could do any good until I understood the voice and saw that it was running me, that I was an automaton. . . . It's incredible to know that the voice prevented me from doing this [writing a biography], even took over my real self image. . . . I feel as if I've been reprieved from a lifelong sentence.
>
> James Masterson (1985, p. 68)
> (from the journal of a borderline patient)

> From the deliberate and stubborn silence she depended upon to survive her painful childhood, Sharon has created a new voice that is all her own.
>
> John A. Chabot (1997, p. 189), *A New Lease on Life*[1]

To understand suicide prevention, one must understand the psychodynamics that predispose self-destructive thought processes. In cases of hereditary predisposition and biological determinants, one can only approach the problem genetically and use the appropriate medical procedures. In the large majority of cases, however, I believe that psychological factors are predominant in the causality of depression, self-destructive behavior, and alienation from self.

---

1. This quote is taken from John Chabot's interview with Sharon as it appears in his book *A New Lease on Life* (1997). Chabot's interview is a follow-up of the case study of Sharon reported in Chapter 2.

My primary concern is in understanding suicide in relation to the destructive thought processes that govern action. But where do these voices come from? Several years ago, while visiting a friend, a psychologist, I was explaining the methods of Voice Therapy when his wife declared, "I know what you're talking about. I had these angry voices myself." At one time in her life, she revealed, she had experienced extremely nasty and hostile thoughts toward herself but had found a method of dealing with the problem. I was interested and asked her how she did it. She went on to say that she had screamed them away, shouting as loud as she could, "Get away! Get the hell out of my head!" Her method was effective and put an end to the voices as far as she was concerned. Of interest, she didn't associate these thoughts in any way with psychological pain or personal relationships. Instead, she thought that they were related to mysterious external sources such as unusual negative ion concentrations or changes in atmospheric pressure.

In my opinion, her denial of the psychological origin of her voice attacks would have a negative effect on her life. Although, on the surface, this woman seems to have devised an effective means of dealing with her voice attacks, her approach was naive because she failed to confront the source of these attacks in relation to her own personal development. Unlike my friend's wife, most subjects who use Voice Therapy techniques become painfully aware that these voices evolved from problems in early interpersonal relationships. My associates and I have found that destructive thought patterns are closely related to parental attitudes and communications that have been incorporated into the personality. This link to parents' hostile, neglectful behaviors toward the patient becomes obvious in Voice Therapy, and patients themselves connect their voice attacks to family interactions in their developmental years.

Guidelines for Primary Prevention in Childhood[2]

As noted earlier, patterns of defense that were developed early in life, and were appropriate for dealing with stress at the time, later become the core problems for people in their adult lives. Given the effects that negative introjects have on people, what can we do about defenses in relation to preventive mental hygiene?

Because the primary sources of negative thought processes that control self-destructive, suicidal behavior can be found in the abuses of childhood, it

---

2. The material in this section is taken primarily from *Compassionate Child-Rearing*, published by Plenum (Firestone, 1990b). Used with permission.

is logical that the primary prevention of suicide should be addressed in the context of the child's early environment. The guidelines that follow include several basic principles regarding child-rearing practices that help provide the basis for the healthy development of children, that is, (a) a secure and loving parental climate; (b) teaching children to avoid developing inward, self-nurturing habit patterns; and (c) curtailing disciplinary measures that inculcate the image of the child as "bad."

A Secure and Loving Parental Climate

Love-food. The concept of *love-food* refers to both affection and control. All children require love, regulation, and control to become happy, self-regulating, and self-directed adults. I have concluded that in the earliest developmental phase, the mother (or primary caretaker) ideally would be able to nurture her infant without undue anxiety and would have empathy toward the child. I refer to the operations of ideal parenting as providing a psychonutritional product called "love-food," which implies both the emotional maturity of parents and their desire to provide for the need gratification of the infant and young child. Love-food is necessary for survival in both the physical sense and the psychological sense. If parents are immature, weak, or inadequate, they will fail to provide basic security for the child even though they may have the best of intentions.

Parents as positive role models. Parents who value their own lives and experiences act as positive role models in setting the emotional climate for their children's development of self-esteem and sense of well-being. Parental integrity, openness, and honesty are as necessary for the child's emotional development as food and drink are for their physical survival. In addition to the benefit of having parents who serve as good role models, children need adults who will relate to them openly and directly in terms of their real thoughts and feelings. Parents' honest, direct communication with their children about the parents' feelings helps break the idealization of parents and family that is typically maintained at the child's expense.

Toxic personality traits in parents not only have a profoundly destructive effect on children directly, but these negative qualities are also passed on to succeeding generations through the process of identification and imitation. Parents who themselves lead dishonest, empty, dull lives will be unable to offer themselves as adequate role models for their children. The quality of the parents' relationship with each other also contributes to or detracts from the child's sense of security and strongly affects his or her ability to sustain close relationships as an adult. The child who grows up in an atmosphere created by loving yet mutually independent parents who do not subordinate themselves one to the other has a much better opportunity to develop his or her full potential and will not be afraid of closeness and intimacy as an adult. On the other hand, couples who have formed a fantasy bond have little energy or emotional sustenance to offer their children.

Sexual rivalry and aggression in the family system. The extent to which the parents' relationship is based on mature sexuality and real companionship is an important determinant of children's subsequent adjustment. Too often couples form a fantasy bond that is exclusive of outside relationships; hence the child born into that relationship is often perceived as a competitor *within the family system.* Rivalrous feelings toward the child of the same sex will be exceptionally strong in parents who are immature, narcissistic, and overly possessive. These insecure parents often have unconscious death wishes toward this intimate intruder or "enemy." Children internalize this aggression and unconsciously adopt their parents' hostile point of view. As they grow older, they often feel the most self-hating and self-destructive in competitive situations and have a tendency to back down or turn against themselves.

There are other reasons parents feel angry and resentful toward their children. Parents' defenses are threatened by their offspring; the innocence and aliveness of the child reawaken emotional pain that parents suffered in their own childhoods. Children also represent a dependency burden that threatens immature parents. In addition, the helplessness and vulnerability of the child remind parents of their own fears and inadequacies. In each of these cases, parents tend to harbor intense aggressive feelings toward the child that are unacceptable to them and therefore are suppressed or relegated to the unconscious. Manifestations of this hostility, however, are imposed on the child in the form of punitive child-rearing practices or through more subtle forms of emotional maltreatment. The internalization of parental hostility and malice through the defense of identifying with the aggressor is a primary causative factor in suicide.

Teaching Children to Avoid Developing Inward, Self-Nurturing Habit Patterns

Avoiding isolation. Disciplinary techniques that foster isolation and an inward, self-protective posture in children should be strenuously avoided (Endnote 1). Many experts advise parents to remove a child who is acting out or throwing a tantrum and isolate him or her in another room until he or she is calm. I strongly disagree with this method (referred to by professionals as "time-out") because being left alone to "cry out" their rage only encourages children's hostile fantasies and increases their anger. This disciplinary method teaches children to seek isolation whenever they are frustrated or angry and leads them to become progressively more inward, self-protective, and secretive.

Parents should strive to "let their child be," that is, to avoid constant evaluations and comments, either positive or negative, on their child's posture, mannerisms, way of speaking, and other personality characteristics. This form of parental intrusiveness leads to extreme self-consciousness and social unease in adolescents and adults as well as an exaggerated need for isolation and self-protection.

Allowing freedom of expression. When parents allow their children to speak their minds freely, a new style of family interaction becomes possible that more successfully meets the basic needs of all family members for harmonious social affiliation. To accomplish this goal, parents should reward children for expressing their opinions, for stating their perceptions, and for asking questions about so-called forbidden subjects. In helping their children to become outward and open in their communication, it is especially important that parents not react defensively to the child's perception of them or other family members. Sensitive parents also respect the child's right to his or her feeling reactions—to cry or feel angry about unpleasant or distressing family interactions. Allowing children an opportunity for self-expression offers a method for healing psychic wounds and is vital to the child's continuing psychological growth. Parents can show by their own words and actions that angry feelings can be verbalized instead of being acted out behaviorally or in critical, sarcastic comments. The suppression of a child's angry responses leads to passive-aggressive, withholding patterns that characterize an inward lifestyle.

Avoidance of mixed messages. Parents who strive to act responsibly and with integrity in their own lives, who do not allow hypocrisy or double standards to compromise their self-respect, are providing their children with a blueprint for mental health. In contrast, parents whose lives are characterized by dishonesty and whose communications contain mixed messages mystify children and can fracture their sense of reality. In my opinion, the truth must be upheld in family life or there will be serious consequences. Children are acutely sensitive to variation in parental behavior and, if forced to "swallow" parents' duplicity, illusions, and lies, suffer severe blows to their own integrity. In relation to painful topics such as death, parents have a natural desire to protect their children and spare the children's feelings; however, their attempts to do so often cause more damage than simply facing issues squarely Children who are aware of the realities of life, as well as the shortcomings of the adults around them, have a better basis for coping with stresses as adults.

Discouraging addictive and destructive habit patterns. Children should be discouraged from developing self-nurturing, addictive habit patterns including excessive eating, television viewing, video-game playing, and other such compulsive behaviors. Parents should take note if their child is suddenly putting on weight or spending an inordinate amount of time alone in his or her room. Adults need to provide their children with a variety of experiences in which they can actively participate with others rather than allowing them to spend their time involved in isolated activities.

It is of the utmost importance that parents not involve themselves in addictive habit patterns that later will be imitated by their offspring. Parents who succumb to addictions such as alcohol, drugs, and addictive personal relationships set an example of unhealthy self-indulgence and, by their actions, promote the use of soothing mechanisms to avoid psychological pain.

Expressions of negative power on the part of children, such as temper tantrums used for manipulation, need to be dealt with firmly. Parents would, ideally, help their children learn that it is not appropriate to cry when they are angry. In this way, they show children that chronic whining or crying is a manipulation that is unacceptable. Children should also be taught that it is never adaptive to castigate or hate themselves for wrongdoing; rather, that it is much more constructive to work on changing their behavior in the future.

Supporting the development of constructive behaviors. Parents should encourage their offspring to develop a sense of responsibility for their lives and an active posture of mastering and coping with the world. It is important to help children develop positive attitudes toward both work and avocation. Children are capable of entering into productive work in the home at an early age, and as they get older, they can expand their participation into more important household and business functions. Treating children as contributing members of the family by providing them with responsibilities not only is respectful but acts as an effective discipline.

Children should be encouraged to develop their own interests, careers, and values. Ideally, parents would not impose their interests on their children but would expose them to many experiences and allow them to discover their own. Parents should not attempt to coerce or manipulate them into career choices. It is critical for parents to "let go" of their children as they grow older; otherwise, as adults, they will tend to equate independence with defiance and respond with unnecessary guilt when moving toward autonomy and independence.

Parents should teach their children that friendships are as important as family relationships. Friendships are often more rewarding because friends are generally selected on the basis of positive qualities and compatible interests. Parents should actively avoid conveying to children suspicious or paranoid attitudes toward others, either by words or by example. Critical or prejudicial attitudes toward those who are different than oneself or one's family or cultural background generate fear, suspicion, and cynicism in children.

Avoiding Disciplinary Measures That
Inculcate the Image of the Child as "Bad"

Most children grow up feeling that they are bad or unlovable. Parents must, at all costs, avoid labeling the child as bad, evil, or essentially hostile, for example, as "the angry one," "the troublemaker," "the difficult one," and so on. These characterizations stigmatize the child and induce those very behaviors for which the child will later hate him- or herself. To avert this outcome, parents need to understand that few rules are necessary to achieve the goal of socializing children. However, those rules that *are* necessary should be consistently upheld. Parents should clearly state their restrictions to the child and, as the child matures, they can explain the reasoning behind such limits. It is more effective to reward children for good behavior and keep punishment to a minimum. A combination of verbal approval, tangible rewards, affection, genuine acknowledgment, and some form of negative consequence for undesirable behavior is conducive to effectively disciplining children without making them feel they are bad or undeserving of love.

Parents should never shake, hit, beat, or physically abuse their child. Harsh, sadistic punishment can set up lifelong fears in the child and create strong tendencies to provoke mistreatment from others that persist into adult life.

Children need reassurance that they are worthwhile after they have been disciplined. Parents should stress that it was the child's *behavior* that was undesirable, not that he or she was a bad person, and that objectionable behavior can be changed. Moralistic training procedures based on the premise that children are bad or sinful have a crippling effect by causing children to turn against themselves. They should not be taught that they are bad or selfish for having wants or needs; such desires are an essential part of their personal identity. If they progressively turn their backs on their wants and learn to sacrifice themselves for others out of a sense of obligation or guilt, they are in effect surrendering a basic part of their identity. As emphasized earlier, giving up priorities, special interests, and points of identity are serious indications of suicide intent.

Battles of the will are best avoided because they degrade the child and reinforce an image of being bad. These unnecessary power plays that force conformity and submission in children can be prevented if parents refrain from issuing ultimatums or arbitrarily taking a rigid stand. I am not suggesting, however, that parents adopt an overly permissive attitude that fosters regressive behavior, destructive acting out, or "parent abuse." Parents need to discover the required balance, which is to a large extent dependent on their maturity and self-control. When parents *do* find themselves in a power struggle, they must refrain from exploding in anger at their child. Irrational expressions of rage frighten children and reinforce an image of the parent as out of control and ineffective or weak. The parent who accepts his or her own anger and feels comfortable expressing it in a controlled manner is neither feared nor seen as inadequate by the child.

In conclusion, the child-rearing practices discussed here are fundamental to encouraging the child to take the reasonable risks necessary for character development while discouraging him or her from developing a closed, inward orientation toward life. The parents' attitudes in this regard are paramount. If mothers and fathers are defensive and self-protective, they will encourage self-protective postures in their children. To teach a child to live "the good life," parents would have to genuinely value themselves, accept their own feelings and priorities, and actively participate in fulfilling their own lives (Endnote 2).

Dimensions of a Lifestyle That Counters Suicidal Trends

Case of Sharon

How can individuals who have been damaged by their early programming challenge the suicidal process that exists, to varying degrees, within each person? I have already described the techniques of Voice Therapy that counteract self-destructive trends in patients. By emancipating themselves from destructive family ties and negative parental prescriptions, people can often develop the courage necessary to remain separate and gradually develop their own ideals, values, and sense of identity. In learning to deal with intensified voice attacks aroused by their movement toward individuation and by holding on to the new territory, they can ultimately liberate themselves from self-destructive propensities that once overpowered them.

This process of progressive individuation and separation was exemplified in Sharon's life in the years following her suicide attempt. The material in this section was excerpted from *A New Lease on Life* by John Chabot (1997). The book describes the recovery process in eight individuals the author interviewed, each of whom had made one or more serious suicide attempts during their lives.[2] Chabot's chapter about Sharon traces her recovery from her attempted suicide in the autumn of 1976 to the present day. In the intervening years, Sharon devoted time to working with her friends in an ongoing business venture. She also acquired a master's degree in psychology and became a psychological assistant to a clinical psychologist. Chabot's discussion delineates the specific dimensions of Sharon's lifestyle that facilitated her recovery and enabled her to achieve a new level of understanding and meaning in life.

Sharon's "journey" toward fulfilling the unique goals that now give her life meaning was undertaken in the context of long-standing friendships and a lifestyle conducive to her regaining the ground she had lost during her suicidal crisis. The specific dimensions of that lifestyle represent sound mental health principles and can be generalized beyond her process of recovery. The aspects of "good living" described below directly challenge internalized prohibitions of the voice and, when applied more generally, would enhance the well-being of most people.

The Therapeutic Value of Friendship

Friendship fulfills the basic need of human beings for social affiliation and is vital in counteracting negative injunctions of the voice that foster isolation and alienation. Friendship is based on choice rather than obligation. A trusted friend who possesses the qualities one admires can become an ally in one's personal development. Meaningful communication with a close friend or friends on an everyday basis diminishes the frequency of self-attacks, disrupts self-denying behavior, and challenges tendencies toward living an inward, self-protective lifestyle. Chabot (1997) writes:

---

2. Many thanks to Dr. John Chabot for his compilation of and sensitive commentary on Sharon's recovery story. From *A New Lease of Life* by John A. Chabot. Copyright 1997 by Fairview Press. Reprinted by permission of Fairview Press.

[Following her suicide attempt], Sharon knew her immediate recovery could not depend upon reconciliation with her family. Instead, she would seek to repair her strained relationships with the Seattle friends who had become such a valuable and vital part of her life since her break from home. These were the friends she had successfully eluded in pursuing her secret plan to end her life. These were the friends she was embarrassed to face after her plan failed. And these were the friends who would become her new family, supporting her dramatically changing sense of herself.

Sharon observes that the end of her individual therapy with Tom opened a new world of possibilities for her in connecting to people. From the posture of stubborn silence that marked her initial entrance into therapy, Sharon emerged from her cocoon to become a more open, passionately engaging butterfly. She felt ready to relate to more people, to take on a larger world than the constricted life she had been leading up to that point. (p. 179)

[Here are Sharon's own words]: "I love the energy and vitality and honesty and sensitivity to each other and to ourselves. . . . [We] are struggling to live our lives as independent people, capable of forming close, meaningful relationships, as unencumbered as we each can be by the painful, destructive patterns of our past lives.

"I feel supportive of the ideas by which we are trying to live our lives and want to share this support by struggling to live my life as honestly and openly as I can. I feel touched to realize that there are people I feel deeply for, real friends who support my independence—the live part of myself—who want to be alive themselves." (p. 181)

"I would say this group of people is as much a cross section of people as you would find anywhere, with one difference: open communication," Sharon observes. "What ties us together more than anything else as a group of friends is an open communication among everybody. This has a very high value for us, and is very much practiced all the time, just in casual interaction and more formally. We actually set aside time to get together and talk among ourselves. The same kinds of things happen there that happen everywhere, both good and bad. In that sense, it's not ideal. But in a way, I see it as the closest to utopia I can imagine." (p. 184)

Sharing Activities and Adventure

Viewing life as a gift, a unique opportunity, and an adventure opens up the possibility of moving toward more freedom of choice rather than continually restricting one's choices. Movement toward the unfamiliar can be frightening, yet exciting, and brings out new facets of one's personality. Disrupting routine habit patterns invariably leads to a more adventurous life. Being open to spontaneous activity represents an alive choice in contrast to preserving deadening conformity and conventionality. Until people give up their destructive thinking and behaviors and break with their dulling routines, they will continue to maintain a false sense of security and an illusion of self-sufficiency that severely impairs their ability to take action in the interpersonal world.

> Sharon beams, her face brightening as she excitedly relates the fantastic adventures she has shared with her friends over the years. Each summer the group plans ambitious backpacking and mountain climbing expeditions that have taken them to many areas of the United States, as well as mountain ranges in Canada and other continents around the world. (pp. 184-185)
>
> More than mastering the mountains, these adventures have played a major role in strengthening the cohesive bonds of this group over the years. . . . In facing the mountains and renewing her commitment to her friends, Sharon felt she was no longer running away from her past or from her parents. Instead, she was climbing toward a more hopeful, more fulfilling future, a brighter summit with new possibilities for openness, understanding, and trust, in herself and others. (pp. 184-186)
>
> Sharon again emphasizes how her suicide attempt affected her whole community of friends: it brought into sharper focus the value of openness, respect, and responsibility for one another. "If there's any one precipitating event that is a breeding ground for suicide," Sharon explains, "I see it as isolation." Her group of friends function as an antidote to isolation and alienation, connecting each individual to a larger and more encompassing sense of purpose and meaning with shared values and shared responsibilities. (Chabot, 1997, p. 186)

Search for Meaning and Transcendental Goals

Involvement with other people or goals outside one's narrow range of experience is not only a sound mental health principle but also reflects a truly moral, philosophical position. From Sharon's perspective, approaching humanity with compassion that went beyond her own private motives gave her life meaning as she progressed toward a more life-affirming posture and renounced suicide as a viable alternative.

> Sharon's recovery depended greatly on her willingness to repair the emotional bonds with Kevin [her husband] and her closest friends. Her most significant failure, she later realized, was the fact that she shut herself off from the group in order to act out her self-destructive fantasies and impulses. She failed to trust her friends enough to be open and honest with them at a time when she most needed to be. . . .

"My recovery took a long time. . . . I think that people don't worry about me anymore. That was something that I talked about for a long time [her suicide attempt]. That set up a fear in people." Sharon acknowledges that her friendships were changed significantly by her attempt at suicide. "People were glad that I survived, but angry at me for what I had done. This was like a big event in this group of people. A huge event . . . but I think people wanted to give me a chance—and they did—to try to come back to life."

Coming back to life meant coming to terms with the self-destructive fantasies full of rage that Sharon had entertained since she was three years old. "That was the biggest part of my recovery," she resolutely declares. "I knew I could never ever, ever, do that again. It was not an option. And I had a rage with that. I was furious at that. It was for other people's [her friends] sake. It wasn't for my own personal life that I had a feeling. But I knew that I couldn't do it again: put these people through what they went through, ever. And I couldn't make them worry. A lot of my efforts were devoted to trying to help them not worry about me, which took a long time. But that's what saved me, really. That's also what the rage was at. I hated that somebody was so important to me that I couldn't do it. More important than myself. That was my rage."

To let go of the option of suicide, Sharon had to let go of that rage. "I had such rage that I never knew what to do with it. I was so terrified that I was going to act on it. It wasn't conscious, but it was, like, in my blood, in my bones, in my body. Trying not to do this thing. Trying not to kill. And I ended up killing somebody, or almost killing somebody. I was provoked to the point that I had to kill." . . .

"I felt like I was raised to be a murderer. I felt like a murderer. I was also raised by someone—my mother—who I felt, in retrospect, really wanted to get rid of me. She really wanted to get rid of me for her own reasons which I tried to understand sometimes, but she really, really wanted to get rid of me forever. I think she wanted me dead." (Chabot, 1997, pp. 182-184)

The emphasis in Sharon's friendship circle on humanistic values gave members a good feeling about themselves that counteracted their negative voices and thereby contributed to their overall mental health. The kindness and concern for each other and for other people that characterized their lives added mature and active dimensions to Sharon's life.

Consideration of Existential Issues and Spiritual Values

Over the years, there have been losses suffered within . . . [Sharon's group of friends], but each has further underlined the importance of sharing emotional experiences. . . . Tears well up as Sharon describes the impact of . . . [one friend's] death.

"It was agony, just agonizing to see this happen, and that's all we talked about, really, for a long time. Because I was shocked for somebody to die. I didn't think one of us would die, especially someone who was thirty-four. That's so young." Sharon seems to forget that she was barely thirty when she attempted to accomplish her own tragic death some twenty years before. . . .

Sharon pauses to contemplate the larger picture of life and death. "How do you live a life that has a death sentence at the end?" she asks rhetorically. "How do you make things worthwhile even though you know you're going to lose everything?" . . .

"You can say, Who cares anyway? You're going to lose everything. Why make anything matter? Or the other choice is, Look, this is the only time I have. Who knows how much time I have? I want to make every second count.

"Is that really a choice? Is that really a viable choice? I mean, it's hard sometimes because you want to go the other way, you know, not caring. Why bother? Or, God, everything matters, every second. But I would say, definitely, I've chosen to make everything count. Everything matters. I do believe that the choice to take is to make every minute worthwhile." (Chabot, 1997, pp. 186-187)

Developing One's Unique Priorities

In pursuing her renewed commitment to living life to the fullest—making every minute, every second count—Sharon reflects on the life-affirming choices that have provided direction, value, and purpose to her life. "Trying to pursue whatever kinds of things excite me," she insists, "is of high value." But this, in turn, spawned a number of questions for Sharon. ". . . What do I like to do? What are the idiosyncratic things that make me who I am and different from the next person? What is it that's really me? What do I love to do? . . . And I try to define the questions more," she continues. "I try to pursue them as much as I can, to develop myself like I started to in therapy. To continue that process. I feel like it never stopped. It's a way of life I've adopted." (Chabot, 1997, pp. 187-188)

Extended Family System

It is extremely important for children to grow up in a family atmosphere that extends beyond the couple's influence. In general, the nuclear family is, metaphorically speaking, too "inbred" to provide optimal environmental conditions for growth and individuation. Most couples are in collusion, living out a fantasy bond that represents a unified but not necessarily healthy point of view. Their range of feeling and understanding is generally too narrow to provide the child with a true perspective of his or her value as a human being. Concerned outsiders, adults who are friends of the family, or family members who are more removed from everyday caretaking functions are often more objective and better role models than the child's parents. Their relationship to the child is more personal than it is role-playing, is less judgmental, involves fewer projections, and is less hampered by parental do's and don'ts. Parents usually relate to their offspring as products or extensions of themselves and inadvertently focus ambivalent attitudes toward themselves on their children. Very often patients report that if it were not for a favorite relative, teacher, or friend of the family, they would have faced a hopeless situation psychologically.

> In her ongoing search to discover who she is and what she wants from her new life, Sharon acknowledges that becoming a mother has provided a significant source of purpose, value, and direction. She and Kevin became the proud parents of David fifteen years ago, and Beth four years after that. The children were assimilated into their growing group of friends, who shared a common interest in raising their children as part of a cohesive extended family.
>
> "It's very much a shared responsibility," Sharon explains, "shared among everyone for the well-being of each and all of our kids." . . .
>
> "I feel like I'm participating in creating what I see as the best environment for their growth that I can offer. I try to respect the children as individuals. I don't feel like I own them. They have a good deal of freedom to come and go, where they want to go within boundaries, but still they have a pretty free rein. I feel like I'm offering them the best thing that I know, and I really believe it is."
>
> Sharon pauses to ponder her own childhood once again, how difficult it was growing up without the active and open encouragement to be independent and self-assured, without the necessary ingredients to feel truly loved and cared for as an individual. It has taken many difficult years for Sharon to discover and truly believe in her own ability to offer with confidence the best that she knows . . .
>
> In the twenty years since Sharon . . . attempted suicide, she has learned much about what is most vital in her life. . . . She has grown to be an articulate and fully expressive participant in a community where open communication and shared responsibility are the core qualities of healthy relationships. "I've learned that I'm capable of speaking honestly, no matter what. If it's painful or not, the truth is worth saying," Sharon states. "Speaking openly to me is of very high value. Being amongst people where that is allowed and that right is protected is of very high value."
>
> Speaking honestly and openly remains the cornerstone of Sharon's continuing recovery. It provides an antidote to suicidal despair, a life-affirming connection to others, and a channel for greater insight and personal

growth. But more than the value to herself as part of her healing, Sharon is acutely aware of how important open, trusting communication is to her own children. (Chabot, 1997, pp. 188-189)

Learning to live the "simple life" without melodramatic reactions makes people painfully aware of their limitation in time, yet it makes them value each moment spent together as precious and irretrievable. Although it is difficult to define the dimensions of the "simple life" or a "good life," as well as a nondramatic style of relating that enhances both the adult's and the child's sense of well-being, one can begin by delineating what the simple family life is not: It is not intrusive, toxic, overcomplicated, or restrictive. As in Sharon's circle of friends, there is a sharing and concern for each other's individuality. Each person feels free to communicate his or her wants directly without expending unnecessary energy in power struggles or trivial disagreements, and each is supportive of the goals of the others, separate from his or her own needs.

John Chabot (1997), in concluding the story of Sharon and her passage from the depths of a suicidal "trance" to a life-affirming lifestyle, wrote,

Opening this window into her life and allowing others in has created a whole new world of possibilities for Sharon, and now for her children and her ever expanding family of friends. As part of her own healing journey, Sharon has discovered her special place within a family. She is finally home where she belongs. (pp. 189-190)

Summary[3]

Looking back at over 20 years of Voice Therapy practice and application to theory has led me to the following conclusion: Whereas in-depth psychoanalysis and object-relations theory and practice reveal that core experiences of childhood trauma produce defensive depersonalization and foster an essential split in self and object representations, my therapeutic technique of bringing internal voices to the surface directly exposes the developmental atmosphere and emotional climate of the family that have had a powerful influence on the child's and later the adult's perspective in life. The unconscious elements and affects of the antilibidinal ego or split within the self are lived out in Voice

---

3. This summary was taken from a speech delivered at the Evolution of Psychotherapy Conference, December 1995, Las Vegas, Nevada.

Therapy sessions. Patients become aware that voices are introjected parental attitudes and feelings that restrict and invalidate their natural destiny.

It is not only the family that affects the voice process; painful existential realities also affect the antiself system. Interpersonal traumas suffered early in the developmental cycle are reinforced by death anxiety as the child discovers his or her life is finite.

Understanding the voice process elucidates the self-destructive machinations of the personality and points the way to a successful resolution. Therapeutic success involves identifying self-destructive voices, releasing the associated affect, and restructuring one's life in the direction of individuation and personal fulfillment. It involves challenging habitual responses and going against internalized negative parental prescriptions. It necessitates the courage to break with fantasy bonds or illusions of connection. Voice Therapy helps an individual to pursue personal goals in the real world as contrasted with a reliance on fantasy gratification. It is a motivating force in developing a creative, adventurous lifestyle in which the self predominates.

I should add that the theory and methodology of Voice Therapy have value in understanding the core of resistance to any form of psychotherapeutic movement or constructive behavioral change. This type of therapeutic venture, by counteracting the dictates of the negative voice and disrupting fantasies of connection, offers people a unique opportunity to fulfill their human potential and thereby give life its special meaning.

Understanding the findings of clinical research conducted with patients, associates, and friends led to the development of hypotheses that are now being tested with more rigorous research methods. As noted earlier, our first foray into this area led to the development of an instrument to identify those individuals at risk for acting out suicidal impulses. Another instrument to assess violence potential has been deemed valuable by personnel in the criminal justice and probationary systems. We plan to study domestic violence and develop a voice scale to identify both perpetrators and victims, and are confident that this scale will prove as effective as the suicide scale. Another research study in the planning stages involves investigating how voices affect all aspects of personal relationships.

Adults who have been subject to physical abuse in childhood go on to act out violence on their children. The voice is the intergenerational link in passing down abusive child-rearing practices (sexual, physical, and emotional). Clinical investigations into the voice process have led to the discovery of the intrapsychic mechanism that is primarily responsible for the transmission of negative parental attitudes, traits, and defensive behaviors through succeeding generations. These partly conscious thoughts and attitudes can be accessed and measured and are therefore predictive of future behavior.

Through the last 20 years, I have moved from clinical theorizing to hypothesis development and empirical studies that have predictive value. More significantly, because the voice process is central to the way people conduct their everyday lives, I feel that Voice Therapy theory and research have great potential for predicting human behavior and helping to avert negative consequences.

My associates and I are able to predict behavior from voice segments and to predict voices underlying erratic or self-destructive behavior from the individual's actions and lifestyle. We have been able to identify the sources of these voices in faulty family interactions and in the impact of existential issues on the child's and adult's adjustment. The methodology is based on understanding an underlying theory of separation anxiety and the process of defense. The theory suggests a preventive mental hygiene program of parent education and implies a way to lead a more constructive life based on acting against the common dictates of the voice. In addition, the Firestone Assessment of Self-Destructive Thoughts (FAST), based on the voice, has potential in measuring therapeutic progress, no matter what form of therapy is administered. Successful cases should demonstrate a definitive change in the predominance of voice attacks.

The primary resistance to Voice Therapy theory and methodology is based on pervasive protective attitudes toward the family and the defensive process in general as it is manifested in our culture. My position is not that the nuclear family is inherently detrimental to human growth and development, but that it has in many ways evolved into a destructive institution. If one maintains an idealized picture of the family, this way of thinking constitutes a serious resistance to the understanding of ideas that expose the damaging aspects of family relationships and how they are internalized. However, blaming or accusing parents is not my focus. In relation to parents, I recognize that they too were part of this chain of victimization.

The theory also challenges defenses and offers no solace in the sense that it provides no "loopholes." It offers no illusions, no means of escaping existential despair or the vicissitudes of life. As patients progress in Voice Therapy, they are brought into a real world where existential issues are more poignant and painful. After recovering aspects of themselves and regaining emotional vitality, patients are more aware of the inevitable loss of self through death. As I have noted in other writings, the resistance to the theory involves the fear of breaking with parental introjects and the fantasy bond because these security maneuvers operate to cut off painful feelings, but only at the expense of one's personal development.

The way that human beings function and the way they are impaired are closely related to negative internal prescriptions. Therefore, the theory is an important tool of psychotherapy in that it has both predictive capability and therapeutic value as well as having merit as the basis for a preventive mental health program. It is my hope and the hope of my associates that our empirical research will break through the resistance to the unconventional aspects of Voice Therapy ideology and focus attention on the work. We feel that Voice Therapy theory and methodology represent a major advancement in psychology because the approach points the way toward coping with negative thought processes and restrictive, destructive elements of the personality, and suggests the way toward a better life.

Endnotes

1. These guidelines refer more to parental attitudes that predispose action rather than rigid, how-to-do-it, practical techniques. These suggestions were derived from a series of parenting seminars in which my associates and I and parents discussed pragmatic approaches to child rearing based on sound mental health principles; they are described in depth in chapters 10 and 11 in *Compassionate Child-Rearing* (Firestone, 1990b).

2. For an in-depth discussion of the broad mental health principles and the philosophical position underlying lifestyles that counter suicidal propensities, see Chapter 18, "The Good Life," in *Combating Destructive Thought Processes: Voice Therapy and Separation Theory* (Firestone, 1997).

Appendix

Supplementary Resource Material

Available From the Glendon Association (Phone: 800-663-5281)

1. Supplement to *Combating Destructive Thought Processes: Voice Therapy and Separation Theory* by Robert W. Firestone: A comparative review of the author's theoretical position with respect to psychoanalytic and object-relations theory

2. Documentary Videos (produced by the Glendon Association and Geoff Parr):

   Suicidology
   The Inner Voice in Suicide (1985)*
   Microsuicide: A Case Report (1985)*
   Teenagers Talk About Suicide (1987)*

   Voice Therapy: Theory and Methodology
   Voice Therapy With Dr. Robert Firestone (1984)*
   Videotapes for Professional Training in Voice Therapy Methodology:
   Voice Therapy: A Group Session (1986)
   "Sonya"—An Individual Session (1992)
   Voice Therapy Session: A New Perspective on the Oedipal Complex (1992)
   Voice Therapy: A Training Session (1992)

   Existential Issues
   Defenses Against Death Anxiety (1990)
   Life, Death & Denial (1990)

---

*Discussion videotape also available.

Overall Theoretical Approach
    The Fantasy Bond Video Supplement (1985)
    "Inwardness": A Retreat From Feeling (1995)*

Couple Relationships and Sexuality
    Closeness Without Bonds (1986)*
    Bobby & Rosie: Anatomy of a Marriage (1989)*
    Sex & Marriage (1990)
    Sex & Society: Everyday Abuses to Children's Emerging Sexuality
        (1989)

    Professional Training Videotapes:
    Sex & Society: Part II (1990)
    Voices in Sex (1990)
    Voices About Relationships (1995)

Compassionate Child Rearing: Resources for Parents
    The Inner Voice in Child Abuse (1986)*
    Parental Ambivalence (1987)
    Hunger Versus Love: A Perspective on Parent-Child Relations (1987)
    The Implicit Pain of Sensitive Child-Rearing (1988)
    Children of the Summer (1993)
    Invisible Child Abuse (1994)
    Teaching Our Children About Feelings (1984)

    Professional Training Videotape:
    *Therapeutic Child-Rearing: An In-Depth Approach to Compassionate
        Parenting* (1987)

3. *Compassionate Child-Rearing—A Parenting Education Program:* Instructors guidelines, parents' workbooks, videotapes, and in-service training for professionals who offer parent education classes

Available From the Psychological Corporation (Phone: 800-211-8378)

The *Firestone Assessment of Self-Destructive Thoughts (FAST)*, a new instrument useful as a screener for persons entering psychological treatment: FAST scores indicate areas in which the client is experiencing the greatest degree of distress, allowing the clinician to focus his or her interventions.

References

Abramson, L. Y., Metalsky, G. I., & Alloy, L. B. (1989). Hopelessness depression: A theory-based subtype of depression. *Psychological Review, 96,* 358-371.

Achte, K. A. (1980). The psychopathology of indirect self-destruction. In N. L. Farberow (Ed.), *The many faces of suicide: Indirect self-destructive behavior* (pp. 41-56). New York: McGraw-Hill.

Ainsworth, M. D. S., Blehar, M. C., Waters, E., & Wall, S. (1978). *Patterns of attachment: A psychological study of the strange situation.* Hillsdale, NJ: Lawrence Erlbaum.

Anthony, S. (1971). *The discovery of death in childhood and after.* Harmondsworth, England: Penguin Education.

Arieti, S., & Bemporad, J. R. (1980). The psychological organization of depression. *American Journal of Psychiatry, 137,* 1360-1365.

Bachman, J. G., & Johnston, L. D. (1978). *The Monitoring the Future project: Design and procedures* (Monitoring the Future Occasional Paper 1). Ann Arbor: University of Michigan, Institute for Social Research.

Baker, F. M. (1989). Black youth suicide: Literature review with a focus on prevention. In M. R. Feinleib (Ed.), *Report of the Secretary's Task Force on Youth Suicide: Vol. 3. Prevention and interventions in youth suicide* (DHHS Pub. No. ADM89-1623, pp. 177-195). Washington, DC: U.S. Department of Health & Human Services, Alcohol, Drug Abuse, and Mental Health Administration.

Balint, M. (1985). *Primary love and psycho-analytic technique.* London: Maresfield Library. (Original work published 1952)

Balswick, J. O. (1982). Male inexpressiveness: Psychological and social aspects. In K. Solomon & N. B. Levy (Eds.), *Men in transition: Theory and therapy* (pp. 131-150). New York: Plenum.

Bartholomew, K. (1990). Avoidance of intimacy: An attachment perspective. *Journal of Social and Personal Relationships, 7,* 147-178.

Bateson, G., Jackson, D. D., Haley, J., & Weakland, J. H. (1972). Toward a theory of schizophrenia. In G. Bateson, *Steps to an ecology of mind* (pp. 201-227). New York: Ballantine. (Original work published 1956)

Beavers, W. R. (1977). *Psychotherapy and growth: A family systems perspective.* New York: Brunner/Mazel.

Beck, A. T. (1976). *Cognitive therapy and the emotional disorders.* New York: New American Library.

Beck, A. T. (1978a). *Beck Depression Inventory.* San Antonio, TX: Psychological Corporation.

Beck, A. T. (1978b). *Beck Hopelessness Scale.* San Antonio, TX: Psychological Corporation.

Beck, A. T. (1987). *Beck Anxiety Inventory.* San Antonio, TX: Psychological Corporation.

Beck, A. T. (1991). *Beck Suicide Inventory.* San Antonio, TX: Psychological Corporation,

Beck, A. T., Rush, A. J., Shaw, B. F., & Emory, G. (1979). *Cognitive therapy of depression.* New York: Guilford.

Beck, A. T., Schuyler, D., & Herman, I. (1974). Development of suicidal intent scales. In A. T. Beck, H. L. P. Resnik, & D. J. Lettieri (Eds.), *The prediction of suicide* (pp. 45-56). Philadelphia: Charles Press.

Beck, A. T., Steer, R. A., & Brown, G. (1993). Dysfunctional attitudes and suicidal ideation in psychiatric outpatients. *Suicide and Life-Threatening Behavior, 23,* 11-20.

Beck, A. T., Steer, R. A., Kovacs, M., & Garrison, B. (1985). Hopelessness and eventual suicide: A 10-year prospective study of patients hospitalized with suicidal ideation. *American Journal of Psychiatry, 142,* 559-563.

Becker, E. (1964). *The revolution in psychiatry: The new understanding of man.* New York: Free Press.

Becker, E. (1973). *The denial of death.* New York: Free Press.

Bedrosian, R. C., & Beck, A. T. (1979). Cognitive aspects of suicidal behaviors. *Suicide and Life-Threatening Behavior, 9,* 87-96.

Benedek, T. (1970). The psychobiology of pregnancy. In E. J. Anthony & T. Benedek (Eds.), *Parenthood: Its psychology and psychopathology* (pp. 137-151). Boston: Little, Brown.

Berlin, I. N. (1986). Suicide among Native American adolescents. In R. Cohen-Sandler (Ed.), *Proceedings, Nineteenth Annual Meeting, American Association of Suicidology, Atlanta, Georgia, April 3-6, 1986* (p. 1-2). Denver, CO: American Association of Suicidology.

Berman, A. L., & Cohen-Sandler, R. (1982). Suicide and the standard of care: Optimal vs. acceptable. *Suicide and Life-Threatening Behavior, 12,* 114-122.

Berman, A. L., & Jobes, D. A. (1991). *Adolescent suicide: Assessment and intervention.* Washington, DC: American Psychological Association.

Berman, A. L., & Schwartz, R. H. (1990). Suicide attempts among adolescent drug users. *American Journal of Diseases of Children, 144,* 310-314.

Bettelheim, B. (1983). Afterword. In M. Cardinal, *The words to say it* (pp. 297-308). Cambridge, MA: Van Vactor & Goodheart.

Beutler, L. E., & Clarkin, J. F. (1990). *Systematic treatment selection: Toward targeted therapeutic interventions.* New York: Brunner/Mazel.

Birtchnell, J. (1983). Psychotherapeutic considerations in the management of the suicidal patient. *American Journal of Psychotherapy, 37,* 24-36.

Blanck, G., & Blanck, R. (1974). *Ego psychology: Theory & practice.* New York: Columbia University Press.

Blatt, S. J. (1995). The destructiveness of perfectionism: Implications for the treatment of depression. *American Psychologist, 50,* 1003-1020.

Bloch, D. (1978). *"So the witch won't eat me": Fantasy and the child's fear of infanticide.* Boston: Houghton Mifflin.

Boldt, M. (1989). Defining suicide: Implications for suicidal behavior and for suicide prevention. In R. F. W. Diekstra, R. Maris, S. Platt, A. Schmidtke, & G. Sonneck (Eds.), *Suicide and its prevention: The role of attitude and imitation* (pp. 3-13). Leiden, Netherlands: E. J. Brill.

Bongar, B. (1991). *The suicidal patient: Clinical and legal standards of care.* Washington, DC: American Psychological Association.

Bongar, B. (1992). Guidelines for risk management in the care of the suicidal patient. In B. Bongar (Ed.), *Suicide: Guidelines for assessment, management, and treatment* (pp. 268-282). New York: Oxford University Press.

Bongar, B., & Beutler, L. E. (Eds.). (1995). *Comprehensive textbook of psychotherapy: Theory and practice.* New York: Oxford University Press.

Bonner, R. L. (1990). A "M.A.P." to the clinical assessment of suicide risk. *Journal of Mental Health Counseling, 12,* 232-236.

Bonner, R. L., & Rich, A. R. (1987). Toward a predictive model of suicidal ideation and behavior: Some preliminary data in college students. *Suicide and Life-Threatening Behavior, 17,* 50-63.

Boszormenyi-Nagy, I. (1965). A theory of relationships: Experience and transaction. In I. Boszormenyi-Nagy & J. L. Framo (Eds.), *Intensive family therapy: Theoretical and practical aspects* (pp. 33-86). New York: Harper & Row.

Bowen, M. (1978). *Family therapy in clinical practice.* New York: Jason Aronson.

Bowlby, J. (1973). *Attachment and loss: Vol. 2. Separation: Anxiety and anger.* New York: Basic Books.

Bowlby, J. (1980). *Attachment and loss: Vol. 3. Loss: Sadness and depression.* New York: Basic Books.

Brazelton, T. B., & Cramer, B. G. (1990). *The earliest relationship: Parents, infants, and the drama of early attachment.* Reading, MA: Addison-Wesley.

Brennan, K. A., & Shaver, P. R. (1993). Attachment styles and parental divorce. *Journal of Divorce & Remarriage, 21,* 161-175.

Briere, J. (1996). *Therapy for adults molested as children: Beyond survival* (Rev. ed.). New York: Springer.

Briere, J., & Runtz, M. (1987). Post sexual abuse trauma: Data and implications for clinical practice. *Journal of Interpersonal Violence, 2,* 367-379.

Brooks, M., & Reiner, C. (1973). *The complete 2000 year old man* [CD]. Los Angeles, CA: Rhino Records.

Bugental, J. F. T. (1976). *The search for existential identity.* San Francisco: Jossey-Bass.

Canetto, S. S. (1992-1993). She died for love and he for glory: Gender myths of suicidal people. *Omega, 26,* 1-17.

Canetto, S. S. (1994). Gender issues in the treatment of suicidal individuals. *Death Studies, 18,* 513-527.

Canetto, S. S., & Feldman, L. B. (1993). Covert and overt dependence in suicidal women and their male partners. *Omega, 27,* 177-194.

Cantor, P. C. (1989). Intervention strategies: Environmental risk reduction for youth suicide. In M. R. Feinleib (Ed.), *Report of the Secretary's Task Force on Youth Suicide: Vol. 3. Prevention and interventions in youth suicide* (pp. 285-293). Washington, DC: U.S. Department of Health and Human Services.

Centers for Disease Control and Prevention. (1994). Programs for the prevention of suicide among adolescents and young adults. *Morbidity and Mortality Weekly Report, 43*(RR-6), 3-12.

Chabot, J. A. (1997). *A new lease on life: Facing the world after a suicide attempt.* Minneapolis, MN: Fairview.

Chemtob, C. M., Hamada, R. S., Bauer, G., Kinney, B., & Torigoe, R. Y. (1988). Patients' suicides: Frequency and impact on psychiatrists. *American Journal of Psychiatry, 145,* 224-228.

Chemtob, C. M., Hamada, R. S., Bauer, G., Torigoe, R. Y., & Kinney, B. (1988). Patient suicide: Frequency and impact on psychologists. *Professional Psychology: Research and Practice, 19,* 416-420.

Clance, P. R., & Imes, S. A. (1978). The impostor phenomenon in high achieving women: Dynamics and therapeutic intervention. *Psychotherapy: Theory, Research, & Practice, 15,* 241-247.

Clark, D. C. (1992). Narcissistic crises of aging and suicidal despair. In D. Lester (Ed.), *Proceedings, Silver Anniversary Conference, American Association of Suicidology, Chicago, Illinois, April 1-4, 1992* (pp. 236-238). Denver, CO: American Association of Suicidology.

Clark, D. C. (1993). Narcissistic crises of aging and suicidal despair. *Suicide and Life-Threatening Behavior, 23,* 21-26.

Clark, D. C., & Clark, S. H. (1992). Psychological autopsy of elderly suicide. In D. Lester (Ed.), *Proceedings, Silver Anniversary Conference, American Association of Suicidology, Chicago, Illinois, April 1-4, 1992* (p. 235). Denver, CO: American Association of Suicidology.

Clopton, J. R., & Baucom, D. H. (1979). MMPI ratings of suicide risk. *Journal of Personality Assessment, 43,* 293-296.

Cloward, R. A., & Piven, F. F. (1979). Hidden protest: The channeling of female innovation and resistance. *Journal of Women in Culture and Society, 4,* 651-669.

Colt, G. H. (1991). *The enigma of suicide.* New York: Simon & Schuster.

Conroy, P. (1986). *The prince of tides.* Boston: Houghton Mifflin.

Conwell, Y., Henderson, R. E., Flannery, C. J., & Caine, E. D. (1991). Suicide and aging, psychological autopsy findings. In D. Lester (Ed.), *Proceedings, 24th Annual Meeting, American Association of Suicidology, Boston, Massachusetts, April 17-21, 1991* (pp. 15-16). Denver, CO: American Association of Suicidology.

Cook, D. R. (1986). *Inventory of Feelings, Problems, and Family Experiences.* Menomonie: University of Wisconsin.

Crook, M. (1989). *Teenagers talk about suicide* (Rev. ed.). Toronto, Canada: NC Press Limited.

Cull, J. G., & Gill, W. S. (1988). *Suicide Probability Scale (SPS) manual.* Los Angeles, CA: Western Psychological Services.

D'Augelli, A. R., & Dark, L. J. (1994). Lesbian, gay, and bisexual youths. In L. D. Eron, J. H. Gentry, & P. Schlegel (Eds.), *Reason to hope: A psychosocial perspective on violence & youth* (pp. 177-196). Washington, DC: American Psychological Association.

De La Rosa, D., & Maw, C. E. (1990). *Hispanic education: A statistical portrait 1990.* Washington, DC: Office of Research, Advocacy, and Legislation, National Council of La Raza.

Deutsch, C. J. (1984). Self-reported sources of stress among psychotherapists. *Professional Psychology: Research and Practice, 15,* 833-845.

Deykin, E. Y., Alpert, J. J., & McNamarra, J. J. (1985). A pilot study of the effect of exposure to child abuse or neglect on adolescent suicidal behavior. *American Journal of Psychiatry, 142,* 1299-1303.

Dick, R. W., Beals, J., Manson, S. M., & Bechtold, D. W. (1992). Psychometric properties of the Suicidal Ideation Questionnaire in American Indian adolescents. In D. Lester (Ed.), *Proceedings, Silver Anniversary Conference, American Association of Suicidology, Chicago, Illinois, April 1-4, 1992* (pp. 103-108). Denver, CO: American Association of Suicidology.

Dorpat, T. L., & Ripley, H. S. (1967). The relationship between attempted suicide and committed suicide. *Comprehensive Psychiatry, 8,* 74-79.

Dorwart, R. A., & Chartock, L. (1989). Suicide: A public health perspective. In D. Jacobs & H. N. Brown (Eds.), *Suicide: Understanding and responding* (pp. 31-55). Madison, CT: International Universities Press.

Dublin, L. I. (1963). *Suicide: A sociological and statistical study.* New York: Ronald.

Dubus, A. (1975). *Separate flights.* Boston: David R. Godine.

Dunne, E. J., McIntosh, J. L., & Dunne-Maxim, K. (Eds.). (1987). *Suicide and its aftermath: Understanding and counseling the survivors.* New York: Norton.

Durkheim, É. (1951). *Suicide: A study in sociology* (J. A. Spaulding & G. Simpson, Trans.). New York: Free Press. (Original work published 1897)

Eisenthal, S. (1974). Assessment of suicidal risk using selected tests. In C. Neuringer (Ed.), *Psychological assessment of suicide risk* (pp. 134-149). Springfield, IL: Charles C Thomas.

Elliott, C. A., Kral, M. J., & Wilson, K. G. (1990). Suicidal concerns among native youth. In D. Lester (Ed.), *Proceedings, 23rd Annual Meeting, American Association of Suicidology, New Orleans, Louisiana, April 25-29, 1990* (pp. 283-285). Denver, CO: American Association of Suicidology.

Ellis, A. (1973). *Humanistic psychotherapy: The rational-emotive approach.* New York: Julian.

Ellis, E. R., & Allen, G. N. (1961). *Traitor within: Our suicide problem.* Garden City, NY: Doubleday.

Elmer, E. (1967). *Children in jeopardy: A study of abused minors and their families.* Pittsburgh, PA: University of Pittsburgh Press.

Exner, J. E., Jr., & Wylie, J. (1977). Some Rorschach data concerning suicide. *Journal of Personality Assessment, 41,* 339-348.

Fairbairn, W. R. D. (1952). *Psychoanalytic studies of the personality.* London: Routledge & Kegan Paul.

Fairbairn, W. R. D. (1952). A revised psychopathology of the psychoses and psychoneuroses. In W. R. D. Fairbairn, *Psychoanalytic studies of the personality* (pp. 28-58). London: Routledge & Kegan Paul. (Original work published 1941)

Farberow, N. L. (1980a). Indirect self-destructive behavior: Classification and characteristics. In N. L. Farberow (Ed.), *The many faces of suicide: Indirect self-destructive behavior* (pp. 15-27). New York: McGraw-Hill.

Farberow, N. L. (1980b). Introduction. In N. L. Farberow (Ed.), *The many faces of suicide: Indirect self-destructive behavior* (pp. 1-12). New York: McGraw-Hill.

Favazza, A. R., & Eppright, T. D. (1986). *Survey on Self-Harm.* Columbia: University of Missouri.

Feeney, J. A., & Noller, P. (1990). Attachment style as a predictor of adult romantic relationships. *Journal of Personality and Social Psychology, 58,* 281-291.

Feldman, M. J., & Hersen, M. (1967). Attitudes toward death in nightmare subjects. *Journal of Abnormal Psychology, 72,* 421-425.

Felner, R. D., Adan, A. M., & Silverman, M. M. (1992). Risk assessment and prevention of youth suicide in schools and educational contexts. In R. W. Maris, A. L. Berman, J. T. Maltsberger, & R. I. Yufit (Eds.), *Assessment and prediction of suicide* (pp. 420-447). New York: Guilford.

Ferenczi, S. (1955). Confusion of tongues between adults and the child. In M. Balint (Ed.), *Final contributions to the problems and methods of psycho-analysis* (E. Mosbacher et al., Trans.) (pp. 156-167). New York: Basic Books. (Original work published 1933)

Fierman, L. B. (Ed.). (1965). *Effective psychotherapy: The contribution of Hellmuth Kaiser.* New York: Free Press.

Fingerhut, L. A., Ingram, D. D., & Feldman, J. J. (1992). Firearm and nonfirearm homicide among persons 15 through 19 years of age. *Journal of the American Medical Association, 267,* 3048 3053.

Finkelhor, D. (with Araji, S., Baron, L., Browne, A., Peters, S. D., & Wyatt, G. E.). (1986). *A sourcebook on child sexual abuse.* Beverly Hills, CA: Sage.

Firestone, R. W. (1957). *A concept of the schizophrenic process.* Unpublished doctoral dissertation, University of Denver.

Firestone, R. W. (1984). A concept of the primary fantasy bond: A developmental perspective. *Psychotherapy, 21,* 218-225.

Firestone, R. W. (1985). *The fantasy bond: Structure of psychological defenses,* New York: Human Sciences Press.

Firestone, R. W. (1986). The "inner voice" and suicide. *Psychotherapy, 23,* 439-447.

Firestone, R. W. (1987a). Destructive effects of the fantasy bond in couple and family relationships. *Psychotherapy, 24,* 233-239.

Firestone, R. W. (1987b). The "voice": The dual nature of guilt reactions. *American Journal of Psychoanalysis, 47,* 210-229.

Firestone, R. W. (1988). *Voice Therapy: A psychotherapeutic approach to self-destructive behavior.* New York: Human Sciences Press.

Firestone, R. W. (1990a). The bipolar causality of regression. *American Journal of Psychoanalysis, 50,* 121-135.

Firestone, R. W. (1990b). *Compassionate child-rearing: An in-depth approach to optimal parenting.* New York: Plenum.

Firestone, R. W. (1990c). Prescription for psychotherapy. *Psychotherapy, 27,* 627-635.

Firestone, R. W. (1990d). Voice therapy. In J. Zeig & W. Munion (Eds.), *What is psychotherapy? Contemporary perspectives* (pp. 68-74). San Francisco: Jossey-Bass.

Firestone, R. W. (1994). Psychological defenses against death anxiety. In R. A. Neimeyer (Ed.), *Death anxiety handbook: Research, instrumentation, and application* (pp. 217-241). Washington, DC: Taylor & Francis.

Firestone, R. W. (1997). *Combating destructive thought processes: Voice Therapy and separation theory.* Thousand Oaks, CA: Sage.

Firestone, R. W., & Catlett, J. (1989). *Psychological defenses in everyday life.* New York: Human Sciences Press.

Firestone, R. W., & Firestone, L. (1996). *Firestone Assessment of Self-Destructive Thoughts manual.* San Antonio, TX: Psychological Corporation.

Firestone, R. W., & Seiden, R. H. (1987). Microsuicide and suicidal threats of everyday life. *Psychotherapy, 24,* 31-39.

Firestone, R. W., & Seiden, R. H. (1990a). Psychodynamics in adolescent suicide. *Journal of College Student Psychotherapy, 4,* 101-123.

Firestone, R. W., & Seiden, R. H. (1990b). Suicide and the continuum of self-destructive behavior. *Journal of American College Health, 38,* 207-213.

Fournier, R. R., Motto, J., Osgood, N., & Fitzpatrick, T. (1991). Rational suicide in later life. In D. Lester (Ed.), *Proceedings, 24th Annual Meeting, American Association of Suicidology, Boston, Massachusetts, April 17-21, 1991* (pp. 7-8). Denver, CO: American Association of Suicidology.

Frankl, V. E. (1959). *Man's search for meaning* (Rev. ed.). New York: Washington Square Press. (Original work published 1946)

Frederick, C. J. (1985). An introduction and overview of youth suicide. In M. L. Peck, N. L. Farberow, & R. E. Litman (Eds.), *Youth suicide* (pp. 1-16). New York: Springer.

Fremouw, W. J., de Perczel, M., & Ellis, T. E. (1990). *Suicide risk: Assessment and response guidelines.* New York: Pergamon Press.

Freud, A. (1966). *The ego and the mechanisms of defense* (Rev. ed.). New York: International Universities Press.

Freud, A. (1989). *Normality and pathology in childhood: Assessments of development.* London: Karnac Books and the Institute of Psycho-Analysis. (Original work published 1966)

Freud, A., & Burlingham, D. (1944). *Infants without families: The case for and against residential nurseries.* New York: International Universities Press.

Freud, S. (1955). Studies on hysteria, case histories, Frau Emmy von N. In J. Strachey (Ed. and Trans.), *The standard edition of the complete psychological works of Sigmund Freud* (Vol. 2, pp. 48-105). London: Hogarth. (Original work published 1893)

Freud, S. (1955). Group psychology and the analysis of the ego. In J. Strachey (Ed. and Trans.), *The standard edition of the complete psychological works of Sigmund Freud* (Vol. 18, pp. 63-143). London: Hogarth. (Original work published 1921)

Freud, S. (1957a). A case of paranoia running counter to the psycho-analytic theory of the disease. In J. Strachey (Ed. and Trans.), *The standard edition of the complete psychological works of Sigmund Freud* (Vol. 14, pp. 261-272). London: Hogarth. (Original work published 1915)

Freud, S. (1957b). Thoughts for the times on war and death. In J. Strachey (Ed. and Trans.), *The standard edition of the complete psychological works of Sigmund Freud* (Vol. 14, pp. 273-302). London: Hogarth. (Original work published 1915)

Freud, S. (1957c). Some character-types met with in psycho-analytic work. In J. Strachey (Ed. and Trans.), *The standard edition of the complete psychological works of Sigmund Freud* (Vol. 14, pp. 311-333). London: Hogarth. (Original work published 1916)

Freud, S. (1961). The ego and the id. In J. Strachey (Ed. and Trans.), *The standard edition of the complete psychological works of Sigmund Freud* (Vol. 19, pp. 12-67). London: Hogarth. (Original work published 1923)

Freud, S. (1963). Introductory lectures on psycho-analysis, Part III. General theory of the neuroses. In J. Strachey (Ed. and Trans.), *The standard edition of the complete psychological works of Sigmund Freud* (Vol. 16, pp. 243-463). London: Hogarth. (Original work published 1917)

Freud, S. (1964). Analysis terminable and interminable. In J. Strachey (Ed. and Trans.), *The standard edition of the complete psychological works of Sigmund Freud* (Vol. 23, pp. 209-253). London: Hogarth. (Original work published 1937)

Freud, S. (1967). Scientific meeting on April 27, 1910 (M. Nunberg, Trans.). In H. Nunberg & E. Federn (Eds.), *Minutes of the Vienna Psychoanalytic Society: Vol. 2. 1908-1910* (pp. 498-506). New York: International Universities Press.

Friday, N. (1977). *My mother/my self: The daughter's search for identity.* New York: Delacorte.

Friedman, R. S. (1989). Hospital treatment of the suicidal patient. In D. G. Jacobs & H. N. Brown (Eds.), *Suicide: Understanding and responding: Harvard Medical School perspectives on suicide* (pp. 379-402). Madison, CT: International Universities Press.

Fromm, E. (1947). *Man for himself: An inquiry into the psychology of ethics.* New York: Rinehart.

Gable, R. K. (1983). Malpractice liability of psychologists. In B. D. Sales (Ed.), *The professional psychologists's handbook* (pp. 457-494). New York: Plenum.

Garbarino, J., & Gilliam, G. (1980). *Understanding abusive families.* Lexington, MA: Lexington.

Garbarino, J., Guttman, E., & Seeley, J. W. (1986). *The psychologically battered child.* San Francisco: Jossey-Bass.

Garner, D. M., & Olmsted, M. P. (1984). *Eating Disorder Inventory manual.* Odessa, FL: Psychological Assessment Resources.

Gibson, P. (1989). Gay male and lesbian youth suicide. In M. R. Feinleib (Ed.), *Report of the Secretary's Task Force on Youth Suicide: Vol. 3. Prevention and interventions in youth suicide* (DHHS Pub. No. ADM89-1623, pp. 110 139). Washington, DC: U.S. Department of Health & Human Services, Alcohol, Drug Abuse, and Mental Health Administration.

Gilpin, A., & Hays, R. D. (1990). *Scalogram analysis program* [Computer program]. Durham, NC: Duke University Press.

Goldenberg, D. (1995). *Self-destructive cognition in severely anxious and depressed patients.* Unpublished doctoral dissertation, California Graduate Institute, Los Angeles.

Goldring, N., & Fieve, R. R. (1984). Attempted suicide in manic-depressive disorder *American Journal of Psychotherapy, 38,* 373 383.

Gove, W. R., & Hughes, M. (1980). Reexamining the ecological fallacy: A study in which aggregate data are critical in investigating the pathological effects of living alone. *Social Forces, 58,* 1157-1177.

Grotstein, J. S. (1981). *Splitting and projective identification.* Northvale, NJ: Jason Aronson.

Guntrip, H. (1961). *Personality structure and human interaction: The developing synthesis of psycho-dynamic theory.* New York: International Universities Press.

Guntrip, H. (1969). *Schizoid phenomena: Object-relations and the self.* New York: International Universities Press.

Gutheil, T. G. (1980). Paranoia and progress notes: A guide to forensically informed psychiatric recordkeeping. *Hospital & Community Psychiatry, 31,* 479-482.

Hamilton, E. W., & Abramson, L. Y. (1983). Cognitive patterns and major depressive disorder: A longitudinal study in a hospital setting. *Journal of Abnormal Psychology, 92,* 173-184.

Harvey, J. C. (1984, August). *The imposter phenomenon: A useful concept in clinical practice.* Paper presented at the annual meeting of the American Psychological Association, Toronto, Canada.

Hatton, C. L., Valente, S. M., & Rink, A. (1977). *Suicide: Assessment and intervention.* New York: Appleton-Century-Crofts.

Hawkins, D. F. (1990). Explaining the black homicide rate. *Journal of Interpersonal Violence, 5,* 151-163.

Hawton, K. (1986). *Suicide and attempted suicide among children and adolescents.* Beverly Hills, CA: Sage.

Hays, R. D., Hayashi, T., & Stewart, A. L. (1989). A five-item measure of socially desirable response set. *Educational and Psychological Measurement, 49,* 629-636.

Heckler, R. A. (1994). *Waking up, alive: The descent, the suicide attempt, and the return to life.* New York: Ballantine.

Hendin, H. (1981). Psychotherapy and suicide. *American Journal of Psychotherapy, 35,* 469-480.

Hendin, H. (1982). *Suicide in America.* New York: Norton.

Hendin, H. (1995). Assisted suicide, euthanasia, and suicide prevention: The implications of the Dutch experience. In M. M. Silverman & R. W. Maris (Eds.), *Suicide prevention: Toward the year 2000* (pp. 193-204). New York: Guilford.

Hewitt, P. L., Flett, G. L., & Weber, C. (1994). Dimensions of perfectionism and suicide ideation. *Cognitive Therapy and Research, 18,* 439-460.

Hill, H. M., Soriano, F. I., Chen, S. A., & LaFromboise, T. D. (1994). Sociocultural factors in the etiology and prevention of violence among ethnic minority youth. In L. D. Eron, J. H. Gentry, & P. Schlegel (Eds.), *Reason to hope: A psychosocial perspective on violence & youth* (pp. 59-97). Washington, DC: American Psychological Association.

Hinton, J. (1975). The influence of previous personality on reactions to having terminal cancer. *Omega, 6,* 95-111.

Holinger, P. C., & Offer, D. (1982). Prediction of adolescent suicide: A population model. *American Journal of Psychiatry, 139,* 302-307.

Holinger, P. C., Offer, D., Barter, J. T., & Bell, C. C. (1994). *Suicide and homicide among adolescents.* New York: Guilford.

Holinger, P. C., Offer, D., & Ostrov, E. (1987). Suicide and homicide in the United States: An epidemiologic study of violent death, population changes, and the potential for prediction. *American Journal of Psychiatry, 144,* 215-219.

Hubert, D., & Addis, B. (Producers). (1983). *Suicide* [Film]. Los Angeles: UCLA Center for the Health Sciences, Behavioral Sciences Media Laboratory.

Hughes, T., & McCullough, F. (Eds.). (1982). *The journals of Sylvia Plath.* New York: Ballantine.

Humphry, D. (1991). *Final exit: The practicalities of self-deliverance and assisted suicide for the dying.* Eugene, OR: Hemlock Society.

Ikiru, E. (1985, April). The voice inside me. *Saturday Night,* pp. 30-39.

Jackson, D. N. (1970). A sequential system for personality scale development. In C. D. Spielberger (Ed.), *Current topics in clinical and community psychology* (Vol. 2, pp. 61-96). New York: Academic Press.

Jacobs, D. (1989). Psychotherapy with suicidal patients: The empathic method. In D. Jacobs & H. N. Brown (Eds.), *Suicide: Understanding and responding* (pp. 329-342). Madison, CT: International Universities Press.

Jacobs, D., & Klein, M. E. (1993). The expanding role of psychological autopsies. In A. A. Leenaars (Ed.), *Suicidology: Essays in honor of Edwin S. Shneidman* (pp. 210-247). Northvale, NJ: Jason Aronson.

Janov, A. (1970). *The primal scream: Primal therapy: The cure for neurosis.* New York: G. P. Putnam.

Jobes, D. A., & Berman, A. L. (1993). Suicide and malpractice liability: Assessing and revising policies, procedures, and practice in outpatient settings. *Professional Psychology: Research and Practice, 24,* 91-99.

Kachur, S. P., Potter, L. B., James, S. P., & Powell, K. E. (1995). *Suicide in the United States, 1980-1992* (Violence Surveillance Summary Series, No. 1). Atlanta, GA: National Center for Injury Prevention and Control, Centers for Disease Control.

Kaiser, H. (1965). The problem of responsibility in psychotherapy. In L. B. Fierman (Ed.), *Effective psychotherapy: The contribution of Hellmuth Kaiser* (pp. 1-13). New York: Free Press. (Original work published 1955)

Kaplan, H. S. (1979). *Disorders of sexual desire and other new concepts and techniques in sex therapy.* New York: Brunner/Mazel.

Kaplan, L. J. (1984). *Adolescence: The farewell to childhood.* New York: Simon & Schuster.

Karpel, M. (1976). Individuation: From fusion to dialogue. *Family Process, 15,* 65-82.

Kastenbaum, R. (1974, Summer). Childhood: The kingdom where creatures die. *Journal of Clinical Child Psychology,* pp. 11-14.

Kaufman, G., & Raphael, L. (1984). Relating to the self: Changing inner dialogue. *Psychological Reports, 54,* 239-250.

Kendra, J. M. (1979). Predicting suicide using the Rorschach Inkblot Test. *Journal of Personality Assessment, 43,* 452-456.

Klaus, M. H., & Kennell, J. H. (1976). *Maternal-infant bonding.* St. Louis, MO: C. V. Mosby.

Kohut, H. (1971). *The analysis of the self* (The Psychoanalytic Study of the Child, Monograph No. 4). New York: International Universities Press.

Kohut, H. (1977). *The restoration of the self.* New York: International Universities Press.

Koop, C. E. (1976). *The right to live, the right to die.* Wheaton, IL: Tyndale House.

Kramer, R. (1995). "The 'bad mother' Freud has never seen": Otto Rank and the birth of object-relations theory. *Journal of the American Academy of Psychoanalysis, 23,* 293-321.

Kreitman, N. (Ed.). (1977). *Parasuicide.* London: John Wiley.

Kreitman, N., Philip, A. E., Greer, S., & Bagley, C. R. (1969). Parasuicide. *British Journal of Psychiatry, 115,* 746-747.

Kushner, H. I. (1985). Women and suicide in historical perspective. *Journal of Women in Culture and Society, 10,* 537-552.

Laing, R. D. (1961). *Self and others.* Harmondsworth, England: Penguin.

Laing, R. D. (1967). *The politics of experience.* New York: Ballantine.

Laing, R. D. (1969). *The divided self.* London: Penguin. (Original work published 1960)

Laing, R. D. (1972). *The politics of the family and other essays.* New York: Vintage. (Original work published 1969)

Laing, R. D. (1976). *The facts of life: An essay in feelings, facts, and fantasy.* New York: Pantheon.

Laing, R. D., & Esterson, A. (1970). *Sanity, madness, and the family: Families of schizophrenics.* London: Penguin. (Original work published 1964)

LeBonniec, Y., & Guillon, C. (1982). *Suicide mode d'emploi: Histoire, technique actualité.* Paris, France: Alain Moreau.

Leenaars, A. A. (1994). Crisis intervention with highly lethal suicidal people. In A. A. Leenaars, J. T. Maltsberger, & R. A. Neimeyer (Eds.), *Treatment of suicidal people* (pp. 45-59). Washington, DC: Taylor & Francis.

Leonard, C. V. (1967). *Understanding and preventing suicide.* Springfield, IL: Charles C Thomas.

Lester, D. (1970). Attempts to predict suicidal risk using psychological tests. *Psychological Bulletin, 74,* 1-17.

Lewis, J. M., & Looney, J. G. (1983). *The long struggle: Well-functioning working-class black families.* New York: Brunner/Mazel.

Lidz, T. (1972). The influence of family studies on the treatment of schizophrenia. In C. J. Sager & H. S. Kaplan (Eds.), *Progress in group and family therapy* (pp. 616-635). New York: Brunner/Mazel. (Original work published 1969).

Lifton, R. J. (1989). Suicide: The quest for a future. In D. Jacobs & H. N. Brown (Eds.), *Suicide: Understanding and responding* (pp. 459-469). Madison, CT: International Universities Press.

Lifton, R. J., & Olson, E. (1976). The human meaning of total disaster: The Buffalo Creek experience. *Psychiatry, 39,* 1-18.

Linehan, M. M. (1981). A social-behavioral analysis of suicide and parasuicide: Implications for clinical assessment and treatment. In J. F. Clarkin & H. I. Glazer (Eds.), *Depression: Behavioral and directive intervention strategies* (pp. 229-294). New York: Garland.

Linehan, M. M. (1993). *Cognitive-behavioral treatment of borderline personality disorder.* New York: Guilford.

Linehan, M. M., Goodstein, J. L., Nielsen, S. L., & Chiles, J. A. (1983). Reasons for staying alive when you are thinking of killing yourself: The Reasons for Living Inventory. *Journal of Consulting and Clinical Psychology, 51,* 276-286.

Linehan, M. M., & Nielsen, S. L. (1981). Assessment of suicide ideation and parasuicide: Hopelessness and social desirability. *Journal of Consulting and Clinical Psychology, 49,* 773-775.

Litman, R. E. (1967). Sigmund Freud on suicide. In E. S. Shneidman (Ed.), *Essays in self-destruction* (pp. 324-344). New York: Jason Aronson.

Litman, R. E. (1994). The dilemma of suicide in psychoanalytic practice. *Journal of the American Academy of Psychoanalysis, 22,* 273 201.

Litman, R. E., & Farberow, N. L. (1983). Emergency evaluation of suicidal potential. In E. Shneidman, N. L. Farberow, & R. E. Litman (Eds.), *The psychology of suicide* (pp. 259-291). New York: Jason Aronson.

MacNeil-Lehrer Productions, WNET, WETA. (1987, March 12). *Open door policy? Teen suicide: Fall from grace* (Transcript 2989 of the MacNeil/Lehrer NewsHour). New York: Author.

Mahler, M. S. (1974). Symbiosis and individuation: The psychological birth of the human infant. In R. S. Eissler, A. Freud, M. Kris, & A. J. Solnit (Eds.), *The psychoanalytic study of the child* (Vol. 29, pp. 89-106). New Haven, CT: Yale University Press.

Mahler, M. S. (1979). On sadness and grief in infancy and childhood: Loss and restoration of the symbiotic love object. In *The selected papers of Margaret S. Mahler, M.D.: Vol. 1. Infantile psychosis and early contributions* (pp. 262-279). New York: Jason Aronson. (Original work published 1961)

Mahler, M. S., Pine, F., & Bergman, A. (1975). *The psychological birth of the human infant: Symbiosis and individuation.* New York: Basic Books.

Maltsberger, J. T. (1986). *Suicide risk: The formulation of clinical judgment.* New York: New York University Press.

Maltsberger, J. T. (1988). Suicide danger: Clinical estimation and decision. *Suicide and Life-Threatening Behavior, 18,* 47-54.

Maltsberger, J. T. (1991). Psychotherapy with older suicidal patients. *Journal of Geriatric Psychiatry, 24,* 217-234.

Maltsberger, J. T., & Buie, D. H. (1989). Common errors in the management of suicidal patients. In D. Jacobs & H. N. Brown (Eds.), *Suicide: Understanding and responding* (pp. 285-294). Madison, CT: International Universities Press.

Maris, R. W. (1981). *Pathways to suicide: A survey of self-destructive behaviors.* Baltimore, MD: Johns Hopkins University Press.

Maris, R. W. (1992). Overview of the study of suicide assessment and prediction. In R. W. Maris, A. L. Berman, J. T. Maltsberger, & R. I. Yufit (Eds.), *Assessment and prediction of suicide* (pp. 3-22). New York: Guilford.

Maris, R. W. (1995). Suicide prevention in adults (age 30-65). In M. M. Silverman & R. W. Maris (Eds.), *Suicide prevention: Toward the year 2000* (pp. 171-179). New York: Guilford.

Maslow, A. H. (1968). *Toward a psychology of being* (2nd ed.). New York: Van Nostrand Reinhold.

Masterson, J. F. (1985). *The real self: A developmental, self, and object relations approach.* New York: Brunner/Mazel.

May, R. (1958). The origins and significance of the existential movement in psychology. In R. May, E. Angel, & H. F. Ellenberger (Eds.), *Existence: A new dimension in psychiatry and psychology* (pp. 3-36). New York: Basic Books.

McGrath, E., Keita, G. P., Strickland, B. R., & Russo, N. F. (1990). *Women and depression: Risk factors and treatment issues.* Washington, DC: American Psychological Association.

McIntosh, J. L. (1990). Older adults: The next suicide epidemic? In D. Lester (Ed.), *Proceedings, 23rd Annual Meeting, American Association of Suicidology, New Orleans, Louisiana, April 25-29, 1990* (pp. 305-308). Denver, CO: American Association of Suicidology.

McIntosh, J. L. (1995). Suicide prevention in the elderly (age 65-99). In M. M. Silverman & R. W. Maris (Eds.), *Suicide prevention: Toward the year 2000* (pp. 180-192). New York: Guilford.

McIntosh, J. L., Hubbard, R. W., & Santos, J. F. (1985). Suicide facts and myths: A study of prevalence. *Death Studies, 9,* 267-281.

Melville, H. (1943). *Moby Dick; Or, the whale.* New York: Heritage. (Original work published 1851)

Menninger, K. (1938). *Man against himself.* New York: Harcourt, Brace & World.

Meyer, R. G., Landis, E. R., & Hays, J. R. (1988). *Law for the psychotherapist.* New York: Norton.

Michalik, D. R. (1988, April). *Client suicide: Therapist experience and resolution*. Paper presented at the 21st Annual Meeting of the American Association of Suicidology, Washington, DC.

Miles, C. P. (1977). Conditions predisposing to suicide: A review. *Journal of Nervous and Mental Disease, 164,* 231-246.

Milgram, S. (1974). *Obedience to authority: An experimental view.* London: Tavistock.

Miller, A. (1984). *For your own good: Hidden cruelty in child-rearing and the roots of violence* (2nd ed.) (H. & H. Hannum, Trans.). New York: Farrar, Straus, Giroux. (Original work published 1980)

Miller, G. A. (1985). *The Substance Abuse Subtle Screening Inventory manual.* Spencer, IN: Spencer Evening World.

Miller, M. L., Chiles, J. A., & Barnes, V. E. (1982). Suicide attempters within a delinquent population. *Journal of Consulting and Clinical Psychology, 50,* 491-498.

Miranda, J., & Persons, J. B. (1988). Dysfunctional attitudes are mood-state dependent. *Journal of Abnormal Psychology, 97,* 76-79.

Moscicki, E. K. (1995). Epidemiology of suicidal behavior. *Suicide and Life-Threatening Behavior, 25,* 22-35.

Murphy, G. E. (1984). The prediction of suicide: Why is it so difficult? *American Journal of Psychotherapy, 38,* 341-349.

Murray, H. A. (1938). *Explorations in personality: A clinical and experimental study of fifty men of college age.* New York: Science Editions.

Murray, H. A. (1943). *Thematic Apperception Test (TAT).* Cambridge, MA: Harvard University Press.

Nagy, M. H. (1959). The child's view of death. In H. Feifel (Ed.), *The meaning of death* (pp. 79-98). New York: McGraw-Hill. (Original work published 1948)

Naidu v. Laird, No. 77, 1987, 539 A.2d 1064 (1988) Del. LEXIS 93.

National Center for Health Statistics. (1996). [Suicide deaths and rates per 100,000, United States, 1987-1993]. Unpublished data.

Neimeyer, R. A., & Pfeiffer, A. M. (1994). The ten most common errors of suicide interventionists. In A. A. Leenaars, J. T. Maltsberger, & R. A. Neimeyer (Eds.), *Treatment of suicidal people* (pp. 207-224). Washington, DC: Taylor & Francis.

Nelson, F. L., & Farberow, N. L. (1982). The development of an indirect self-destructive behaviour scale for use with chronically ill medical patients. *International Journal of Social Psychiatry, 28,* 5-14.

Neuringer, C. (1974). Suicide and the Rorschach: A rueful postscript. *Journal of Personality Assessment, 38,* 535-539.

Nietzsche, F. (1966). *Beyond good and evil* (W. Kaufmann, Trans.). New York: Vintage. (Original work published 1886)

Norman, M. (1983). *'Night, mother.* New York: Hill and Wang.

Nunberg, H., & Federn, E. (Eds.). (1967). *Minutes of the Vienna Psychoanalytic Society: Vol. 2. 1908-1910* (M. Nunberg, Trans.). New York: International Universities Press.

Orbach, I. (1988). *Children who don't want to live.* San Francisco: Jossey-Bass.

Orbach, I. (1989). Familial and intrapsychic splits in suicidal adolescents. *American Journal of Psychotherapy, 43,* 356-367.

Orbach, I., Lotem-Peleg, M., & Kedem, P. (1995). Attitudes toward the body in suicidal, depressed, and normal adolescents. *Suicide and Life-Threatening Behavior, 25,* 211-221.

Osgood, C. E., Suci, G. J., & Tannenbaum, P. H. (1957). *The measurement of meaning.* Urbana: University of Illinois Press.

Pagels, E. (1988). *Adam, Eve, and the serpent.* New York: Random House.

Pagels, E. (1995). *The origin of Satan.* New York: Random House.

Parr, G. (Producer). (1984). *Voice therapy with Dr. Robert Firestone* [Video]. Santa Barbara, CA: Glendon Association.

Parr, G. (Producer). (1987a). *Panel discussion on teenage suicide* [Video]. Santa Barbara, CA: Glendon Association.

Parr, G. (Producer). (1987b). *Teenagers talk about suicide* [Video]. Santa Barbara, CA: Glendon Association.

Paykel, E. S., Myers, J. K., Lindenthal, J. J., & Tanner, J. (1974). Suicidal feelings in the general population: A prevalence study. *British Journal of Psychiatry, 124,* 460-469.

Pfeffer, C. R. (1985). Observations of ego functioning of suicidal latency-age children. In M. L. Peck, N. L. Farberow, & R. E. Litman (Eds.), *Youth suicide* (pp. 39-47). New York: Springer.

Pfeffer, C. R. (1986). *The suicidal child.* New York: Guilford.

Pfeffer, C. R. (1989). Life stress and family risk factors for youth fatal and nonfatal suicidal behavior. In C. R. Pfeffer (Ed.), *Suicide among youth: Perspective on risk and prevention* (pp. 143-164). Washington, DC: American Psychiatric Press.

Pfeffer, C. R., Conte, H. R., Plutchik, R., & Jerrett, I. (1980). Suicidal behavior in latency-age children: An outpatient population. *Journal of the American Academy of Child Psychiatry, 19,* 703-710.

Plutchik, R., & van Praag, H. M. (1990). Psychosocial correlates of suicide and violence risk. In H. M. van Praag, R. Plutchik, & A. Apter (Eds.), *Violence and suicidality: Perspectives in clinical and psychobiological research* (pp. 37-65). New York: Brunner/Mazel.

Pokorny, A. D. (1960). Characteristics of forty-four patients who subsequently committed suicide. *Archives of General Psychiatry, 2,* 314-323.

Poland, S. (1989). *Suicide intervention in the schools.* New York: Guilford.

Radloff, L. S. (1977). The CES-D Scale: A self-report depression scale for research in the general population. *Applied Psychological Measurement, 1,* 385-401.

Raimy, V. (1975). *Misunderstandings of the self.* San Francisco: Jossey-Bass.

Rank, O. (1929). *The trauma of birth.* London: Kegan Paul. (Original work published 1923)

Rank, O. (1972). *Will therapy and truth and reality* (J. Taft, Trans.). New York: Knopf. (Original work published 1936)

Resnick, P. J. (1969). Child murder by parents: A psychiatric review of filicide. *American Journal of Psychiatry, 126,* 325-334.

Reynolds, W. M. (1985). *Suicide Ideation Questionnaire.* Unpublished manuscript, University of Wisconsin, Madison.

Rheingold, J. C. (1964). *The fear of being a woman: A theory of maternal destructiveness.* New York: Grune & Stratton.

Rheingold, J. C. (1967). *The mother, anxiety, and death: The catastrophic death complex.* Boston: Little, Brown.

Rich, A. R., Bonner, R. L., & Reimold, A. (1986, August). *Suicidal ideation in college students: Support for a vulnerability model.* Paper presented at the annual meeting of the American Psychological Association, Washington, DC.

Richman, J. (1984). The family therapy of suicidal adolescents: Promises and pitfalls. In H. S. Sudak, Α. B. Ford, & N. B. Rushforth (Eds.), *Suicide in the young* (pp. 393-406). Boston: John Wright/PSG Inc.

Richman, J. (1986). *Family therapy for suicidal people.* New York: Springer.

Richman, J. (1993). *Preventing elderly suicide: Overcoming personal despair, professional neglect, and social bias.* New York: Springer.

Roberts, A. R. (1975). Self destruction by one's own hand: Suicide and suicide prevention. In A. R. Roberts (Ed.), *Self-destructive behavior* (pp. 21-77). Springfield, IL: Charles C Thomas.

Robinson, R. (1989). *Survivors of suicide.* Santa Monica, CA: IBS Press.

Rochlin, G. (1967). How younger children view death and themselves. In E. A. Grollman (Ed.), *Explaining death to children* (pp. 51-85). Boston: Beacon.

Rosberg, J., & Karon, B. P. (1959). A direct analytic contribution to the understanding of postpartum psychosis. *Psychiatric Quarterly, 33,* 296-304.

Rose, D. T., & Abramson, L. Y. (1992). Developmental predictors of depressive cognitive style: Research and theory. In D. Ciochetti & S. L. Toth (Eds.), *Rochester Symposium on Developmental Psychopathology: Vol. 4. Developmental perspectives on depression* (pp. 325-349). Rochester, NY: University of Rochester Press.

Rose, D. T., Abramson, L. Y., Hodulik, C. J., Halberstadt, L., & Leff, G. (1994). Heterogeneity of cognitive style among depressed inpatients. *Journal of Abnormal Psychology, 103,* 419-429.

Rosen, J. N. (1953). *Direct analysis: Selected papers.* New York: Grune & Stratton.

Rosenbaum, M., & Richman, J. (1970). Suicide: The role of hostility and death wishes from the family and significant others. *American Journal of Psychiatry, 126,* 1652-1655.

Rothbard, J. C., & Shaver, P. R. (1994). Continuity of attachment across the life span. In M. B. Sperling & W. H. Berman (Eds.), *Attachment in adults: Clinical and developmental perspectives* (pp. 31-71). New York: Guilford.

Rubin, T. I. (with Rubin, E.). (1975). *Compassion and self-hate: An alternative to despair.* New York: David McKay.

Rush, A. J., & Beck, A. T. (1978). Cognitive therapy of depression and suicide. *American Journal of Psychotherapy, 32,* 201-218.

Sabbath, J. C. (1969). The suicidal adolescent: The expendable child. *Journal of the American Academy of Child Psychiatry, 8,* 272-289.

Sadoff, R. L. (1975). *Forensic psychiatry: A practical guide for lawyers and psychiatrists.* Springfield, IL: Charles C Thomas.

Sandbek, T. J. (1993). *The deadly diet: Recovering from anorexia and bulimia* (2nd ed.). Oakland, CA: New Harbinger.

Sansonnet-Hayden, H., Haley, G., Marriage, K., & Fine, S. (1987). Sexual abuse and psychopathology in hospitalized adolescents. *Journal of the American Academy of Child & Adolescent Psychiatry, 26,* 753-757.

Satir, V. (1972). *Peoplemaking.* Palo Alto, CA: Science and Behavior Books.

Satir, V. (1983). *Conjoint family therapy* (3rd ed.). Palo Alto, CA: Science and Behavior Books.

Searles, H. F. (1961). Schizophrenia and the inevitability of death. *Psychiatric Quarterly, 35,* 631-665.

Sechehaye, M. A. (1951). *Symbolic realization: A new method of psychotherapy applied to a case of schizophrenia* (B. Wursten & H. Wursten, Trans.). New York: International Universities Press.

Seiden, R. H. (1965). Salutary effects of maternal separation. *Social Work, 10,* 25-29.

Seiden, R. H. (1966). Campus tragedy: A study of student suicide. *Journal of Abnormal Psychology, 71,* 389-399.

Seiden, R. H. (1984a). Death in the west: A regional analysis of the youthful suicide rate. *Western Journal of Medicine, 140,* 969-973.

Seiden, R. H. (1984b). The youthful suicide epidemic. *Public Affairs Report, 25,* 1-8.

Shaffer, D. (1974). Suicide in childhood and early adolescence. *Journal of Child Psychology and Psychiatry, 15,* 275-291.

Shafii, M., Carrigan, S., Whittinghill, J. R., & Derrick, A. (1985). Psychological autopsy of completed suicide in children and adolescents. *American Journal of Psychiatry, 142,* 1061-1064.

Shapiro, J. P. (1996, April 15). Expanding a right to die. *U.S. News & World Report,* p. 63.

Shaver, P. R., & Hazan, C. (1993). Adult romantic attachment: Theory and evidence. In D. Perlman & W. Jones (Eds.), *Advances in personal relationships* (Vol. 4, pp. 29-70). London: Jessica Kingsley.

Shengold, L. (1989). *Soul murder: The effects of childhood abuse and deprivation.* New Haven, CT: Yale University Press.

Shneidman, E. S. (1966). Orientations toward death: A vital aspect of the study of lives. *International Journal of Psychiatry, 2,* 167-200.

Shneidman, E. S. (1972). Foreword. In A. C. Cain (Ed.), *Survivors of suicide* (pp. ix-xi). Springfield, IL: Charles C Thomas.

Shneidman, E. S. (1981). Psychotherapy with suicidal patients. *Suicide and Life-Threatening Behavior, 11,* 341-348.

Shneidman, E. S. (1985). *Definition of suicide.* New York: John Wiley.

Shneidman, E. S. (1989). Overview: A multidimensional approach to suicide. In D. Jacobs & H. N. Brown (Eds.), *Suicide: Understanding and responding* (pp. 1-30). Madison, CT: International Universities Press.

Shneidman, E. S. (1993). *Suicide as psychache: A clinical approach to self-destructive behavior.* Northvale, NJ: Jason Aronson.

Shneidman, E. S. (1996). *The suicidal mind.* New York: Oxford University Press.

Shneidman, E. S., & Farberow, N. L. (1957). Some comparisons between genuine and simulated suicide notes in terms of Mowrer's concepts of discomfort and relief. *Journal of General Psychology, 56,* 251-256.

Slaby, A. E. (1994). *Handbook of psychiatric emergencies* (4th ed.). Norwalk, CT: Appleton & Lange.

Slawson, P. F., Flinn, D. E., & Schwartz, D. A. (1974). Legal responsibility for suicide. *Psychiatric Quarterly, 48,* 50-64.

Smith, K., & Eyman, J. (1988). Ego structure and object differentiation in suicidal patients. In H. D. Lerner & P. M. Lerner (Eds.), *Primitive mental states and the Rorschach* (pp. 175-202). Madison, CT: International Universities Press.

Soriano, F. I., & Ramirez, A. (1991). Unequal employment status and ethnicity: Further analysis of the USPI-ESPI model. *Hispanic Journal of Behavioral Sciences, 13,* 391-400.

Soubrier, J. (1993). Definitions of suicide. In A. A. Leenaars (Ed.), *Suicidology: Essays in honor of Edwin S. Shneidman* (pp. 35-41). Northvale, NJ: Jason Aronson.

Srole, L., Langner, T. S., Michael, S. T., & Opler, M. K. (1962). *Mental health in the metropolis: The midtown Manhattan study.* New York: McGraw-Hill.

Stenback, A. (1980). Depression and suicidal behavior in old age. In J. E. Birren & R. B. Sloane (Eds.), *Handbook of mental health and aging* (pp. 616-652). Englewood Cliffs, NJ: Prentice Hall.

Stromberg, C. D., Haggarty, D. J., Leibenluft, R. F., McMillian, M. H., Mishkin, B., Rubin, B. L., & Trilling, H. R. (1988). *The psychologist's legal handbook.* Washington, DC: Council for the National Register of Health Service Providers in Psychology.

Strunk, R. C., Mrazek, D. A., Fuhrmann, G. S. W., & LaBrecque, J. F. (1985). Physiologic and psychological characteristics associated with deaths due to asthma in childhood. *Journal of the American Medical Association, 254,* 1193-1198.

Styron, W. (1979). *Sophie's choice.* New York: Bantam.

Szasz, T. S. (1961). *The myth of mental illness: Foundations of a theory of personal conduct.* New York: Hoeber-Harper.

Szasz, T. S. (1963). *Law, liberty, and psychiatry: An inquiry into the social uses of mental health practices.* New York: Collier.

Szasz, T. (1978). *The myth of psychotherapy: Mental healing as religion, rhetoric, and repression.* Garden City, NY: Anchor.

Szasz, T. S. (1987). Justifying coercion through theology and therapy. In J. Zeig (Ed.), *The evolution of psychotherapy* (pp. 413-429). New York: Brunner/Mazel.

Szasz, T. S. (1989). A moral view on suicide. In D. Jacobs & H. N. Brown (Eds.), *Suicide: Understanding and responding* (pp. 437-447). Madison, CT: International Universities Press.

Tomer, A., & Eliason, G. (1996). Toward a comprehensive model of death anxiety. *Death Studies, 20,* 343-365.

United Nations Department of Public Information. (1992, August). *United Nations principles for older persons* (United Nations DPI-1261). New York: Author.

van Praag, H. M., Plutchik, R., & Apter, A. (Eds.). (1990). *Violence and suicidality: Perspective in clinical and psychobiological research.* New York: Brunner/Mazel.

Watzlawick, P., Bavelas, J. B., & Jackson, D. D. (1967). *Pragmatics of human communication: A study of interactional patterns, pathologies, and paradoxes.* New York: Norton.

Weakland, J. H. (1977). "The double-bind theory" by self-reflexive hindsight. In P. Watzlawick & J. H. Weakland (Eds.), *The interactional view: Studies at the Mental Research Institute, Palo Alto, 1965-1974* (pp. 241-248). New York: Norton. (Original work published 1974)

Weissman, M. M., Klerman, G. L., Markowitz, J. S., & Ouellette, R. (1989). Suicidal ideation and suicide attempts in panic disorder and attacks. *New England Journal of Medicine, 321,* 1209-1214.

Wexler, J., & Steidl, J. (1978). Marriage and the capacity to be alone. *Psychiatry, 41,* 72-82.

Whitaker, C. A., & Malone, T. P. (1981). *The roots of psychotherapy.* New York: Brunner/Mazel.

White-Bowden, S. (1985). *Everything to live for.* New York: Poseidon.

Willi, J. (1982). *Couples in collusion: The unconscious dimension in partner relationships.* Claremont, CA: Hunter House. (Original work published 1975)

Winnicott, D. W. (1958a). Primitive emotional development. In D. W. Winnicott, *Collected papers: Through paediatrics to psycho-analysis* (pp. 145-156). London: Tavistock. (Original work published 1945)

Winnicott, D. W. (1958b). The observation of infants in a set situation. In D. W. Winnicott, *Collected papers: Through paediatrics to psycho-analysis* (pp. 52-69). London: Tavistock. (Original work published 1941)

Winnicott, D. W. (1965). The parent-infant relationship. In D. W. Winnicott, *Maturation processes and the facilitating environment: Studies in the theory of emotional development* (pp. 37-55). Madison, CT: International Universities Press.

Wise, M. G., & Rundell, J. R. (1988). *Concise guide to consultation psychiatry* (2nd ed.). Washington, DC: American Psychiatric Press.

Wright, R. (1995, August 28). The evolution of despair. *Time,* pp. 50-54, 56-57.

Wynne, L. C., Ryckoff, I. M., Day, J., & Hirsch, S. I. (1958) Pseudo mutuality in the family relations of schizophrenics. *Psychiatry, 21,* 205-220.

Yalom, I. D. (1980). *Existential psychotherapy.* New York: Basic Books.

Name Index

Abramson, L. Y. , 62-63, 87
Achte, K. A., 61, 124
Adan, A. M., 83
Addis, B., 257
Ainsworth, M. D. S., 197n11
Allen, G. N., 177n4
Alloy, L. B., 62-63
Alpert, J. J., 103n5
Anthony, S., 196n5
Apter, A., 228
Arieti, S., 63, 64

Bachman, J., 230
Bagley, C. R., 67n1
Baker, F. M., 73-74
Balint, M., 11n3, 61
Balswick, J. O., 102
Barnes, V. E., 79
Barter, J. T., 98
Bartholomew, K., 214n1
Bateson, G., 211
Baucom, D. H., 81n4
Bauer, G., 252n9
Bavelas, J. B., 211
Beals, J., 76
Beavers, W. R., 211, 212, 214n2
Bechtold, D. W., 76
Beck, A. T., 63, 64, 66, 79, 87, 222, 223, 230, 231, 245
Becker, E., 10, 125, 142, 144, 156, 189, 214
Bedrosian, R. C., 79

Bell, C. C., 98
Bemporad, J. R., 63, 64
Benedek T., 177n5
Bergman, A., 186
Berlin, I. N., 76
Berman, A. L., 86-87, 103n1, 233, 234, 236, 251, 252n3
Bettelheim, B., 30
Beutler, L. E., 247
Birtchnell, J., 233-234
Blanck, G., 199
Blanck, R., 199
Blatt, S. J., 87
Blehar, M. C., 197n11
Bloch, D., 102
Boldt, M., 120n6
Bongar, B., 236, 247, 252n3
Bonner, R. L., 81n5, 218, 233
Boszormenyi-Nagy, I., 200
Bowen, M., 210
Bowlby, J., 9, 63, 64, 186, 197n11
Brazelton, T. B., 177n5
Brennan, K. A., 214n1
Briere, J., 103n5, 245
Brooks, M., 154
Brown, G., 87
Bugental, J. F. T., 11n3
Buie, D. H., 220, 243
Burlingham, D., 186

Caine, E. D., 114
Canetto, S. S., 70, 80n1

Cantor, P. C., 86, 87, 93
Carrigan, S., 81n5
Catlett, J., 113
Centers for Disease Control, 82, 126
Chabot, J. A., 279, 279n, 287-288, 289,
     290, 291, 293
Chartock, L., 232n4
Chemtob, C. M., 252n9
Chen, S. A., 73
Chiles, J. A. , 79
Clance, P. R., 171
Clark, D. C., 107, 108, 119n4
Clark, S. H., 108, 119n4
Clarkin, J. F., 247
Clopton, J. R., 81n4
Cohen-Sandler, R., 236, 252n3
Colt, G. H., 234, 250
Conroy, P., 198
Conte, H. R., 80
Conwell, Y., 114
Cook, D. R., 230
Cramer, B. G., 177n5
Crook, M., 82, 93
Cull, J. G., 78, 79, 223, 230

Dark, L. J., 99
D'Augelli, A. R., 99
Day, J., 211
De La Rosa, D., 75
Derrick, A., 81n5
Deutsch, C. J., 234
Deykin, E. Y., 103n5
Dick, R. W., 76
Dorpat, T. L., 68
Dorwart, R. A., 232n4
Dublin, L. I., 83
Dubus, A., 150
Dunne, E. J., 252n8
Dunne-Maxim, K., 252n8
Durkheim, E., 65, 124

Eisenthal, S., 81n4
Eliason, G., 11n4

Elliott, C. A., 76
Ellis, A., 62
Ellis, E. R., 177n4
Elmer, E., 177n5
Emery, G., 64
Eppright, T. D., 230
Esterson, A., 61, 211
Exner, J. E., Jr., 81n4
Eyman, J., 115

Fairbairn, W. R. D., 9, 11n3, 52, 163, 181
Farberow, N. L. , 61, 65, 66, 78, 113, 124,
     131, 198, 228
Favazza, A. R., 230
Federn, E., 217
Feeney, J. A., 200, 214n1
Feldman, J. J., 73
Feldman, L. B., 80n1
Feldman, M. J., 177n3
Felner, R. D., 83
Ferenczi, S., 9, 30, 61, 62
Fierman, L. B., 163
Fieve, R. R., 68
Fine, S., 103n5
Fingerhut, L. A., 73
Finkelhor, D., 99
Firestone, L., 8, 28, 79, 107, 217, 219n,
     232n1, 246, 252n6
Firestone, R. W., 8, 9, 11n1, 28, 34n1,
     34n2, 66, 67, 79, 81n3, 82, 103n3,
     107, 108, 113, 123, 160n, 182, 183,
     184, 186, 195n2, 196n3, 196n9,
     197n13, 217, 218, 219n, 221, 225,
     232n1, 246, 252n6, 275n1, 276n4,
     296n1, 296n2
Fitzpatrick, T., 116
Flannery, C. J., 114
Flett, G. L., 103n4
Flinn, D. E., 252
Fournier, R. R.,116, 118
Frankl, V. E., 11n3, 56
Frederick, C. J., 34n3
Freud, A., 9, 30, 61, 186

Freud, S., 46, 59, 61, 115, 141, 144, 158,
        160, 195n2, 196n7
Friday, N., 175
Fromm, E., 156
Fuhrmann, G. S. W., 152

Gable, R. K., 234
Garbarino, J., 9, 196n10
Garner, D. M., 230
Garrison, B., 79
Gibson, P., 99
Gill, W. S., 78, 79, 223, 230
Gilliam, G., 196n10
Gilpin, A., 230
Goldenberg, D, 224.
Goldring, N., 68
Goodstein, J. L., 79
Gove, W. R., 44
Greer, S., 67n1
Grotstein, J. S., 61, 62
Guillon, C., 117
Guntrip, H., 9, 11n3, 62, 163
Gutheil, T. G., 252n2
Guttman, E., 9

Halberstadt, L., 63
Haley, G., 103n5
Haley, J., 211
Hamada, R. S., 252n9
Hamilton, E. W., 62-63
Harvey, J. C., 87
Hatton, C. L., 78
Hawkins, D. F., 73
Hawton, K., 83
Hayashi, T., 230
Hays, J. R., 235
Hays, R. D., 230, 231
Hazan, C., 200
Heckler, R. A., 15, 22, 43, 45-46, 54, 64,
        198
Henderson, R. E., 114
Hendin, H., 99, 116-117, 120n8, 234
Herman, I., 222

Hersen, M., 177n3
Hewitt, P. L., 103n4
Hill, H. M., 73
Hinton, J., 10
Hirsch, S. I., 211
Hodulik, C. J., 63
Holinger, P. L., 86, 98, 228
Hubbard, R. W.,104
Hubert, D. 257
Hughes, M. M., 44
Humphry, D., 117

Ikuru, E., 123
Imes, S. A., 171
Ingram, D. D., 73

Jackson, D. D., 211
Jackson, D. N., 221
Jacobs, D., 177n1, 245
Jacobson, E., 199
James, S. P., 68
Janov, A., 10, 195n2, 196n7, 196n9, 276n6
Jerrett, I., 80
Jobes, D. A. , 87, 233, 234, 251
Johnston, L. D., 230

Kachur, S. P., 68, 70, 73, 75, 80, 104
Kaiser, H., 182, 199
Kaplan, H. S., 205
Kaplan, L. J., 130, 131
Karon, B. P., 176
Karpel, M., 182, 200
Kastenbaum, R., 196n5
Kaufman, G., 63
Kedem, P., 98
Keita, G. P., 70
Kendra, J. M., 81n4
Kennell, J. H., 177n5, 177n7
Kinney, B., 252n9
Klaus, M. H., 177n4, 177n7
Klein, M. E., 61, 177n1
Klerman, G. L., 69
Kohut, H., 9, 199, 248

Koop, C. E., 117, 217
Kovacs, M., 79
Kral, M. J., 76
Kreitman, N., 67n1
Kushner, H. I., 80n1

LaBrecque, J. F., 152
LaFramboise, T. D., 73
Laing, R. D., 11n3, 24, 31, 35, 61, 149,
    182, 196n10, 200, 201, 211
Landis, E. R., 235
Langner, T. S., 214n2
LeBonniec, Y., 117
Leenaars, A. A., 232n2, 251, 255, 256,
    275n3
Leff, G., 63
Leonard, C. V., 234
Lester, D., 78
Lewis, J. M., 74
Lidz, T., 152
Lifton, R. J., 120n10, 155, 246, 247
Linehan, M. M., 66, 79, 230, 245
Litman, R. E., 65, 124, 198, 245, 246
Looney, J. G., 74
Lotem-Peleg, M., 98

MacNeil-Lehrer Productions, 37
Mahler, M. S., 9, 164, 186, 199
Malone, T. P., 25
Maltsberger, J. T., 46, 62, 115, 220,
    236-237, 243
Manson, S. M., 76
Maris, R. W., 68, 103n1, 105, 107, 109
Markowitz, J. S., 69
Marriage, K., 103n5
Maslow, A. H., 10, 11n3, 144-145
Masterson, J. F., 279
Maw, C. E., 75
McGrath, E., 70
McIntosh, J. L., 104, 107, 114, 116,
    252n8
McNamarra, J. J., 103n5
Melville, H., 59

Menninger, K., 60, 65, 66, 115, 124
Metalsky, G. I., 62-63
Meyer, R. G., 235
Michael, S. T., 214n2
Michalik, D. R., 234
Miles, C. P., 68, 70
Milgram, S., 146
Miller, A., 9, 196n10
Miller, M. L., 79
Miranda, J., 63
Motto, J., 116
Mrazek, D. A., 152
Murphy, G. E., 78
Murray, H. A., 81n4, 275n2
Myers, J. K., 70

Nagy, M. H., 196n5
National Center for Health Statistics, 68
Neimeyer, R. A., 243
Nelson, F. L., 131
Neuringer, C., 78, 80n4
Nielsen, S. L., 79
Nietzsche, F., 60
Noller, P., 200, 214n1
Norman, M., 135
Nunberg, H., 217

Offer, D., 86, 98, 228
Olmsted, M. P., 230
Olson, E., 120n10, 155
Opler, M. K., 214n2
Orbach, I., 71, 98, 118
Osgood, C. E., 81n4
Osgood, N., 116
Ostrov, E., 228
Ouellette, R., 69

Pagels, E., 143, 158
Parr, G., 84, 94, 94n1, 276n4, 297
Paykel, E. S., 70
Persons, J. B., 63
Pfeffer, C. R., 70, 71, 80, 98, 177n2
Pfeiffer, A. M., 243

Philip, A. E., 67n1
Pine, F., 186
Piven, F. F., 80n1
Plath, S., 59
Plutchik, R. 80, 98, 228
Pokorny, A. D., 78
Poland, S., 94, 252n8
Potter, L. B., 68
Powell, K. E., 68

Raimy, V., 63
Ramirez, A., 75
Rank, O., 10, 111, 119, 124, 125, 146, 160,
    162, 181
Raphael, L., 63
Reimold, A., 81n5
Reiner, C., 153
Resnick, P. J., 177n6
Reynolds, W. M., 80
Rheingold, J. C., 103, 111, 175, 176,
    177n5
Rich, A. R., 81n5
Richman, J., 32, 86, 106, 107, 114, 115,
    119n1-3, 120n5, 148-149, 192, 198,
    229, 252n7
Rink, A., 78
Ripley, H. S., 68
Roberts, A. R., 234
Robinson, R., 248
Rochlin, G., 196n5
Rosberg, J., 176
Rose, D. T., 87
Rosen, J. N., 195n1
Rosenbaum, M., 32, 229,
    234
Rothbard, J. C., 214n1
Rubin, T. L., 140
Rundell, J. R., 252n4
Runtz, M., 103n5
Rush, A. J., 63, 64
Russo, N. F., 70
Ryckoff, I. M., 211

Sabbath, J. C., 34n3
Sadoff, R. L., 252n1
Sandbek, T. J., 131
Sansonnet-Hayden, H., 103n5
Santos, J. F., 104
Satir, V., 211
Schuyler, D., 222
Schwartz, D. A., 252
Schwartz, R. H., 103
Searles, H. F., 10
Sechehaye, M. A., 159
Seeley, J. W., 9
Seiden, R. H. , 44, 66, 80, 82, 87, 94,
    94n1, 123, 152
Shaffer, D., 37, 70
Shafii, M., 81n5
Shapiro, J. P., 120n7
Shaver, P. R., 200, 214n1
Shaw, B. F., 64
Shengold, L., 196n10
Shneidman, E. S., 15, 37, 59, 60, 65, 66,
    78, 87, 105, 107, 110, 139n3, 159,
    177n1, 234, 253, 254, 256, 275n2,
    275n3
Silverman, M. M., 83
Slaby, A. E., 220
Slawson, P. E., 252
Smith, K., 115
Soriano, F. I. , 73, 75
Soubrier, J., 59-60, 66, 117
Srole, L., 214n2
Steer, R. A., 79, 87
Steidl, J., 182, 200
Stenback, A., 104
Stewart, A. L., 230
Strickland, B. R., 70
Stromberg, C. D., 235
Strunk, R. C., 152
Styron, W., 155
Suci, G. J., 81n4
Szasz, T. S., 61, 117, 118, 120n9, 248

Tannenbaum, P. H., 81n4
Tanner, J., 70

Tomer, A., 11n4
Torigoe, R. Y., 252n9

United Nations Department of Public
    Information, 119

Valente, S. M., 78
van Praag, H. M., 98, 228

Wall, S., 197n11
Waters, E., 197n11
Watzlawick, P., 211
Weakland, J. H. , 211
Weber, C., 103n4

Weissman, M. M., 69, 232n6
Wexler, J., 182, 200
Whitaker, C. A., 25
White-Bowden, S., 248, 249
Whittinghill, J. R., 81n5
Willi, J., 182
Wilson, K. G., 76
Winnicott, D. W., 9, 29, 164, 186
Wise, M. G., 252n4
Wright, R., 103n2
Wylie, J., 81n4
Wynne, L. C., 211

Yalom, I. D., 10, 11n3

Subject Index

Abuse. *See* Child abuse
Accident-proneness, 135
Addiction, voices that encourage, 128,
    130-132
Addictions composite, FAST factor
    analysis, 226
Addictive attachment, 132-134
Addictive habits, 46-47
    discouraging in children, 284
    intergenerational transmission of, 88
    recognizing, 49
Addictive substances. *See* Alcoholism;
    Alcohol use; Drug use; Substance
    abuse
Adolescents:
    anger in, 94
    drug use by, 98
    eating disorders, 85-86, 87-88
    guilt in, 90-91
    isolation of, 87, 88-89
    perfectionism in, 89-90
    self-attacks in, 89-90, 92, 93, 100
    self-destructive behavior in, 86, 87, 88,
        97-98, 99
    sexual orientation, 99, 100
    substance abuse by, 85-86, 87-88
    voices, 93, 100
    See also Adolescent suicide
Adolescent suicide, 78, 82-103
    cluster suicide, 82, 94
    contributing factors, 86-87, 93-94
    demographics, 82-83, 84
    homosexuality and, 99

risk assessment, 83
sexual abuse and, 99
sexuality and, 98-102
signs of, 83, 96
See also Adolescents
African Americans:
    hostile thoughts toward others, 136-137
    suicide in, 73-74
Age, suicide and, 78, 105, 106
Aggression:
    appropriate, 25
    of defended individual, 39
    in family systems, 282
    of minority populations, 76-77
Aggressor, identification with. *See*
        Identification with the aggressor
Alcoholism:
    manipulativeness and, 139
    self-attacks and, 97-98
    suicide demographics and, 68
    See also Substance abuse
Alcohol use, 46, 86
Alienation, 64, 83-84
Ambivalence, in suicidal individuals, 97
Anger:
    in adolescents, 94
    of family and friends after a suicide, 250
    guilt and, 153-154
Anorexia, 130
Antiego, 28
Antilibidinal ego, 9, 62
Antiself system, 9, 23, 25-33
    in the elderly, 108

suicide as triumph of, 60
Antisuicide contracting, 241-242, 259-260
Anxiety, 25-26
    adolescents, 102
    fantasy bond and, 214
    fear of loss and, 169
    inwardness, 38-39, 56
    See also Death anxiety; Separation anxiety
Automatic thoughts, 63

Beck Depression Inventory, 79
Beck Hopelessness Scale, 79
Beck Suicide Inventory, 79
Bender-Gestalt test, 78, 81n4
Binge-eating, 130
Bipolar disorders, suicide and, 68-69
Bisexuality. *See* Sexual orientation
Blacks. *See* African Americans
Bulimia, 85, 130

Career choice, 149-150
Career success, regression following,
    171-173
Chicanos. *See* Hispanics
Child. *See* Children
Child abuse:
    acting out as suicide, 30-31
    emotional abuse, 189-192
    fragmentation of self, 25-26, 28, 29-33
    identification with the aggressor, 29-30
    kinship groups and, 103n2
    reasons for, 190-191
    sexual abuse, 99
    suicide and, 103n5
    voice process in victims of, 294-295
Child discipline, 282-283, 285-286
Childhood suicide, 70-73
    microsuicide, 127
    parental suicide and, 249
    predicting, 80
    preventive measures, 280-286
    signs of, 57, 71
Child rearing. *See* Parenting methods

Children:
    addictive and destructive habit patterns,
        284
    avoiding isolation, 282-283
    constructive behaviors, 284-285
    death anxiety in, 165
    defenses of, 10, 95-96
    demonic possession of, 29
    depressive states and, 63-64
    disciplining, 282, 285-286
    discovery of death by, 186-187, 196n5
    ego splitting in, 71-72, 163-164
    emotional pain of, 9, 10, 24, 95-96
    fantasy bond in, 34n2, 164
    freedom of expression for, 283
    humanness of, 191-192
    identification with the aggressor, 29-30,
        61-62
    inwardness in, 38-39, 56
    mixed messages from parents, 283-284
    negative feelings toward self, 57, 72
    negative parental introjects, verbalization
        of, 71-73
    negative parental traits and defenses,
        147-148, 193-194
    regression in, 71
    scapegoated child, 71
    self/antiself division, 25-26, 29-30
    self-attacks in, 57
    sense of self, 54
    separation, 162, 164-165, 185-186
    separation anxiety, 125
    sexual rivalry in, 282
    suicide. *See* Childhood suicide
    as symbol of immortality, 191
    unwanted, 155
    value system development in, 24-25
    See also Adolescents; Adolescent suicide;
        Child abuse; Childhood suicide
Chronic illness:
    depression and, 112
    right to die, 116-118
Chronic suicide, 124
Cluster suicide, 82, 94
Cognitive approaches, to suicide, 62-65

Cognitive processes, in depressive states, 63-65
Cognitive therapy, for suicide patient, 245
Cognitive triad, 245
College students, suicide in, 87, 145
Collusion, within the fantasy bond, 200-201, 206-208
Compulsive habit pattern, 47
Countertransference, 237, 243, 246
Crisis intervention:
    acceptable standard of care, 235-245
    antisuicide contracting, 241-242, 259-260
    developing options and constructive action, 256
    errors, 243-245
    establishing rapport, 253-255
    guilt and, 256-259
    hospitalization, 241-242
    initial intake interview, 236-237, 240, 257-261
    model of, 255-256
    See also Psychotherapy; Suicide risk assessment; Suicide treatment
Cynicism, 52-54
    adolescence, 100

Dating, 102
DBT. See Dialectic Behavior Therapy
Death:
    discovery of by children, 186-187, 196n5
    fear of, 10, 11
    of parents, 109-110
Death anxiety:
    case studies, 17-24
    in children, 165
    children as defense against, 191
    death of a parent, 109-110
    defense against, 111, 191
    in the elderly, 107, 111
    existentialism and, 10, 11n5
    fantasy bond and, 132
    guilt and, 142-143
    individuation and, 10
    microsuicide and, 125-126

origin of, 186-187, 196n5
    regression and, 165-167
    voices and, 111-113
Death guilt, 120n10
Death wishes, after failed suicide, 32
Defended individual, 38-39
Defenses:
    antiself system and, 25
    childhood distress and, 10, 95-96
    fantasy bond as, 183-185, 214
    fear of death, 187, 196n6
    function of, 11n4
    goal pursuit or inwardness, 187-188, 214
    maladaptive, 9-10
    overreliance on, 188-189
    personal relationships affected by, 188-189
    as psychopathology, 9-10, 16
    regression as, 162-168
Depersonalization, fragmentation of personality, 26, 29-30
Depression:
    in adolescents, 86
    chronic illness and, 112
    cognitive style and, 63
    suicide demographics and, 69
    women and, 70
Depressive states, 63-65
Despair, 54-56
Dialectic Behavior Therapy (DBT), 245
Direct self-destructive behavior (DSDB), 66
Disengagement from life, 111-114
Distrust, 53
Division of the mind, 24-29
Documentation, 240
Domestic violence, voices leading to, 137
Drug use, 46-48, 86
    in adolescents, 98
    in the elderly, 108
    manipulativeness of, 139
    See also Substance abuse
DSDB. See Direct self-destructive behavior
Dysfunctional family:
    adolescents and, 83, 88, 93, 95
    guilt in victims of, 145-146

identifying with the aggressor, 61-62, 77
self-denying or martyred parent in, 138
self-destructiveness and, 32-33, 77
as suicide precursor, 64, 83
voice process and, 9, 72-73

Eating disorders:
    as addictive behavior, 130
    in adolescents, 85-86, 87-88
Ego, self system, 28
Ego splitting, 71-72, 163-164
Elderly suicide, 78, 104-120
    chronic nature of, 107
    factors in, 105-108, 119n4
    prevention of, 115-116
    psychodynamics of, 110-113
    sexuality and, 108
    signs of, 107-108
    suicide pacts, 119n3
    treatment of, 114-116
Embryonic suicide, 124
Emotional child abuse, 189-192
Ethnic minorities, suicide demographics
    for, 73-76
Euthanasia, 116-117, 120n8
Existential conflict, 17
Existential despair, 56
Existential guilt, 12, 143-145, 156-157
Existentialism:
    death anxiety and, 10, 11n5
    emotional pain and, 9, 11n3
Existential psychotherapy:
    death anxiety and life satisfaction, 11n5
    suicide treatment, 246-247
Extended family system, 291-293
Eye contact, lack of, 203

Family:
    dysfunctional. See Dysfunctional family
    extended family system, 291-293
    fantasy bond in, 210-212
    individuation in, 145-147
    involvement in treatment, 240-241

sexual rivalry and aggression in, 282
thought control in, 146-147
Family contact, guilt after, 152
Family secrets, betrayed in therapy, 153
Family therapy, 115
Fantasy bond, 9, 26, 28, 34n2, 164, 214
    in the adult, 199-201
    in children, 163, 164
    collusion within, 200-201, 206-208
    couple relationships and, 26, 132-134,
        200-210
    death anxiety, 132
    as defense system, 183-185, 214
    development, 199
    family and, 210-212
    intimacy and, 209-210
    in marriage, 26, 132-134, 200-210
    psychodynamics of, 198-201
    psychotherapy, identifying and
        challenging, 213
    separation anxiety and, 132
    separation leading to guilt, 145
Fantasy gratification, 51-52, 56
FAST. See Firestone Assessment of
    Self-Destructive Thoughts
Fear of death. See Death anxiety
Fear of loss, anxiety and, 169
Feeling release sessions, FAST, 263-264
Feelings:
    diminished sense of, 120n10
    psychic numbing, 120n10
    withholding, 49-50, 108
Firearms, as suicide weapon, 68, 69, 83,
    103n1
Firestone Assessment of Self-Destructive
    Thoughts (FAST), 79-80, 217-232,
    246
    exploratory factors, 224-226
    feeling release sessions, 263-264
    history and development of, 217-221
    studies, 221-224, 230-232
    theoretical basis of, 221
    understanding results of, 226-228
    use with the elderly, 107
    "voice" statements in, 8, 228-229

Firestone Voice Scale for Violence
(FVSV), 228-229
Fragmentation:
object relations approach, 62
signs of, 39
under stress, 26, 29-33
Friendship:
characteristics of, 212-213
therapeutic value of, 287-288
withdrawal from, 44-46, 88-89, 91
FVSV. *See* Firestone Voice Scale for
Violence

Garden of Eden myth, 142
Gay youth. *See* Sexual orientation
Gender, suicide and, 68-70, 73-76, 106
Gratification, in fantasy, 51-52, 56
Group therapy, 115, 265
Guilt:
about valuing one's life, 155
in adolescents, 90-91
after contact with family members, 152
anger and, 153-154
betraying family "secrets" in therapy, 153
career choice and, 149-150
crisis intervention and, 256-259
death anxiety and, 142-143
death guilt, 120n10
existential guilt, 12, 143-145, 156-157
of family and friends after a suicide, 250
individuation and independence, 145-149
neurotic guilt, 143-156, 159n4
religious training and, 141-142, 143
self-consciousness as precursor of,
168-169
self-destructive habit patterns and, 86, 87,
97-98
sexual guilt, 154-155
suicide and, 140-159
surpassing the same-sex parent, 150-151
survivor guilt, 155-156
voices, 158
Guns, as suicide weapon, 68, 69, 83, 103n1

Hallucinations, 17
Hidden suicide, 124
High achievers, suicide in, 87-89
Hispanics, suicide, 74-75
Homosexuality, adolescent suicide, 99
Hopelessness, 54-56, 90, 107
FAST test for, 226
Hospitalization, 241, 243

Identification with the aggressor, 29-30,
61-62, 77
Illness:
depression and, 112
right to die, 116-118
Inadequacy, feeling of, 91, 108
Incompetency, feeling of, 91
Independence, guilt about, 145-149
Indifference, 52
Indirect self-destructive behavior (ISDB),
66
Indirect suicide, 124
Individuation:
death anxiety and, 10
existential issues in, 9
guilt about, 145-149
voices attacking, 147-149
Inferiority, feeling of, 108
Installment-plan suicide, 124
Intake interview, 236-237, 240, 257-261
Internalized rage, of minority populations,
76-77
Intimacy, fantasy bond and, 209-210
Inwardness, 35-36, 56-57
case study, 40-58
choosing defenses, 187-188
comfort of, 48
conditions conducive to, 38-39
in the elderly, 107-108
manifestations of, 40-58
signs of, 36-38
ISDB. *See* Indirect self-destructive
behavior
Isolation:
in adolescents, 87, 88-89

as child discipline tactic, 282-283
comfort of, 48
corrective procedures for, 44
of a couple, 119n2
in the elderly, 108
inwardness and, 42-44
self-denial and, 127-130
voices that predispose to, 127-130

Latinos. *See* Hispanics
Lesbianism. *See* Sexual orientation
Liability, 252n1
Libidinal ego, 62
Living alone, 44, 69
Loss, 64, 106, 110, 125
Love-food, 197n13, 281
Low self-esteem, 52, 127-130

Malpractice, 234, 252n1
Managed health care, 243
Manipulation:
    microsuicide, 138-139
    by parents, 147
Marriage:
    as crisis for women, 175
    fantasy bond in, 26, 132-134, 200-210
    regression precipitated by, 174-175
    role reversal in, 101-102
Masculinity, insecurity about, 101, 102
Masked suicide, 124
Melancholia, 61
Mental health, manifestations of healthy
    individual, 38, 41
Mental illness, 16
    suicide and, 60-62
    suicide demographics and, 68-70
Microsuicide, 28, 66, 123-139
    continuum of, 127
    death anxiety and, 125-126
    defined, 123
    dynamics of, 126-127
    in the elderly, 113
    manipulative aspects of, 138-139

progressive self-denial and, 123
separation anxiety and, 124-125
voices and, 127-139
Middle age, 111-116
Minnesota Multiphasic Personality
    Inventory (MMPI), as suicide
    predictor, 81n4
Minorities:
    hostile thoughts toward others, 136-137
    suicide in, 73-78
Mixed messages, from parents, 283-284
Motherhood, regression in women
    precipitated by, 175-176
Motivation, lack of, 54

Native Americans, suicide, 75-76
Negative anxiety, 25-26
Negative feelings toward self:
    in children, 57, 72
    continuum of, 219
    in the elderly, 111-113
    giving voice to, 4-7
    incorporating, 7, 62
    integral part of psyche, 15, 95
    second-person voice, 139n2, 196n4
    Voice Therapy and, 63
    See also Self-attacks; Voices
Negative identification, 110
Negative voices. *See* Self-attacks; Voices
Neurosis, fragmentation of self, 26
Neurotic guilt, 143-156, 159n4
    about valuing one's life, 155
    after contact with family members, 152
    betraying family "secrets" in therapy, 153
    career choice and, 149-150
    defined, 144
    individuation and independence, 145-149
    sexual guilt, 154-155
    surpassing the same-sex parent, 150-151
    survivor guilt, 155-156
Nurturing oneself in inward state, 56

Object relations theory, 9, 11n3, 61-62, 293

Older people, suicide in. *See* Elderly
    suicide
Omnipotence, 110, 164
Original sin, 141, 143
Overwork, as addictive behavior, 131

Pain, 9
    antiself system and, 25
    defense system, 10, 185, 186-187
    origin of psychological pain, 182-183
Panic disorders, suicide and, 69
Paranoia, 53, 54, 137
Parasuicide, 66, 67n1, 124
Parental abuse. *See* Child abuse
Parenting methods:
    discipline, 282-283, 285-286
    love-food, 197n13, 281
    predisposing to suicide, 96, 98, 109
    preventing suicide, 98
    secure and loving parental climate,
        281-282
    See also Child abuse
Parents:
    child abuse. *See* Child abuse
    death of, 109-110
    guilt induced by visit with, 152
    guilt-inducing manipulation by, 147
    internalized, 30-31
    mixed messages from, 283-284
    negative parental traits and defenses,
        147-149, 193-194
    as positive role model, 281-282
    role reversal in marriage, 101-102
    self and antiself systems, 24-29
    self-destructive behaviors imitated by
        children, 72, 88
    of suicidal patients, 62
    surpassing same-sex parent, 150-151
Partial suicide, 65, 66, 124
Passivity, 52, 137
Perfectionism, 87, 89-90, 103n4
Personal goals, 28
Personal relationships:
    addictive, 132-134

affected by defenses, 188-189
    retreating from, 46, 52
Perturbation, 65, 69, 101, 107
Physical abuse:
    voice process, 294-295
    See also Child abuse
Physician-assisted suicide, 116-117
Positive anxiety, 25-26
Postvention, 248-251, 252n8
Pregnancy, regression in women
    precipitated by, 175-176
Primal Therapy, 10
Progressive self-denial, 43, 129
    death anxiety and, 11, 110-111
    microsuicide, 123
    self-attacks, 134
    voices, 111-113
Projective identification, 62
Pseudoindependence, 164
Psychache, 15, 105, 106
Psyche:
    ego splitting, 71-72
    fragmentation of self, 25-26, 29-33, 62
    identification with the aggressor, 29-30,
        61-62
    self and antiself system, 24-33
Psychiatric coercion, 117, 120n9
Psychiatric Rating Scale, predicting
    suicide potential with, 78, 81n4
Psychic numbing, 120n10
Psychoanalytic approach:
    emotional pain and, 9
    split ego, 71-72, 163
    to suicide, 61-62, 65, 66
    to suicide treatment, 246, 293
Psychological autopsy, 177n1
Psychological tests, suicide potential,
    78-79, 81n4; *See also* Firestone
    Assessment of Self-Destructive
    Thoughts
Psychopathology. *See* Mental illness
Psychotherapist:
    antisuicide contracting with,
        241-242
    countertransference of, 237, 243, 246

encouraging survival, 52
guilt, care not to induce, 256-259
isolation undesirable, 251
knowledge of community resources,
    242
paranoid distortions, helping with,
    53, 54
personality of, 247-248
primary goal of, 273
self-attacks, response to, 266
as survivor, 251, 252n9
technical and personal competence of,
    242-243
as "transitional object," 52
voices, understanding and
    acknowledgment of, 253
See also Crisis intervention; Suicide
    treatment
Psychotherapy:
acceptable standard of care in, 235-245
anger at parents, guilt and, 154
cognitive approach to, 246
documentation of, 240
errors in, 243-245
establishing rapport in, 253-255
existential psychotherapy, 246-247
family involvement in, 240-241
family secrets betrayed in, 153
fantasy bond identified and challenged by,
    213
FAST. *See* Firestone Assessment of
    Self-Destructive Thoughts
goals of, 195
hospitalization, 241-242
manipulation in, 273
primary goal of, 273
psychoanalytic approach to, 246
regression in, 162-163
resistance in, 194-195, 294
self-attacks, response to, 266
suicidal crisis and, 233-234
team approach in, 240
termination of, 162-163, 274
See also Crisis intervention; Suicide
    treatment

Rage:
of minority populations, 76-77
toward self, 135
Rapport, with therapist, 253, 255
Rational Emotive Therapy, 62
Reasons for Living Inventory (RFL), 79
Regression:
bipolar causality, 160-162
case study, 171-173
in children, 71
death anxiety and, 165-167
as defense mechanism, 162-168
defined, 163
dependency of others and, 173-174
following career successes, 171-173
following hospitalization, 243
positive events and, 161-162, 165-166,
    168-170
separation anxiety and, 164-168
Religious training, guilt and, 141-142, 143
Resistance, psychotherapy, 194-195, 294
Right to die, 116-118, 248
Risk assessment, for suicide. *See* Suicide
    risk assessment
Risk-taking behavior, 135
Role models, parents as, 281-282
Rorschach test, predicting suicide potential
    with, 78, 81n4
Running away, 44-46, 89

Schizophrenia:
fragmentation of self, 26
hallucinations, 157
as method of self-destruction, 60
suicide demographics, 70
voices, dual function of, 48
Search for meaning, 56, 290-291
Self:
and antiself, 24-33
fragmentation under stress, 26, 29-33
sense of, 1, 54
suicide as renunciation of, 16
Voice Therapy and, 10

Self-annihilating composite, FAST factor analysis, 226
Self-annihilating thoughts, leading to suicide, 128, 134-136
Self-attacks, 6-8, 28
    addictive habits and, 47
    in adolescents, 89-90, 92, 93, 100
    in alcoholics, 97-98
    antiself system and, 26
    in children, 57, 72
    corrective procedures for, 53-54
    escalation of, 135
    family experiences and, 72-73
    feeling unwanted and unloved, 155
    regression and, 170
    second-person voice, 139n2, 196n4
    self-denial and, 134
    sexuality and, 100
    stages of, 28
    in suicidal trance, 253
    therapist response to, 266
    See also Negative feelings toward self
Self-consciousness, precursor to guilt reactions, 168
Self-criticism, 52
Self-defeating composite, FAST factor analysis, 226
Self-denial, 43, 129
    death anxiety and, 110-111
    self-attacks and, 134
    voices that predispose to, 127-130
Self-destructive behavior, 65-66
    in adolescents, 86, 87, 88, 97-98, 99
    continuum of, 127, 128
    in the elderly, 105, 110-113
    guilt and, 86, 87, 97-98
    hostile thoughts toward others, 136-137
    imitation of parents, 72, 88
    interrelatedness of, 126
    as microsuicide, 28, 66, 123-139
    in minority populations, 77
    range of, 65-66
    regression and, 170
Self-expression, in children, 283
Self-hatred, 135

Self-image, 52-54, 56, 108
Selfishness, 155
Selflessness, 155
Self system, 24-33
Separation, childhood development, 162, 164-165, 185-186
Separation anxiety:
    fantasy bond and, 132
    microsuicide and, 124-125
    in psychotherapy, 163
    regression and, 164-168
Sexual abuse, of children, 99
Sexual guilt, 154-155
Sexuality:
    adolescent suicide and, 98-102
    elderly suicide and, 108
    fantasy bond and, 209
Sexual orientation, in adolescence, 99, 100
Sexual rivalry, in family systems, 282
Shame, 52, 87, 158n1
SIQ-JR, 80
Slow suicide, 124
Social isolation. See Isolation
Sorrow, 64
Split ego, regression and, 71-72, 163-164
Starting a family, 198
Street person, 89
Stress:
    fragmentation of self, 25-26, 29-33
    inwardness, 38-39, 56
Substance abuse:
    by adolescents, 85-86, 87-88, 98
    in the elderly, 108
    manipulativeness of, 139
Suicidal ideation, 28, 65
    in the elderly, 107
    perfectionism and, 103n4
    as predictor of actual suicide, 79
    in women, 70
Suicidal signs, 37, 56-57, 61, 78
    addictive routines and substances, 46-49
    adolescents, 83, 96
    in adolescents, 83
    in children, 57, 71
    cognitive constriction, 65

denial of priorities, 44-46
in the elderly, 107-108
fantasy gratification, 51-52
hopelessness and despair, 54-56
indifference, 52
inwardness, 35-42
isolation, 42-44
lack of motivation, 54
negative self-image, 52-54
passivity, 52
perturbation, 65, 69, 101, 107
psychological features, 65
rational thought, 65
withdrawal from relationships, 44-46
withholding personal feelings, 49-50
Suicidal spiral, 90-91, 95-96
Suicidal trance, 15, 22, 23, 33
abandonment of friendships, 44
antisuicide contracting, 241-242, 260
preventing, 260
voice attacks in, 253
withdrawal from social contact, 43-44
Suicide:
as acting out of parental abuse, 30-31
in adolescents. *See* Adolescent suicide
African Americans, 73-74
age and, 78, 105, 106
case studies, 17-24
in children. *See* Childhood suicide
cluster suicide, 82, 94
cognitive approaches, 62-65
in college students, 87, 145
cry for help before, 234
defined, 59-61
demographics, 68-70, 73-78, 82-83, 84,
    104, 105
in the elderly. *See* Elderly suicide
ethnic minorities, 73-78
gender and, 68-70, 73-76, 106
genetic inheritability, 16
gradual self-destruction, 124
guilt and, 140-159
in high achievers, 87-89
Hispanics, 74-75
human dignity and, 120n6

identification and imitation, 16
loss leading to, 64
malpractice issues, 234, 252n1
mental illness and, 60-62
methods of, 69, 83
microsuicide, 28, 66, 113, 123-139
Native Americans, 75-76
negative voices and, 11
object-relations approach, 61-62
parasuicide, 66, 67n1, 124
partial suicide, 66
physician-assisted, 116-117
positive events precipitating, 49, 80
postvention, 248-251, 252n8
presuicidal state, 87
psychache and, 15, 105, 106
psychoanalytic approach, 61-62, 65, 66
reactions to, 249-250
as renunciation of self, 16
right to die, 116-118, 248
risk factors, 68-70
self-annihilating thoughts leading to, 128,
    134-136
self-destructive behavior, range of, 65-66
sexual abuse and, 99, 103n5
sexuality and, 98-102, 108
of the spirit, 11
suicide pacts, 119n3
survivors, impact on, 248-251
therapists as survivors, 251, 252n9
women and, 68-70, 73-76
See also Suicidal ideation; Suicidal signs;
    Suicidal trance; Suicide prevention;
    Suicide risk assessment; Suicide
    treatment
Suicide Ideation Questionnaire, 80
Suicide pacts, in the elderly, 119n3
Suicide prevention, 33, 56-58, 279-296
addictive patterns, recognizing, 49
caring about something, 56, 290
in childhood, 280-286
child-rearing practices, 98
communication, encouraging, 44
in the elderly, 115-116
encouraging survival, 52

existential issues, 289-291
extended family, 291-293
fantasy process, exposing and
    discouraging, 52
firearms, removing, 103n1
friendships, 52, 287-288
isolation, correcting, 44
kindness and generosity, accepting, 50
lifestyle that counters suicidal trends,
    286-293
patients' interests, encouraging, 46,
    288-289
psychiatric coercion, 117, 120n9
relationships, not retreating from, 46, 52
rights of individual, 117-118, 120n6
search for meaning, 56, 290-291
self-attacks, understanding and
    discouraging, 49, 53-54, 115
sharing activities and adventure, 188-189
social context, 44
substance abuse, discouraging, 49
survival as goal, 52
withholding behavior, recognizing, 50
See also Crisis intervention; Voice
    Therapy
Suicide Probability Scale (SPS), 79
Suicide recovery, 23, 32
Suicide risk assessment, 78-80, 236-240
adolescents, 83
in children, 80
crisis intervention, 255
FAST. See Firestone Assessment of
    Self-Destructive Thoughts
parent's suicide, 249
See also Suicidal signs
Suicide treatment, 233-252
antisuicide contracting, 241-242,
    259-260
case management, 233-252
clinical interview, 257-261
cognitive behavioral, 245
consultation, 240
cry for help, 234
documentation, 240
in the elderly, 116-118

errors, 243-245
existential framework, 246-247
family involvement, 240-241
FAST test. See Firestone Assessment of
    Self-Destructive Thoughts
guilt, 256-259
hospitalization, 241
initial intake interview, 236-237, 240
malpractice issues, 234, 252n1
manipulation in, 273
object-relations theory, 9, 11n3, 293
psychoanalytic approach, 246, 293
standards of care, 235-245
Voice Therapy, 2-7, 10, 17, 26, 33,
    162-163, 253-276, 274
See also Crisis intervention;
    Psychotherapist; Psychotherapy
Superego, 24, 28
Survivor guilt, 120n10, 155-156
Survivors:
postvention strategies, 250-251,
    252n8
reaction of, 249-250
Symbiotic partnership, 119n2

Teenagers. See Adolescents
Termination, Voice Therapy, 162-163, 274
Thematic Apperception Test (TAT),
    predicting suicide potential with,
    78, 81n4
Therapist. See Psychotherapist
Time-out, as child discipline, 282-283

Value systems, 24
Valuing one's life, 155
Victimization, 137
Voice attacks. See Self-attacks
Voice process, 2, 9, 22, 72
child abuse, 294-295
defense system and, 184
depressive state and, 67
split ego, 163-164
therapists' understanding of, 33, 293

Voices, 126
    addiction regulation, 128
    addictive habit patterns and, 48
    adolescents, 93, 100
    attacking individuation, 147-149
    in children, 57, 72
    continuum of negative thought patterns,
        219
    cycle of addiction and, 128, 130-132
    dangerous risks and, 135
    death anxiety, 111-113
    defensive uses of, 2
    defined, 16-17
    domestic violence and, 137
    of guilt, 158
    hallucinations different from, 17
    hostile thoughts toward others,
        136-137
    identifying with Voice Therapy, 263
    internalized voices, bringing to the
        surface, 263
    life and death struggle, 17-24
    low self-esteem, 127-130
    microsuicidal behavior, 123
    in middle age, 111
    as negative thought patterns, 17
    parental death wishes, 32-33
    progressive self-denial, 111-113
    self-denial, 127-130
    sexuality, 100
    suicidal trance, 15, 22, 23
    verbalizing, 276n4
    withholding and, 50
    See also Negative feelings toward self;
        Self-attacks

Voice Therapy, 17, 253-254, 274-275,
        293-294
    automatic thoughts, 63
    background and evolution of, 2 7
    benefits of, 33
    case study, 266-272
    in the elderly, 115-116
    group interaction, 265
    methods, 262-266, 272-273
    psychoanalytic roots of, 67
    purpose of, 10
    resistance to, 294
    results of, 184
    termination, 162-163, 274
    theory of, 10, 17, 26, 33
    See also Suicide prevention; Suicide
        treatment

Withdrawal, 129
Withholding:
    correcting, 50
    in the elderly, 108
    inwardness and, 49
    in the workplace, 50
Women:
    marriage as crisis, 175
    motherhood, regression and,
        175-176
    suicide and, 68-70, 73-76
Worthlessness, 90-91

Youth. See Adolescents; Children

About the Author

Robert W. Firestone, Ph.D., is affiliated with the Glendon Association in Santa Barbara, California, a nonprofit organization dedicated to the development and dissemination of concepts and practices in psychotherapy. He completed his doctoral dissertation, *A Concept of the Schizophrenic Process,* in 1957 and received his doctorate in clinical psychology from the University of Denver that same year. From 1957 to 1979, he was engaged in the private practice of psychotherapy as a clinical psychologist working with a wide range of patients, amplifying his original ideas on schizophrenia, and applying these concepts to a comprehensive theory of neurosis. In 1979, he joined the Glendon Association, which has made possible a longitudinal study that provided supporting data for his theory and an understanding of the fantasy bond as manifested in normal couples and family relationships. His major works, *The Fantasy Bond: Structure of Psychological Defenses, Voice Therapy: A Psychotherapeutic Approach to Self-Destructive Behavior,* and *Compassionate Child-Rearing: An In-Depth Approach to Optimal Parenting,* describe how couples form destructive bonds that impair their psychological functioning and have a damaging effect on their child-rearing practices. His studies of negative thought processes and their associated affect have led to the development of an innovative therapeutic methodology to uncover and contend with aspects of destructive cognition. In recent years, he has applied his concepts to empirical research and to developing the Firestone Assessment of Self-Destructive Thoughts (FAST), a scale that assesses suicide potential. In addition to his contributions to the mental health field, he serves as a consultant to several large corporations.